Safety and Security in Tourism

Recovery Marketing after Crises

Edited by Noel Scott, Eric Laws and
Bruce Prideaux

 Routledge
Taylor & Francis Group

LONDON AND NEW YORK

First published 2010 by Routledge
2 Park Square, Milton Park, Abingdon, Oxon, OX14 4RN

Simultaneously published in the USA and Canada
by Routledge
711 Third Avenue, New York, NY 10017

Routledge is an imprint of the Taylor & Francis Group, an informa business

© 2010 Taylor & Francis

First issued in paperback 2013

Typeset in Times by Value Chain, India

British Library Cataloguing in Publication Data
A catalogue record for this book is available from the British Library

ISBN13: 978-0-4158-5046-9 (pbk)
ISBN13: 978-0-7890-3783-1 (hbk)

Safety and Security in Tourism

Natural disasters, wars and conflicts, epidemics, and other major crises can devastate a tourism service or destination. Though there is an extensive literature and research base on preparation for, and coping with tourism crises, there is a gap in information on how to best market and recover from the destruction caused to tourism businesses and destinations. This book fills the gap by comprehensively examining how to rebuild the market for a tourism service or destination after a catastrophe. This important book presents leading experts from around the world providing useful instruction on effective ways to plan for future crisis response and strategies for recovering business.

A crisis for the tourism industry may arise from several types of destructive occurrences, from natural physical destruction of important infrastructure to acts of terrorism. Because of the broad range of potential problems, there is no single strategy to deal with crises. The book explores a wide range of catastrophes, from Hurricane Katrina to tsunamis to war, taking a detailed look at management and administrative strategies which can help stimulate tourism recovery. This book explores catastrophic risks, risk perceptions, mediating the effects of natural disasters on travel intention, and various marketing strategies designed to bring customers back. This volume may become one of the most crucial resources in a tourism professional's library. The book is extensively referenced and includes several tables and figures to clearly explain data.

This book is essential reading for tourism researchers, tourism educators, tourism industry managers, and tourism industry administrators.

This book was published as a special issue of the *Journal of Travel & Tourism Marketing*.

Noel Scott is a Senior Research Fellow in the School of Tourism, The University of Queensland, Australia.

Eric Laws is an Adjunct Professor at James Cook University, Australia.

Bruce Prideaux is Professor of Marketing and Tourism Management and Deputy Dean of the School of Postgraduate Studies at James Cook University, Australia.

Contents

1. Tourism Crises and Marketing Recovery Strategies   1
    Noel Scott, Eric Laws and Bruce Prideaux

2. Stealth Risks and Catastrophic Risks: On Risk Perception and Crisis
    Recovery Strategies   15
    Pedro Moreira

3. Mediating the Effects of Natural Disasters on Travel Intention   29
    Xinran Lehto, Alecia C. Douglas and Jungkun Park

4. Tourism Crisis Management and Organizational Learning: The Role of
    Reflection in Developing Effective DMO Crisis Strategies   45
    Deborah Blackman and Brent W. Ritchie

5. The Role of Market Orientation in Managing Crises During the Post-Crisis Phase   59
    David Martín-Consuegra, Águeda Esteban and Arturo Molina

6. A Cautionary Tale of a Resort Destination's Self-Inflicted Crisis   73
    Steven Pike

7. Communicating Tourism Crises Through Destination Websites   83
    Serena Volo

8. London Tourism: A 'Post-Disaster' Marketing Response   95
    Adele Ladkin, Alan Fyall, John Fletcher and Richard Shipway

9. Understanding the Potential Impact on the Image of Canada as a
    Weekend Travel Destination as a Result of Western Hemisphere Travel
    Initiative Passport Requirements   113
    Wayne W. Smith, Barbara A. Carmichael and Nicole M. Batovsky

10. Branding Post-Conflict Destinations: Recreating Montenegro After the
    Disintegration of Yugoslavia   127
    Andriela Vitic and *Greg Ringer*

11. Tourism Market Recovery in the Maldives After the 2004 Indian Ocean Tsunami   139
    Jack C. Carlsen and Michael Hughes

12. Market Segmentation in Time of Crisis: A Case Study of the MICE
    Sector in Thailand   151
    Kom Campiranon and Charles Arcodia

13. Post Crisis Recovery: The Case of After Cyclone Larry   163
     Bruce Prideaux, Alexandra Coghlan and Fay Falco-Mammone

14. The Heart Recovery Marketing Campaign: Destination Recovery After a
    Major Bushfire in Australia's National Capital   175
     E. Kate Armstrong and Brent W. Ritchie

15. Crisis Management: A Case Study from the Greek Passenger Shipping Industry   191
     Outi Niininen and Maria Gatsou

16. Crisis Management Planning to Restore Tourism After Disasters:
    A Case Study from Taiwan   203
     Yu-Chin Huang, Yung-Ping Tseng and James F. Petrick

17. Repositioning a Tourism Destination: The Case of New Orleans After
    Hurricane Katrina   223
     Harsha E. Chacko and Marianne Hawkins Marcell

18. Backpacking Your Way into Crisis: An Exploratory Study into Perceived
    Risk and Tourist Behaviour Amongst Young People   237
     Philippa Hunter-Jones, Alice Jeffs and Denis Smith

19. Crisis Management in Tourism: Preparing for Recovery   249
     Christof Pforr and Peter J. Hosie

20. Developing a Research Agenda for Tourism Crisis Management,
    Market Recovery and Communications   265
     Jack C. Carlsen and Janne J. Liburd

    Index   277

Tourism Crises and Marketing Recovery Strategies

Noel Scott
Eric Laws
Bruce Prideaux

SUMMARY. The recent frequency and intensity of crises and disasters affecting the tourism industry has resulted in a growing body of research into their causes, effects and management, as the bibliographies of the ensuing papers catalogue. To date, most papers and collections of research have taken a broad approach, describing the origins of a particular event which triggered a tourism crises, followed by an examination of the differential effects of the crisis on local residents, staff, tourists and tourism organizations or the environment and infrastructure. They have also discussed rescue efforts and the complexity of management tasks in the immediate aftermath of an event, often pointing to the need for preplanning to mitigate the consequences of any future disaster. Other researchers have contributed directly to the academic debate about how to theorise tourism crisis management, often by drawing on the wider crisis management literature.

The present collection of research differs in that it focuses on one phase of the tasks which managers face after the immediate consequences of a crisis have been dealt with. This phase addresses the question of how to rebuild the market for a tourism service or a destination which has experienced a significant catastrophe, and how to learn from the experience in planning for future crisis response strategies. It is suggested in this paper that the challenges are actually more varied and complex than is implied by the suggestion, found in much of the literature, that the task is about 'restoring normality.' The chaos and complexity experienced in the aftermath of a crisis raise general issues of how organizations learn and adapt to change.

INTRODUCTION

What does it actually mean for a tourism organisation to suffer a crisis and to recover from it? In the case of natural disasters such as earthquakes, hurricanes or tsunamis, the devastation to life and property is all too evident, both to those in the locality and to global audiences who may be described as remote witnesses through the medium of TV, press and internet

Noel Scott (E-mail: noel.scott@uq.edu.au) is a Lecturer in the School of Tourism and Leisure Management at The University of Queensland (11 Salisbury Road, Ipswich, 4305, Queensland, Australia). Eric Laws (E-mail: e.laws@runbox.com) is Adjunct Professor of Tourism Studies at James Cook University (P.O. Box 6811, Cairns, QLD Australia). Bruce Prideaux (E-mail: bruce.prideaux@jcu.edu.au) is the Chair of Marketing and Tourism Management at James Cook University (P.O. Box 6811, Cairns, QLD Australia).

coverage. Similarly, the suffering and ruin caused by acts of terrorism as well as disasters involving transport, communications and other infrastructure is immediately visible to the global community through the media. The media also rapidly draws attention to the outbreak of a war or insurgency, and on epidemics, thereby turning tourists' travel intentions to alternative destinations. In all these cases the need for rescue, clear up operations and rebuilding is self-evident. It is also widely understood that a further set of management responses are required at a later stage to inform the public and industry partners that tourism services have resumed and that recovery is taking place.

In developing this volume, we have focused on the specific skills and understandings that can assist in post crisis tourism recovery. As the papers in this collection demonstrate, there is more to recovery than the restoration of normal services. Although each crisis has its own distinct causes, impacts and pattern of recovery, it is evident from the papers which follow and from the wider tourism crisis literature that certain tourism organisations are more resilient than others in terms of the speed of recovery and/or their ability to adapt to change in the post crisis period. An organizations' vulnerability to crises and the effectiveness of their recovery efforts vary in ways, and for reasons which are not yet fully understood.

Earlier studies of crises (including previous work by the present editors; Laws, Prideaux and Chon, 2007; Laws and Prideaux, 2005; Prideaux, Laws and Faulkner 2003; Campiranon and Scott, 2007) have focussed on management of the crisis itself and have highlighted how a crisis precipitates a complex and changing situation where the pre-existing rules of action for the organisation are suspended and other tasks take priority. These other tasks lack the normal clarity of organisational procedures, and at first glance many appear to be difficult to prioritise on the basis of past experience. There may be no consensus about what to do, how to do it and who should be undertaking the work. In these situations, leadership becomes a critical issue, both within an organisation and in terms of co-ordinating and directing the multitude of stakeholders participating in recovery. In summary then, crises are chaotic, dynamic and dangerous

and are events where leadership becomes a key factor in prioritization, redirection and creation of new patterns of post event activity.

In this paper the editors of this volume argue that tourism crisis recovery may mean a change to the pre-existing ways of operating. The standard means of measuring recovery by the success of an organisation in restoring business flows to an earlier trend line may not be adequate because this benchmark it does not take into account the adaptation that may take place during the crisis and ensuing recovery period processes. The consequences for an organisation of a crisis (beyond its immediate impacts in terms of suffering, damage, and loss of business) are often more fundamental and may necessitate changes to the way the organisation operates, forces it to create new networks, and even stimulate the development of new business opportunities or social objectives.

The objectives of this paper are to: present a summary of theoretical understanding of tourism crisis management from the perspective of crisis recovery with a particular emphasis on the systems approach and the role of networks; to introduce the other papers in this collection; and to contribute an adjustment to Faulkner's (2001) model of disaster management to incorporate that role of marketing in post crisis recovery. This aspect of the paper is summarised in Figure 4.

TOURISM CRISIS RECOVERY–
AN OVERVIEW

From the practical perspective of managers, the general challenge of the recovery phase is to restore operations to normal, but increasingly there is evidence of more radical, strategic thinking in reshaping the offer as social and tourism infrastructure, equipment and even staff may have to be replaced, new patterns of operation developed and new markets sought. It is in this context that viewing tourism as a system has a number of advantages. It is interesting that the Chinese word for crisis (shown in Figure 1) is composed of two symbols meaning "danger" and "opportunity." Some destinations, including a number of Thai resorts devastated by the 2004 Boxing Day Tsunami, have

FIGURE 1. The Chinese Word for Crisis Is Composed of Characters Meaning Opportunity and Disaster

used the event as an opportunity to restructure by identifying new market segments and in some cases discouraging some market sectors they feel are less desirable. This usually equates to 'moving up market.' A related recovery strategy focuses on rebuilding high margin sectors such as MICE (Campiranon and Arcodia, below).

The focus of much of the existing research has been on the events leading up the crisis which then results in a perturbation of the normal state, followed by the steps required to restore the 'normal' situation. In their review of different perspectives on the study of crises and their development of propositions for further study, Pearson and Clair (1998:6) discuss the outcome of a crisis as a system being restored to its normal state. This approach views the crisis as distinct from the remainder of the environment in which the organization functions, with the consequences of the crisis affecting internal technical and social elements of the tourism system operating at the time of the onset of the disaster or crisis event. Restoration in this view is achieved through a series of steps or stages. An alternative view is to consider crisis events from a systems perspective where a change such as a crisis event causes changes to other parts of the system. In many cases these changes have system wide implications that prevent a return to the pre-crisis specifications of the system.

The previous discussion has conceptualized the study of crises and disasters by using a view of tourism systems in which there exist networks of organizations. Three implications of this should be considered. First a systems view questions the boundaries that should be used to study crisis and disasters. Second, the idea of complexity or chaos theory can add new insights to recovery. Third, a social network view provides a different perspective focusing on the interactions between organizations. Together, the implications point to the need to review existing models and incorporate new perspectives from the lessons learnt during recent disasters and crises.

The Role of Boundaries

A systems perspective is useful as it highlights another range of effects or impacts of crises that have not been sufficiently recognised within the tourism literature. Scott and Laws (2006) discussed the idea of system resilience, of change in system states and in improvements or degeneration in the overall system of tourism as a result of a crisis. These ideas were also identified and explored in a paper using floods in Katherine, Australia as a case study to examine how a disaster may lead to a positive change in a destination's tourism (Faulkner & Vikulov, 2001).

Within a system the impact of an event such as a crisis is felt to either a greater or lesser scale by all members of the system. The implication of this is that the effects of a crisis may be transferred across system boundaries by organizational relationships. As a simple example, a baggage handlers' strike at one airport may delay passengers, impose costs on airlines in accommodating passengers, moving luggage and rescheduling flights, and result in extra stress for airport staff. However it may also have follow-on effects at distant airports and cause a loss of business to hotels in those destinations. Systems theory perspectives can therefore assist to identify the range of stakeholders involved, and lead to a study of factors influencing speed of recovery, the intensity of effects and the factors causing the effect (see Armstrong and Ritchie; Carelsen and Hughes; and Vitic and Ringer, below).

Complexity or Chaos Theory

Complexity or chaos theory provides an insightful paradigm for the investigation of rapidly changing complex situations where multiple influences impact on non-equilibrium systems. In these conditions of uncertainty, there is a need to incorporate contingencies for the unexpected into policy framework that may result in adaptation of the system itself. Chaos theory demonstrates that there are elements of system behaviour that are intrinsically unstable and not amenable to formal forecasting. If this is the case, a new approach to forecasting is required. Possible ways forward may include political audits and risk analysis to develop a sense of the possible patterns of events that may emerge. In this sense future tourism activity may be forecast using a series of scenarios. The latter may involve the use of a scenario building approach incorporating elements of van der Heijden's (1997) strategic conversion model, elements of the learning organisation approach based on a structured participatory dialogue (Senge, 1990) or elements of risk management described by Haimes et al. (2002). Which ever direction is taken, there are a number of factors that must be identified and factored into considerations of the possible course of events in the future. A typical large scale disruption precipitates complex movements away from the previous relationships which often trend towards stability and partial equilibrium. Keown-McMullan (1997: 9) noted that organisations will undergo significant change even when they are successful in managing a crisis situation. It is apparent that traditional Newtonian (linear) thinking with its presumption of stability is not able to adequately explain the impact of crises where the previous business trajectory is altered and a new state emerges.

Richardson's (1994) analysis of crisis management in organisations provides another perspective on community adjustment capabilities by drawing on "single" and "double loop" learning approaches (Argyris and Schon, 1978). In the former, the response to disasters involves a linear reorientation 'more' or less in keeping with traditional objectives and traditional responses (Richardson, 1994, 5). Alternatively, the double loop learning approach challenges traditional beliefs about what society and management is and what it should do. This approach recognises that management systems can themselves engender the ingredients of chaos and catastrophe, and that managers must also be more aware and proactively concerned about organisations as the creators of crises. Pike (below) presents a cautionary tale of a destination which suffered a crisis through its inability to recognise that changing government policy could adversely affect it. As Blackman and Ritchie (below) point out, lessons can be learned from the experience of a crisis, or from studying other destinations and organisations which have experienced serious disruption. For example, the absence of any post crisis recovery planning and action following the 1994 volcanic eruption in Rabaul, Papua New Guinea resulted in a slow decline of a destination that was internationally recognised as a dive location. Today, formerly busy hotels lie abandoned and tourism investment has moved elsewhere. Morea (below) argues that crisis recovery requires different approaches depending on whether the onset and impacts of the crisis are sudden or spread over a longer period. Only in this way can impacts of crisis be mitigated and prospects for long term recovery can be more assured (Faulkner and Vikolov 2001).

Social Networks

The third implication of viewing crisis recovery from a systems perspective arises from the view that destinations are networks of stakeholders which may be reconfigured into more efficient structures following a crisis. This is slightly different to the view of Faulkner and Vikulov (2001), who suggested a disaster may have a positive outcome but this was primarily due to new infrastructure rather than realignment or creation of new social networks. Crises may also lead to a more cohesive industry-wide or community-wide response mechanisms, better information flows and indeed the development of new organizational structures (Quarantelli, 1988). The emphasis on the flow of information as a critical issue in crisis management leads to the idea of social network analysis as a means of analysing the structure of this 'flow' of information through communication channels. This is an important element of crisis recovery that needs to be further analysed. For example, Pikkemaat and Peters (2005, 99) discussed the significant role of networks in tourism innovation. 'All experts agree on the most promising vehicle for innovation which is cooperation, alliances and/or networks in various fields such as technology, marketing distribution, and human resources sharing.' In recovering from a crisis the need is often for innovative solutions and clear leadership rather than merely focussing on rebuilding.

As will be demonstrates later in Figure 4 and Subphase 5C in particular, crises may lead to adaptation of the system and its related networks. In this context, an organizational network can be described as a set of interacting organizations that exchange information, share customers, or exchange resources. In the tourism context this involves many companies involved in transport, accommodation, attractions, etc., working together to produce a product. From this perspective, tourism recognises tourism destinations are interactive networks of suppliers of services (Scott & Laws, 2004) that change over time.

As Scott and Cooper (2005) point out, the concept of organizational networks originated in the early sociological writings of Simmel (1908) and the social anthropological work of Radcliffe Brown (1935). These writers developed a structural view on social interaction which highlighted the importance of social organizations, relationships and interactions in influencing individual decisions. Structures are recurring patterns of social relations (Thatcher, 1998). This view may be contrasted with a rationalist perspective that focuses on the attributes and actions of individuals or organizations (Brinton Milward & Provan, 1998).

Social network analysis seeks to define and quantify these relationships. The work of Moreno (1934) indicated that social configura-

tions had definite structures which could be described in 'sociograms' to visualise the flow of information between organizations or the friendships between individuals. This led to the development of graph theory where the relationships between individuals in groups are represented as points and lines and the resulting patterns are described.

Later developments led to the identification of groups of individuals with similar patterns of relationships (blockmodels) and to the use of statistical methods such as multidimensional scaling to transform relationships into social distance and map them in social space. Social network analysis relates the relationships of the individual to the pattern of the network, and provides insight into the interactions between the two (Stokman, 2002). Social network analysis is philosophically related to systems theory (Boulding, 1956), where the properties of the system are derived from the interaction of many components.

Social network analysis delivers a number of useful outcomes. It provides a means of visualizing complex sets of relationships and through simplifying them delivers a useful method for promoting effective collaboration within a group, supporting critical junctures in networks that cross functional, hierarchical, or geographic boundaries; and ensuring integration within groups following strategic restructuring initiatives (Cross et al., 2002). The use of standard methods and questions enables networks of relationships to be compared between regions or over time facilitating the study of dynamic situations. A more ambitious aim is to offer a structural analysis and suggestions for improving network characteristics such as communication flows. As a result, social network analysis overlaps and informs the study of inter-organizational collaboration and cooperation, networks and strategic alliances. It has been used in studies of inter organizational relationships and in the development of policy (Tyler & Dinan, 2001; Coleman, 2002; Pforr, 2002). A social network has been defined as a specific set of linkages among a defined set of persons, with the additional property that the characteristics of these linkages as a whole may be used to interpret the social behaviour of the persons involved (Mitchell, 1969).

From a social network perspective, the tourism system is a network of organizations. The effect of a disaster or crisis is to place stress on these relationships. This stress is also systemic to the extent that the impact of a disaster on one organization or destination may in turn lead to a flow-on effect on others. One reason for this is that competition between companies and destinations is intense and the effect of disaster in one destination will have an effect on related or neighbouring destinations (Lepp and Gibson, 2003). Thus the effect of Severe Acute Respiratory Syndrome on Australian tourism destinations was to reduce international visitor numbers from Asia but boost domestic tourism to popular national destinations. A number of authors have examined the effect of a crisis on organizations outside the initial crisis area. Litvin and Alderson (2003), for example, examined the effect of the 9/11 crisis on the Charleston Convention and Visitors Bureau. In that case effective management was able to avert the full extent of the impact by switching promotion expenditure to different markets.

The effect of a crisis on the destination, conceptualized as a network of organizations, is shown in Figure 2. In this example a crisis has the effect of changing the network of relationships between organizations, potentially through loss of some members or the introduction of new ones. In State A (left hand cluster) firms have loose networks often operating independently. In the post crisis situation the need to work together to overcome the effects of the crisis forges new networks creating the situation illustrated in State B (right hand cluster). As a consequence, a crisis may create potentially unpredictable consequences in destination markets.

A related view is that the nature of other relationship types such as cooperation and alliances between stakeholders is important in minimizing or averting the effects of a disaster through better crisis management (Pearson & Clair, 1998; Pforr and Hosie, below). This is related to the established management approach of scanning for problems and avoiding or minimizing their impacts. But it is also related to

FIGURE 2. Conceptualization of the Effect of a Crisis on a Destination System

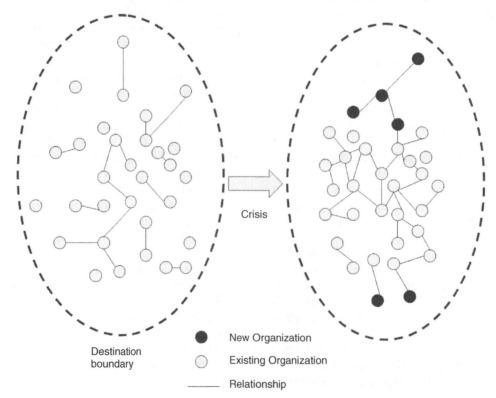

the idea that a network of organizations that cooperate together may be able to better manage the effects of a crisis. This approach is similar to the socio-technical systems perspective and has been examined in a study of social networks and a crisis in the construction sector (Loosemore, 1998).

PHASES OF CRISIS MANAGEMENT

From the preceding discussion, it is apparent that new perspectives on the operations of the post recovery phase have emerged and these need to be incorporated into existing models where possible. Coles (2003) notes that both Sonmez (1998) and Boyd (2000) offer conceptualisations of recovery in which, after falls in demand induced by terrorism, tourism production and consumption, levels come full circle back to those enjoyed before the event. Such expectations echo the advice offered by the World Tourism Organisation (WTO, 1998: 156) which can be described as the standard perspective on recovering from a crisis through a series of remedial steps. The WTO phase model summarised in Figure 3 advises users how to deal with media and tourist responses to the incident, how to mitigate negative impacts of loss of visitors to the area, and the use of media techniques to restore 'the normal pattern.' However, this model in its attempt to be accessible glosses over important complexities in crisis management. As Coles (2003, 177-178) noted "First . . . crises associated with terrorism are likely to be different to other forms of crisis. Second, the model's inherent linearity and the reduction of recovery to a set of practically automatic steps is stark. Finally, and most importantly, it views the events as practically ring-fenced temporally, so there is a "normal pattern" to which production and consumption can return."

Other models show the sequence of rescue, restoration of infrastructure and then the rebuilding of markets. These phase models share the premise that recovery equates to a return to normal operations, with a resumption of the actual or predicted trend of growth in the organisation's business activities. The crisis is itself regarded as the unit of analysis in these approaches.

In the field of tourism research relatively few studies have applied established crisis models. One of the most comprehensive tourism disaster management frameworks in tourism was developed by Faulkner (2001) who synthesised crisis situations based on research by Fink (1986: 20), Keown-McMullan (1997: 9) and Weiner and Kahn (1972: 21) and identified a number of phases in crisis situations as illustrated in Figure 4.

The alternative systems perspective is based on the idea of a continuously evolving system where (gradual) change is endemic but a crisis may suddenly result in a fundamentally different state. From this perspective a return to normality is not necessarily the required (or even desired) endpoint. A crisis is seen as the result of one form of change and the effects of a crisis are not confined to its immediate temporal or geographical vicinity. These changes may be positive or negative but certainly the subsequent state may be different from proceeding ones, and importantly, the changes that occur were unplanned from the perspective of the organisations strategic management. In these terms the effect of a disaster as a catastrophic change event is much more likely to trigger a change of state than other 'lesser' events. This perspective is presented in the case study of a flooding disaster in Katherine (Faulkner & Vikulov, 2001) previously referred to. In that case the disaster was seen as leading to the opportunity to change the quality of accommodation and other infrastructure in the tourism sector. However the opportunities for realignment of the system through changes to or development of new networks were not considered.

A DISASTER MANAGEMENT FRAMEWORK

In this paper we elaborate on phase 5 of Faulkner's model by indicating that longer term recovery consists of three sub-phases, 5A–recovery of damaged infrastructure; 5B–marketing responses; and 5C–adaptations to the system itself. In his original work Faulkner considered the long term recovery phase as important but did not elaborate to any great extent. In terms of the research reported in this volume it is necessary to examine this phase of the

FIGURE 3. Phase Model of a Tourism Crisis

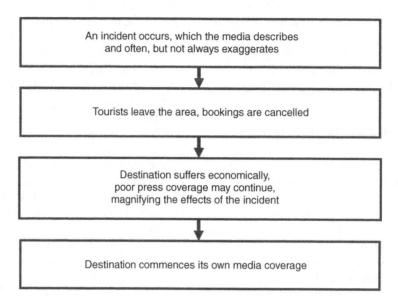

Based on WTO 1998, page 156.

model in more detail with a view to identify specific subphases in the long term recovery phase.

In many cases the three subphases identified above have to occur simultaneously and are often the responsibility of different groups of individuals and authorities who may or may not be acting in a coordinated manner. For example, in the case of Cyclone Larry hitting Northern Queensland in 2006 (see Prideaux et al., below) Subphases 5A (Recovery of damaged infrastructure) and 5B (Marketing) were implemented simultaneously but by different groups. This may lead to confusion but in cases where there is the potential for further loss of life and damage to property, Phase B can be expected to receive relatively little attention by the authorities, forcing marketing authorities to initiate their own activities. Later and once the danger to life and property has past more attention can be focused on Subphase B which will then evolve into Subphase C when the new realities become apparent. Subphase B is a critical element of Phase 5 for even if damaged infrastructure is rebuilt the failure to convince travellers that the destination is reopened for business will result in market failure and economic loss.

It is entirely likely that during Phase 5 the firms and organisations involved in re-establishing the destination will develop new networks as suggested in Figure 4. If this is the case, the previous system will undergo change and a new system will emerge that will, to a greater or lesser extent, differ from the shape and composition that existed in the pre crisis period.

A fuller understanding of the range of recovery challenges may therefore be obtained from more advanced theoretical perspectives which see the organisation as a member of one or more functional networks which are usually characterised as dynamic and complex. This perspective is evolutionary, and does not presume that there is a single solution to a crisis in which the recovered state is a resumption of normal patterns of operation. Instead, the analysis is concerned with the effects of a crisis on methods of operations, relationships with network partners, the ways in which these develop as responses to the crisis, and the emergence of new states of operation which may include some previous partners as well as new partners. In this mode of analysis, interest focuses on a number of issues including: the system and its

FIGURE 4. Faulkner's Tourism Disaster Management Framework (Simplified)

Stage	Phase
1	Pre-event phase: disaster contingency plans, scenarios or probability assessments play a major role in the disaster management strategy
2	Prodromol phase: the disaster is imminent and warning systems and command centres are established. In this second phase contingency plan actions are initiated.
3	Emergency phase: disaster effects are felt and actions are necessary to protect people or property in the tourism destination.
4	Intermediate phase: short-term and immediate needs of people have to be addressed by emergency and rescue teams. A clear media communication strategy is crucial in this phase.
5	Long-term (recovery) phase: the damaged infrastructure has to be rebuilt and environmentally damaged areas have to be reconstructed.. • 5A- recovery of damaged infrastructure; Includes roads, water, electricity, hotels, transport and other services • 5B - marketing responses: by individual firms, DMOs, STOs, NTOs • 5C – adaptations to the system itself: as rebuilding occurs
6	Resolution phase: this phase corresponds to Smith's (1990) feedback loop where existing assessment methods or contingency plans are improved.

Source Based on Faulkner 2001

boundaries and their permeability; on the networked and social relationships on which the organisation depends; a historical perspective which can be used to understand the ways in which social relationships may amplify the psychological support or vulnerability of the organisation as it deals with a crisis; and finally on the sources and forms of leadership that are used to deal with crisis situations. This also raises the question of how organisations cooperate, and how they learn from and share experiences. Many of the papers which follow present detailed analysis of these issues (see particularly Smith, Carmichael and Batovsky; Moreira; Pike; Blackman and Ritchie; Carlsen and Hughes; Carlsen and Liburd, below).

THE EFFECT OF CRISES ON INTENTIONS TO TRAVEL

A major aspect of the special challenges of post crisis recovery can be understood by examining the reasons why a tourist service or destination suffers loss of business after a crisis (see Prideaux, Coglan and Falco-Mammone, below). In some situations, such as destruction in areas prone to wind storms (hurricanes, typhoons and cyclones) there is a need to analyse the significance of an organisation's market orientation to enhance the success of their recovery efforts (Martin-Consuegra, Esteban and Molina, (below). Tourism is usually a discretionary activity, and one which tourists choose over alternative ways of spending time and money. Confidence needs to be restored to a level where intending visitors believe that disruption has been minimised and their holiday investment of time and money is safe. If visitors perceive that there is a risk they are more than likely to select an alternative destination as highlighted by Hunter-Jones, Jeffs and Smith (below). There are also conditions which lead tourists to decide not to travel, or to avoid particular destinations (Floyd et al., 2003). This will be of particular concern in Subphase 5B of Figure 4.

Chief amongst the avoidance factors are risks to tourists themselves, and the likelihood of being in regions where epidemics or wars are raging, or which are in turmoil. In contemporary society, the 24 hour news services such as CNN feature and repeat scenes of devastation and disaster, so that potential travellers rapidly become aware of incidents occurring literally on the other side of the world. Thus the destination suffering a crisis becomes in effect 'demarketed' under a deluge of negative, if not hostile, publicity. In one example of this effect Vitic and Ringer (below) discuss the need for Montenegro to overcome its 'clouded image' after its recent period of conflict. Further, mis-

takes or delays in responding to the needs of those enmeshed in the drama of a disaster stimulate more adverse media interest, and increasingly, governments in countries which generate tourist flows feel compelled to issue advice to their own nationals against travelling to destinations under stress. This can have significant impacts as highlighted by Smith, Carmicheal and Batovsky (below) in their analysis of the impacts of the US Government's new Western Hemisphere Travel Initiative Passport requirements on Canada as a transborder weekend destination.

At the core of these recovery approaches is an acknowledgement of the need to change travellers' (mis) perceptions of the destination or organisation. Volo (below) questions whether an individual destination can achieve this through its website. A more comprehensive marketing strategy, particularly at the destination level, that also includes promotion, advertising and public relations is required. Attention to funding and long term monitoring of the effectiveness of this strategy is also required.

Floyd et al. (2003, 32-34) note that five groups of risk factors are pertinent to travel decision: war and political instability, health concerns, crime, terrorism, and natural disasters. They found that "Travel experience emerged as the most significant predictor of travel intentions." Critiquing the Travel Industry Association of America's persuasive advertising campaign they point out that "intentions to travel in the 12 months following 9-11 were to the risk of family, friends and associates disapproving of vacation choices. Referring Pearce's Travel Career Ladder, they recommend that recovery marketing should target experienced travellers who "would require less attention to safety and security issues."

Thus, a communications-led approach intended to ameliorate travellers' perceptions of risk in a specific area is often a key element in tourism recovery strategies. See Ladkin, Fyall, Fletcher and Shipway; Niineinen and Gatsou; Chacko and Marcell; Carlsen and Hughes; and Armstrong and Ritchie for analyses of recent marketing led recovery programmes (below). Lehto, Douglas and Park (below) analyse the advantages of working with destination stakeholders to mediate natural disasters.

DISCUSSION

In this paper crisis is set within a wider systems perspective. In its normal state a system is seen in dynamic balance, given that at any time there will be a number of factors affecting it such as technological change and changes in consumer preferences. Any change to one part of the system may have an effect on other parts of the system. Where these impacts are small and recognised, as occurs when new technologies are introduced, the system usually responds in a predictable manner. When unpredictable events such as a crisis impacts on the system's stability, balance and predictability are lost until a new level of balance is achieved. The foregoing discussion emphasises the editors' view that the outcome of a crisis may not be a return to a normal situation, as parts of the system are likely to have changed. It is pertinent to this discussion that Carlsen and Liburd (below) call for the re-analysis of previously published case studies arguing that they are an important source of knowledge which could provide better insights into crisis recovery management when re-examined from this perspective.

An issue highlighted in this collection of studies is the measurement of the success of a tourism crisis recovery programme. The blunt instruments of visitor arrivals and visitor spending do not: adequately differentiate between recovery of different market segments; indicate the variable recovery rates of stakeholders; identify changes to the tourism system; or assist in understanding the resilience or otherwise of the system. Most crucially, there appears to be no way of measuring a tourism organisation's ability to learn from past crises, either one it has experienced directly or those which have afflicted partners or competitors. Yet improved responsiveness to future crisis situations, as well as the potential to recover from them more rapidly, depends on a full understanding of the complexity and dynamics of crisis situations and a willingness to take a positive approach to solving future problems.

This paper challenges the standard perspective that recovering from a crisis requires only a series of remedial steps to return to the previous normality. The WTO phase model discussed earlier is typical of this approach, first dealing with casualties of the incident, then restoring infrastructure and later rebuilding markets. As demonstrated in this collection of papers this is often not the case. Accordingly, a fuller understanding of the range of challenges that may occur requires more advanced theoretical perspectives which see the organisation as a member of a wider system operating in the context of a variety of partner organisations and as a member of one or more dynamic and complex functional networks. This perspective is evolutionary, and does not presume that there is a unique solution to a crisis. Instead, the analysis is concerned with the effects of a crisis on operations, relationships with network partners, the ways in which these develop as responses to the crisis, and the emergence of new states of operation, with some previous partners disconnected and others joining the new state. In this mode of analysis, interest focuses on the following aspects of the system: its boundaries and their permeability; the networked and social relationships on which the organisation depends; the historical perspectives give understanding to the ways in which social relationships may amplify the psychological support or vulnerability of the organisation as it deals with a crisis; and on the sources of and forms of leadership that are required to deal with crisis situations. This also raises the questions of how organisations cooperate, and how they learn from and shared experience.

CONCLUSION

The major objective of this collection of research, and of this editorial paper, is to focus the attention of researchers and managers on the recovery phase following a tourism crisis. However, as noted earlier, there is a burgeoning literature on general tourism crisis management, and it is important to recognise that considerable advances have been made in preplanning to avoid or to mitigate future disasters.

While some of the crises which trigger the need for tourism recovery marketing originate as humanitarian crises and require urgent responses to the immediate needs of residents as well as tourists, others have their genesis in nature. Initially, the responsibility of managers is to deal with the humanitarian aspects of crisis to the best of their abilities. Attention must then be given to the infrastructure that supports the tourism industry and importantly, its marketing to alter the perceptions of visitors that the destination is again open for business. Early recovery of the tourism sector is important particularly for countries and regions that depend on tourism.

The papers in this collection demonstrate that new theoretical insight can be gained by examining how organisations achieve recovery as members of dynamic functional networks. This evolutionary perspective is concerned with the way that organization and the system in which they operate adapts to the pressures and opportunities presented by the crisis.

It is apparent that no ideal template exists or will ever be devised to deal with crises because of their varied nature. It is also apparent that understanding the impact of crisis on organisations and destinations is the key to effective post event recovery. Unfortunately, the future will bring with it new crises and disasters and these will in turn be reported in future academic discourses. It is the hope of the authors of this paper and indeed of the papers that comprise this volume, that the learning recorded here will be used as a base for future disaster and crises research and will assist organisations and destinations to better plan and implement post crisis recovery marketing.

REFERENCES

Anderson, B., Prideaux, B. and Brown, G. (2007) Responding to the Crises of 2001: the Australian Experience in Laws, E., Prideaux, B. and Chon, K. (eds.) *Crisis Management in Tourism*, CABI: Wallingford.

Boulding, K. E. (1956). General Systems Theory; the skeleton of science. *Management Science, 2*(3), 56-68.

Brinton Milward, H., & Provan, K. G. (1998). Measuring network structure. *Public Administration, 76,* 387-407.

Britton, S., & Clarke, W. (Eds.). (1987). *Ambiguous alternative: Tourism in small developing countries.* Suva, Fiji: University of the South Pacific.

Buhalis, D. (2000). Marketing the competitive destination of the future. *Tourism Management, 21*(1), 97-116.

Burstein, P. (1991). Policy domains: Organization, culture and policy outcomes. *Annual Review of Sociology, 17,* 327-350.

Coleman, W. D. (2002). Policy Networks. In *International Encyclopedia of the Social & Behavioral Sciences.*

Coles, T. A Local Reading of a Global Disaster: Some Lessons on Tourism Management from an Annus Horribilis in South West England. *Journal of Travel and Tourism Marketing, 15/*2-3, 173-197, 2003.

Cross, R., Borgatti, S. P., & Parker, A. (2002). Making invisible work visible: Using social network analysis to support strategic collaboration. *California Management Review, 44*(2), 25-46.

Faulkner, B. (2001). Towards a framework for tourism disaster management. *Tourism Management, 22*(2), 135-147.

Faulkner, B., & Russell, R. (2001). Turbulence, chaos and complexity in tourism systems: A research direction for the new millennium. In B. Faulkner, G. Moscardo & E. Laws (Eds.), *Tourism in the 21st Century: Lessons from Experience* (pp. 328-349). London: Continuum.

Faulkner, B., & Vikulov, L. (2001). Katherine, washed out one day, back on track the next: A post-mortem of a tourism disaster. *Tourism Management, 22*(4), 331-344.

Fink, S. (1986). *Crisis Management.* New York: American Association of Management.

Floyd, M. Gibson, H. Pennington-Grey, L. and Thapa, B. The Effect of Risk Perceptions on Intentions to Travel in the aftermath of September 11, 2001. Journal of Travel and Tourism Marketing, 15/2-3, 19-38, 2003.

Huang, J. H., & Min, J. C. H. (2002). Earthquake devastation and recovery in tourism: the Taiwan case. *Tourism Management, 23*(2), 145-154.

Keown-McMullan, C. (1997). Crisis: When does a molehill become a mountain? *Disaster Prevention and Management, 6*(1), 4-10.

Laws, E., & Cooper, C. (1998). Inclusive tours and commodification: the marketing constraints for mass-market resorts. *Journal of Vacation Marketing, 4*(4), 337-352.

Laws, E. Prideaux, B. and Chon, K. (2007). Crisis Management in Tourism: Challenges for Managers and Researchers in Laws, E., Prideaux, B. and Chon, K. (eds.) *Crisis Management in Tourism,* CABI: Wallingford.

Litvin, S. W., & Alderson, L. L. (2003). How Charleston got her groove back: A Convention and Visitors Bureau's response to 9/11. *Journal of Vacation Marketing, 9*(2), 188-197.

McKercher, B., & Chon, K. (2004). The Over-Reaction to SARS and the Collapse of Asian Tourism. *Annals of Tourism Research, 31*(3), 716-719.

Mansfield, Y. and Pizam, A. Editors. Tourism, Security and Safety: From Theory to Practice. Butterworth Heineman, Burlington, MA, 2006.

Mitchell, J. C. (1969). The concept and use of social networks. In J. C. Mitchell (Ed.), *Social networks in ur-*

ban situations. Manchester: University of Manchester Press.

Moreno, J. (1934). *Who Shall Survive?* New York: Beacon Press.

Murphy, P. E., & Bayley, R. (1989). Tourism and disaster planning. *Geographical Review*, *79*(1), 36-46.

Pearson, C. M., & Clair, J. A. (1998). Reframing crisis management. *Academy of Management Review*, *23*(1), 59-76.

Pikkemaat, B. and Peters, M. (2005) Towards the measurement of innovation–A pilot study in the small and medium sized hotel industry. *Journal of Quality Assurance in Hospitality and Tourism*, *6*(3-4), 89-112.

Pforr, C. (2002). The 'makers and shapers' of tourism policy in the Northern Territory of Australia: A policy network analysis of actors and their relational constellations. *Journal of Hospitality and Tourism Research*, *9*(2), 134-151.

Prideaux, B. and Laws, E. (2007), Reflections and Further Research Priorities, in Laws, E., Prideaux, B. and Chon, K. (eds.) *Crisis Management in Tourism*, CABI: Wallingford.

Prideaux, B., Laws, E., & Faulkner, B. (2003). Events in Indonesia: exploring the limits to formal tourism trends forecasting methods in complex crisis situations. *Tourism Management*, *24*(4), 475-487.

Quarantelli, E. L. (1988). Disaster crisis management–a summary of research findings. *Journal of Management Studies*, *25*(4), 373-385.

Radcliffe-Brown, A. R. (1935). ON the concept of function in social science. *American Anthropologist*, *37*(3), 394-402.

Russell, R., & Faulkner, B. (1999). Movers and shakers: Chaos makers in tourism development. *Tourism Management*, *20*(4), 411-423.

Scott, N., & Cooper, C. (2005). The network structure of a regional tourism organization: Application of the social network theory in one region of Queensland. Paper presented at the Sharing Tourism Knowledge: 15th International Research Conference of the Council for Australian University Tourism and Hospitality Education, Alice Springs.

Scott, N., & Laws, E. (2004). *Stimulants and inhibitors in the development of niche markets–The whale's tale.* Paper presented at the CAUTHE 2004, Brisbane.

Scott, N., & Laws, E. (2004). Whale watching–the roles of small firms in the evolution of a new Australian niche market. In R. Thomas (Ed.), *Small Firms in Tourism: International Perspectives* (pp. 153-166). London: Elsevier.

Simmel, G. (1908). *Soziologie* (1968 edition). Berlin: Dunker and Humblot.

Stokman, F. N. (2002). Networks: Social. In *International Encyclopedia of the Social & Behavioral Sciences*.

Thatcher, M. (1998). The development of policy network analyses from modest origins to overarching frameworks. *Journal of Theoretical Politics*, *10*(4), 389-416.

Turner, B. A. (1976). The organizational and inter-organizational development of disasters. *Administrative Science Quarterly*, *21*, 378-397.

Tyler, D., & Dinan, C. (2001). The role of interested groups in England's emerging tourism policy network. *Current Issues in Tourism*, *4*(2-4), 210-252.

Weiner, A., & Kahn, H. (1972). Crisis and arms control. In C. F. Hermann (Ed.), *International crises: Insights from behaviour research* (pp. 21). New York: The Free Press.

Stealth Risks and Catastrophic Risks:
On Risk Perception and Crisis Recovery Strategies

Pedro Moreira

SUMMARY. What individuals do in the present is to a certain degree influenced by their vision of the future, which comprises a dimension of risk perception. This study compares the risk perception of stealth risks and catastrophic risks to the development of a tourism destination. The main distinction between the two types of risk relies on the distribution of the consequences over a longer or shorter timeline. In the case of stealth risks the consequences are diffused whilst in the case of catastrophic risks the consequences are concentrated in time, suggesting the hypothesis that catastrophic risks would be perceived as higher risks to tourism development than stealth risks, given the higher visibility of the consequences. A second hypothesis compares the risk perceptions of the tourists and residents to the tourism development of the destination. The data shows that stealth risks are considered higher risks than catastrophic risks and reveal a wide consistency in the risk perceptions of tourists and residents. These results and other aspects of risk perception as the sense of personal invulnerability and the effect of gender are explored and confronted with the literature and implications to destination management and travel and tourism research are discussed.

INTRODUCTION

Risk is a perception of the future, a perception of a threatening scenario. A risk scenario does not exist yet and it is therefore a mental model of the future built over a mental representation of the reality. One of the core elements of the definitions of risk is the distinction between what is real and what is possible (Markowitz, 1991, Evers and Nowotny, 1987, referred by Renn, 1992).

Nevertheless, perceptions of the future affect decisions, and decisions affect what the future is going to become. Until the terrorist attacks of September 11, 2001 in the United States, some images of the future had little influence over the decision to buy a flight ticket. After the bombings of October 12th, 2002 in Bali, Indonesia, flights and hotel reservations dropped abruptly, and the consequences had a long term impact on the island economy. In November of 2002 the first known cases of the Severe Acute Respiratory Syndrome (SARS) were recorded and through 2003 the outbreak spread from Southern China and rapidly affected travellers and destinations worldwide.

Pedro Moreira (E-mail: pedro@ift.edu.mo) is a Lecturer in Management and Social Sciences at Institute for Tourism Studies (Colina de Mong-Ha, Macau).

Risk is now an explicit component of travel and tourism related decisions.

Not all risks are, however, so strong in terms of impact and as clearly defined in time. Other risks exist that affect silently but relentlessly the development of tourism destinations. Stealth risks' impacts are sustainable negative impacts that threaten long term development. One of the distinct and dangerous characteristics of these risks is their apparent invisibility in terms of risk perception, leading to the unawareness or underestimation of their consequences until it is already too late.

This paper presents a contrasting perspective between the perceptions of stealth risks and catastrophic risks among tourists and residents in an Asia Pacific destination. The Pacific Ocean is the centre of a zone of enormous potential for tourism growth. However, the Pacific is far from being a route exempt of risks. The "Pacific Ring of Fire" is an arc of frequent earthquakes and intense volcanic activity and the range of natural hazards extends to extreme weather, an exotic wildlife that includes a wide number of dangers, and tropical diseases. Human sources of danger include risks related with political and social instability, underdevelopment, uncontrolled or non sustained development, war, terrorism, crime, accidents and pollution. Asia Pacific is replete of wonderful and unique destinations although it requires some spirit of adventure. On the other hand, risk adds uniqueness to the tourism experience and evokes memories of the lost challenges faced by the first explorers.

The tourism development of the Asia Pacific region in the recent years justifies not only a close attention to its characteristic risks but also to new risks that can arise in the future. Great dangers and catastrophic events might not be the only risks affecting the sustainable growth of tourism. Some risks characterise economical success, and are predictable consequences of progress and prosperity.

Beyond its structural dimension of probability, risk can be defined as a function of both the level of the consequences associated with a specific risk source and the period of time over which these consequences materialize. *Ceteris paribus*, the extension of the same level of consequences over a long period is expected to produce different risk perceptions than if these consequences are concentrated in a short period of time. Gradual evolutions of known problems or the degradation of the present conditions do not apparently have the impact of extreme catastrophic events and could therefore become progressively more dangerous, slowly evolving to a point where nothing can be done to avoid the worst consequences. Is this true in terms of risk perception? Are catastrophic risks considered higher risks than stealth risks? In addition, if the risk perceptions of tourists and residents are significantly different, the implications introduce the possibility that a dual management of the risk factors might be required, and that the differences between the internal and external image of the destination should be looked at attentively.

A model of crisis recovery integrating the perception of the reality will be suggested as a form of creating a deeper understanding of the nature of risk and an improvement of the response to crisis and disasters, and a ranking of the most feared risks for residents and tourists will be presented, pointing out the major concerns about one city specifically (Macau SAR, PR China) but also opening a line of research to future comparisons with risk perceptions in other tourism destinations.

RISK AND RISK PERCEPTION

The term risk can be used to express hazard, probability, consequence, or a potential adversity or threat (Slovic and Weber, 2002). Risk is a social construction emerging as a response to danger and uncertainty, and it is always a subjective evaluation (Slovic, 1992). This approach implies an understanding that both the probability and consequences that are generally considered the core dimensions of risk are subjective evaluations or perceptions. General definitions presenting risk as the probability of hazard occurrence (Smith, 1992) or "the probability of a adverse future multiplied by its magnitude" (Adams, 2003:69), are now complemented with this view of risk including the perceptive dimensions of loss potential (Jones and Hood, 2002). Although risk perception is an intuitive evaluation of risk (Slovic, 1987, 1998), it is the perceived risk that determines the behaviours (Weinstein, 1988, Sjoberg,

2000, both referred by Brug, Aro, Oenema, Zwart, Richardus and Bishop, 2004). That way, even an incorrect or clearly wrong perception of risk will influence behaviours in the same way that decisions are consistently affected by judgment biases.

Previous research also indicates the existence of a biased sense of personal invulnerability in risk perception. Brug et al. (2004) found that one in each three of the respondents of their study thought that their risk of contracting SARS was lower in comparison to other individuals of the same age and gender, with less than one in each ten respondents perceiving a higher personal risk. When the same subjects were asked about their worries of getting SARS themselves, family members acquiring it or the possibility of SARS cases in their homeland (Netherlands), in all the three questions the affirmative answers were lower than 10 per cent. Brug et al. (2004) also report an effect of gender in risk percentage with women exhibiting a high risk perception associated with SARS than men. These results are coherent with the initial hypothesis proposed by Mitchell and Vassos (1997) that male individuals would perceive a lower risk than female individuals, but this hypothesis was then rejected in face of contradictory results.

Research on risk perception (Fischhoff, 2002) shows that: (1) risk perceptions might be very different from quantitative risk analysis; (2) we know very little about the integration of human fantasies and rational knowledge; and (3) risk estimates can express the risk perceptions associated with a risk factor as well as the uncertainty of the knowledge about the risk factor.

The dimension of the consequences does not influence risk perceptions in such a consistent way as it influences objective risks estimations. Risk characteristics like the controllability of the risk factors, previous information or experience, or the circumstance of the risks being voluntary or imposed affects what we consider to be the major threats in our vision of the future. Fischhoff, Slovic, Lichtenstein, Read and Combs (1978), identified nine characteristics that influence the perception of an overall acceptable level of risk (Figure 1).

Back then, the original study intended to analyse the risk perceptions of medical X-rays and nuclear power, but this framework might be extensible to a broader scope of risk research. In this article we are especially interested in the influence on risk perception of the relationship between the timeline length and the intensity of the consequences, which differentiates stealth risks (long timeline and diffused, low intensity) from catastrophic risks (short timeline and concentrated, high intensity). This timeline length-consequences intensity relationship is comparable to the chronic or catastrophic effects of X-rays or nuclear power and, apparently, there would be a basis to expect that the results in terms of risk perception could be similar. In the study of Fischhoff et al. (1978), nuclear power was perceived to hold a much higher risk than X-rays and, from the nine dimensions, the chronic-catastrophic dimension was the dimension that registered the higher rating difference in the comparison between X-rays and nuclear power. These results suggest that this dimension might be one of the most powerful dimensions differentiating high from low risk perceptions.

REAL RISK, RISK PERCEPTION AND CRISIS RECOVERY STRATEGIES

"Many raised their arms to the gods, others, more numerous, declared that the gods were no longer, and that this was the last night on earth. Some magnified the real dangers with imaginary and false terrors." Pliny's (the younger) letter to Tacitus de-

FIGURE 1. Risk Characteristics Influencing Risk Perception (derived from Fischhoff et al., 1978)

Voluntary	Involuntary
Chronic	Catastrophic
Common	Dread
Consequences not fatal	Consequences fatal
Known to exposed	Not known to exposed
Immediate	Delayed
Known to science	Not known to science
Not controllable	Controllable
New	Old

scribing the eruption that destroyed Pompeii and Herculaneum in A.D. 79 (from Carolis and Patricelli, 2003:82)

"(. . .) disaster is the impossible that happens." Denis (1995:14)

Risk perception is an element of the general perceived image of products or services and was found to have a critical impact on organisational results (e.g., "airlines perceived as being unsafe, lose market and suffer long-term decline" (Mowen, 1990, in Siomkos, 2000:101)). Siomkos (2000), on a study involving 329 airline travellers, confirmed that airline safety perceptions are strong determinants of consumer response. The results showed that different types of consumers respond differently to the same reality. Business travellers decisions were found to be less vulnerable to declines in safety perception when compared with travellers flying for pleasure, probably under the influence of the travel frequency, "since frequent travellers have already accepted the existence of a risk when flying" (Siomkos, 2000:107). According with Shrader-Frechette (1991), two reasons for high risk perceptions could be due to: (1) the catastrophic consequences of an event; and (2) the imposition of the risk, by contrast with a risk which is taken voluntarily. Schrader-Frechette (1991) also suggests that

new risks or unusual situations of risk are associated with cautious approaches and that usual or recurrent risks are faced with lesser concern. This might lead us to an important point, that the frequency of occurrence of a risk event in the past influences the risk perception and defines the amount of attention and caution applied to future risks of the same nature.

Continued exposure to risk might alter the risk tolerance, raise and consolidate the levels of risk that are tolerated and make necessary the perception of very high risks before changes are produced on decisions and behaviours. It is legitimate to suggest that, if the risks are perceived to remain stable, the isolated effect of repeated exposure will have as a consequence that the risk perception will tend to stabilise and progressively decline over time. With this natural tendency in mind the image recovery efforts should be directed to decrease the time length of the post crisis divergence between the risk and the risk perception thus faster reaching the period of decline and convergence of the risk and the risk perception (Figure 2) and the image recovery evolution after a crisis or disaster should show a consistent decrease of the risk perception over time (Figure 3).

After some turbulence following a crisis or disaster and as a result of the response and recovery initial measures the risk and the risk per-

FIGURE 2. Real Risk and Risk Perception Trends After a Crisis or Disaster

Risk and risk perception short and medium term trend   **Risk and risk perception long term trend**

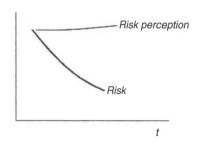
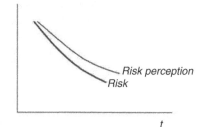

FIGURE 3. Image Recovery Evolution

Crisis
Disaster   *Phase I: High risk perception*   *Phase II: Low risk perception*

                                                                                                                t

ception will tend to stabilize. Assuming that the risks decrease progressively as a result of a successful crisis response, the risk perception will follow that decrease, or instead remain high or even increase if the image recovery is unsuccessful. If both the risk and the risk perception decrease as the recovery process progresses this is an indication that the recovery is successful and well balanced and that the crisis response was both effective and perceived as effective. If there is a lack of balance and the risk perception remains high this will mean that the effort of recovery is not being perceived as effective. This unbalance might be attributed to several factors as the lack of information, the distortion of the information and the lack of confidence in the sources of the information or a risk perception so consolidated in the past that the new information is not able to produce significant changes. The importance of the information and communication management in the recovery process is recognised by several authors (Hale, Dulek, Hale, 2005, Horsley, Barker, 2002, Drabek, 2000 in Cavlek, 2002, Siomkos, 2000, Sönmez, 1998) and, in our perspective, the crises recovery strategies aim two fundamental lines of action: (1) actions over the reality; and (2) actions over the mental image or the perception of the reality. These two lines of action can also be approached as strategies to decrease real risk and risk perception.

Throughout and after the recovery, and accordingly with the effectiveness of that recovery, four scenarios are possible (Figure 4). The first scenario, involving high real risk and high risk perception is a sign that the recovery strategies both over the reality and over the perception of the reality are not being effective and such high levels of both variables should appear associated with low numbers of arrivals and sales. The second scenario is an unbalanced and dangerous scenario with high real risk and low risk perception. This unbalance can be the result of a recovery strategy that was strongly focused on image recovery without achieving effective progresses in the reduction of the risk. The positive image might support good business figures for a while but the recovery will not be sustainable and it might be a matter of time until this situation evolves into a scenario type I. The third scenario is also unbalanced, but in an inverse way, with a low real risk combined with a high risk perception. In this case the effective efforts to decrease risk were not sufficient to produce a decrease in the risk perception, due to insufficient, incorrect or inadequate information made available, or to a consolidated high risk perception that might be attributed to the proximity of the crisis height, to the magnitude of the losses, or to a loss of confidence in the recovery success. Finally, the fourth scenario is a scenario in which both the real risk and the risk perception are low. This is the ideal scenario of recovery with a balanced combination of real risk and risk perception in low levels, as a result of an effective recovery strategy.

The suggested model defines two priorities in managing the response to crises and disasters:

FIGURE 4. Real Risk and Risk Perception Scenarios After the Crisis or Disaster Recovery

		Risk Perception	
		High	Low
Real Risk	High	Scenario I High real risk High risk perception	Scenario II High real risk Low risk perception
	Low	Scenario III Low real risk High risk perception	Scenario IV Low real risk Low risk perception

(1) *Response to the objective impacts of the crisis or disaster*, with loss control and recovery measures.

(2) *Response to the subjective impacts of the crisis or disaster*, on issues involving the destination image, the confidence of the custumers, and the response commitment of the professionals and of the investors.

It seems difficult that tourism operators, or even private or public organisations representing the tourism industry could prepare in advance responses for events that are characterised by a given degree of unpredictability and by an external origin (e.g., medical emergencies like the severe acute respiratory syndrome or the bird flu pandemic, terrorist attacks, political instability, social unrest, or natural disasters of extraordinary scale like the December 2004 tsunami). However, it can be argued that there are general lines of action that can be applied in the design of general emergency plans capable of responding to common characteristics of crises and disasters.

Risk can also be described including the concept of vulnerability. Risk (R), would be a function of hazard (H) and vulnerability (V): R = H*V (Wisner, Blaikie, Cannon, Davis, 1994). This concept of vulnerability is clearly related to the present state of the individuals and to the problems that are placed before them, either if perceived or not (Shiels, 1991:3, defines disaster as "a damaging and unsought failure of intelligence and judgment").

If it is true that tourism is highly vulnerable to the influence of external factors (McIntosh, Goeldner, Ritchie, 1995) it is often also true that

"(. . .) it is extremely difficult to isolate the contributions to tourism development of a single factor or separate the effects of one factor from another" (Liu, 1995:28). The cultural perspective of risk suggests that "risk taking and risk aversion, shared confidence and shared fears, are part of the dialogue on how to organise social relations" (Douglas & Wilavsky, 1982:8). Douglas and Wildavsky (1982) present risk as a social construct and argue that most of risk assessment has the purpose of ranking risks, in order to establish priorities for action.

The perception of risk determines our decisions and responses to risk. Research confirms that people respond to perceived risks (Fischhoff, Slovic and Lichtenstein, 1982) and want to be informed about potential risks (Alfidi, 1971, Weinstein, 1979, both referred by Fischhoff, Slovic, Lichtenstein, 1982), and therefore the failure to perceive negative consequences in conditions in which the necessary information is available can be considered one of the characteristics of preventable disasters (Shiels, 1991).

The real risk and risk perception inconsistent trends presented in Figure 5 are the possible consequences of a management deficit in one of the risk response priorities proposed by our model and are, although for different reasons, the most damaging pre or post crisis trends, involving the unrealistic perception of risks that will nevertheless influence decisions and behaviour as if those risks were real, or real but unperceived risks in which case the absence of perception might contribute to the increase of the real risk and to a suboptimal response if the decisions do not take into account the loss possibilities involved.

FIGURE 5. Real Risk and Risk Perception Inconsistent Trends

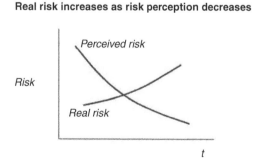

Real risk increases as risk perception decreases

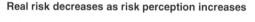

Real risk decreases as risk perception increases

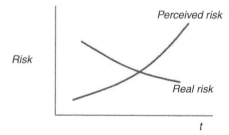

Sensitivity to hazards is a combination of exposure and vulnerability (Smith, 1992), but there is a long history of human response to adversity (e.g., "attempts to defend individual buildings against earthquakes date back at least 2,000 years," Smith, 1992:4). Risk recovery is always a challenge since "the essence of risk management lies in maximising the areas where we have some control over the outcome while minimising the areas where we have absolutely no control over the outcome and the linkage between effect and cause is hidden from us" (Bernstein, 1996:197). Although some crises and disasters are by its nature virtually inevitable, the proposed model highlighting the two major response priorities addressing the real risks and the risk perception might contribute to a better understanding of the true extension of risk and of the possible losses associated with crises and disasters and to the management of the risks that can be managed either in terms of prevention or of crisis response.

RISK PROBABILITY AND IMPACT TIMELINE: STEALTH RISKS AND CATASTROPHIC RISKS

The distinction between stealth risks and catastrophic risks shares similarities with the chronic-catastrophic dimension, one of the nine risk characteristics identified by Fischhoff et al. (1978), and with the delayed effect-immediate effect dimension presented by Slovic (1987).

What distinguish catastrophic risks are the immediate impact of high intensity consequences and the concentration of the direct consequences over a short timeline. Our definition of catastrophic risks involves the possibility of sudden negative impacts or changes in the present reality and includes serious accidents (e.g., an airplane crash or an industrial accident), disasters (e.g., an epidemic disease outbreak, a terrorist attack) or extreme events commonly termed as 'acts of God' (e.g., an earthquake or a typhoon).

Stealth risks include the gradual increase of neutral or negative present conditions (e.g., crime levels) and the gradual degradation of neutral or positive present conditions (e.g., air quality). In the case of the stealth risks the consequences intensity is diffused over a long timeline and these seem to be therefore less visible risks, more difficult to detect and acknowledge.

It would be then acceptable to hypothesise *a priori* that stealth risks would be considered lower risks than catastrophic risks, due to the intensity concentration of the consequences over a reduced timeline in the later ones.

Paradoxically, our results show a different pattern, with the stealth risks being consistently considered higher risks than the catastrophic risks, which might indicate a predominance of the extension of the time length over the concentration of the consequences in defining what is perceived as a higher risk.

METHODOLOGY

The individual interviews for data collection took place in Macau SAR, PR China, during April 2004. The sample included 300 respondents (150 tourists and 150 residents). The percentages' distribution for the age was the following: 49% were 25 years old or less, 28% were between 26 and 35, 14% between 36 and 45, and the remaining 9% were 46 or older. The gender distribution was 44% male and 56% female respondents. The place of residence percentages show 50% of the respondents residing in Macau, 31% in Hong Kong, 15% in Mainland China and the remaining 4% in other countries or territories. The place of birth distribution is also dominated by Macau (37%), followed by Hong Kong (32%), Mainland China (26%) and Taiwan (1%), with 5% of the respondents referring other places of birth (Sri Lanka, United States of America, Australia, New Zealand, Malaysia, Portugal and United Kingdom).

The research approach of the study can be integrated in what is generally termed as the psychometric paradigm of risk perception, and previous studies offer evidence that perceived risk is quantifiable and predictable (Slovic and Weber, 2002). The first part of the bilingual questionnaire (English and Chinese) included a list of 20 sources of risk and a 9 point rating scale, with extremes defined as low risk and high risk. The risk sources' list was specifically created for this study (some risks are specific to this city) and the 20 items were presented inter-laced in the questionnaire (one stealth risk item followed by a catastrophic risk item) to reduce possible biases generated by the item sequence. The respondents were asked to attribute a rate from 1 to 9 to each item, according with their perception of the high or low risk involved to the development of the city as a tourism destination.

The second part of the questionnaire in-cluded a set of questions related with the per-ception of risk vulnerability and with the com-parison between crises over short and long periods of time.

RESULTS

The results show a clear consistency be-tween the risk perception of tourists and resi-dents. From the twenty specific risks that the re-spondents were invited to rate, only three presented significant risk perception differ-ences (Table 1). All the differences were related to stealth risks and the direction of the differ-ences was also consistent, showing a higher risk rate expressed by the residents than by the tourists. In the first two cases ("gradual degra-dation of the air quality due to pollution" and

"gradual degradation of the city hygiene lev-els"), the differences can be explained in terms of the general concerns of the residents with the degradation of the quality of live, compre-hensively not so important for the tourists due, among other possible factors, to their rela-tively low length of stay in the city. In the third case ("gradual degradation of the city interna-tional image"), the difference can be due to the recognition of the importance of a positive in-ternational image, especially critical in face of the city's strong economic dependency of tourism.

Compared with the basic reference of the proposed 1 to 9 low risk-high risk rating scale, the risk perception did not reach extreme values either in the lower or in the higher ranges of the scale. The graphic in Figure 6 illustrates the concentration of the ratings in the central range contrasting with the blank areas both on the lower and higher extremes of risk perception. In the set of risks that the respondents were asked to rate no risks were considered extremely high or extremely low and the higher rate was attrib-uted to an "epidemic disease outbreak" risk, which is comprehensible due to the still vivid memories of the recent crisis that affected Southeast Asia, China, and specifically the nearby city of Hong Kong.

TABLE 1. Risk Perception Means: Tourists vs. Residents

	Tourists	Residents	t	df	p
Typhoon	4.3	4.3			n. s.
Gradual degradation of the air quality due to pollution	**4.6**	**5.1**	−2.1	298	.05
Earthquake	4.1	4.2			n. s.
Gradual increase of crime levels	6.0	5.9			n.s.
Flood	4.2	3.9			n. s.
Gradual degradation of the city hygiene levels	**5.3**	**5.9**	−2.4	298	.05
Terrorist attack	5.4	5.5			n. s.
Gradual increase of river and sea pollution	4.6	4.8			n.s.
Epidemic disease outbreak	6.5	7.0			n.s.
Gradual degradation of residents attitude towards tourists	**5.1**	**5.4**			n.s.
Airplane crash	3.5	3.5			n. s.
Gradual increase of the prices of products and services	5.0	5.0			n.s.
Jet Foil accident	3.7	3.3			n.s.
Gradual degradation of the city green areas	4.3	4.5			n.s.
Tour bus accident	4.3	4.2			n.s.
Gradual increase of the number of tourists	4.7	4.6			n. s.
Industrial accident	2.8	3.0			n.s.
Gradual degradation of the city international image	**4.6**	**5.6**	−3.9	298	.01
Urban or forestall fire	3.4	3.1			n. s.
Gradual increase of traffic and traffic accidents	4.8	5.0			n.s.

As showed in Table 2, the stealth risks were considered significantly higher risks in both groups (tourists and residents) and these results were reflected in the means of the total sample.

No significant differences were found in risk perception between genders, either for stealth risks or for catastrophic risks. The male means were lower than the female means for both types of risks but not lower enough to confirm the hypothesis of a gender effect in risk perception.

Considering that both involved the same losses, from an individual perspective, short period crises were preferred over long period crises (91% vs. 9%, p < .01). These results are consistent with the perception that, still considering the same losses, at a city level, crises that develop over long periods of time are greater

threats than crises that are concentrated in short periods (64% vs. 34%, p < .01).

Table 3 presents the ten higher risks to tourism development in the perception of tourists and residents. In both groups, there is an 8 to 2 ratio between stealth and catastrophic risks. The first risk is directly related with health and safety, a crucial factor in the competitiveness of tourism destinations considered of top importance by the respondents after the recent SARS outbreak. The only other catastrophic risk in the list ('terrorist attack') has become since September 11, 2001 an ever present major threat to tourism. All the remaining top risks were stealth risks, which impacts affect the sustainable development of a tourism destination, showing the awareness of both tourists and resi-

FIGURE 6. Risk Perception Means: Tourists vs. Residents

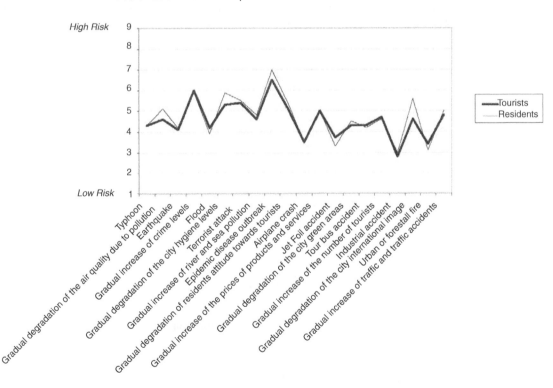

TABLE 2. Risk Perception Means: Catastrophic Risks vs. Stealth Risks

	Catastrophic Risks	Stealth Risks	t	df	p
Tourists	4.2	4.9	6.9	148	.01
Residents	4.2	5.2	9.9	147	.01
Total	4.2	5.1	11.8	296	.01

dents to the need of a careful management of these dimensions.

The sense of personal invulnerability effect was confirmed with only 8% of the respondents believing that the risks presented in the questionnaire would have a prime effect on themselves and their families and friends (Figure 7). The vast majority (66%) considered the residents to be most vulnerable to the risks presented and only 26% considered the tourists the most affected group.

CONCLUSIONS

The central questions of this study were to find if tourists and residents in a tourism destination would have different risk perceptions and if the risk perceptions of immediate impact catastrophic risks would be higher than the risk perceptions of delayed impact stealth risks.

The first question was suggested by the obvious differences between tourists and residents in terms of permanence at the destination and also by the different fundamental concerns of the two groups about the harmonious future development of the city.

The second question is justified by the difference of the distribution of the risk consequences over time. The concentration of the consequences over a shorter timeline might lead to a perception of a higher risk in the case of catastrophic risks, and the diffusion of the risk consequences over a longer timeline in the case of the stealth risks, might lead to the perception of a lower risk.

The fundamental question would be if the timeline of the consequences affects the risk perception, i.e., considering the same consequences, do we fear more hazards that take place in short or in long periods of time? The results show a preference for short period crises over long period crises with effects both at an individual and at a city level, confirming the differences that associated stealth risk with higher risk perceptions than catastrophic risks,

TABLE 3. Top Ten Risk Ranking

Tourists		Residents
Epidemic disease outbreak	①	Epidemic disease outbreak
Gradual increase of crime levels	②	Gradual increase of crime levels
Terrorist attack	③	Gradual degradation of the city hygiene levels
Gradual degradation of the city hygiene levels	④	Gradual degradation of the city international image
Gradual degradation of residents attitude towards tourists	⑤	Terrorist attack
Gradual increase of the prices of products and services	⑥	Gradual degradation of residents attitude towards tourists
Gradual increase of traffic and traffic accidents	⑦	Gradual degradation of the air quality due to pollution
Gradual increase of the number of tourists	⑧	Gradual increase of the prices of products and services
Gradual degradation of the air quality due to pollution	⑨	Gradual increase of traffic and traffic accidents
Gradual increase of river and sea pollution	⑩	Gradual increase of river and sea pollution

FIGURE 7. Perception of Risk Vulnerability

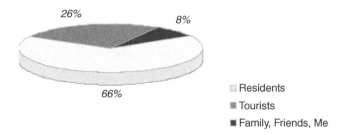

☐ Residents
▨ Tourists
■ Family, Friends, Me

and supporting the argument that "individuals (...) ignore low probability events by assuming that they are below a threshold worth worrying about" (Kunreuther, 1992:307).

Previous research indicates that there is a biased sense of personal invulnerability in risk perception (Brug et al., 2004). Our results also show this effect with only a very small percentage of the subjects recognising that this set of risks would affect more their families, their friends and themselves than others. Recently, Brug et al. (2004) reported an effect of gender on risk perception with women reporting higher perceptions of risk associated with SARS than men. These results are coherent with the initial hypothesis proposed by Mitchell and Vassos (1997) that male individuals would perceive a lower risk than female individuals, a hypothesis that was later rejected in face of contradictory results. Our study did not identify significant differences in risk perception due to a gender effect. In face of the inconsistent data available so far, further research seems to be needed in order to clarify if risk perceptions are in fact influenced by gender.

Assuming that 'objective risk' or 'real risk' is an empty concept (Slovic, 1992), and that the perception of risk, albeit inherently subjective, is a more correct assessment of risk, there is a question that might be raised. Could this evaluation be used to assess the frontier between acceptable and unacceptable risk? Although we can not answer that question with a clear yes, the risk factors that scored risk perceptions equal or above the reference means for each one of the groups (tourists and residents) should be more closely monitored.

Risk perceptions have impacts and can generate much wider losses than the direct losses caused by the original harmful events. Through a process designated by social amplification of risk (Kasperson, Renn, Slovic, Brown, Emel, Goble, Kasperson and Ratick, 1988; Slovic, 1992; Slovic and Weber, 2002), the final losses mediated by risk perception are considered highly unpredictable and can far exceed the most pessimistic estimations, due not to an objective factor of risk but to an entirely subjective one.

The extension of the consequences over longer periods, rather than lowering the perceived risk due to the diffusion of the impacts, increase the risk perception due to the longer ex-

posure to the negative effects of the risk factors. Although these results were found both in the tourists and in the residents groups, different implications might be drawn in terms of destination management and public policy decisions.

The importance of risk perception in the field of tourism has been recognised by several studies (e.g., Rohel, Fesenmaier, 1992, Sönmez, Graefe, 1998, Floyd, Pennington-Gray, 2004). The development and success of a tourism destination depends on the perceived image that tourists and residents have of the present reality and of the future. As the future is by definition unknown there is always a factor of risk to be considered. But what influences risk perception? What types of risk are considered higher risks and prioritary in terms of intervention? This paper presents preliminary answers to these questions, with the results indicating that risk perception is influenced not only by the magnitude of the impacts and by the probability of occurrence but also by the distribution of the impacts over time. Stealth risks were considered higher risks than catastrophic risks and, for this specific destination, the top ten risk ranking offers a first diagnosis of the risk perception and of the prime concerns of tourists and residents, information that might be considered of importance in the area of destination management and planning. Our findings are so far limited to the specificity of the risk perception in one tourism destination and in this study a major part of the sample was composed by either Macau or Hong Kong residents. This geographical concentration might be a possible source of biases and future studies in the same city or in other destinations might contribute to confirm the results now presented and extend the data available to test the hypotheses for a wider validity or bring new evidence to this research area.

Other potential research implications include the further development of the questionnaire as an instrument for the diagnostic and assessment of risk perception. The possibility of generating different versions of the questionnaire adapted to other tourism destinations or to specific products or services opens a wide range of possibilities in the study of risk perception and of its influence in the fields of crisis management and destination image.

REFERENCES

Adams, J. (2003) *Risk*. London: Routledge.

Alfidi, J. (1971). Informed consent: a study of patient reaction. *Journal of the American Medical Assotiation*, 1971, 216, pp. 1325-1329.

Bernstein, P. (1996). *Against the gods: The remarkable story of risk*. New York: John Wiley.

Brug, J., Aro, A., Oenema, A., Zwart, O., Richardus, J. and Bishop, G. (2004) SARS risk perception, knowledge, precautions, and information sources, the Netherlands. *Emerging Infectious Diseases*, 10 (8), pp. 1486-1489.

Carolis, E., Patricelli, G. (2003). *Vesuvius A.D. 79: The destruction of Pompeii and Herculaneum*. Los Angeles: Getty.

Cavlek, N. (2002). Tour operators and destination safety. *Annals of Tourism Research*, 29(2), pp. 478-496.

Denis, H. (1995). Scientists an disaster management. *Disaster Prevention and Management*, 4(2), 14-19.

Douglas, M., Wildavsky, A. (1982). *Risk and culture: An essay on the selection of technical and environmental dangers*. California: University of California Press.

Drabek, T. (2000). *Emergency management, principles and applications for tourism, hospitality and travel management*. FEMA–Federal Emergency Management Agency <www.fema.gov/emi/edu/higher.htm>.

Evers, A., Nowotny, H. (1987). Über den Umgang mit Unsicherheit. Die Entdeckung der Gestaltbarkeit von Gesellshaft. Frankfurt: Suhrkamp.

Fischhoff, B. (2002). Risk perception, risk communication, risk taking. *The Journal of Psychology and Financial Markets*, 3(2), 102-111.

Fischhoff, B. Slovic, P., Lichtenstein, S. (1982). Lay foybles and expert fables in judgements about risk. *American Statistician*, 36(3), 240-255.

Fischhoff, B., Slovic, P., Lichtenstein, S., Read, S. and Combs, B. (1978) How safe is safe enough? A psychometric study of attitudes towards technological risks and benefits. *Policy Sciences*, 9, pp. 127-152.

Floyd, M., Pennington-Gray, L. (2004). Profiling risk perceptions of tourists. *Annals of Tourism Research*, 31(4), pp. 1051-1054.

Hale, J., Dulek, R., Hale, D. (2005). Crisis response communication challenges. Building theory from qualitative data. *Journal of Business Communication*, 42(2), pp. 112-134.

Horsley, S., Barker, R. (2002). Toward a synthesis model for crisis communication in the public sector: An initial investigation. *Journal of Business and Technical Communication*, 16(4), pp. 406-440.

Jones, D. and Hood, C. (2002) Introduction. In C. Hood and D. Jones (Eds.) *Accident and Design: Contemporary debates in risk management* (pp. 113-139). London: Routledge.

Kasperson, R., Renn, O., Slovic, P., Brown, H., Emel, J., Goble, J., Kasperson, J., Ratick, S. (1988). The social amplification of risk: A conceptual framework. *Risk Analysis*, 8(2), pp. 177-187.

Kunreuther, H. (1992). A conceptual framework for managing low probability events. In S. Krimsky and D. Golding (Eds.) *Social theories of risk*, pp. 301-320. Westport: Praeger.

Liu, Z. (1995). Tourism development: A system analysis. In A. Seaton, C. Jenkins, R. Wood, P. Dieke, M. Bennett & L. MacLellan (eds.) *Tourism: The State of the Art* (pp. 20-30). Chichester: John Wiley.

Markowitz, J. (1991). *Kommunikation über Risiken: Eine Problemskizze*. Unpublished manuscript, University of Bielefeld.

McIntosh, R., Goeldner, C., Ritchie, J. (1995). *Tourism: Principles, practices, philosophies*. New York: Wiley.

Mitchell, V., Vassos, V. (1997) Perceived risk and risk reduction in holiday purchases: A cross-cultural and gender analysis. *Journal of Euro-Marketing*, 6 (3), pp. 47-79.

Mowen, J. (1990). *Consumer Behaviour*. New York: Macmillan Publishing Company.

Renn, O. (1992) Concepts of risk: A classification. In S. Krimsky and D. Golding (Eds.) *Social theories of risk* (pp. 53-79). Westport: Praeger.

Rohel, W., Fesenmaier, D. (1992). Risk perceptions and pleasure travel: An exploratory analysis. *Journal of Travel Research*, 2(4), pp. 17-26.

Shields, F. (1991). *Preventable disasters: Why governments fail?* Savage: Rowman and Littlefield.

Shrader-Frechette, K. (1991). *Risk and rationality*. Berkeley: Univerisity of California Press.

Siomkos, G. (2000). Managing airline disasters: The role of consumer safetu perceptions and sense-making. *Journal of Air Transport Management*, 6, 101-108.

Sjöberg, L. (2000). Factors in risk perception. *Risk Analysis*, 20, pp. 1-11.

Smith, K. (1992) *Environmental hazards: Assessing risk and reducing disaster*. London: Routledge.

Slovic, P. (1987) Perception of risk. *Science*, 236, pp. 280-285.

Slovic, P. (1992) Perception of risk: Reflections on the psychometric paradigm. *in* S. Krimsky and D. Golding (Eds.) *Social theories of risk*. Westport: Praeger; pp. 117-152.

Slovic, P. (1998) Perception of risk. In R. Löfstedt and L. Frewer (Eds.) *Risk and Modern Society* (pp. 31-43). London: Earthscan.

Slovic, P., Lichtenstein, S., Read, S., Combs, B. (1978). How safe is safe enough? A psychometric study of attitudes towards technological risks and benefits. *Policy Sciences*, 9, 127-152.

Slovic, P. and Weber, E. (2002) *Perception of risk posed by extreme events*. Paper prepared for discussion at the conference "Risk Management Strategies in an Uncertain World," Palisades, New York, April 12-13.

Smith, K. (1992). *Environmental hazards: Assessing risk and reducing disaster*. London: Routledge.

Sönmez, S., Graefe, A. (1998). Determining future travel behaviour from past travel experience and perceptions of risk and safety. *Journal of Travel Research*, 37, pp. 171-177.

Weinstein, N. (1979). Seeking reassuring or threatening information about environmental cancer. *Journal of Behavioural Medicine*, 16, pp. 220-224.

Weinstein, N. (1988). The precaution adoption process. *Health Psychology*, 7, pp. 355-386.

Wisner, B., Blaikie, P., Cannon, T., Davis, I. (1994). *At risk*. London: Routledge.

Mediating the Effects of Natural Disasters on Travel Intention

Xinran Lehto
Alecia C. Douglas
Jungkun Park

SUMMARY. Emotional correlates of affective reactions towards a natural disaster and their influence on future travel intention to seaside destinations were explored using the PAD (Pleasure-Arousal-Dominance) Emotion Model. The results from a structural equation modeling process support the proposition that a natural disaster influences significantly the affective responses to the emotional states of pleasure, arousal and dominance. The PAD affect changes in return impact to varying degrees the intentions of a traveler to visit a seaside destination. The pleasure domain is found to exert the strongest impact on intention. Practical implications for tourism recovery are elaborated.

INTRODUCTION

Episodes of disaster and crises tend to have a staggering effect on the psyche of tourists and their behavior towards and within the system. The recent major events that have devastating impacts on tourism have led to increasing academic scrutiny about crisis management. Much of the discussions have dealt with this issue from the supply perspectives, proposing both proactive planning frameworks and reactive crisis management systems (Prideaux, 2003; Santana, 2003; Coles, 2003). Other research provides quantitative measures of the impact of crises or forecasts of their impact (Eugenio-Martin et al., 2005; Huan et al., 2005). A key component of effective crisis management, however, pertains to management of visitor perception and perception change.

Although tourists' image towards a destination has traditionally been regarded as resistant to change and relatively persistent (Morrison, 2003), perception changes can occur after natural disaster occurrences due to their devastating

Xinran Lehto (E-mail: xinran@purdue.edu) is Assistant Professor in the Department of Hospitality and Tourism Management at Purdue University (700 West State Street, West Lafayette, IN 47907-2059, USA). Alecia C. Douglas (E-mail: acdougla@purdue.edu) is a Graduate Research Assistant in the Department of Hospitality and Tourism Management at Purdue University (700 West State Street, West Lafayette, IN 47907-2059, USA). Jungkun Park (E-mail: park4@purdue.edu) is Assistant Professor in the Department of Consumer Sciences and Retailing at Purdue University (812 West State Street, West Lafayette, IN 47907-2060, USA).

effects. Should tourists become victims of a natural disaster, the negative impact on the image of the destination concerned can be both serious and long-lasting (Obasi & Frangialli, 1998). Although turnaround and recovery from a natural disaster is a complex issue, the role of marketing communication in regaining tourist confidence is undeniable. Subsequent to a disaster, destinations are faced with not only the daunting tasks of rebuilding infrastructure, facilities and communities, but also image recovery. Marketing communication can play a central role for economic recovery and changing potential customers' misperception (Pottorff & Neal, 1994). Effective communication strategies, however, are formulated based on accurate assessments of the psychology of the customers towards the disaster, especially their attitudinal and affective responses towards such an event.

Natural events occurring on a large scale can quickly accelerate from a disaster to a crisis situation for the destination, significantly affecting the image. It has been noted that an individual's affective reaction to an environmental change can impact their behavior or behavioral intention. The purpose of this research was to contribute to the understanding of consumers' affective reactions towards a tourism destination after a natural disaster and their influences on future visit intention. The PAD (pleasure, arousal, and dominance) Model, initially proposed by Mehrabian and Russell (1974) and its scales were adopted as a conceptual framework for this study to measure the degree and pattern of emotional changes as a result of natural disaster.

NATURAL DISASTERS IN TOURISM

As defined by Scott and Laws (2005) a disaster refers to "situations where an enterprise (or collection of enterprises in the case of a tourist destination) is confronted with sudden unpredictable a catastrophic change over which it has little control." Key characteristics of disasters (Faulkner, 2001) include: "(1) a triggering event; (2) a high threat environment with short response times; (3) a perception of an inability to cope by those directly affected, at least in the short term; (4) a turning point where the situa-

tion is responded to; and (5) characterized by "fluid, unstable, dynamic" situations" (Fink, 1986: 20).

While there have been propositions of various frameworks on crisis management, limitations in the capacity and ability to handle complex and critical situations as they arise have been observed by Santana (2003) as a deficiency in tourism disaster management. This is largely due to the sensitivity of tourism products to disruptions arising from political unrest, economic crises, military disturbances and cultural affairs (Prideaux, 2003). A review of major news headlines in the last ten years can validate the nature and origins of disruptions to the operation and development of tourism.

On December 26, 2004, the tsunami, one of the deadliest and most devastating natural disasters ever in modern history, struck eight countries in South Asia, Southeast Asia and East Africa. This unexpected tragedy caused losses totaling billions of dollars in damage to the tourism industry and as many as 250,000 deaths with miles and miles of coastline decimated (Zhang, 2005; Stanley, 2005). Within the same year, four hurricanes struck Florida and parts of the Caribbean resulting in significant damage to the infrastructure of the region's tourism industry (Laws & Prideaux, 2005). Just three years prior, the vulnerability of the tourism industry was exposed by the September 11 terrorist attacks on the U.S in 2001 (Prideaux, 2003). On September 21, 1999, a massive earthquake measuring 7.3 on the Richter scale hit Chinese Taipei, Nantou county resulting in 2,455 casualties, 8,000 injuries and 38,935 homes completely destroyed (Wilks & Stewart, 2004). Damages were estimated at US$11.4 billion in this major tourism region of Chinese Taipei. Several other disasters such as the Foot and Mouth Disease (FMD), SARS, and the El Nino weather phenomenon in Southeast Asia have resulted in major threats to the viability and vitality of the tourism industry including changes in the travel behavior of certain travelers (Coles, 2003; Dombey, 2003; Cushnahan, 2003).

Disasters of this magnitude although occurring infrequently have increased public awareness of the threats associated with activities and sectors within the tourism industry (Santana, 2003). Even with evidence that tourism developments are likely to be exposed to the sudden-onset of natural disasters, in particular beach and coastal areas (Obasi & Frangialli, 1998), it seems unusual to think about tourism and disaster simultaneously (Santana, 2003). This is because the thought of tourism naturally evokes feelings of enjoyment, pleasure, relaxation, and safety while conversely, disasters arouse distress, fear, anxiety, trauma, and panic in individuals (Santana, 2003).

Disruptions to one aspect of the industry can create ripple effects throughout the entire system due to what Laws and Prideaux (2005) identify as the global scale of tourism, the interconnectedness of its sub sectors, and the resultant complexity of the industry. Because of the interconnectedness of the industry, tourist areas place a large number of businesses, communities and travelers at risk when components of the supporting infrastructure are affected. The effect on the tourism industry post-disaster period is largely dependent on several factors. Prideaux (2003) identifies these factors as: "(1) the internal cultures and modus operandi of organizations responding to the disaster; (2) the ability of various organizations to work cooperatively to solve the problem; (3) the ability of normally bureaucratic hierarchical organizations to respond swiftly and decisively; (4) the manner in which the media cover the situation; (5) the resources available to the public sector to respond to the disaster; and (6) the ability of the private sector to continue to trade during and after the disaster." Bearing these factors in mind, the likely outcome of a crisis may not be a return to normalcy, or, even if specific components of the tourism system do return to normalcy, the remaining parts may have undergone some changes (Scott & Laws, 2005). Regardless of the unpleasantness of the topic, it should also to be acknowledged that crises (whether natural or man-made) have been and continue to be a part of organizational operations and directly or indirectly affect all concerned (communities, visitors, regulators, promoters, and so forth). Where communities have considerable economic dependence on tourism related activities, their vulnerability to crisis occurrence is significantly increased, given that they need to maintain a positive image of attractiveness for continued success (Santana, 2003).

DESTINATION IMAGE

Image has long been considered as an attitudinal construct representing an individual's beliefs, feelings, and general impressions about an object or destination (Crompton, 1979; Echtner and Ritchie, 1991). It is agreed upon by researchers in several disciplines that the image construct is evaluated on both the cognitive and affective levels. According to Baloglu and McCleary (1999), evaluations of a cognitive nature pertains to the beliefs or knowledge held of a destination's attributes while affective evaluations are those feelings toward, or attachment to the characteristics of the destination.

Benefits inherent in the consumption of tourism services have always been of an experiential nature. Tourists not only engage in activities while vacationing but also shape their actions while at the destination (Padgett & Douglas, 1997). As travel products are comprised of various attributes and characteristics it is likely that a vacationer will develop multiple attitudes toward a given product (Leisen, 2001). For instance, a travel destination might consist of natural attractions such as mountains, beaches or volcanoes and cultural showcases such as unique architecture, artifacts and other features. It is the perception of these various attributes within the destination that is held in one's mind that will fuse to create a composite image imprint (Gartner, 1986). Multiple attributes inherently define the tourism product and helps to distinguish it from the many destination alternatives.

One of the most significant roles of a travel destination's image is its profound impact on the travel decision-making process (Chon 1990, 1992; Echtner & Ritchie 1991; Stabler 1988; Telisman-Kosuta 1989; Baloglu & McClearly, 1999a; Leisen, 2001; Kim & Richardson, 2003). Researchers have clearly illustrated how the perceived image of a destination is positively correlated to a travel purchase decision (Mayo 1973; Mayo & Jarvis 1981), clearly indicating the importance of a destination's image as a critical selection factor (Woodside & Lysonski, 1989). Connotations derived from the image are largely associated with the traveler's expectation from the experience at the destination. In the minds of consumers, this image could be in one of three stages ranging from creation to change to confirmation/reinforcement. Leisen (2001) argues that travelers can envision the type of experience based on any positive or negative emotions about the destination before they actually consume the travel product.

Because behavior is the result of these perceived images, the traveler's vacation choice of a given destination depends to a large extent on the positive image (Baloglu & McCleary, 1999; Chon, 1991; Woodside & Lysonski, 1989). The determinant in the traveler's choice process is the image associated with the destination rather than the destination itself. According to Woodside and Lysonski (1989), affective associations toward a destination are usually based on more positive images if a traveler intends to visit but are based on more negative for a destination the traveler has decided not to visit. On the other hand, a neutral image may be as a result of lack of awareness of the destination and as such, individuals holding neutral or weak images of a destination might not consider the destination in their choice process (Woodside & Lysonski, 1989).

Destination images are shaped in the traveler's mind through synthesis and analysis of information gathered over a period of time. As images held by individuals are crucial to a destination's marketing success, marketers are likely to pay particular attention to the effect of image on travel intention (Leisen, 2001). In fact, issues related to image formation and change and their influences on behavior have commanded marketing researchers' undivided attention and destination marketers have allocated a great deal of time, financial resources and effort to creating desirable images to help entice prospective travelers to visit their destinations (Baloglu & McClearly, 1999b).

RISK ON TRAVEL INTENTION

Not to be ignored from the decision-making process is the consideration of natural disaster which falls under the category of exogenous factors affecting travel destination choice (Sirakaya, McLellan, & Uysal, 1996). The tourism industry frequently experiences natural and man-made disasters that leave a devastating effect on the industry in a given area. Weakened or negative images of a destination can be a direct consequence of these catastrophic events. The degree of risk associated with an infected destination can significantly alter the perceived benefits to be derived from an intended travel experience. By nature, tourism is tied to the concept of risk in such a way that tourist behavior and destination image are significantly influenced by the tourist's perceptions of security, risk and safety (Hall, Timothy, & Duval, 2003). According to Crompton (1979) and Gartner and Hunt (1987), there is a general acceptance that perceived risk and perceived safety help potential travelers to form a lasting destination image which later becomes critical in the destination choice process.

According to the World Tourism Organization (2003), there are four major sources of risk with the potential of affecting tourism destinations: (1) the human and institutional environment outside the tourism sector; (2) the tourism sector and related commercial sectors; (3) the individual traveler (personal risks); and (4) physical or environmental risks (natural, climatic, epidemic). Whether acting collectively or independently, these risks not only threaten the safety and security of tourists but also create a ripple effect endangering the livelihood of host communities. Of particular interest for this study are those environmental risks with catastrophic proportions resulting from natural disasters. Wilks and Stewart (2004) imply that the traveler's vacation could be jeopardized if they are exposed to dangerous situations such as natural disasters and epidemics arising from the physical environment.

From an academic standpoint, risk as it relates to safety and security in travel and tourism has been a recurring theme since the 1980s and has gained considerable attention in the post 9/11 era. Floyd et al. (2003) in their extensive review of the literature on risk narrowed the body of research to four major risk factors pertinent to tourism: (1) war and political instability; (2) health concerns; (3) crime; and (4) terrorism. Noticeably absent from these major risk factors are those natural occurrences. However in recent years researchers (Faulkner, 2001; Mazzocchi & Montini, 2001) have recognized the growing influence that natural disasters had on tourism demand. By and large, regardless of the source of a potential risk, travelers are more likely to pay attention to issues relating to their personal safety and security particularly during the travel decision-making process.

Perceived risk can be characterized as a function of uncertainty and its consequences. Functional risk, psychological risk, social risk, financial risk, time risk, and physical risk are the risk categories typically employed. With respect to applications in tourism, Sonmez and Graefe (1996) examined the relationship between ten different types of risk and the resultant overall risk perceptions of U.S international vacation travelers. According to this research, significant predictors of overall risk perception involve the risk of being exposed to terrorist acts, having problems with transportation or accommodation, being entrapped in a country's political turmoil and or being generally dissatisfied with the travel experience. Tourists are high involvement customers as tourism products are expensive and risky and as tourists generally lack of knowledge for making sound decisions. Hence, it is understandable that tourists associate travel with various types of risk and consequently tend to engage in activities such as active search for information as a means of reducing risk and improving decision-making (Maser & Weiermair, 1998).

From the traveler's perspective, safety and security were extremely important concerns when choosing to visit a destination (Poon & Adams, 2000; Floyd et al., 2003). In their research on the effects of safety on travel intention, Floyd et al. (2003) support the theory of protection motivation by Rogers (1975). This theory holds that individuals will engage in protective behavior when there is (a) a high potential and magnitude for danger; (b) a high probability of occurrence exists; (c) selecting alternatives to avoiding threat; and (d) increased control over the outcome of the chosen alternative. An earlier study on travel and risk by Roehl and Fesenmeier (1992) revealed that travelers have varying degrees of perception about risk with some tending to be more risk averse than others. To some extent, even the portrayal of a risky vacation situation through ad photos may create excitement in some individuals, for example, adventure travelers, whereas others may experience feelings of fear

(Hem, Iversen, & Nysveen, 2002). Tourists perceiving fear are most likely to avoid visiting the destination therefore the image perceived of the destination can negatively impact the intention to visit a place (Hem, Iversen, & Nysveen, 2002).

IMPACT OF EMOTIONAL REACTION TO A NATURAL DISASTER ON TRAVEL INTENTION

To examine environmental influences on behavior, this study employs Mehrabian and Russell's (1974) pleasure, arousal, and dominance (PAD) affective responses to capture the dimensions of emotional reactions to the tsunami on seaside destinations. The original PAD scales pursued parallels among the semantic differential factors and emotions by proposing a measurement of positive versus negative states as measured by pleasure-displeasure, the emotional equivalent of high-low evaluation of a stimuli (Mehrabian & Russel, 1974, in Mehrabian, 1995). The second dimension of affect was measured by the level of physical and/or mental arousal, or in other words, an individual's arousal-nonarousal. Likewise, rounding off the emotional scale is the exploration of emotions relating to the feelings of control and influence over others as opposed to feeling controlled or being influenced by external circumstances by the dominance-submissive dimension thereby examining the negative correlate of a stimulus' potency. As such, factors exploring evaluation, activity, and potency (Osgood, Suci, & Tannenbaum, 1957) correspond to the emotional dimensions of pleasure, arousal and dominance respectively (Mehrabian & de Wetter, 1987).

Specifically designed to focus on emotionally based connotative and metaphorical meanings (Mehrabian, 1995), the PAD scales provides support for examining emotions as they relate to the stimuli, situations or activities (Mehrabian et al., 1997) surrounding an individual's environment. Moreover, several combinations of the various levels of pleasure-arousal-dominance can sufficiently explain an individual's emotional state (Mehrabian & de Wetter, 1987). Pleasure is assessed from a respondent's verbal assessment of their responses to the environment whether they feel happy rather than unhappy, pleased or annoyed, satisfied or unsatisfied, contented or melancholic, hopeful or despairing and relaxed or bored. Likewise, arousal is assessed by verbal reactions to whether respondents feel stimulated rather than relaxed, excited rather than calm, frenzied rather than sluggish, jittery rather than dull, wide-awake rather than sleepy and aroused rather than un-aroused. Lastly, dominance is reflected verbally if respondents feel more in control as opposed to being controlled, influential as opposed to influenced, in control as opposed to cared-for, important as opposed to awed, dominant as opposed to submissive and autonomous as opposed to guided towards the environment under examination.

By employing the use of standardized scores on the pleasure-arousal-dominance scale, any emotional state can be subjected to measurement on this basis (Mehrabian, Wihardja & Ljunggren, 1997). In addition, Mehrabian et al. (1997) posit that any situational occurrences, events or activities influencing a representative sample of individuals can be described in terms of an aggregate of scores explaining pleasure, arousal, and dominance. For the proposed study, the PAD scale was modified in the context of the travel literature to appropriately measure the emotional responses to a naturally occurring event having a catastrophic effect on a destination. This exploratory study utilizes primary data to determine the relationship between the change in the affective dimensions of

pleasure, arousal and dominance as a result of the tsunami and behavioral intention to travel to seaside destinations.

Several propositions were developed for exploring the proposed relationship between affect and intent. The basic propositions are that pleasure, arousal, and dominance before the tsunami will be significantly different from after the tsunami (*proposition 1*); the change in pleasure, arousal, and dominance will influence the future travel intention to seaside destinations (*proposition 2*); and the degrees of influence on intent by pleasure, arousal and dominance vary (*proposition 3*). Accordingly, a structural model was developed to explain the relationship among pleasure, arousal, and dominance variables and their impacts on travel intention. Figure 1 illustrates the proposed study model.

METHODOLOGY

Survey Development and Sampling

Being that the survey developed for this study examined the effects of a natural disaster on the behavioral intention of visitors to a destination, particularly seaside attractions, the pleasure, arousal and dominance measures were employed to predict future travel intention. The survey instrument developed consisted of 67 questionnaire items. As such, the survey explored the dimensions of emotions, experience,

FIGURE 1. Proposed Study Model

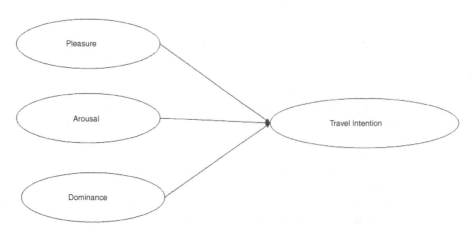

perception and attitude and behavioral intention towards traveling to a seaside destination following the tsunami. Affective items measuring pleasure, arousal and dominance were adopted from Mehrabian and Russell's (1974) *"Approach to Environmental Psychology"* after some adjustments to fit in the context of travel and tourism. All items measuring affective aspects were tested on a 7-point Likert-type scale ranging from "strongly disagree" to "strongly agree." More specifically, respondents were asked to report on their emotions both before and after the tsunami, as measured by 16 pre-tsunami PAD measures and 16 post-tsunami PAD measures. The data was collected online using a Web-based survey over two week period in February, 2005. The survey was administered to convenient sample of undergraduate students at a prominent Mid-Western university in the US (N = 265).

Statistical Analysis

The study took on a two step procedure. First, the before and after Tsunami PAD comparisons were conducted by employing Paired-Sample t-tests on the 16 pairs of emotional state measures. These series of bi-variate tests were followed by a Structural Equation Modeling (SEM) process to assess the influence of the change of affect on travel intention to seaside destinations. The measures for the constructs in the structural model were developed based upon relevant literature. Analysis of the proposed model began with the Statistical Package for the Social Sciences (SPSS 12.0) software which is used to conduct normality and descriptive analysis followed by model construction using CFA in AMOS 5.0. Structure model testing was performed as the final step to test the proposed conceptual model. In determining the best model, the following goodness-of-fit statistics were analyzed: chi-square, the related degrees of freedom, and the p value. For additional support of the final model, absolute indexes of fit such as normed-fit index, the classical criterion of choice, and the comparative fit index (CFI) are reported. An NFI and CFI value closer to 1.00 indicates a good model fit (Hu & Bentler, 1995). The root mean square error of approximation (RMSEA) which takes into account the error of approximation in the population is also reported. Ideally, a value less than .05 would indicate a good model fit (Browne & Cudeck, 1993).

RESULTS

Paired-Samples t-Test

Sixteen paired-sample t-tests were conducted to identify significant changes in the mean scores of the 16 before and after tsunami PAD measures (Table 1); the t values, together with mean scores, standard deviation, and standard errors were reported. All 16 pairs of statements with the exceptions of "Pre_Arousing and Post_Arousing" (P = 0.057) and "Pre_Submissive and Post_Submissive" (P = 0.229) were found to be significantly different at 0.05 P value level as shown in Table 1. In the domain of "pleasure," all tests concurred that there was a decline in pleasure, fun and peace associated with visiting a seaside destination post tsunami. On the other hand, there was an increase in "boredom" as revealed in the negative mean difference. In the domain of "arousal," it was the consensus of the respondents that seaside destinations after the Tsunami tsunami were not as calming, relaxing or at ease, implying a heightened level of arousal. For the feelings associated with "dominance," the sense of feeling helpless and risky increased, indicating a decreased sense of being in control. Overall, the pair t-test results are in support of the first study proposition which states that pleasure, arousal, and dominance before the tsunami would be significantly different from after the tsunami.

Model Measurement

Variables in the proposed model are normally distributed or close to normal distribution with the absolute value of skewness index < 3 (Kline, 2005). Prior to testing the proposed conceptual model, a first order confirmatory factor analysis was performed to evaluate the appropriateness of measurements for the three PAD latent constructs, i.e., pleasure, arousal and dominance. As there are three latent variables in the structural model, only a three-factor structure was tested. As previously mentioned,

TABLE 1. Paired Sample T-Test Comparisons of PAD

Measures	Before Tsunami			After Tsunami			Paired Samples Test				
	Mean	Std. Dev	Std. Error Mean	Mean	Std. Dev	Std. Error Mean	Mean Diff.	Std. Dev. Diff.	Std. Error Mean	t	Sig 2 Tailed
Pleasure											
Pleasurable	6.21	1.256	.082	5.91	1.323	.086	.308	.869	.057	5.418	.000
Fun	6.25	1.219	.080	5.90	1.351	.088	.355	.971	.063	5.589	.000
Peaceful	5.97	1.294	.085	5.65	1.383	.090	.329	1.056	.069	4.768	.000
Boring	1.91	1.373	.090	2.14	1.384	.090	−.231	1.186	.078	−2.977	.003
Quality Time	5.63	1.406	.092	5.51	1.418	.093	.115	.879	.057	2.009	.046
Arousal											
Relaxing	6.17	1.247	.082	5.79	1.361	.089	.380	.920	.060	6.325	.000
Exciting	6.05	1.296	.085	5.77	1.401	.092	.282	.979	.064	4.406	.000
Arousing	5.48	1.311	.086	5.35	1.319	.086	.124	.992	.065	1.911	.057
Stimulating	5.69	1.359	.089	5.48	1.356	.089	.205	1.028	.067	3.053	.003
Ease	5.50	1.442	.094	5.28	1.437	.094	.226	1.238	.081	2.799	.006
Calming	5.94	1.312	.086	5.60	1.411	.092	.338	1.081	.071	4.777	.000
Dominance											
Helpless	2.87	1.619	.106	3.42	1.742	.114	−.551	1.610	.105	−5.238	.000
Dangerous	2.50	1.466	.096	3.30	1.735	.113	−.808	1.634	.107	−7.560	.000
Risky	2.69	1.528	.100	3.35	1.727	.113	−.658	1.650	.108	−6.100	.000
Submissive	3.73	1.578	.103	3.82	1.505	.098	−.094	1.194	.078	−1.205	.229
Sense of Control	4.21	1.461	.096	3.97	1.491	.097	.248	1.405	.092	2.700	.007

the model was evaluated based on indices assessing a number of distinct aspects of model fit, including NFI, the CFI, the chi-square statistic, and the RMSEA.

Affect changes in the three domains of emotional status were measured by the differences in response to the 16 PAD statements. Scores for 'before the tsunami' were subtracted from scores for 'after the tsunami' to create the new set of 'affect change' variables. The resulting 16 'change' variables created were then entered for structure model for testing. A series of model modifications starting from the initial model was conducted resulting with insignificant paths being dropped. As such, the most improved fit was achieved after multiple times of revision and refinement of the model presented in Figure 2. The final model therefore provided a much improved fit of the data where $\chi^2 = 57.617$, $df = 32$, P-value = .004, NFI = .904, CFI = .954, and RMSEA = .059.

Guided by the CFA fit indexes, adjustments were made and 10 measurement items were re-

tained for the structural model testing. The measurements of each construct were explained as per Table 2. The pleasure construct was measured by three indicators: change in "fun," "pleasure" and "boredom." The variable "boring" was transformed into reversed direction to avoid negative correlation. Arousal changes was represented by four indicators: "relaxing," "exciting," "calming" and "stimulating." Change in "dominance" was measured using changes in "dangerous," "helpless" and "submissive."

Structural Model Specification

The proposed conceptual model (refer to Figure 1) was tested to arrive at a final model explaining the effect of a natural disaster such as the tsunami on the intentions of potential travelers to visit a seaside destination. The final model (refer to Figure 3) provided a reasonable fit of the data ($\chi^2 = 103.28$, $df = 49$, P-value = .002, NFI = .872, CFI = .941, RMSEA = .055).

FIGURE 2. CFA Model

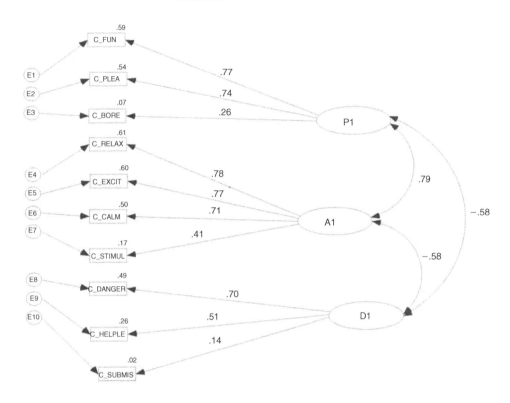

TABLE 2. Variables Used for Model

Construct	Items	Names
Pleasure (P1)	Taking a vacation to a beach destination is fun.	C_Fun
	Taking a vacation to a beach destination is pleasurable.	C_Plea
	Taking a vacation to a beach destination is always boring.	C_Bore
Arousal (A1)	Taking a vacation to a beach destination is exciting.	C_Excit
	Taking a vacation to a beach destination is calming.	C_Calm
	Taking a vacation to a beach destination is stimulating	C_Stimul
	Taking a vacation to a beach destination is relaxing.	C_Relax
Dominance (D1)	I feel submissive in front of the sea.	C_Submis
	Taking a vacation to a beach destination is dangerous.	C_Danger
	I feel helpless in front of the sea.	C_Helple
Intention	How likely will you be to vacation at a seaside destination in the coming year?	VISITTHI

The significane of the chi-square indicates that that the hypothesized model does not mirror the pattern of covariance contained within the raw data (Bagozzi and Yi, 1988). However, the Normed Chi-Square (χ^2/df) which takes into account of the degree of freedom is reasonable at 2.1 (Below the acceptable value of below 3). All other indices show the revised model fits quite well to the data with the exception of the NFI index which is less than .90 and the RMSEA which is greater than .05. NFI values greater than .90 reflects a good model fit. However, it is assumed that the NFI index was influenced by the relatively small sample size (N = 256). In this case, the CFI becomes the index of choice since it is not sensitive to the sample size (Bentler, 1990). In addition, as for the generally considered model fit indices, when GFI is

FIGURE 3. Structural Equation Model of PAD on Intention

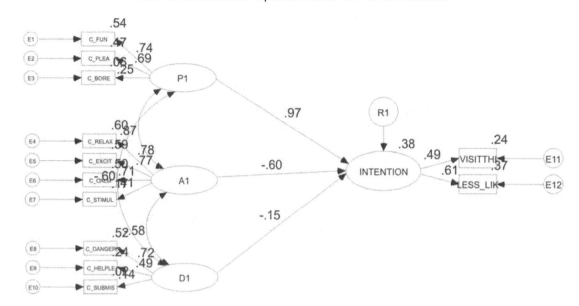

TABLE 3. Maximum Likelihood Estimates

Parameters			Unstandardized Estimate	Standardized Estimates	S.E.	Critical Ratio
C_Bore	←	P1	.478	.258	.139	3.446***
C_Plea	←	P1	1.000	.736		
C_Fun	←	P1	1.170	.770	.128	9.108***
C_Stimul	←	A1	.583	.408	.102	5.733***
C_Calm	←	A1	1.067	.709	.108	9.866***
C_Excit	←	A1	1.055	.774	.093	11.314***
C_Relax	←	A1	1.000	.781		
C_Helple	←	D1	.714	.507	.168	4.251***
C_Danger	←	D1	1.000	.699		
C_Submis	←	D1	.143	.137	.089	1.609***

*** p < .005

greater than 0.9 and AGFI is greater than 0.8, the goodness-of-fit is satisfactory (Hayduk 1987). In this research, not only GFI is .944, but also AGFI is .911, indicating a reasonable fit. In addition, a CFI value of 0.941, which is over the desired criterion of 0.9, shows a good fit for the data applied to the proposed model. The RMSEA was 0.055, which is above the standard of 0.05 recommended by Browne and Cudeck (1993), but it is approximately close to a value of 0.05, which represents reasonable errors of approximation in the population (Byrne, 2001). Thus, the analysis of these model fit indices suggested a reasonably acceptable fit of the proposed structural model to the data.

When the final model was examined, both the arousal factor and the dominance factor had a negative relationship with intention to travel. The path coefficients for these relationships were −.60 and −.15 respectively. The negative path coefficient from "arousal" to "intention" indicates that when a visitor feels overly stimulated or aroused, he or she tends to be less likely to visit a seaside destination. Further, the negative coefficient from "dominance" to "intention" (−0.60) attests to the tendency that when tourists perceive a destination to be risky or dangerous, and thus feeling insecure and not in control, it is less likely that the intention to visit will be favorable. Conversely, the pleasure factor had a strong positive relation to intention with a path coefficient of .97. This indicates that the more fun, pleasure and less boredom perceived by the visitor to the potential seaside destination, the greater the likelihood for the traveler to visit the destination.

DISCUSSION AND CONCLUSION

Tourism is one of the most susceptible and vulnerable industries to the effects of a wide range of events and crises occurring both naturally and man-made. While the global flow of tourists continues to increase, events with magnitudes such as the 2004 Tsunami and the September 11th attacks lead to significant shifts in tourism flow. In addition to devastated infrastructure and attractions, the affected destinations also suffer from the resulting negative affect on the part of the tourists. This study attempted to measure the influence of a natural disaster such as the tsunami on the likelihood of a visitor traveling to a seaside destination. Aimed at presenting an understanding of the importance of examining the impact of naturally occurring disasters frequenting the tourism industry, the study used a structural model to explain the relationship among pleasure, arousal, and dominance correlates with travel intention. The impact of the tsunami was measured on several dimensions including an assessment of the influence on a traveler's reported response to the emotional correlates. In today's world with the increased levels of disturbances from both man-made and natural causes, it becomes necessary to examine the influence of the tsunami by comparing both before and after mean scores to determine if there were significant changes in the traveler's affective response to pleasure, arousal, and dominance. Further, this study provides empirical evidences to the proposition that that changes in pleasure, arousal, and dominance influence visitors future travel intention to seaside destinations. The results obtained from the paired sample t-test and the proposed and refined models support these study propositions.

Evidently, the paired samples test results show that the negatively worded statements such as boring, helpless, dominance, risky,

and submissive increased after the tsunami impacted seaside destinations. An increase in these emotional correlates indicates that changes in perception in the affective dimension of seaside destinations occurred. These affective changes, being an important part of a destination image, can induce an overall negative evaluation of a seaside destination. In fact, past research has showed that the affective dimension of an image can impact the cognitive dimension of a destination, and thus impacting negatively destination choices (Li et al., 2006). As apparent in this research, the respondents felt that a change in the affective image of the destination due to the influence of the natural disaster could result in their potential experience being negative. This study shows that the negativity can potentially be derived from three dimensions: dominance, arousal and pleasure.

From the dominance dimension, it seems that a natural disaster evokes increased feelings of overwhelm and danger. These sentiments could be shaped largely by the magnitude of the devastation. The intense and sometimes sensational media reporting could have played a significant role influencing in consumers' cognition that the devastation of the tsunami. Visitors' anticipation of an overwhelming recovery process could seriously deter their intention to re-patronize. The structural equation model results show that the path coefficient from "dominance" to "intention" is negative, implying that that dominance has an inverse relationship with travel intention. This is consistent with the literature that the more risky or dangerous a destination is perceived, the less likely the traveler would visit the destination. This risk of the destination is evaluated in the traveler's decision making process and reflected in the decreased likelihood of visit intent (Poon & Adams, 2000; Floyd et al., 2003).

From the destination's perspective, one of the first marketing messages should be intended to restore confidence in the minds of potential visitors. As discussed by Pottorff and Neal (1994), one of the biggest myths about disaster is that those impacted by the disaster tend to panic. Although Pottorff and Neal's assessment is from the angle of the hospitality industry, the tendency to panic is apparent through the expressed sentiments affiliated with the dominance dimension. Destination marketers should therefore ensure that messages communicated after the disaster are effective at persuading visitors that the destination is safe. Additionally, marketing messages should serve to defray any misinformation prevalent in media which has the potential to significantly affect the rate of economic recovery for the destination.

The emotional reactions derived from the arousal dimension also bear significant implications for tourism recovery. One interesting observation is that as a result of over-arousal or stimulation, the consumers appear to have lost some of the common sentiments towards a seaside destination such as "relaxing," "ease" and "calming." At the same time, other common traits associated with a seaside destination such as "exciting" and "stimulating" seem to have lost their lustre as illustrated by the decreasing mean values of those measurement items. The flow theory (Csikszentmihalyi, 1975, 1987) that has been extensively utilized in recreation and tourism areas seem to provide some conceptual support for this phenomenon. According to Csikszentmihalyi, to achieve optimal experience, a balance is required between the challenges perceived in a given situation and the skills a person brings to that situation.

When a challenge becomes so overbearing that an individual's skills can not respond, the flow experience will be disrupted. Although arousal can positively influence visits to a destination, too much stimulation resulting from natural disasters can discourage visitors. In fact, the structural model results demonstrated a significant negative relationship between increased arousal and intention to visit. In this sense, feeling over aroused broke the balance a visitor needs in order to enjoy the excitement and stimulations that seaside destinations can offer. The consumer's reaction to the arousal dimension certainly present challenges to tourism destinations as to regain tourist's confidence. There have been discussions in tourism literature about potentially taking advantage of the consumer's psychology of mass convergence. Pottorff and Neal (1994) in their discussion of marketing implications for post-disaster tourism destinations posited that disasters sometimes actually attract visitors that may be curious about the damage left behind. This approach to utilize visitor's mass convergence

tendency could be effective to tourists who are driven by novelty, curiosity and competence.

The paired sample t-tests showed that the pleasure domain of the PAD suggested an overall decline in all measurement items. The perceived decrease in the pleasure domain can be very detrimental to destinations as it is strongly related to intention for future visit. In fact, the structural equation model results show that higher perceived level of pleasure would greatly impact positive intention to visit a seaside destination. As the path coefficients (0.97 for "pleasure" versus $-.6$ for arousal and $-.15$ for dominance) from the structural equation model attest, the pleasure dimension of affect is undoubtedly most influential among all three PAD constructs. The fact that pleasure has a strong positive relationship with intention to travel suggest that the more the perceived pleasure that can be experienced at a seaside destination, the more likely the traveler would visit the destination. This research certainly underscores the importance of targeting consumers with marketing schemes that highlight the pleasure dimension. The fact is, while time could erase some of the initial emotions felt such as danger and loss of control from the consumers, bringing back the reassurance of a pleasurable experience can be much more challenging. The return of pleasurable affect is contingent upon the actual physical recovery of the infected destinations. A natural disaster with the magnitude of the tsunami left many communities and tourist resort areas decimated, the usual tourist activities and facilities supporting these activities that are attractive to a seaside destination would no longer exist. As such visitors traveling to these destinations even months after the event may find that activities are extremely limited or non-existent due to the rate of recovery efforts in the affected areas.

As is attested by this research, an individual's behavioral intention as it relates to travel is influenced by a destination's image. Weakened image of a destination can be a result of the degree of increased risk associated with the destination. It can significantly alter the perceived benefits to be derived from an intended travel experience. As a result, image restoration is a critical part of destination recovery. A practical consequence of this research is drawing attention to the marketing implications of the study findings for the destination management organizations and governing bodies in charge of national tourism policy formulation. It is important to recognize that the impact of such a natural disaster affects not only the immediate communities, livelihood of local people, disruption of natural environment which are all important stakeholders at any given destination, but also the minds of the potential travelers. The later will need great attention in the recovery process. It has long been the challenge for marketers to get into the psyche or 'black box' of their consumers and this research opens the gateway for exploring more about travelers to a seaside destination and their perception of naturally occurring events on their intention to visit. This research demonstrates the importance of managing image and image recovery after a crisis situation. It serves as a call for active research into issues relating to the effects of natural disasters on the consumers of the tourism product in the affected areas. It therefore becomes necessary for conducting such research so as to determine effective marketing action and strategies of a proactive and reactive nature for communicating the readiness of the destination before the imminent disaster as well as changing the destination image and the perceived risk associated after the occurrence of the disaster. This is not to imply that destinations with prior experience with devastating natural disasters have not implemented marketing efforts. However, linking the perceptions and perception changes of the traveler to the destination is important for destinations to effectively manage image formation and change. From a crisis management perspective, a crisis recovery system that is built upon better understanding of consumer psychology in the face of environmental changes can be more effective than one that is built upon suppliers frame of mind.

LIMITATIONS AND FUTURE RESEARCH

The results from the modeling process support the proposition that a natural disaster influence significantly the affective responses to the emotional states of pleasure, arousal and dominance. The PAD affect changes in return impact to varying degrees the intentions of a traveler to

visit a seaside destination. In determining the model development procedure, it must be restated that the proposed model took into consideration the affective responses to the emotional states in the context of the travel literature and while all 16 states were explored, only 10 best explained the relationship under study. As the travel literature is broad, it should also be noted that the model did not consider the "universe" of all affective responses that may be associated with the intention of a traveler to visit a seaside destination after the impact of a major natural disaster. A second limitation of this research is the fact that this research is based on convenient sample size and the data was collected at one point in time after the tsunami. As affect could change over time, it takes longitudinal data to account for that change. In fact, it could be interesting to examine the residual effect of the disaster at various time periods and compare the relativity in emotional turnaround in the different domains of pleasure, arousal and dominance. Some domains could see faster return to normalcy than others.

REFERENCES

Bagozzi RP, Yi Y. (1998). On the evaluation of structural equation models. *Journal of the Academy of Marketing Science*, 16(1), 74-94.

Baloglu, S. (1999). A path analytic model of visitation intention involving information sources, socio-psychological motivations, and destination image. *Journal of Travel and Tourism Marketing*, 8(3), 81-90.

Baloglu, S., & McClearly, K. (1999a). A Model of Destination Image Formation. *Annals of Tourism Research*, 26, 868-897.

Baloglu, S., & McClearly, K. (1999b). U.S. international pleasure travelers' images of four Mediterranean destinations: a comparison of visitors and non-visitors. *Journal of Travel Research*, 38, 144-152.

Bentler, P. M. (1990). Comparative indexes in structural models. Psychological Bulletin, *107*, 238-246.

Biel, A. (1997). Discovering brand magic: The hardness of the softer side of branding. *International Journal of Advertising*, 16, 199-210.

Browne, M. & Cudeck, R. (1993). Alternative ways of assessing model fit. In K. A. Bollen & J.S. Long (Eds.). *Testing structural equation models*. Newbury Park, CA: Sage.

Byrne BM. Structural Equation Modeling with AMOS. Rahwah, NJ: Lawrence Erlbaum Associates, 2001.

Cassedy, K. (1991). *Crisis management planning in the travel and tourism industry: A study of three destina-*

tions and a crisis management planning manual. San Francisco: PATA.

Chon, K. (1991). Tourism Destination image modification process: marketing implications. *Tourism Management,* 12, 68-72.

Coles, T. (2003). A local reading of a global disaster: some lessons on tourism management from an *annus horribilis* in South West England. *Journal of Travel & Tourism Marketing,* 15(2/3), 173-197.

Cooper, M. (2005). Japanese tourism and the SARS epidemic of 2003. *Journal of Travel & Tourism Marketing,* 19(2/3), 119-133.

Crompton, L. (1979). Motivations for pleasure vacation. *Annals of Tourism Research,* 6, 408-24.

Csikszentmihalyi, M. (1975). *Beyond bordom and anxiety.* San Francisco: Jossey-Bass.

Csikszentmihalyi, M. (1987). *The flow experience.* In M. Eliade (Ed.), The Encyclopedia of Religion (Vol, 5, pp. 361-363). New York: Mcmillan.

Cushnahan, G. (2003). Crisis management in small-scale tourism. *Journal of Travel & Tourism Marketing,* 15(4), 323-338.

Dombey, O. (2003). The effect of SARS on the Chinese tourism industry. *Journal of Vacation Marketing,* 10(1), 4-10.

Echtner, C., & J. Brent Ritchie (1991). The meaning and measurement of destination image. *Journal of Tourism Studies,* 2(2), 2-12.

Eugenio-martin, J. L., Sinclair, M.T., & Yeoman, I. (2005). Quantifying the effects of tourism crises: an application to Scotland. *Journal of Travel and Tourism Marketing,* 19 (2/3), 23-36.

Fakeye, P. & Crompton, J. (1991). Image difference between prospective, first-time and repeat visitors to the lower Rio Grande Valley. *Journal of Travel Research,* 30(2), 10-16.

Faulkner, B and Vikulov, S. (2001). Katherine, washed out one day, back on track the next: a post-mortem of a tourism disaster. *Tourism Management,* 22(4), 331-344.

Faulkner, B. (2001). Towards a framework for tourism disaster management. *Tourism Management,* 22, 135-147.

Fink, S. (1986), *Crisis Management.* New York, Association of Management.

Floyd, M. F., Gibson, H., Pennington-Gray, L. & Thapa, B. (2003). The effect of risk perceptions on intentions to travel in the aftermath of September 11, 2001. *Journal of Travel & Tourism Marketing,* 15(2/3), 19-38.

Gallarza, M. G., Saura, I. G., & Garcia, H. C. (2001). Destination image towards a conceptual framework. *Annals of Tourism Research,* 29(1), 56-78.

Gartner, W. (1986). Temporal influences on image change. *Annals of Tourism Research,* 13, 635-644.

Gartner, W. C. & Hunt, J. D. (1987). An analysis of state image change over a twelve-year period (1971-1983). *Journal of Travel Research,* 16, 15-19.

Goodrich, J. (1978). A new approach to image analysis through multidimensional scaling. *Journal of Travel Research,* 16(3), 3-7.

Gunn, C. (1972). Vacationscape. Texas: University of Texas Press.

Guthrie, J. & P. Gale (1991). Positioning ski areas. *In* New Horizons Conference Proceedings, pp. 551-569. Calgary: University of Calgary.

Hall, Timothy, & Duval, (2003). Security and tourism: towards a new understanding? *Journal of Travel & Tourism Marketing,* 15(2/3), 1-18.

Hayduk LA. Structural Equation Modeling with LISLEL: Essentials and Advances, Johns Hopkins Univ. Press. Baltimore, MD, 1987.

Hem, L. E., Iversen, N. M., & Nysveen, H. (2002). Effects of ad photos portraying risky vacation situations on intention to visit a tourist destination: moderating effects of age, gender, and nationality. *Journal of Travel & Tourism Marketing,* 13(4), 1-26.

Henderson, J. C. (1999). Managing the Asian financial crisis: tourist attractions in Singapore. *Journal of Travel Research,* 38(2), 177-181.

Hu, L. & Bentler, P. M. (1995). Evaluating Model Fit. In R. H. Hoyle, Ed. Structure Equation Modeling: Concepts, Issues, and Applications, Thousand Oaks: Sage.

Huan, T-C, Beaman, J. & Shelby, L. (2003). No-escape natural disaster Mitigating imacts on tourism. *Annuals of Tourism Research,* 31 (2), 255-273.

Klara, R. (1998). Hawaii K-O. *Restaurant Business,* 97(10), 26.

Kline, R. (2005). *Principles and practice of structural equation modeling* (2nd ed). New York; The Guilford Press.

Kim, H. & Richardson, S. L. (2003). Motion picture impacts on destination images. *Annals of Tourism Research,* 30(1), 216-237.

Laws, E. & Prideaux, B. (2005) Crisis Management: A Suggested Typology. *Journal of Travel & Tourism Marketing,* 19(2/3), 1-8.

Leisen (2001). Image segmentation: the case of a tourism destination. *Journal of Services Marketing,* 15(1), 49-66.

Li, M., Cai, L. A., Lehto, X. Y., & Zhang, L. (2006). An examination of the relationship between destination image, travel motivation and loyalty. Proceedings of 2006 International Society of Travel and Tourism Educators (ISTTE) Conference. Las Vegas, Nevada. October 12-14.

Maser, B., & Weiermair, K. (1998). Travel decision-making: from the vantage point of perceived risk and information preferences. *Journal of Travel & Tourism Marketing,* 7(4), 107-121.

Mayo, E. (1973) Regional images and regional travel behavior. Proceedings Travel Research Association Fourth Annual Meeting, Sun Valley, ID, pp. 211-218.

Mayo, E. & Jarvis, L. (1981). The psychology of leisure travel. Boston: CBI.

Mazzocchi, M., and Montini, A. (2001). Earthquake effects on tourism in central Italy. *Annals of Tourism Research*, 28, 1031-1046.

Mehrabian, A. & Russell, J. A. (1974). An Approach to Environmental Psychology. Cambridge: M.I.T. Press.

Obasi, B. & Frangialli, F. (1998). Preface. In: World Tourism Organization and World Meteorological Organization, *Handbook on Natural Disaster Reduction in Tourist Areas*. Madrid: WTO.

Poon, A. & Adams, E. (2000). How the British will travel 2005. *Tourism Intelligence*, Germany: International Bielefeld.

Pottorff, S. M. & Neal, D. M. (1994). Marketing implications for post-disaster tourism destinations. *Journal of Travel & Tourism Marketing*, 3(1), 115-122.

Prideaux, B. (2003). The need to use disaster planning frameworks to respond to major tourism disasters: analysis of Australia's response to tourism disasters in 2001. *Journal of Travel & Tourism Marketing*, 15(4), 281-298.

Roehl, W. S. & Fesenmaier, D. R. (1992). Risk perceptions and pleasure travel: An exploratory analysis. *Journal of Travel Research*, 2, 17-26.

Rogers, R. W. (1975). A protection motivation theory of fear appeals and attitude change. *The Journal of Psychology*, 91, 93-114.

Santana, G. (2003). Crisis management and tourism: beyond the rhetoric. *Journal of Travel & Tourism Marketing*, 15(4), 299-321.

Scott, N. & Laws, E. (2005). Tourism crises and disasters: enhancing understanding of system effects. *Journal of Travel & Tourism Marketing*, 19(2/3), 151-160.

Siguaw, J.A., Mattila, A., & Austin, J.R. (1999). The brand-personality scale: An application for restaurants. *Cornell Hotel and Restaurant Administration Quarterly*, 40(3), 49-55.

Sirakaya, E., McLellan, R. W., & Uysal, M. (1996). Modeling vacation destination decisions: a behavioral approach. *Journal of Travel & Tourism Marketing*, 5(1/2), 57-75.

Woodside, A., & S. Lysonski 1989 A General Model of Traveler Destination Choice. *Journal of Travel Research*, 27(4),8-14.

World Tourism Organization (2003). *Safety and Security in Tourism: Partnerships and Practical Guidelines for Destinations*. Madrid: WTO.

Wilks, J. & Stewart, M. (2004). *Tourism risk management for the Asia Pacific region: an authoritative guide for managing crises and disasters*. Apec international centre for sustainable tourism.

Zhang, H.Q. (2005). Impact of the tsunami on Chinese outbound tourism. *International Journal of Contemporary Hospitality Management*, 17(5), 433-435.

Tourism Crisis Management and Organizational Learning: The Role of Reflection in Developing Effective DMO Crisis Strategies

Deborah Blackman
Brent W. Ritchie

SUMMARY. To date limited attention has been provided on the review stage of the crisis management framework, despite the importance of organizational learning for developing effective tourism crisis strategies. Using the concepts of double loop learning (Argyris and Schon, 1996), doubting (Blackman and Henderson, 2004) and Preskill and Torres (1999) core processes of evaluative enquiry, the paper discusses the possible application of critical evaluative inquiry and managed reflection by DMOs. The paper recommends that DMOs question their existing knowledge, assumptions and beliefs through reflection and dialogue with stakeholders and collect and analyse information, not just related to confirming the success of crisis strategies, but to assesses the likely impact of alternatives. Challenging existing mental models and capturing this emergent knowledge should enable DMOs to develop even better tourism crisis communication strategies in the future.

INTRODUCTION

Faulkner (2001) notes an increasing number of disasters and crises which affect the tourism industry, ranging from natural to human influenced incidents. In recent years the global tourism industry has experienced many crises and disasters including terrorist attacks, political instability, economic recession, biosecurity threats and natural disasters. Lee and Harrald (1999:184) state that "natural disasters can disrupt the supply and distribution chains for even the best prepared businesses . . . service businesses are increasingly vulnerable to electrical, communication and other critical infrastructure failures." This vulnerability can also be exposed through human induced behaviour most evident by September 11th 2001 and the Bali Bomb Attack, which dramatically impacted upon the tourism and travel industry. Faulkner

Deborah Blackman is Associate Professor in the Division of Business, Law and Info Science, University of Canberra, ACT, 2601, Australia (E-mail: Deborah.Blackman@canberra.edu.au). Brent W. Ritchie is Director in the Centre for Tourism Research, University of Canberra, ACT, 2601, Australia (E-mail: Brent.Ritchie@canberra.edu.au).

(2001) and Ritchie (2004) argue that there is a lack of research on crisis or disaster phenomena in the tourism industry, on the impacts of such events on both the industry and specific organizations, and the responses of the tourism industry to such incidents. However, increased recognition of disaster management, recovery, and organizational continuity (Lee and Harrald, 1999) because of crisis events has led to more recent tourism crisis management research (see for instance Frisby, 2002; Hooper, 2002; Stafford et al., 2002; Pine and McKercher, 2004; Fall and Massey, 2005; Evans and Elphick, 2005).

Several authors note the ability of crises or disasters to act as turning points for destinations and businesses (Faulkner, 2001; Burnett, 1998; Kash and Darling, 1998). As Faulkner (2001: 137) notes "crises and disasters have transformational connotations, with each such event having potential positive (e.g., stimulus to innovation, recognition of new markets, etc.), as well as negative outcomes." Burnett (1998) suggests that crises create heroes or leaders who emerge to help direct a destination or organization facing such crises back to normality or an improved state. An improved state is possible because of the ability of an organization or destination to learn from crises and disasters, make policy changes, and adapt and modify strategies that did not work effectively. Therefore, at the resolution stage of crisis and disaster management, a feedback loop back to proactive planning and prevention is possible and an important part of crisis management.

However, questions have been raised as to whether individuals or destinations as a whole really learn anything from tourism crises and shocks (Miller and Ritchie, 2003) and what tools or approaches destination managers use to facilitate this learning process. Furthermore, questions remain as to whether learning results in policy changes through organizational learning and reflection, and how reflection is used in adjusting or developing new policies and strategies to deal more effectively with tourism related crises and shocks. This process of review, appraisal of crisis management and marketing activities to provide feedback to future crisis management activities appears under researched and thus understood, yet reviewing strategies is vital for developing effective future strategies for crisis communication and recovery marketing.

This paper argues that the role of organizational learning in enhancing the potential effectiveness of crisis management strategies has, hitherto, been understated particularly in examining destination marketing organization (DMO) responses, yet DMOs are particularly important in implementing crisis communication and recovery marketing activities (Henderson, 1999). The key role of DMOs in a crisis or disaster is related to two key activities: crisis communication with key stakeholders or publics and the development and implementation of crisis recovery marketing strategies. As noted in Armstrong and Ritchie (in this volume) and Henderson (1999), crisis communication is a key role of DMOs to reduce negative media coverage, bring together the public and private sector and implement consistent messages and recovery marketing techniques. This includes working with internal stakeholders (staff), and external stakeholders including government, tourism industry, tourists or potential tourists, the media and other DMOs. However, this paper notes that the review of DMO activities in crisis situations is often internally focused and lacking in critical and managed reflection, which may impede the development of emergent knowledge, and thus, organizational learning.

In the paper the relationship between strategic development frameworks and organizational learning will be outlined, with special emphasis upon the role of critical evaluation and reflection as processes that enable applicable, situated knowledge to be developed. Such processes can be applied to destination marketing organizations (DMOs) and the paper provides an outline of key questions destination managers could incorporate in order to embed reflection and organizational learning in their review of tourism crises. Using the concepts of double loop learning (Argyris and Schon, 1996), doubting (Blackman and Henderson, 2004) and Preskill and Torres (1999) core processes of evaluative enquiry, the paper discusses the possible application of critical evaluative inquiry and managed reflection by DMOs at the resolution phase of tourism crises in order to enhance organizational learning.

ROLE OF ORGANIZATIONAL LEARNING IN EFFECTIVE CRISIS POLICY FORMATION

For an organization to develop and move forward those within it need to develop policies and strategies, which will enable all those involved to understand the projected destination and be able to set up tactics and plans that will ensure that all actions support the desired outcome. In order for such strategies to be developed there are usually five phases: (1) analysis of the current operating environment; (2) development of potential strategic directions and choices; (3) the selection of a particular strategic direction; (4) implementation and control of the strategy throughout the organization; and, finally, (5) evaluation and feedback of the strategic choice in order to learn how to improve current implementation and future choices (Richardson and Richardson, 1992; Viljoen, 1994). Using a strategic management framework and the crisis and disaster lifecycle, Ritchie (2004) developed a model which outlined how such a strategic framework could be applied to crisis and disaster management (Figure 1). Despite Ritchie (2004) highlighting the concept of organizational learning at the resolution and feedback stage of crisis management and its importance to future crisis preparation and planning, only limited studies have highlighted organizational learning.

One of the few studies to note organizational learning and feedback was that of Faulkner and Vikulov (2001) who tested a tourism disaster management framework developed by Faulkner (2001) using the case of the 1998 Katherine floods in Australia. The authors encouraged respondents to reflect on lessons learnt through the disaster by posing three major questions in their research:

1. With the benefit of hindsight, is there anything you or any other part could have done which would have enabled you to cope with the situation more effectively?
2. Has the experience of the floods resulted in any permanent changes to your firm/agency's approach to management planning?

3. Have there been any permanent changes in the planning and organization of the destination as a whole?

Based on their application of the framework they revised the tourism disaster framework to include a reappraisal of the marketing, planning and policy regime at the review/resolution stage. However, no discussion occurred on how any review should occur, who should be involved and what the principal ingredients are in the review.

Henderson (2003) is also one of the few tourism crisis management researchers to explicitly note the importance of organizational learning by including it as her final stage in airline crisis management directly after the resolution phase of a crisis. However, no feedback loop from learning to crisis preparation was specifically indicated in her model. Henderson (2003:281) suggests that "[r]esolution, even if only partial, provides an opportunity for review and reflection leading to reforms in pursuit of improvements in structures and systems and a heightened preparedness for future crises." She also noted, in writing about Singapore Airline's (SIA) response to the flight SQ 006 crash, that there was an assumption that SIA's management conducted a review but questioned whether it was conducted formally or informally. Furthermore, no discussion occurred as to how it was carried out, despite reassurances about preventing further accidents and assertions made by the company that no effort would be spared to uncover the full circumstances of the crash (Henderson 2003:283).

This illustrates that in order for such a model to work, those involved with the strategy planning and preparation need to understand the issues and the environment involved, make informed choices and effectively review their actions in order to make new choices. Whilst organizational learning is used explicitly within the model of some authors (Faulkner, 2001; Henderson, 2003; Ritchie, 2004) it is clear that a knowledge management process should assist destination marketing organizations in making better crisis communication and recovery marketing strategies in a way that is beneficial to the organization and their stakeholders.

Organizational learning has been defined in many ways (Prange, 1999; Blackman, 2005)

FIGURE 1. Crisis and Disaster Management: A Strategic and Holistic Framework

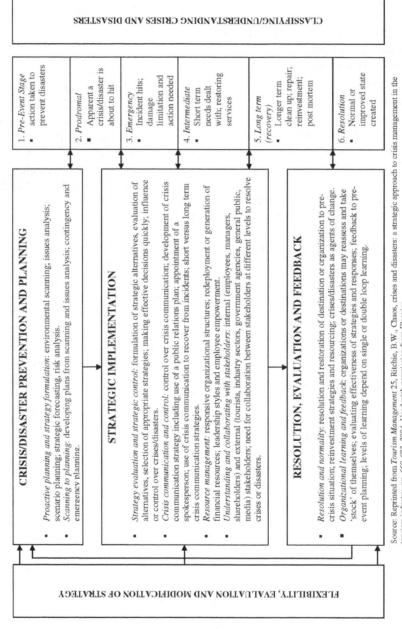

Source: Reprinted from *Tourism Management* 25, Ritchie, B.W., Chaos, crises and disasters: a strategic approach to crisis management in the tourism industry, pp. 669-683, 2004. Used with permission from Elsevier.

but a common thread is that it is a set of processes that enable organizational behaviour to change in some way as a result of new knowledge that has been developed. Such new knowledge enables the re-evaluation of currently understood ideas and beliefs and leads to the possibility of change. It can be argued that, without the creation of new knowledge, no change will ever be possible (Blackman, 2005; Cook and Brown, 1999). In terms of Figure 1 there will need to be learning at all stages of the strategic crisis management process, However, for effective evaluation and feedback, long term learning from current experience needs to be captured and understood in order to ensure that (a) the same mistakes/problems do not re-occur and (b) that new strategies are increasingly better informed. Without such learning the same problem can occur again even though it has been 'managed' and 'dealt with' previously. Previous research has illustrated that DMOs involved in crisis communication and recovery marketing activities may not use this experience to develop crisis management strategies (such as Australian Capital Tourism after the bushfires discussed in an article in this volume). Furthermore, Ritchie et al. (2003) noted that despite going through the Foot and Mouth Outbreak, regional and local agencies suggested that future crisis plans would not be established because of the unpredictability of planning for tourism crises. However, other DMOs such as in Malaysia and South Carolina have developed crisis management plans as a result of previous crisis and disaster experiences (Henderson, 1999; Soñmez and Backman, 1992).

Differences in organizational learning may be due to the cultural context, organizational culture and perhaps even the way that learning and reflection are managed by such organizations. This can be described by what Argyris and Schon (1996) describe as single loop learning, where the values and norms underpinning a strategy or action are left unchallenged and unchanged, preventing organizations learning from their errors and, potentially, leading to failure. As a result they advocate double loop learning which will promote inquiry, challenge current assumptions and actions, and leading to new theories-in use and better foresight (Figure 2).

The example commonly given to explain the difference between single and double loop learning is taken from cybernetics (Argyris 1991, 1999). A thermostat reacts to the condition "too hot" or "too cold" by turning heat on or off as appropriate to maintain a fixed temperature. This is single loop learning, since the thermostat does not question why either state is unsatisfactory. The single loop learning commences with a mismatch between expectations and experiences (the temperature is not as set) which leads to a required action. This can be corrected in a straightforward, single loop process which does not add to the stock of knowledge, since it only applies what was already known. It is not even necessary for the thermostat to know why or how its actions create changes in temperature. If the thermostat could ask questions, and wondered why it was set for a particular temperature, or what the significance of temperature was in the wider scheme of things, it would be commencing double loop learning as shown in Figure 2, as it would be beginning to develop consciousness in its routines and thus is examining the problem.

Single and double loop learning has been mentioned in the crisis management literature

FIGURE 2. Double Loop Learning

Source: Adapted from Argyris et al. (1985) in Anderson (1997).

by authors such as Richardson (1994), discussions on organizational foresight (Blackman and Henderson, 2004) and could be applied to tourism crisis management. In particular, the concept could be applied to how DMOs evaluate their crisis communication and marketing activities. As Faulkner and Vukulov (2001:343) suggest "... it [loop learning] emphasises the importance of a fundamental reassessment of the destination's management and planning approaches at the post-disaster stage if the positive enduring effects are to be accentuated and the negatives ameliorated." However, DMOs reappraisal of the destination crisis marketing and communication strategies should not simply be an internal process, but a process involving all stakeholders and should be as important as the implementation of crisis communication and marketing strategies and thus be provided with relevant resources.

In organizational terms double loop learning is the difference between responding to a problem in a formulaic, procedures driven way, versus considering why the problem is occurring and capturing such understanding for future use. Subsequently, without a form of *managed reflection* it may not be possible for an organization to acquire the new knowledge that it needs in order to be able to develop effective strategies. It is by reflecting that new ways of conceptualising the problem can be developed which will lead to the development of new-theories in-use. As Miller and Ritchie (2002:165) note, "double-loop learning requires a paradigmatic shift as a result of the experience and so emergent knowledge is produced and ultimately new understanding is derived ... [c]onversely, and as evidenced by history, those who suffer the effects of a disaster react to events and are contained to single-loop actions, if not single-loop thinking, unless a larger body can enforce the necessary changes to prevent the events repeating themselves." A larger body may be related to external forces such as regulation, government policies or changes from other external stakeholders.

REFLECTION AS A PART
OF THE LEARNING PROCESS

In the previous section we established that, in order to be effective in the long term, organiza-

tions need to undertake systematic strategy development which is underpinned by effective learning processes. One of these processes is ongoing reflection enabling new knowledge to be recognised, captured and reused when needed. It is important that this is an ongoing process that ensures that knowledge is constantly updated as the use of incorrect or incomplete knowledge is potentially extremely dangerous (Gibb, 2002; Chapman and Ferfolja, 2001). Preskill and Torres (1999:92) argue that what is needed is evaluative enquiry which requires that organization members "critically consider what they think, say and do in the context of the work environment." They use the term because evaluation is used to seek answers and information about an object or outcome which should include, not only the action or object itself, but also the values, standards and assumptions that relate to it. By critically evaluating all the aspects of strategy formulation, implementation and outcomes it should be possible to gain important knowledge for the future and change the currently held collective mental models of organizational members. Seven processes are outlined as making up the core of evaluative enquiry and are identified in Table 1.

Whilst reflection is listed above as a process within evaluative enquiry, it could be argued that it also equates with the process of evaluative inquiry itself. Reflection is the process whereby knowledge, beliefs, assumptions and processes are considered in order to establish how they influence behaviour and understanding and, consequently, experiences. The importance of reflection can be understood if the way that knowledge is developed and considered. It is increasingly argued that knowledge is constructed within organizations by making inquiries into situations of uncertainty (Dewey in Elkjaer, 2004) and developing new theories about such situations. This occurs through reflection upon the relationship between how the problem or situation is defined and the chosen resolution. What is important here is the notion that learning will be contextual and needs to be related to both the organization and the organizational community in order to develop knowledge that is relevant and useful for the situation being studied or developed. Furthermore, in many cases reflection does not occur because people are too busy–for it to be

TABLE 1. Crises Evaluation Processes Using Core Processes of Evaluative Enquiry

Asking Questions	■ Questions that ask about alternatives ■ Questions that ask why what was done has to be right ■ Questions that ask why what was done could not be wrong ■ Questions that frame alternatives that could have happened ■ Were there unexpected consequences from the actions taken ■ How does one action compare with another
Identifying and challenging values, beliefs and assumptions	■ The key here is to identify assumptions about the solutions and the choices made. ■ Why was the strategy chosen accepted–what did it assume about the context.
Reflection	■ All stakeholders need to have the opportunity to feed in to the dialogue and challenge values, beliefs and assumptions.
Dialogue	■ All stake holders need to be included in discussions about the new strategy. ■ All need to be involved in setting the questions for the next stage. ■ Alternative scenarios need to be developed–even if they were ones that were rejected at the time to allow further evaluation at this stage.
Collecting, analyzing and interpreting data	■ Too often data is collected that will show why what happened worked, thus data should be collected about alternatives–even ideas previously rejected. ■ Data should be collected by a variety of stakeholders, not just the project team.
Action planning and implementation	■ A variety of scenarios should be developed and evaluated and incorporated into future tourism crisis communication and recovery strategies and plans. ■ These should be communicated to stakeholders and publics and tested through simulations, media training exercises and audits.

Source: Adapted from Preskill and Torres (1999).

effective it must be a managed process which seeks to understand why things did or did not work in a particular set of circumstances.

In terms of crisis communication and recovery strategies developed by DMOs, reflection will need to occur at every stage of the crisis management framework in order to challenge the currently accepted norms which might otherwise lead to mental models constricting the range of possibilities (Blackman and Henderson, 2004; Chapman and Ferfolja, 2001). However, the most important time for reflection, as indicted by the frameworks of Faulkner (2001), Henderson (2003) and Ritchie (2004), will be at the end of the crisis as a form of evaluating crisis communication and recovery strategies. As indicated earlier this is posited in some of the literature but there is little detail as to how this should actually occur.

This matters as often evaluation, which should be a double loop learning process lead-

ing to new knowledge, is actually a self-reflexive process which merely acts to confirm the knowledge already understood (Blackman and Henderson, 2004). Those involved seek out ideas and information that supports the actions already in place and does not challenge the current givens and mind set (Mellahi et al., 2002). This is illustrated in the tourism crisis publications written by representatives from DMOs who present research and data on the number of press releases, media interviews, value and extent of media coverage or recovery marketing funds gained (see Hopper, 2002; Frisby, 2002) to justify their decisions. However, these data only seek to confirm and illustrate the success of implemented tourism crisis communication and recovery strategies, without collecting data on possible alternative actions or even inaction. What is needed is a process of doubting (Blackman and Henderson, 2004) that will actively explore the current context and the nature of the solutions that were chosen compared to other possible scenarios and implement managed scepticism or double loop doubting. We argue that the traditional approach to evaluating DMO crisis activities are unlikely to create new knowledge, and yet if the status quo is to change and more effective policies and strategies are to be developed new knowledge and ideas will be vital. As identified in Figure 3, Cook and Brown (1999) argue that there are four distinctive types of knowledge based upon the social context and the locus of the knowledge (i.e., internal or external to those holding it).

They argue that for new knowledge to be created the existing knowledge needs to be moved from square to square (the order may vary) in order to generate new knowledge in the other squares. This dance generates the process of knowing which leads, in turn, to the generation of something new. Thus, evaluation processes will need to ensure that such movement between knowledge types occurs. Below we will expand on the notion of evaluative enquiry in order to (a) consider how to avoid reflexivity and (b) to ensure that new knowledge develop-

ment is actively encouraged. Table 1 provides recommendations for applying the process to effective crisis strategy evaluation, based upon the lack of research and attention devoted to the organizational learning part of Figure 1. The section below expands upon each of these ideas, developing a set of recommendations for DMOs to embed a more reflective and critical review of their tourism crisis communication and recovery strategies. DMOs should consider these components with respect to their major activities during a tourism crisis: crisis communication with key publics and recovery marketing activities.

CRISIS ORGANIZATIONAL LEARNING FOR DMOS

Asking Questions

When evaluating DMOs crisis communication strategies it is very tempting to consider what action worked and to frame questions in a way that support the current mental models, as discussed previously. If evaluation is to be truly

FIGURE 3. Four Forms of Knowledge

	Individual	*Group*
Explicit	**Concepts** Including things an individual can know, learn and express explicitly (concepts, rules and equations).	**Stories** Typically expressed explicitly as a group through stories about how work is done or about famous successes or failures. Also can include metaphors or phrases with meaning for a particular group.
Tacit	Skill that are tacit and used in making use of concepts, rules and equations. **Skills**	Most difficult to define. Various social and physical artefacts such as different types of things (products) and activities (ways of doing tasks) and meanings in literary artefacts. **Genres**

Source: Adapted from Cook and Brown (1999:391).

effective the questions will need to challenge the status quo and encourage a form of mild scepticism (Blackman and Henderson, 2004). Questions should ask about alternatives and rather than ask whether what was done was right, there should be questions that ask why what was done could not be wrong–a form of falsification. Questions that frame alternatives that could have happened should be used to enable a wider range of discussion to evolve. Such questions may be asked prior to choosing and implementing crisis recovery strategies, but will be dependent upon the speed and intensity of the crisis and whether adequate information is available to the DMO to assist decision making. As noted below, and in Table 1, all steps must involve external stakeholders as well as internal stakeholders. Based on previous suggestions for crisis communication and recovery marketing (Berry, 1998; Coombs, 1999) questions could include: was the response of the DMO quick enough? Were the messages consistent for all stakeholders? Were appropriate communication strategies developed for all stakeholders (government, tourists, industry, media) and were communication channels accessible? Were DMOS proactive or reactive at communicating with stakeholders? For instance, only 60% of Tourist Information Centres in the South East of England had e-mail facilities during the Foot and Mouth Outbreak and only six out of ten Regional Tourist Boards had websites (DCMS, 2001), yet the national DMO used e-mail as a major crisis communication channel for stakeholders.

Questions can be used to move tacit or explicit individual knowledge to a group owned set of understandings considering the DMO as an organization but also the 'tourism industry' as a group. By developing questions that will elicit what each individual or stakeholder currently believes happened and why, new stories can be generated that can then be discussed. One technique may be to get each stakeholder to do a self-interview and answer the framing questions individually in a relatively formal manner–i.e., written. These can then be shared. By doing this, pre-judging will not occur during the discussions, as can otherwise occur. Comments from the British Hospitality Association in 2001, before the Foot and Mouth Outbreak and recovery marketing had ended, stated that

the response was too little too late (Cotton, 2001). Perhaps these public statements were premature and unproductive prior to any re-appraisal at the resolution and review stage of the crisis.

The questions can also be seen to be looking at comparisons and consequences. Such discussions are argued by Davenport and Prusak (1998) to be two ways of developing new knowledge. The idea is not to rank one idea as better than another but to look at each (even if one was initially rejected) as serious alternatives and evaluate the differences emerging as a series of potential outcomes. The comparisons may also help to identify and challenge some of the assumptions and beliefs being made as a basis for decision making.

Identifying and Challenging Values, Beliefs and Assumptions

One of the hardest things to do will be to open the shared mental models and surface the beliefs and assumptions that have been used as the basis for the decision-making by the DMO during the crisis. Those involved in crisis communication and recovery will need to look at each decision point and explore why they chose that particular action–what was the conversation that occurred and what does it indicate about what they believed at that time. What will be hard will be to keep the conversation open–it will be tempting to keep remaking the decisions and re-judging the events to justify the decision. This is not the point of this section–the validity of the decision is not in question–what matters is why it was taken. It is likely that a third party facilitator will be needed to talk to as many stakeholders as possible and develop an understanding of the knowledge assumptions in place. Certain assumptions may have been made about the likely impact of a crisis on the image or reputation of a destination because of a lack of information, preparedness or organizational beliefs of the DMO. Therefore, DMOs should consider what assumptions were in place and challenge these for developing more effective strategies in the future. On what basis were these values, beliefs and assumptions based? They should reflect on these and involve stakeholders where possible to provide critical reflection.

Reflection

This is where all the stakeholders need to compare the espoused theories-in-action with the actual theories-in-use (Argyris and Schon, 1996). Espoused theory is the theory that is put forward to explain what is done and to justify a particular pattern of activity, whereas theory-in-use is that which is implicit in the performance of the given activity. The latter is much harder to achieve and must be constructed from evidence gained by observing and analyzing what was actually done. It is easy to assume that an action emerges from espoused theory but this is often not the case–especially at a time of crisis when reaction may take over from consideration. Thus, reflection on the theory-in-use will matter as if it is different from espoused theory, and this is not what is desired, this may be a serious area for reconsideration. It may be that policy and culture do not match, for example, or that different stakeholders do not actually espouse the same theory. Differences that emerge will be a part of the dialogues to emerge. In order to consider these two areas it may require someone who was less involved to track the actual actions and determine what the theory-in-use really was.

Dialogue

During the crisis it is likely that a very wide range of stakeholders will have been involved in trying to overcome the problems. However, it has been noted that the DMO usually takes a coordination role (Henderson, 1999; Stafford et al., 2002). It is, therefore, important that all these parties are involved in the conversations (Davenport and Prusak, 1998) that occur as a consequence of the reflective process.

Dialogue or conversation is not about sending reports from one place to another, but is about situating the current knowledge. Nonaka and Konno (1998) describe socially based knowledge generation and note that participation in a social situation defines what is knowledge and what is information. Knowledge is described as useful only at a specific time and place if it is to be of value. Knowledge that is separated from its situation reverts to information to be communicated between situations. This processual perspective of knowledge

(Newell et al., 2002) indicates that it is the interaction between the different stakeholders that will enable the new knowledge to be developed within and around the context of the crisis. This movement of knowledge around a wider range of people will again enable the movement of knowledge between types; stories can be compared so that new scenarios and concepts can be developed. People with differing skills and current knowledge will analyse the ideas and develop their own theories-in-use (Argyris and Schon, 1996) as to how such ideas would develop if there was another crisis.

Dialogue has been noted as an important part of crisis recovery, and DMOs have been noted as having an important role to play in developing dialogue and coordinating messages (Stafford et al., 2002; Henderson, 1999). However, few studies have been conducted on the role and mechanisms of dialogue for organizational learning. For instance, Hopper (2002) did note that continuous dialogue with the industry was vital to monitor the impact of the Foot and Mouth Outbreak and also used to discuss recovery marketing options and opportunities. Furthermore, Stafford et al. (2002) noted that dialogue was vital with government officials to help raise funds for crisis recovery activities with respect to 9/11 in Washington D.C., but also government officials were an important part of strategies to encourage visitation through:

- Issuing executive orders to encourage federal agencies to continue to visit and host conferences and conventions in Washington D.C.
- Urging the State Department to communicate with embassies to encourage international travel to Washington D.C.
- Using the cast of the 'West Wing' television program, first lady Laura Bush and other political leaders to promote tourism to the national capital.

As Neilson (2001) notes, significant others can play a decisive role in providing information and encouraging people to visit a destination following negative media events. However, the evaluation and reflection of such activities in tourism crisis recovery appears to be limited. The British national DMO did realise that their previous dialogue with the media, and in particular London-based foreign correspondents, was reactive and that "successful targeting of these individuals was crucial to the success of the [marketing and communication] programme" (Frisby, 2002:99).

Collecting, Analyzing and Interpreting Data

It will be very tempting to start to consider data and seek more confirmatory data early in the reflection process, as noted earlier in the paper. This needs to be avoided. The order of the processes of evaluative enquiry is very important as it is designed to ensure that those involved have taken the time to develop alternative scenarios and will, therefore, gather data about those, as well as the actual choices made. What will be made possible is the opportunity for novel connections (Davenport and Prusak (1998). As Zerman (1995) notes crisis communication should follow four specific functions: (1) research, (2) action, (3) communication, and (4) evaluation. DMOs should consider gathering data and information from internal and external stakeholders and consider critically evaluating the implications of the findings to develop new espoused theory for future crisis communication planning.

Gathering information is vital in the implementation of crisis communication strategies in order for coordination to occur as well as at the end through a formal review. This may also include stakeholders such as government consulate officials in foreign countries as well as foreign journalists and news agencies. How well did the crisis communication strategies meet their goals and needs? What changes could be made in the future to meet the needs of key publics based on their reaction to the strategies?

Action Planning and Implementation

Information and new knowledge from the *managed reflection* and critical enquiry should be then used to develop more effective plans and strategies as noted by the framework outlined by Ritchie (2004). As discussed in the introduction, tourism crises and disasters can lead to transformations and positive outcomes through the generation of new knowledge, relationships and policy. Some destinations have

reduced their reliance on key markets, increased government support and funding for tourism, developed new products and tourism related policies. Examples include Australia after the Asian Economic Crisis (Prideaux, 1999) and the Foot and Mouth Outbreak (Sharpley and Craven, 2001; Miller and Ritchie, 2003). However, such knowledge is likely to be stronger if it has been created through a reflective and critical way at the review stage and used to produce organizational learning. Organizational learning should then lead to the development of better crisis communication and recovery plans which then need to be communicated to stakeholders, tested through simulations and audits, modified and ultimately implemented when the next crisis or disaster occurs.

CONCLUSIONS

This paper has outlined the importance of organizational learning and *managed reflection* at the resolution phase of tourism crises for DMOs. DMOs are vital to destination crisis management because of their role in crisis communication and recovery marketing activities on behalf of the tourism industry. Despite the importance of organizational learning from tourism crises little research and focus has been given to the review of DMO crisis communication strategies. It appears that organizational learning is not carried out in a managed or critical way, reducing the ability to create new knowledge to assist future crisis communication strategies.

The paper has provided an outline of key questions destination managers could incorporate in order to embed reflection and organizational learning in their review of tourism crisis responses. Using the concepts of double loop learning and doubting and the core processes of evaluative enquiry, the paper has discussed the possible application of critical evaluative inquiry and managed reflection by DMOs at the resolution phase of tourism crises. DMOs should question their existing knowledge, assumptions and beliefs through reflection and dialogue with stakeholders and collect and analyse information, not just related to confirming the success of crisis strategies, but to assess the likely impact of alternatives. We argue that emergent knowledge will be created which can be used to help DMOs learn and develop even better crisis communication and recovery strategies which should be tested through simulations and independent audits prior to their future implementation. The core processes of evaluative enquiry could be used at each stage of Ritchie's (2004) crisis and disaster framework by tourism organizations to design and implement better strategies and actions to assist destination response and recovery. However, this will require a major paradigm shift, new mental models and a willingness for DMOs to open themselves up to dialogue and questioning from a range of stakeholders and publics.

Tourism researchers should consider incorporating knowledge management theory and concepts, such as organizational learning, into their tourism crisis research to examine how and why emergent knowledge is created and applied by tourism organizations. The concepts of double loop learning and doubting as tools to gain foresight have value for researchers. Furthermore, future research should also examine the role of *managed reflection* and organizational learning throughout the crisis management model and the extent to which tourism organizations manage knowledge during a crisis through looking for evidence of DMOs questioning, reflecting, creating dialogue with stakeholders and collecting data to assist decision making. Subsequently, the framework outlined in this paper can be used as a basis for future case study research on organizational learning. It is only by using managed reflection processes that DMOs will be able to develop more effective crisis communication strategies.

REFERENCES

Anderson, L. (1997) *Argyris and Schon's theory on congruence and learning* [On line]. Available at *http://www.scu.edu.au/schools/gcm/ar/arp/argyris.html*, Accessed 12th July 2006.

Argyris, C. (1982). *Reasoning, Learning and Action*. San Francisco: Jossey-Bass.

Argyris, C. (1991), Teaching Smart People How To Learn. *Harvard Business Review*, May/June.

Argyris, C. (1999). *On Organizational Learning*. (2nd edition). Oxford, UK, Blackwell Business.

Argyris, C. and Schon, D.A. (1996). *Organizational Learning II: Theory, Method and Practice*. Massachusetts: USA, Addison-Wesley.

Berry, S. (1999). We have a problem...call the press! (crisis management plan). *Public Management*, 81(4), 4-15.

Blackman, D.A. (2005). Knowledge creation and the learning organization. In Murray, P., Poole, D. and Jones, G. *Contemporary Management Issues in Management and Organizational Behaviour*. Melbourne: Thomson.

Blackman, D. and Henderson, S., (2004). Double Loop Doubting: challenging past experience to frame the future. *Futures*, 36(2), 253-266.

Burnett, J. (1998). A strategic approach to managing a crisis. *Public Relations Review*, 24(4), 475-488.

Chapman, J. and Ferfolja, T. (2001). Fatal flaws: The acquisition of imperfect mental models and their use in hazardous situations. *Journal of Intellectual Capital*, 2(4), 398-409.

Cook, S.D.N. and Brown, J.S. (1999). Bridging Epistemologies: The Generative Dance Between Organizational Knowledge and Organizational Knowing. *Organization Science*, 10(4), 381-400.

Coombs, T. (1999). *Ongoing Crisis Communication: Planning, Managing and Responding*. Thousand Oakes, CA: Sage.

Cotton, B. (2001). Foot and mouth: The lessons we must learn. *Tourism: Journal of the Tourism Society*, Autumn (110), 5.

Department of Culture, Media and Sport (DCMS). (2001). Press releases. London (online). Available at: http://www.culture.gov.uk/tourism/search.asp?Name=press releases/tourism/2001/dcms (Accessed 02 January 2002).

Elkjaer, B. (2004). The Learning Organization: an undelivered promise. In Grey, C. and Antonacopoulou, E. (2004). *Essential Readings in Management Learning*. London: Sage.

Evans, N. & Elphick, S. (2005). Models of crisis management: An evaluation of their value for strategic planning in the international travel industry. *International Journal of Tourism Research*, 7, 135-150.

Fall, L. & Massey, J. (2005). The significance of crisis communication in the aftermath of 9/11: A national investigation of how tourism managers have re-tooled their promotional campaigns. *Journal of Travel and Tourism Marketing*, 19(2/3), 79-92.

Faulkner, B. (2001). Towards a framework for tourism disaster management. *Tourism Management*, 22(2), 135-147.

Faulkner, B. & Vikulov, S. (2001). Katherine, washed out one day, back on track the next: A post mortem of a tourism disaster. *Tourism Management*, 22(4), 331-344.

Frisby, E. (2002). Communicating in a crisis: The British Tourist Authority's responses to the foot-and-mouth outbreak and 11th September, 2001. *Journal of Vacation Marketing*, 9(1), 89-100.

Gibb, S. (2002). *Learning and Development: processes, practices and perspectives at work*. Basingstoke, UK: Palgrave Macmillan.

Henderson, J. (1999). Tourism management and the Southeast Asian economic and environmental crisis: A Singapore Perspective. *Managing Leisure*, 4, 107-120.

Henderson, .J. (2003). Communicating in a crisis: Flight SQ 006. *Tourism Management*, 24, 279-287.

Hopper, P. (2002). Marketing London in a difficult climate. *Journal of Vacation Marketing*, 9(1), 81-88.

Kash, T. & Darling, J. (1998). Crisis management: Prevention, diagnosis and intervention. *Leadership and Organization Development Journal*, 15(4), 179-186.

Lee, Y. & Harrald, J. (1999). Critical issue for business area impact analysis in business crisis management: Analytical capability. *Disaster Prevention and Management*, 8(3), 184-189.

Mellahi, K., Jackson, P. and Sparks, L., (2002). An Exploratory Study into Failure in Successful Organizations: The Case of Marks and Spencer. *British Journal of Management*, March, 13(1), 15-30.

Miller, G. & Ritchie, B. (2003). A farming crisis or a tourism disaster? An analysis of the foot and mouth disease in the UK. *Current Issues in Tourism*, 6(2), 150-171.

Neilson, C. (2001). *Tourism and the Media*. Sydney: Hospitality Press Pty Ltd

Newell, S., Robertson, M., Scarborough, H. and Swan, J. (2002). *Managing Knowledge Work*. Basingstoke: Palgrave.

Nonaka, I and Konno, N. (1998). The concept of "ba": Building a foundation for knowledge creation. *California Management Review*, 40(3), 40-54.

Pine, R. & McKercher, B. (2004). The impact of SARS on Hong Kong's tourism industry. *International Journal of Contemporary Hospitality Management*, 16(2), 139-143.

Prange, C. (1999). Organizational Learning - Desperately Seeking Theory. In Easterby-Smith, M., Burgoyne, J. and Araujo, L., (Eds.) (1999). *Organizational Learning and the Learning Organization*. London: Sage.

Preskill, H. and Torres, R.T. (1999). The role of evaluative enquiry in creating learning organizations. In Easterby-

Smith, M., Burgoyne, J. and Araujo, L., (Eds.) (1999). *Organizational Learning and the Learning Organization*. London: Sage.

Prideaux, B. (1994). The Asian financial crisis: Causes and implications for Australia's tourism industry. *Australian Journal of Hospitality Management*, 6(2), 35-44.

Richardson, B. & Richardson, R. (1992). (2nd Edition). *Business planning: An approach to strategic management*. London: Pitman.

Richardson, B. (1994). Crisis management and management strategy - Time to "loop the loop?" *Disaster Prevention and Management*, 3(3), 59-80.

Ritchie, B.W. (2004). Chaos, crises and disasters: a strategic approach to crisis management in the tourism industry. *Tourism Management*, 25, 669-683.

Ritchie, B., Dorrell, H., Miller, D., & Miller, G. A. (2003) Crisis Communication and Recovery for the Tourism Industry: Lessons from the 2001 Foot and Mouth Disease Outbreak in the United Kingdom. *Journal of Travel and Tourism Marketing*, 15(2), 199-216.

Sharpely, R. & Craven, B. (2001). The 2001 Foot and Mouth crisis - rural economy and tourism policy implications: A comment. *Current Issues in Tourism*, 4(6), 527-537.

Soñmez, S. F. & Backman, S. J. (1992). Crisis management in tourist destinations. *Visions in Leisure and Business*, 11(3), 25-33.

Stafford, G., Yu, L. & Armoo, A. (2002). Crisis management and recovery: How Washington, D.C., hotels responded to terrorism. *Cornell Hotel and Restaurant Administration Quarterly*, October, 27-40.

Teodorescu, D. (2006). Institutional Researchers as Knowledge Managers in Universities: envisioning new roles for the IR Profession. *Tertiary Education and Management*, 12, 75-88.

Viljoen, J. (1994). (2nd Edition). *Strategic management: Planning and implementing successful corporate strategies*. Melbourne: Longman.

Zerman, D. (1995) Crisis communication: Managing the mass media. *Information and Computer Security*, 3(5), 25-28.

The Role of Market Orientation in Managing Crises During the Post-Crisis Phase

David Martín-Consuegra
Águeda Esteban
Arturo Molina

SUMMARY. The tourism business around the world, as one of the most susceptible and vulnerable sectors, must often manage and survive global crises. In recent years the global tourism industry has experienced major crises, such as terrorist attacks, political instability, economic recession, biosecurity threats and natural disasters. The most well-known cases bear testimony to the fact that crises are not new to the tourism industry. However, tourism management capabilities and abilities to deal with complex and critical situations are limited. The time has come to develop an understanding of factors that can help tourism businesses prepare a way of getting through such crises by examining the role of market orientation and its antecedents during a post-crisis phase. This paper is concerned with the effects of several organizational factors on market orientation in airlines during the post-crisis phase of the terrorist attacks of "9/11." The results indicate that top management factors, interdepartmental factors and organizational systems have a positive effect on market orientation after a crisis has occurred.

INTRODUCTION

A crisis may occur at any time and place and no tourism organization is immune to such events. In recent years, the global tourism industry has experienced terrorist attacks, the effects of political instability, economic recession, biosecurity threats and natural disasters (Ritchie, 2004). The most well-known cases of such crises, like the Gulf War of 1991, the Foot and Mouth Outbreak of 2001, the "9/11" terrorist attacks in the United States, the 2002 Bali bombing, the SARS Outbreak and the Iraq conflict in 2003, and the bird flu in 2005, bear testimony to this fact. All of these examples are large-scale events that involve numerous stake-

David Martín-Consuegra (E-mail: David.Martin@uclm.es) is Associate Professor in the Marketing Department at University of Castilla-La Mancha (Ronda de Toledo, s/n. 13071-Ciudad Real, Spain). Águeda Esteban (E-mail: Agueda.Esteban@uclm.es) is Professor of Marketing and Head of the Marketing Department at University of Castilla-La Mancha (Ronda de Toledo, s/n. 13071-Ciudad Real, Spain). Arturo Molina (E-mail: Arturo.Molina@uclm.es) is Associate Professor in the Marketing Department at University of Castilla-La Mancha (Ronda de Toledo, s/n. 13071-Ciudad Real, Spain).

holders and are characterized by surprise, threat, uncertainty, time pressure, and extreme emotions. Under these conditions, an organization must provide appropriate and effective responses. Post-crisis is notably the period of recovery and assessment and a point where unique opportunities may be created or additional negative effects occur (Ray, 1999). While a crisis generally means a threat, opportunities may be introduced. In this sense, Meyers (1986) suggests seven potential advantages of a crisis: heroes are born, change is accelerated, latent problems are faced, people can be changed, new strategies evolve, early-warning systems develop, and new competitive edges appear. Thus, literature on crises emphasizes, in general, the need to "better manage" but does not underscore the specifics of this better management (Grewal and Tansuhaj, 2001).

In recent years, market-oriented corporate strategy has been recognized as a pillar of superior competitive advantage by both academics and practitioners. Market orientation emphasizes a business culture and an organization's ability to put the customer's interests first (Kohli and Jaworski, 1990; Narver and Slater, 1990; Deshpande, Farley and Webster, 1993). In this sense, market orientation motivates employees throughout the organization to place the highest priority on the creation and maintenance of superior customer value. So, market-oriented businesses have a competitive advantage in both the speed and effectiveness of their responsiveness to opportunities and threats (Slater, 2001). Despite compelling negative evidence linking market orientation to business performance (Grewal and Tansuhaj, 2001) after a crisis, relatively little progress has been made in developing a theoretical understanding of how organizations can manage their way through crises. However, it seems that a market-oriented corporate strategy is expected to be very useful in post-crisis situations (where unique opportunities may be created or additional negative effects occur). Throughout the last two decades, researchers have investigated several antecedents and consequences of market orientation in order to better understand why some organizations are more market-oriented than the role it has to play within companies. In particular, it has been argued that as part

of enhancing the understanding of market-driven firm performance, the effects of top management, interdepartmental factors and organizational systems on market orientation should be examined in greater depth (Jaworski and Kohli, 1993). In spite of the fact that this construct has been under severe scrutiny from marketing scholars, research has concentrated on the normal course of a firm's business. As a result of this, research has ignored its impact on the firm's ability to manage crises. Therefore, this study takes a firm step in this direction by examining the role of market orientation and its antecedents in helping tourism organizations manage crises during a post-crisis phase.

From within the tourism industry, the airline sector was chosen for this research. The study was focused on the airline sector because the tourism industry has become increasingly dependent on air transportation as one of the most comprehensive and significant factors in contributing to the development of tourism worldwide. Thus, as airlines are integrated into the tourism sector, it is a moment in which to develop an understanding of organizational factors that can help airlines manage their way through such crises. Ray (1999) indicates that airline accidents illustrate the industry's high level of vulnerability to crisis and capture the complexity of crisis management. While an airplane crash tends to be the most visible form of crisis, it is not the only type of crisis the industry encounters. Similarly, the highly complex, competitive, and interdependent nature of the industry places airlines in a chronic crisis phase. Furthermore, sudden market shifts, finances, top-management succession, mergers, strikes, government dictates, air piracy, adverse international events, and in-flight crimes create many crises for airlines. Given this context, this study was carried out after one of the most important global crises (9/11), which has had devastating implications for global airlines and the tourism industry.

In short, a study was conducted to provide a first step towards addressing the importance of the role of market orientation and its antecedents in helping tourism organizations manage crises. This study has two main objectives: (a) to identify and characterize the market orientation of airlines, and (b) to contrast the effects of several organizational factors on market orientation. Consequently, the paper starts with a brief overview of the conceptualisation on crisis and market orientation. This is followed by the development of a set of hypotheses based on the existing literature on both crisis and market orientation. The study will then present the methodology used to collect the primary data and test the hypotheses, followed by the study's results. The results of this study will demonstrate the contingent nature of the influence of organizational factors on market orientation after a crisis has occurred. Finally, the conclusions and the main implications derived from the study are considered and directions for future research are proposed.

LITERATURE REVIEW

Although the tourism industry is quite adept at using proven marketing principles after a crisis has occurred, setbacks due to negative occurrences call for something more than traditional marketing efforts (Sönmez, Apostolopoulos and Tarlow, 1999). The boundaries used to study crisis and disasters should be questioned (Scott and Laws, 2005). There is a need for researchers to develop a theoretical or conceptual framework on crisis management (Ritchie, 2004). In this sense, the tourism industry must adapt and understand marketing strategies, such as market orientation, especially during a post-crisis phase. Market orientation is defined as an organization-wide generation of market intelligence pertaining to current and future customer needs, dissemination of the intelligence among the departments of the organization, and organization-wide responsiveness to this knowledge derived from the market intelligence (Kohli and Jaworski, 1990). That is to say, market-oriented firms are expected to collect, analyze, and use market information in a more systematic, thoughtful and anticipatory manner, which may be very useful during a post-crisis phase. These market orientation dimensions have been previously identified in tourism literature. Tourism managers must anticipate the challenges of an irrational situation (Ray, 1999) and Ritchie (2004) suggests that regular meetings are required to assess the effectiveness of strategies (intelligence generation). Evans and Elphick (2005) point out the importance of sharing the knowledge about the situation and that the whole organization is aware of the framework or recovery strategy (intelligence dissemination). Also, Turner (1994) indicates that critical actions should be implemented (responsiveness). Consequently, market orientation is already included within crisis and disaster strategies as proposed by several authors (i.e., Quarantelli, 1984; Cassedy, 1991; Smith and Spika, 1993; Turner, 1994; Faulkner, 2001; Ritchie, 2004). Thus, since the post-crisis stage may present opportunities or additional negative effects (Ray, 1999), a market orientation strategy may provide managers with a tool to deal more effectively with a crisis situation by defining the company's philosophy, approach, and actions. The post-crisis phase provides a chance for organizational assessment and increased understanding of the system's overall functioning. It is a time to correct problems, develop and implement preventive actions, and introduce needed change (Ray, 1999). However, literature on market orientation has revealed that there are great difficulties for the development of a market orientation. Each firm reveals it has a different degree of market orientation, depending on a set of inner factors defined as antecedents. In this sense, antecedents are defined as a group of variables that affect business activity and restrict or obstruct the development of a market oriented culture or behavior (Kohli and Jaworski, 1990). Since the beginning of the 1950s, numerous studies have focused on the great variety of factors impeding market orientation. A review of the literature connected to this topic has shown that there are many unresolved questions and that the conclusions are highly fragmented.

Research on antecedents or barriers for market orientation may be categorized in two main periods (Harris, 1996). However, a previous period can also be identified in the early 1950s. This previous period coincided with the general acceptance of the marketing concept, which may indicate that there were no barriers to market orientation (Harris, 1999). This classification does not describe both groups as mutually exclusive; rather, it intends to demonstrate the articulation or evolution of the marketing theory. The first period spanned from the late 1950s onwards. It consisted of a sporadic evolution in order to identify specific orientation antecedents, focus mainly on types of employees, employee behaviors and organizational system and structures. This period may itself be divided into two groups (Harris, 1999). The first group makes implicit references to the antecedents to market orientation such as organizational culture (Messikomer, 1987), top management features (Chaganti and Sambharya, 1987), and employees (Kelley, 1990), rather than centering upon the identification of them. The second group includes articles focusing on the identification of one or two of the specific antecedents to market orientation pointed out above (i.e., Felton, 1959; Gummenson, 1991; Ruekert, 1992; Harris and Piercy, 1999; Harris and Ogbonna, 2001). These studies center upon one or two factors alone and consequently do not offer a global vision of all elements impeding the development of market orientation. However, they all share a common element: the importance of control over structures, systems and processes. On the other hand, the second period of research, mentioned above, can be placed from the end of the 1980s onwards. In this period, academic research paid more attention to the concept of market orientation, and as a consequence, more holistic analyses of factor types and strengths of antecedents impeding market orientation were carried out, both from theoretical and empirical perspectives (Harris, 1996). Most of the studies stand out in this research line (i.e., Kohly and Jaworski, 1990, 1993; Morgan, 1990; Morgan and Piercy, 1991; Harris, 1996, 1999, 2000 and 2002). These studies suggest that the major antecedents for the development of a market orientation are organizational structure, internal relations and systems, ignorance, and employees' lack of training.

However, Kohli and Jaworki's study (1990) put forward the most important theoretical work on the antecedents to market orientation. The following inhibitors were identified: interdepartmental dynamics, top management, and organizational systems. Kohli and Jaworski's (1990) model was applied in Saudi Arabia by Bhuian (1998), in Australia by Pulendran, Speed and Widing II (2000) and in the United Kingdom by Tay and Morgan (2002), obtaining very similar results. Other similar models describing antecedents or obstacles have been applied to non-profit organizations; for example, Balabanis, Stables and Phillips (1997) focused on British charity organization, Wood, Bhuian and Kiecker's (2000) work was centered upon charity hospitals and Cervera, Molla and Sanchez's (2001) study dealt with local administration. Other studies centering on the analysis of barriers to market orientation in tourist businesses can be appropriately cited here. Harris and Walkins (1998) focused on the executive attitudes that limited its development in this sector. The study discovered that there was a negative effect on market orientation when the managers were unaware of this concept, when they did not have enough resources, when they did not consider it essential for their business size, when they were deterred by taking risks, when they were focused on short-term objectives, when they did not have the consumer as their main objective, or when they did not have to face competition. In these models, factors described as antecedents were mainly: top management, organization and environment.

Top management emphasis and top management risk aversion as antecedents to market orientation were examined initially by Jaworski and Kohli (1993). The importance of top management emphasis and risk aversion in setting up market orientation behavior among the employees is based on the premise that employees will not have the motivation to be responsive to customer needs until they receive clear signals from the top management (Bhuian, 1998). Thus, leadership is required to provide direction and guidance in dealing with unexpected incidents (Ritchie, 2004). Leadership in dealing with a crisis has been mentioned by Cassedy (1991), Turner (1994) and Faulkner (2001). In addition, Evans and Elphick (2005) indicate that in a volatile sector such as travel, prudently managed airlines should consider the potential risks and managerial responses to external shock at the analysis and formulation phases of the strategic planning process in the post-crisis phase. However, the risk aversion of top managers could in all probability have a negative effect on the motivation to undertake new market-oriented actions (Jaworski and Kohli, 1993) to manage the crisis. Consequently, the following hypotheses can be proposed:

H1: The greater the top management emphasis on a market orientation, the greater its market orientation is during a post-crisis phase.

H2: The greater the risk aversion of top management, the lower its market orientation is during a post-crisis phase.

Jaworski and Kohli (1993) also hypothesize two aspects of interdepartmental dynamics as inhibitors of market orientation: the degree of an organization's interdepartmental conflict and the degree of an organization's interdepartmental connectedness. Collaboration is required between different departments. In the case of a crisis, understanding its impact on internal (business units, staff, departments) and external stakeholders and the relationship between them is critical. Ritchie (2004) suggests that this is because of the inter-relationship and dependency between these groups and a need to develop suitable strategies to resolve any crisis. Also, an organization's response to a crisis is dependent in part on how individuals respond to the stress from the crisis. Jaworski and Kohli (1993) pointed to interdepartmental conflict as an inhibitor of market orientation. Interdepartmental conflict refers to the perception of one party's interests being negatively affected by another department arising from the incompatibility of actual or desired responses. Also, the degree of formal and informal direct contact among employees across departments was posited to affect a market orientation. Therefore, the following hypotheses are proposed:

H3: The greater the interdepartmental conflict, the lower its market orientation is during a post-crisis phase.

H4: The greater the interdepartmental connectedness, the greater its market orientation is during a post-crisis phase.

In addition, organizations must have deliberate strategies to generate and disseminate information that helps to design and introduce a response through the creation of adequate organizational structures and systems. After a crisis has occurred, the turnaround process is also concerned with organizational learning, configuring the structure of the organization to respond effectively, and creating a culture that is responsive and flexible (Evans and Elphick, 2005). Ritchie (2004) suggests that strategies alone will not be effective if an organization does not have an adaptive, flexible or responsive organizational culture. Tribe (1997) indicates that organizational structure and culture tend to evolve reactively after a crisis. So, rigid management structures may not be appropriate. In this sense, management may need to look for freer structures which may help position the organization in relation to the outside environment, allowing for improved monitoring of change and dealing with crises after they occur. According to Jaworski and Kohli (1993), formalization, centralization and an adequate reward system must be considered. The concept of formalization represents the degree to which formal rules, authority relations, communications, and regulations guide employees. Centralization refers to the inverse amount of delegation of decision-making authority throughout an organization and the extent of participation by organizational members in decision making (Aiken and Hage, 1968). Thus, improved and sustained market orientation may require coordinating structures that enhance the management's ability to handle uncertainties in a rapidly changing environment (Kuada and Buatsi, 2005). On the other hand, rewards systems shape the behaviors of employees influencing loyalty to their companies and motivation. It enables firms to satisfy variations in their customers' needs because the requisite skills and knowledge for serving such needs exists within the company thanks to management's priority on their acquisition rather than on task performance. However, Kuada and Buatsi (2005) indicate that while managers are able to maintain centralized control in young and small organizations that operate in relatively stable environments, larger organizations that operate in complex and unpredictable environment constraints customer orientation due to centralization and formalization. Therefore, the following hypothesis is proposed:

H5: The more adequate organizational systems are, the greater its market orientation is during a post-crisis phase.

To sum up, a review of the literature on market orientation antecedents suggests a huge number of multiple, complex and interconnected antecedents which can influence the market orientation of a given firm during a post-crisis period. These antecedents range from attitude and behavior of employees to organization structure. However, four theoretical conclusions are offered from the analysis of market orientation literature. Firstly, employees' and top managers' opinions, attitudes, beliefs and values are the main determinant of a high level of market orientation. Secondly, the systems, structures and strategies of a business are also highly significant for market orientation. Thirdly, these antecedents mentioned above are derived from a business' internal characteristics and depend on their interdepartmental dynamics. Fourthly, there are several external factors that influence structure, organizational systems and interdepartmental dynamics according to what is happening in the competitive environment.

METHOD

Measures

In order to investigate the antecedents of market orientation in the study described here, all measures were adapted from past studies. The survey instrument consisted of three sections. Section 1 included the MARKOR scale, developed by Kohli, Jaworski and Kumar (1993), which was utilized to measure market orientation. MARKOR, which has 20 items covering the three dimensions of the construct, consists of 6 items pertaining to market intelligence generation, 5 to intelligence dissemination and 9 to responsiveness. In line with Jaworski and Kohli's (1993) framework, the responsiveness construct was divided into two parts: design of responses and implementation of responses. In addition, it assessed the extent of a firm's market orientation by treating it as a second-order construct within the three constructs mentioned above. Each item was scored on a five-point scale, ranging from "strongly disagree" to "strongly agree." Section 2 of the questionnaire included questions regarding antecedents of a market orientation. In order to

measure the antecedents of a market orientation, a reduced version of Jaworski and Kohli's (1993) study was used (Bhuian, 1998). Initially, all items related to all antecedents, taken from Jaworski and Kohli's study, were used to develop the questionnaire. This questionnaire was pretested on three senior marketing managers of two national companies. All three respondents showed great concern about the length of the questionnaire and the number of questions. So, the items were reviewed and 17 scale items were selected without sacrificing the content validity of these constructs. The final version of the antecedents included on the questionnaire consisted of 5 items pertaining to the top management construct, 5 to the interdepartmental dynamics construct and 7 to the organizational systems construct. Regarding the top management construct, 2 items measured top management emphasis on market orientation and 3 items measured top management attitude towards risk. The remaining items measured interdepartmental conflict (3 items), interdepartmental connectedness (2 items) and 7 items pertaining to organizational systems (centralization, formalization and reward systems). Finally, section 3 included questions regarding background information, such as size of the organization, years of experience, line of services provided, strategic actions, turnover and profits.

Sample

In order to collect information a postal survey was carried out among international airlines during 2002 and the beginning of 2003. A sample of 234 airlines was drawn from members of the *International Air Transport Association* (IATA), along with the other biggest airlines in the world that are not members of this association (i.e., low cost airlines). Key respondents techniques were employed in the collection of the data as the survey instrument was specialized. The main purpose was to guarantee a global knowledge of the respondents of the firms' internal operations (Nunnally, 1967). A self-administered questionnaire, a letter from the president of an International Tourism Institute, a personalized instruction cover letter explaining the purpose of the survey and a return envelope was sent to the marketing director/

manager of the selected organizations. The manager or the head of marketing was treated as the key informant. This key informant approach implicitly assumes that the head of marketing's individual opinion accurately provides a good indication of their organization's market orientation and marketing philosophy (Kohli and Jaworski, 1990). Respondents were assured of their anonymity. Respondents were also offered a copy of the aggregated results of the survey. To further enhance the response rate, each eight weeks after the initial mailing, a follow-up letter with a questionnaire was mailed. A total 72 responses were received and used for data analysis, yielding a usable response rate of 30.7%. However, it should be noted that although this sample size is small for estimating, in EQS, a measurement model with 7 construct was used. In addition, it can be noted that previous studies of this kind from selected industries used small samples (from 41 to 89 organizations or business units) (Au and Tse, 1995; Chang and Ellis, 1998; Horng and Chen, 1998; Webb, Webster and Krepapa, 2000; Pulendran, Speed and Widing, 2003). Consequently, this limitation is described in the limitations and further research section. The early versus late respondents analysis provide no evidence of non-response bias (Amstrong and Overton, 1977). The chi-square tests and t-test results indicate that there is no significant difference between the early and the late respondents. Thus, nonresponse bias is not a serious problem in this study.

RESULTS

The scales used in this study were subjected to standard reliability and validity checks. The evaluation of the psychometric properties was carried out in accordance with Churchill (1979), Anderson and Gerbing's (1988) two-step approach and Deng and Dart's (1994) methodological suggestions.

Firstly, different analyses of the correlations between the initial scale items were carried out for this purpose, as well as examinations of variance analyses and scale reliability. According to Bagozzi (1981) and Nurosis (1993), nine items were dropped because of their low corrected item-to-total correlations (i.e., < 0.3).

The next step was an exploratory factor analysis to initially assess the psychometric properties of the scale. Exploratory factoring was based upon a principal components analysis with varimax rotation of remaining items. The scale items were purified through an iterative process. Items that did not load heavily on the primary factor (i.e., < 0.5) and items that had significant cross loadings were removed. This resulted in the removal of five more items. After that, the reliability coefficients of most of the scales met the threshold of 0.70 recommended by Nunnally (1967). The reliability coefficient of interdepartmental conflict scale were too low (0.54) and were not acceptable. Therefore, these items were dropped from the subsequent analysis and its respective hypothesis could not be tested.

In order to analyze market orientation unidimensionality, a confirmatory factorial analysis (CFA) was employed sequentially. Several first order successive CFA were carried out in order to estimate various fit models until the most suitable one was obtained (Kohli and Jaworski, 1993; Han, Kim and Srivastava, 1998). Finally, the scale's concept validity evaluation was carried out from both its convergent and discriminant perspective. Convergent validity refers to the degree of agreement in two or more measures of the same construct. A strong correlation among the components would indicate that they are convergent on a common construct, thereby providing evidence of convergent validity. In order to test the convergent validity, the items' substantial convergence in their respective latent variables was analyzed (Gerbing and Anderson, 1988) and the significance of the correlation between dimensions of each concept was determined (Lehmann, Gupta and Steckel, 1999). All correlation coefficients were significant at $P < 0.001$ and all the estimated coefficients of all the indicators were significant ($t > 2.0$). Convergence had been achieved for measures of market orientation as a function of three components. Discriminant validity concerns the degree to which measures of conceptually distinct constructs differ. The discriminatory character of the dimensions was checked proving that the confidence interval of the correlation between each pair of critical dimensions did not include the value 1 (Anderson and Gerbing, 1988). The analysis clearly suggested that the scale had acceptable discriminant validity. In addition, the goodness-of-fit statistics in respect of the construct may also be considered as correct. According to the previous criteria, the MARKOR scale possessed all the desirable psychometric properties of a valid scale. The unidimensionality, reliability and validity of the antecedents can also be accepted, following similar procedures to those previously described. In short, seven constructs, three antecedents and market orientation, along with 23 indicants were included in the following analysis.

The hypotheses formulated previously were evaluated undertaking a structural equation analysis. This technique allows the assessment of the existing casual relationships among the antecedents and a firm's market orientation. The measurement scales used for each concept were the result of the evaluation process described. Because of the size of the sample and the number of variables in the model, a path diagram based on the average scores for each of the constructs was used in the analysis of the data. That is to say, the means of each of the seven constructs were employed as indicators, representing intelligence generation, intelligence dissemination and responsiveness, of the latent market orientation factor, and top management risk aversion, top management emphasis, interdepartmental connectedness and organizational systems of the latent antecedent factors. The final model is a respecified model based on modification indices where a number of error variances were allowed to correlate (Byrne, Shavelson, and Muthen, 1989). The results of the final measurement model indicate that the overall fit of the model was good. All fit indices were above the suggested cut-off values for satisfactory fit. The overall fit of the model is good (see Figure 1). The Comparative Fit Index (CFI = 0.983), the Normed Fit Index (NFI = 0.953), and the GFI Fit Index (GFI = 0.953) are well above the recommended threshold of 0.90 for a satisfactory goodness of fit. Also the Root Mean Square Error of Approximation (RMSEA = 0.069) is below the recommended 0.08 level. Overall, Table 1 presents means, standard deviations, number of indicators, and correlations

among the constructs according to their final operationalization.

Thus, the results allowed testing the hypotheses of the study formulated. Figure 1 reports the factor loadings of the seven constructs. All the estimated coefficients of all the indicators were significant ($t > 2.0$). The results show support for H1. The influence of top management emphasis on market orientation dimensions during a post-crisis phase is positive and statistically significant, as predicted. Therefore, hypothesis 2 which states that the influence of top management has a negative significant influence on market orientation during a post-crisis stage, is supported. Also, in support of hypothesis 4, interdepartmental connectedness has a positive influence on market orientation. The results show support for H5 too. The influence of adequate organizational systems on market orientation is positive and statistically significant. Finally, due to large standardized residuals and error variances, the only non-hypothesized effect found to be significant was the influence of interdepartmental conflicts on market orientation in the airline sector.

CONCLUSIONS

This study represents the first effort reported in literature connected to empirically examine which antecedents determine the degree of a market orientation in the airline sector after a crisis. The present study was conducted to examine the applicability of Jaworski and Kohli's (1993) antecedent framework in airline sector during a post-crisis phase. The principal findings of this research suggest that the antecedents proposed by Jaworski and Kohli (1993) are generalized to airlines during a post-crisis phase. As previously noted, an organization's market orientation after a crisis is dependent on top management behavior, interdepartmental connectedness and adequate organizational systems in order to be market oriented and to avoid interdepartmental conflict. Consequently, the results indicate that internal factors, such as top management involvement, department relationships and organizational systems play an important role in the implementation of market-oriented activities in an airline after a crisis. To this end, a sample of 72

FIGURE 1. Path Diagram of Integrative Model Results

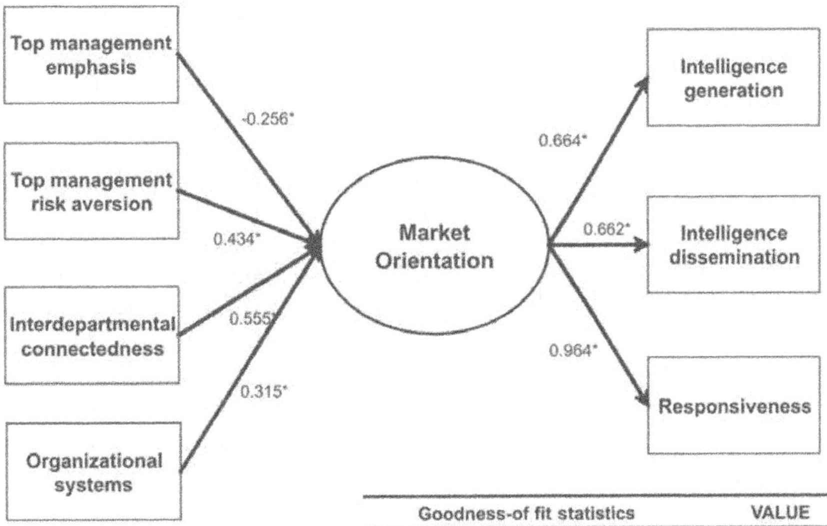

Goodness-of fit statistics	VALUE
Chi-square	16,646 (P=0,15)
Comparative Fit Index (CFI)	0.983
Normed Fit Index (NFI)	0.953
GFI Fit Index (GFI)	0.953
RMSEA	0.069

NOTE: Asterisks indicate significant result.

TABLE 1. Integrative Model Statistics

	Mean	SD	No. of Items	Cronbach's alpha	IG	ID	RE	RA	CO	EM	OS
IG	3.91	0.72	3	0.72	1.000						
ID	4.06	0.65	3	0.75	0.501	1.000					
RE	3.90	0.68	7	0.78	0.674	0.682	1.000				
RA	2.41	0.98	2	0.78	0.403	0.444	0.428	1.000			
CO	3.83	0.94	2	0.85	0.424	0.709	0.732	0.349	1.000		
EM	4.15	0.92	2	0.72	0.485	0.493	0.714	0.419	0.515	1.000	
OS	2.29	0.70	4	0.83	0.425	0.374	0.433	0.369	0.617	0.412	1.000

Intelligence generation (IG), Intelligence dissemination (ID), Responsiveness (RE), Top management risk aversion (RA), Top management emphasis (EM), Interdepartmental connectedness (CO), Organizational systems (OS)

airlines was used to validate the scale of market orientation and its antecedents and examine the relationships of market orientation with its antecedents after "9/11." Owing to the length of Jaworski and Kohli's (1993) scales, this study had to use reduced versions of all the scales. The methods of analysis produced similar results to those reported in Jaworski and Kohli's (1993) study under normal circumstances.

Overall, it is interesting to note within the scale of market orientation that while the responsiveness items appear to be particularly relevant for the airline managers' sample, the items related to intelligence generation and dissemination appear to be less important. This may be because of the importance given to returning to normality through adequate actions by airline managers according to intelligence obtained from the market after a crisis. On the other hand, this does not mean that top airline managers do not consider consumers opinions when developing appropriate activities. Airline managers can probably make a fairly accurate judgment about the wants and needs of the consumers after a crisis and, therefore, intelligence generation through market research is just another way to design and implement the best way of returning to normality.

Furthermore, the results suggest that several factors drive the market orientation of a business. The most important result of the present study is that antecedents identified previously in literature are strongly related to market orientation during a post-crisis stage. In relation to top management antecedents, the amount of emphasis top managers place on market orientation after a crisis appears to affect the market orientation of the organization. In addition, the results also support the claim that a lower top management risk aversion leads to greater market orientation. These findings support the hypothesis that responding to market development after a crisis entails some amount of risk. According to Jaworski and Kohli (1993), if top managers are disinclined to assume risks, the organization is less likely to be responsive to the changing environment. Therefore, top mangers should place more emphasis on being more market oriented and being less averse to risk after a post-crisis stage. Also, the results indicate that connectedness among departments, as expected, promotes market orientation. However, the lack of internal consistency pertaining to the scale of interdepartmental conflict could be due to the fact that airline managers are reluctant to admit to the existence of any conflict in their organizations during the post-crisis phase. In this sense, the good connectedness among departments after the crisis could reduce internal conflicts. Thus, due to the impact of a big crisis, all the departments could be working in the same direction avoiding any conflict that could damage the organization recovery strategy during this period.

Undoubtedly, the tourism industry is one of the most susceptible and vulnerable industries to crises. These kinds of episodes are not confined to any geographical region, as crises respect no political or cultural boundaries (Santana, 2004). From a managerial perspective, the unpredictable nature of this crisis has created a need for understanding management imperatives for different types of crisis. The globalization of the tourism industry has opened organizations up to a wider set of potential risks. Greater exposure to different kinds of crises and disasters all over the world require tourism managers to deal with them effectively. The results of this study suggest that providing airline managers with Jaworski and Kohli's market orientation framework could help organizations manage a crisis. This study provides some guidelines for marketing managers who have to handle a crisis. Managers who implement a market orientation strategy during a post-crisis phase should increase top management emphasis on customer orientation after a crisis. These managers should consider minimizing their risk aversion too. In addition, they have to promote connectedness among departments through adequate organizational systems to increase the generation of market intelligence and the dissemination of intelligence across the organization.

Furthermore, a number of areas for future research are suggested based on above findings and limitations. First of all, despite the fact that the scale used in this study to measure the construct of market orientation was derived from one the most well-known studies in this area, a measurement of market orientation of tourism providers may be developed. As this study has examined the influence of seven antecedents on market orientation in the airline sector during a post-crisis phase, future studies should also consider other antecedent variables presented in literature. In addition, the results of this study may have capitalized on the peculiar characteristics of the data from the airline sector. Therefore, the hypothesized relationships should be tested further with other tourism businesses as well as in other crisis. This is because the degree of market orientation that a business will exhibit will depend partly on the type of crisis it has to control.

Although this study has provided a relevant and notable insight into the effects of some antecedents on market orientation in the airline sector, several limitations must be considered when interpreting the findings. These include the sample size, the fact that the study provides cross-sectional data and the fact that the information was obtained from only one type of respondent. This means that any generalizations of findings to other populations or post-crisis phases must be made with a certain amount of cautions. The need to revisit the properties of the MARKOR scale in particular was noted, along with the impact of a modest sample on test power. An insufficient sample size may cause the solution to be instable, especially when the items are distributed non-normally and are categorical or Likert scales with small ranges. This means that the estimates of factor loadings will have large standard errors, and the model may have difficulty reaching a solution (Kara, Spillan and DeShields, 2004). Working with a larger sample size could perhaps reduce problems with respect to model parameter estimation. The greatest limitation of the study is, however, shared by the vast majority of others in the area. This study, like so many others, employs a cross-sectional analysis. While providing an important insight into the barriers of market orientation, there is certainly a need to investigate the results of those many studies from a longitudinal perspective during the whole post-crisis phase. The data were collected through the key informant approach. Although senior managers could be adequate for reliable and valid data (Tan and Litschert, 1994), the information that a firm generates may not be the only source of information about its levels of market orientation. It might be important to contrast a firm's degree of market orientation as internal information assesses it with its level of market orientation as perceived by customer, competitors, and distributors (Sin et al., 2005). This may be one of the most challenging areas for further research.

Furthermore, this study should be viewed as an initial attempt to isolate the impact of some barriers to market orientation in the airline sector during the post-crisis phase, since the levels of market orientation in the service sector may be influenced by a number of additional variables (Esteban et al., 2002). Additionally, while the multi-cultural nature of the sample added diversity and richness to the study, it may have obscured some uniqueness among the airlines. Within this context, a worthy area of investigation might be to explore the differences in the ways market orientation is applied in various geographical zones. Regardless of these limitations, it is suggested that the findings presented make a positive contribution to the tourism literature related to this area and that tourism business managers can benefit from the insights gained from this study.

REFERENCES

Aiken, M. & Hage, J. (1968). Organizational Independence and Intra-organizational Structure. *American Sociological review*, 33: 912-930.

Anderson, J. C. & Gerbing, D. W. (1988). Structural Equation Modeling in Practice: A Review and Recommended Two-Step Approach. *Psychological Bulletin*, 103(3): 411-423.

Armstrong, J. S. & Overton, T. S. (1977). Estimating Nonresponse Bias in Mail Surveys. *Journal of Marketing Research*, 14 (August): 396-402.

Au, A. K. M. & Tse, A. C. B. (1995). The effect of market orientation on company performance in the service sector: a comparative study of the hotel industry in Hong Kong and New Zealand. *Journal of International Consumer Marketing*, 8(2): 77-87.

Bagozzi, R. P. (1981). Evaluating Structural Equations Models with unobservable variables and measurement error: a comment. *Journal of Marketing Research*, 23 (August): 375-381.

Balabanis, G.; Stables, R. E. & Phillips, H. C. (1997). Market Orientation in the Top 200 British charity organizations and its impact on their performance. *European Journal of Marketing*, 31(8): 583-603.

Bhuian, S. N. (1998). An empirical examination of Market Orientation in Saudi Arabian Manufacturing Companies. *Journal of Business Research*, 43: 13-25.

Byrne B. M.; Shavelson R. J. & Muthen B. (1989). Testing for the equivalence of factor covariance and mean structures: the issue of partial measurement invariance. *Psychological Bulletin*, 105(3): 456-466.

Cassedy, K. (1991). *Crisis management planning in the travel and tourism industry: A study of three destinations and a crisis management planning manua.*, PATA, San Francisco.

Cervera, A.; Mollá, A. & Sánchez, M. (2001). Antecedents and consequences of Market Orientation in public organisations. *European Journal of Marketing*, 35(1/2): 1259-1286.

Chaganti, R. & Sambharya, R. (1987). Strategic Orientation and characteristics of top management. *Strategic Management Journal*, 8(6):393-401.

Chang J. H. N. & Ellis, P. (1998). Market Orientation and business performance: some evidence from Hong Kong. *International Marketing Review*, 15(2): 119-139.

Churchill, G. A. (1979). A Paradigm for Developing Better Measures of Marketing Constructs. *Journal of Marketing Research*, 16 (February): 64-73.

Deng, S. & Dart, J. (1994). Measuring Market Orientation: A Multi-factor, Multi-item Approach. *Journal of Marketing Management*, 10: 725-742.

Deshpande, R.; Farley, J. U. & Webster, F. E. Jr. (1993). Corporate Culture, Customer Orientation, and Innovativeness in Japanese Firms: A Quadrad Analysis. *Journal of Marketing*, 57 (January): 23-37.

Esteban, A.; Millán, A.; Molina, A. & Martín-Consuegra, D. (2002). Market Orientation in service: a review and analysis. *European Journal of Marketing*, 36(9/10): 1003-1021.

Evans, N. & Elphick, S. (2005). Models of Crisis Management: an Evaluation of their Value for Strategic Planning in the International Travel Industry. *International Journal of Tourism Research*, 7: 135-150.

Faulkner, B. (2001). Towards a framework for tourism disaster management. *Tourism Management*, 22: 135-147.

Felton, A. P. (1959). Making the Marketing Concept Work. *Harvard Business Review*, 37 (July/August): 55-65.

Gerbing, D. W. & Anderson, J. C. (1988). An Updated Paradigm for Scale Development Incorporating Unidimensionality and Its Assessment. *Journal of Marketing Research*, 25 (May): 186-192.

Grewal, R. & Tansuhaj, P. (2001). Building Organizational Capabilities for Managing Economic Crisis: The Role of Market Orientation and Strategic Flexibility. *Journal of Marketing*, 65 (April): 67-80.

Gummesson, E. (1991). Marketing-orientation revisited: the crucial role of the part-time marketer. *European Journal of Marketing*, 25 (2): 60-75.

Han, J. K.; Kim, N. & Srivastava, R. K. (1998). Market Orientation and organizational performance: Is innovation a missing link?" *Journal of Marketing*, 62 (October): 30-45.

Harris, L. C. (1996). Cultural obstacles to Market Orientation. *Journal of Marketing Practice: Applied Marketing Science*, 2(4): 36-52.

Harris, L. C. (1999). Barriers to Developing Market Orientation. *Journal of Applied Management Studies*, 8(1): 85-101.

Harris, L. C. (2000). The organizational barriers to developing Market Orientation. *European Journal of Marketing*, 34(5/6): 598-624.

Harris, L. C. (2002). Developing Market Orientation: An Exploration of Differences in Management Approaches. *Journal of Marketing Management*, 18: 603-632.

Harris, L. C. & Ogbonna, E. (2001). Leadership style and Market Orientation: an empirical study. *European Journal of Marketing*, 35(5/6): 744-764.

Harris, L. C. & Piercy, N. F. (1999). Management behavior and barriers to Market Orientation in retailing companies. *The Journal of Services Marketing*, 13(2): 113-131.

Harris, L. C. & Watkins, P. (1998). The impediments to developing a Market Orientation: an exploratory study of small UK hotels. *International Journal of Contemporary Hospitality Management*, 10(6): 221-226.

Horng, S. & Cheng, A. H. (1998). Market Orientation of small and medium-sized firms in Taiwan. *Journal of Small Business Management*, 36 (July): 79-85.

Jaworski, B. & Kohli, A. K. (1993). Market Orientation: Antecedents and Consequences. *Journal of Marketing*, 57 (July): 53-70.

Kara, A.; Spillan, J. E. & DeShields, O. W. Jr. (2004). An empirical investigation of the link between market orientation and business performance in non-profit service providers. *Journal of Marketing Theory and Practice*, 12 (2): 59-72.

Kelley, S. W. (1990). Customer Orientation of bank employees. *International Journal of Bank Marketing*, 8 (6): 25-29.

Kohli, A. K. & Jaworski, B. (1990). Market Orientation: The Construct, Research Propositions, and Managerial Implications. *Journal of Marketing*, 54 (April): 1-18.

Kohli, A. K., Jaworski, B. & Kumar, A. (1993). MARKOR: A Measure of Market Orientation. *Journal of Marketing Research*, 30 (November): 467-477.

Kuada, J. & Buatsi, S. N. (2005). Market Orientation and Management Practices in Ghanaian Firms: Revisiting the Jaworski and Kohli Framework. *Journal of International Marketing*, 13(1): 58-88.

Lehmann, D.R.; Gupta, S. & Steckel, J.H. (1999), *Marketing Research*, Addison-Wesley, New York.

Messikomer, E. E. (1987). Marketing changes the corporate culture: a company study. *Journal of Business and Industrial Marketing*, 2(4): 53-58.

Meyers, G. C. (1986). *When it Hits the Fan: managing the nine crises of business.* Houghton Mifflin, Boston.

Morgan, N. A. (1990). Implementing Marketing: key issues for professional service firms. *Journal of Professional Services Marketing*, 6(1):7-16.

Morgan, N. A. & Piercy, N. F. (1991). Barriers to Marketing Implementation in UK Professional Service Firms. *Journal of Professional Services Marketing*, 8(1): 95-113.

Narver, J. C. & Slater, S. F. (1990). The Effect of a Market Orientation on Business Profitability. *Journal of Marketing*, 54 (October): 20-35.

Nunnally, J. C. (1967). *Psychometric Theory*, McGraw Hill, New York.

Nurosis, M. J. (1993). *SPSS Statistical Data Analysis*, SPSS Inc.

Pulendran, S.; Speed, R. & Widing II, R. E. (2000). The Antecedents and Consequences of Market Orientation in Australia. *Australian Journal of Management*, 25(2): 119-143.

Pulendran, S.; Speed, R. & Widing II, R. E. (2003). Marketing planning, Market Orientation and business performance. *European Journal of Marketing*, 37(3/4): 476-497.

Quarantelli, E. L. (1984). Organisational behaviour in disasters and implications for disaster planning. *Monographs of the National Emergency Training Center*, 1(2): 1-31.

Ray, S. J. (1999). *Strategic Communication in Crisis Management: lessons from the airline industry.* Quorum Books, London.

Ritchie, B. W. (2004). Chaos, crises and disasters: a strategic approach to crisis management in the tourism industry. *Tourism Management*, 25: 669-683.

Ruekert, R. W. (1992). Developing a Market Orientation: An Organizational Strategy Perspective. *International Journal of Research in Marketing*, 9: 225-245.

Santana, G. (2004). Crisis Management and Tourism: Beyond the Rhetoric. *Journal of Travel and Tourism Marketing*, 15(4): 299-321.

Scott, N. & Laws, E. (2005). Tourism Crises and Disasters: Enhancing Understanding of Systems Effects. *Journal of Travel and Tourism Marketing*, 19(2/3): 151-160.

Sin, L.; Tse, A.; Yau, O.; Chow, R. & Lee, J. (2005). Market Orientation, Relationship Marketing Orientation, and Business Performance: The Moderating Effects of Economic Ideology and Industry Type. *Journal of International Marketing*, 13(1): 36-57.

Slater, S. F. (2001). Market Orientation at the beginning of a new millennium. *Managing Service Quality*, 11(4): 230-232.

Smith, D. & Spika, C. (1993). Back from the brink, post crisis management. *Long Range Planning*, 26: 28-38.

Sönmez, S. F.; Apostolopoulos, Y. & Tarlow, P. (1999). Tourism in crisis: managing the effects of terrorism. *Journal of Travel Research*, 38 (August): 13-18.

Tan, J. J. & Litschert, R. J. (1994). Environment-Strategy Relationship and Its Performance Implications: An Empirical Study of the Chinese Electronic Industry. *Strategic Management*, 15 (January): 1-20.

Tay, L. & Morgan, N. A. (2002). Antecedents and consequences of Market Orientation in chartered surveying firms. *Construction Management and Economics*, 20: 331-341.

Tribe, J. (1997). *Corporate strategy for tourism.* Thompson, Suffolk.

Turner, D. (1994). Resources for disaster recovery. *Security Management.* Arlington: Vol. 38, Issue 8, 57-61.

Webb, D.; Webster, C. & Krepapa, A. (2000). An exploration of the Meaning and Outcomes of a Customer-Defined Market Orientation. *Journal of Business Research*, 48: 101-112.

Wood, V. R.; Bhuian, S. & Kiecker, P. (2000). Market Orientation and Organizational Performance in Not-for-Profit Hospitals. *Journal of Business Research*, 48: 213-226.

A Cautionary Tale of a Resort Destination's Self-Inflicted Crisis

Steven Pike

SUMMARY. Rotorua was New Zealand's first tourism destination, rising to prominence a hundred years ago on the back of the central government's vision for a South Pacific spa to rival those of Europe. Government resources were used to develop and support Rotorua's infrastructure and tourism industry, like no other in the British Commonwealth, for the best part of the 20th century. By the 1980s however, Rotorua's tourism industry was in a crisis, and it is posited that the crisis was largely self-inflicted. The paper provides an historical summary of key events leading to the crisis, and subsequent efforts to regain destination competitiveness through a public-private partnership. Written from the perspective of the CEO of the destination's inaugural regional tourism organisation charged with co-ordinating the marketing response to the crisis, the case provides a cautionary tale of how one destination's success as a destination has risen, fallen and risen in line with government intervention.

INTRODUCTION

The primary role of any destination marketing organisation (DMO) is to foster market competitiveness. Since achieving competitiveness is now a major challenge for most destinations (WTTC, 2002), this is as much an issue of significance to individual businesses as it is to DMOs. After all, the success of individual businesses is to a large extent reliant on the competitiveness of that destination (Pike, 2004), particularly in places affected by disasters and crises.

Many DMOs at national and local levels started life as government departments. Although there has been a shift in structure towards limited liability companies, trusts and public-private partnerships, most DMO funding remains from government. Many outside the tourism industry have questioned why taxes should be used in destination marketing to 'subsidise tourism businesses.' A political implication of this has been witnessed in the USA, where lack of Congress support for a national tourism office is a result of a strong political lobby arguing this would represent 'corporate

Steven Pike (E-mail: sd.pike@qut.edu.au) is a Senior Lecturer in the School of Advertising, Marketing & Public Relations at Queensland University of Technology (Gardens Point Campus, 2 George Street, Brisbane, Queensland 4001, Australia).

welfare' (Gatty & Blalock, 1997). Without government intervention, particularly in the form of financial resources, most DMOs would not exist in their current form. Government withdrawal of funding in Colorado, Maine and California in recent years (see Doering 1979, Donnelly & Vaske 1997) provides indications of how destination marketing activities can be curtailed through a drop in budget that cannot be reimbursed through corporate sponsorship or membership levies. For example, Colorado slipped from 3rd to 17th in terms of traveller recognition of state destinations, and visits by pleasure travellers decreased by up to 10% in the short term. In 2003 the governor of California proposed the state tourism office be closed as a cost saving measure when the state faced a $35 billion shortfall (*Inbound*, 13 January 2003, p. 1). Such a withdrawal of government funding can lead to a tourism crisis. In 2006 for example, Tourism Waikato, one of New Zealand's regional tourism organisations (RTO), had its budget unexpectedly cut in half by the local government (see Coventry, 2006, p. 1). Tourism Waikato's Chief Executive Officer lamented: "It's a very gut wrenching situation. Marketing of the whole Waikato will be suspended until funding regenerates."

Increasing attention in the tourism literature is being devoted to destination disaster management. This has been particularly evident in the new millennium, a time when the competitiveness of many destinations has been tested by a diverse range of exogenous events involving terrorism, acts of God, and threats of pandemics. In the case of such 'wildcard events,' described by Hall (2005) as being low probability but high impact, the destination's recovery will depend on the level of preparedness. Hall rightly argued there exists a tendency in tourism to assume the unthinkable will not happen. This may imply a view that the future will continue to evolve as per the past, and in this paper it is argued management's unpreparedness for a different future can lead to a crisis.

A crisis is a self-inflicted situation caused by inept management practises or an inability to adapt to a changing environment (Faulkner, 1999). A disaster on the other hand is a sudden catastrophic event over which the DMO has little or no control. In the emerging literature on destination disaster management, there have

been a number of very useful cases about DMO responses to a wide range of disasters such as cyclones (Faulkner & Vikulov, 2001), Foot and Mouth disease (Frisby, 2002), bush fires (Christine, 1995), travel advisories (Beirman 2003), war (Mansfield, 1999), violence (Leslie, 1999) and terrorism (Hopper, 2002). While destinations in decline have also been mentioned in the literature, including Hamm (Buckley & Witt, 1985), Majorca (Morgan, 1991), Canada (Go, 1987), Bermuda (Conlin, 1995), and Amsterdam (Dahles, 1998), little has been reported about attempts by a destination to recover from such a management crisis. This paper documents a tourism crisis that emerged through the inability by a resort destination's stakeholders to adapt to a changing environment. A historical perspective elucidating the context of the crisis, involving a significant review of archival material, is followed by a reflexive narrative of recovery efforts from the perspective of the inaugural RTO manager appointed to coordinate marketing aspects of the recovery. In this regard the paper joins other practitioner reflections on practical DMO challenges (see for example Curtis, 2001, Frisby, 2002).

The destination of interest is Rotorua, which was New Zealand's first tourism resort area. Singled out by the country's government in the late 1800s as a future 'Sanatorium of the earth,' the area became a beneficiary of levels of support only dreamed of by other New Zealand regions. The New Zealand government built infrastructure, accommodation, spas, tourist attractions and transport, handled the majority of all domestic and overseas promotion, and even operated the local visitor information centre for 90 years. However, Rotorua's star status within the New Zealand tourism industry, which the destination had enjoyed for the best part of a century, declined to such a point that by the late 1980s the local tourism industry was considered to be in a state of crisis.

ROTORUA– SANATORIUM OF THE EARTH!

Rotorua has a short-recorded history by international standards. The township was officially created in 1880, through the British

Crown's 'Fenton Agreement' with the Maori owners. The first non-indigenous visitors were traders (see Cowan, 1935) and missionaries (see Tapsell, 1972) during the 1830s. The first tourist was thought to be naturalist John Bidwell, in 1839, who later published the book *Rambles in New Zealand* (Stafford, 1977). The reason for the early visitation was to experience the Pink and White Terraces. These were impressive silica terraces, probably similar to Turkey's white terraces at Pamukkale, formed from mineral deposits in the geothermally heated water. An attraction for visitors was the opportunity to bathe in the natural recesses of the terraces. There were few other tourist attractions in New Zealand at this time (Reggett, 1972).

The systematic colonisation of New Zealand began in the 1840s (Cushman, 1990), and the first settlement of Europeans at Rotorua occurred in 1856 (Tapsell, 1972). By this time, the potential of Rotorua's geothermal waters was attracting attention. In 1859 the Auckland Provincial Government commissioned Austrian Geologist Dr. Ferdinand Von Hochstetter to document the 'Natural Characteristics of the Thermal Area' in southern Auckland (Reggett 1972, Tapsell 1972). While Von Hochstetter's ensuing report is credited with generating much interest in the region, it was the 1870 visit of the Duke of Edinburgh and accompanying media that stimulated the first real growth of tourist traffic (Steele, 1980). The Duke's visit, along with other luminaries such as Mark Twain, is said to have established Rotorua in the wealthy social circles of America and Europe (Reggett, 1972), and a part of the 'grand tour' of the colonies (Savage, 1986).

Disaster struck in 1886 when Mount Tarawera erupted, destroying three Maori villages and obliterating the terraces. While this was a devastating blow for tourism, within two years Rotorua's annual visitor arrivals were higher than pre-eruption levels (Reggett, 1972). Part of the continued interest in Rotorua was the eruption aftermath and new volcanic craters, which remain attractions today and evidence of Ahmed's (1991) suggestion of a dark side to tourism. Interest was also directed towards the therapeutic values of the remaining geothermal features (Stafford, 1986).

Brown's (1985) analysis of the evolution of 19th century British resort development, noted the medical profession was responsible for much of the initial resort development impetus in that country. In New Zealand it was English balneologist, Dr. Wohlmann, who in 1902, following a tour of European spas, convinced the New Zealand government of the value of the sanatorium concept (Stafford, 1988). Central government planned to develop Rotorua as "a hot water mineral spa on much the same lines as the famous European and English spas such as Vichy, Carlsbad, Bath and Harrogate" (Savage, 1980, p. 5). Wohlmann convinced the government to invest all available resources in the development of one spa, Rotorua, rather than spread resources around the country (Herbert, 1921, p. 7).

The attempt to make Rotorua the great spa of the southern hemisphere floundered in the depression years and World War Two (Rockel, 1980a), and by the 1950s the government had dispensed with the Rotorua sanatorium concept (Stafford, 1988). Rotorua District Council (RDC, 1992) attributed failure to a number of factors, including: long distance from markets, lengthy travel times, slow internal travel options within New Zealand, high plant maintenance costs in the acidic environment, too few people using the facilities, and a relatively strong medical (sanatorium) focus that fell from vogue in the 1920s as modern medicinal practices expanded.

RELIANCE ON GOVERNMENT RESOURCES

No other town in New Zealand has a more complex legislative history than Rotorua (Rockel, 1980b). Although a town board was formed in 1880, the town was to be managed by the New Zealand Department of Tourist & Health Resorts. New Zealand's establishment of a national tourism office (NTO) in 1901 was the first of its kind in the world (Steele, 1980), as was the development of a government operated visitor information network in New Zealand and overseas, named Government Tourist Bureaux (Coventry, 2001). The first office was built in Rotorua in 1903. While the NTO and Government Tourist Bureaux were the most important elements in the promotion of Rotorua during the 20th century, central government also funded almost everything in the development of Rotorua: "No other town in the country enjoyed such support from public funds" (Stafford, 1986, p. 36). It has been claimed Rotorua was the only town in the British Empire to have been completely controlled by central government (Braynart, 1980). Rotorua did not have an independent council, devoid of government representatives, until 1950 (Stafford 1988, Tapsell 1972).

Rotorua's increasingly forced independence from central government from the 1950s coincided with a steady decline in destination image. Signs of Rotorua's impending demise started during the 1960s. One particularly high profile incident occurred in 1965, when the president of the Travel Agents Association of New Zealand described Rotorua as the most squalid place in the country (Steele, 1980). Council had not helped the cause with the development of the town's rubbish tip on the Lake Rotorua foreshore, adjacent to the central business district, and the release of sewerage into the lake after only partial treatment. Little wonder an overseas scientist gained national media coverage when he labelled the lake an 'unflushed toilet' in the 1970s. In 1978, two hundred people attending a tourism conference reached consensus that Rotorua was losing its 'oomph' against other centres (Stafford, 1988).

A private sector response to the image problems in the 1970s was the formation of the Rotorua Promotion Society, which was to be funded by member subscriptions. After a decade of funding uncertainty the organisation succeeded in gaining an RDC grant of $65,000 per annum for three years. In return for this modest sum RDC imposed considerable responsibilities: overseas and domestic promotion, organisation of an annual Christmas carnival, a seven-day a week accommodation booking service, a show ticketing service, promotion of Rotorua as a conference centre, and general visitor enquiries.

The 1980s were a challenging decade for the New Zealand tourism industry due to changing travel patterns. For example, from 1983 to 1988 domestic person nights decreased from 61.4 million to 53.1 million (NZTP, 1989/2), while international visitor arrivals doubled (Pearce 1990). Changes in international arrivals led to a greater diversification of the market. Prior to this, tourism in New Zealand had mostly focused on "passive sightseeing of a range of natural scenic resources" (Cushman, 1990, p. 13). In this era Rotorua was firmly established on the blue ribbon route of coach tour itineraries, and thus assured of a steady flow of group tourists. One of the leading suppliers was central government's own coach tour operation, Tiki Tours. A shift away from coach touring towards self-drive holidays opened up more destinations to travellers and shifted distribution control away from a small group of inbound tour operators, from which Rotorua relied heavily. Drive tourism opened opportunities for less traditional destinations that began to emerge as serious competition to Rotorua. There was also a sense of NTO abandonment of Rotorua in overseas promotion in favour of the South Island's snowy mountain scenes. The changing travel patterns, increased competition, and decline in Rotorua's image led the Rotorua Promotion Society to commission a consultancy to provide a situation analysis of Rotorua at this time. Key points were (PA Hotels and Tourism, 1987):

- Local and national media were biased in their negative publicity.
- Rotorua was developing into a town that was not particularly attractive.
- Rotorua was stagnant, even going backwards, and living on its reputation.
- The Mayor and councillors were not seen to be supporting tourism.
- Poor destination marketing relative to other communities.
- Rotorua did not communicate itself well, and needed professional help.

Denial of the image problems remained strong in the mid-1980s among some civic leaders, perhaps best encapsulated in a quote by Mayor John Keaney: "It is in the interests of other centres to carry out a vendetta against Rotorua to put tourists off coming here" (Rotorua Daily Post, 13/8/86). Keaney was commenting on reports in the *Dominion* newspaper under the heading 'Death of a Tourist town', and related television news. However, such denial by council was ultimately not sustainable given the number of issues compounding the image problems:

- The third highest unemployment in New Zealand, at 13% (Stafford, 1988).
- National media coverage of scientific claims that Rotorua's famous geysers were dying (Hindley, 1989).
- The national recession brought Rotorua commercial property development to a standstill (Stafford, 1988).
- High rent from out of town landlords forced retail closures, leading to an abundance of empty shops in the central business district.
- A run down central business district due to a lack of council investment.

CRISIS ACKNOWLEDGEMENT

The year 1988 proved a watershed in Rotorua's destination life cycle. Frustrated by a lack of funding, industry in-fighting, and inability to reposition the destination's tarnished image, the Rotorua Promotion Society board resigned en masse and abdicated its RDC agreement. Finally acknowledging a tourism crisis, RDC sought comment from the public, with the majority of submissions recommending RDC needed to take control of tourism promotion. Council agreed to the establishment of a Promotion and Marketing Co-ordinator position, to which I was appointed in January 1989:

> In response to Rotorua's serious economic crisis in the late 1980s, the Rotorua District Council initiated a series of strategic changes . . . to employ somebody 'solely' responsible for the tourism and business development of Rotorua. (Ateljevic & Doorne, 2000, p. 28)

Incidentally, I began my DMO career in 1978 as a cadet with the then NZ Tourist & Publicity Department, initially at the Rotorua Government Tourist Bureau. This was Rotorua's visitor information office, and at this time still managed a number of number of facilities such as Waimangu Volcanic Valley, Blue Baths,

Government Gardens, The Bath House, and launches on lakes Rotomahana and Tarawera.

The sense of crisis permeated all of my initial discussions with a wide range of stakeholders, with no semblance of any recovery plan. As noted by Hall (1999), the need for coordination is felt most when there is a lack of it. One of the most obvious problems noted during my initial meetings with industry groups was the disparate nature of the tourism community. There were strong feelings, vented angrily on occasions, that Rotorua Promotion Society promotions had only promoted the larger businesses, referred to as the 'fat cats.' These larger operators explained to me that since they contributed the majority of funding, it was only fair to expect more promotional exposure. This is in keeping with Hall's suggestion to temper expectations of collaborative tourism planning due to the narrow focus of, and dominance by, the larger corporate entities, to the detriment of other community stakeholders. Suspicion reigned, and what was needed was an impartial marketing organisation.

RECOVERY EFFORTS

The expectation of RDC senior management and elected officials was that the council investment (initially $250,000 per annum) should be seen as seed funding for the development of a cooperative private-public fighting fund. There was a clear expectation that a significant industry contribution be forthcoming. It was evident my initial priorities needed to focus on gaining the trust of small businesses and to develop a cooperative approach towards destination promotion. Regarding the former, efforts were made to ensure that no favours were intentionally provided to the larger operators. All new staff were explicitly inducted into this philosophy. Unfortunately, although the office was successful in ensuring equal opportunities for all operators, the political implications were the larger operators felt a loss of control. Clearly all tourism businesses seek to have their product exposed in all campaigns in all markets, and the altruistic philosophy of promoting strengths suited to different markets and segments was challenging to maintain. The staff are to be credited for their determination and courage in this regard. The politics of destination decision making is rarely addressed in the literature, but put simply, can play a major role in frustrating best intended efforts.

The main aims of the recovery were to stimulate co-operative promotions by local operators, enhance tourism awareness among the host community, and improve the destination's tarnished image in key markets. Key initiatives included:

- Stronger links were initiated with the NTO by organising group sales missions to key offshore markets based around NTO participation at trade and consumer travel events. Prior to this time, there was minimal presence by tourism businesses and regions at offshore promotional events.
- Formation of the Rotorua Tourism Forum, which brought together 30 representatives of sector groups, for quarterly meetings about destination issues and presentations by guest speakers such as the NZ Minister of Tourism and NTO CEO. Businesses not involved in formal sector groups were challenged to form groups and to be proactive in developing initiatives to work with the RTO. Successes in this regard included the adventure operators and Maori tourism operators.
- Funding was provided to the Rotorua Promotion Society to participate in domestic travel expos. While the society remained resource poor, a strength was the their voluntary manpower to organise displays at domestic events, which freed RTO staff for other activities.
- An alliance with other RTOs to form 'Top Half NZ,' which linked Rotorua, Auckland and Northland as a macro region in promotions targeting the Australian market.
- A series of double page advertisements was scheduled in the country's most popular newspaper. Each operator was able to obtain equal size exposure, with the proceeds subsidising the accompanying advertorial space.
- A printed destination visitor's guide, which instead of being contracted out to a publisher, as was previously the case, was produced by the office. This carried some

political risk since one of the publishers was also an elected council official. The incentive for advertisers was that the brochure would be used in all domestic and offshore promotions and used to service visitor enquires. This was an important initiative that generated an annual surplus enabling a $100,000 + domestic television advertising campaign each year. Thus, this was tangible evidence of industry contributions to the RDC budget, which in a regime without a room tax, could never be raised by membership subscriptions as previously attempted by the Rotorua Promotions Society.

- Ongoing efforts were made to stimulate tourism awareness among the host community. An early success was a destination-wide open day of tourism attractions. All tourism attractions provided free admission for local residents for a day. The initiative stimulated an ongoing admission structure for locals by attractions. Other activities included regular newspaper columns, radio interviews and talks to schools and service clubs.
- Implementation of a new brand positioning theme, which while designed to reposition the destination image in the domestic market, was used in all markets.
- The establishment of a commercial accommodation monitor to provide performance measures by which RDC could determine some sort of return on investment. It is difficult to quantify Rotorua's rise and fall and rise in terms of visitor statistics, since there were no reliable data for the Rotorua region prior to this. Since 1990, businesses and RDC have enjoyed month by month data, completed by the majority of accommodation houses. The monitor would later become a model for a nationwide commercial accommodation monitor used by all New Zealand RTOs.

In addition to the marketing activities, RDC's commitment to enhancing Rotorua's destination competitiveness has included a combination of infrastructure investments, including:

- A $30 million beautification of the central shopping district and lakefront, and
- Redevelopment of the Government Gardens and Bathhouse
- Development of a new visitor information centre, Convention Centre and exhibition centre
- Commissioning of market feasibility studies that ultimately led to new private sector hotel developments
- Airport runway extensions to enable future international aircraft arrivals

Turning around a negative image does not occur overnight. With the benefit of hindsight, Wahab, Crampon and Rothfield's (1976, p. 92) reflections on negative tourism images were certainly appropriate in Rotorua's case: "It is easy to downgrade a product or allow it to deteriorate; but it is the devil's own work to upgrade a low-image product." It would be an understatement to suggest the task of repositioning Rotorua in the domestic market was recognised as representing a significant challenge. One senior airline official commented at the time: "If you can turn Rotorua around you will be able to write your own ticket!" Even though significant efforts had been made since 1989, Rotorua's negative image was still so serious in 1992 the NTO undertook an analysis of the local tourism industry and infrastructure:

> The study is being carried out in the context of industry concern that Rotorua as one of New Zealand's major tourism hubs could be in decline and unless rejuvenated could lose its focus as a major tourism destination, either as part of the traditional touring circuit or as a regional tourism hub. Taupo has been suggested as a potential challenger to Rotorua's position as the central North Island main tourism hub. (NZTB, 1992, p. 2)

With the increasing funding support of RDC, and increasing industry cooperation, the sole position evolved into an RTO, Tourism Rotorua. Remaining responsible to RDC, the mission statement for the RTO clearly indicates the rationale for the council's ongoing tourism funding: *To enhance the economic base of Rotorua by the vigorous marketing of the district as a tourism destination* (www.rotoruanz.com). The RTO is a public-private partnership. The majority of funding is provided by the RDC, who also employ all RTO staff. For governance purposes, senior management report directly to RDC. However, staff also work with a tourism advisory board, which also includes elected council officials, to develop marketing plans. Additionally, a series of portfolio groups was established to focus on key strategic issues. Portfolio group members are elected by industry to work with RTO staff. The public-private partnership structure has been successful as a mechanism to ensure dialogue remains open between council and industry, and to some extent within industry. The nature of destination politics means it is likely no governance structure will please all stakeholders. For example, should industry board members be selected by the mayor on the basis of ability, a process subject to accusations of bias and favouritism? Or should members be democratically elected, a system that can reward attributes other than ability? The current public-private partnership ensures local government remains in touch with the stakeholders of the city's most economically important industry. Open and formal communication about matters relating to marketing budgets and infrastructure maintenance should ensure no repeat of Rotorua's previous fall from grace.

In 1996, I resigned after seven years with Tourism Rotorua to take up a position in higher education. By this time the organisation comprised a marketing office with six staff and an annual budget of $1 million, a visitor centre with 11 staff and turnover in excess of $3 million, and the redeveloped Rotorua Convention Centre. Later in 1996, Tourism Rotorua released the district's first strategic plan for tourism. By 2006 the RTO budget had increased to $1.6 million.

It is clear the council-led initiatives since 1988 have been successful in improving the destination's image among trade and consumers. For example, by 1997 Tourism Rotorua became the first RTO to achieve a 'distinction' at the New Zealand Tourism Awards for winning the 'Best RTO' award on three occasions. The district has also been a recipient of New Zealand's beautiful city award in 1999, 2000 and 2002. In 2005 Air New Zealand announced plans to name one of its Boeing 747 aircraft 'Rotorua,' and the district's starring role in the NTO's formative years was acknowledged when Tourism New Zealand staged its 2001 centennial celebrations in the city. In the first data from the NZ Regional Visitor Monitor (June, 2006), a new survey of international and domestic visitors managed by the Ministry of Tourism and Tourism New Zealand, 88% of respondents were interested in returning to Rotorua, and 78% indicated they would recommend the destination to friends (Marshall, 2006). The national benchmarks were 85% and 69% respectively.

CONCLUSION

In the emerging literature on destination disaster management, there has been little written on management crises. There is a difference between what constitutes a disaster and what is a crisis (Faulkner, 1999), and not all tourism crises manifest as a result of a sudden exogenous disaster. The purpose of this paper has been to provide a cautionary tale of how one resort destination struggled through a self inflicted tourism crisis. The investigation of aspects of Rotorua's tourism history provides an enhanced understanding of the evolution of New Zealand's first holiday destination, adding to the recent efforts of Ateljevic (1998), Ateljevic and Doorne (2000), Horn, Fairweather and Simmons (2000), and Pike (2002). It could be argued the premise that Rotorua's stakeholders were the authors of the destination's demise is a harsh one given the lengthy time period and range of stakeholders involved. Nevertheless, a crisis did take place through what can retrospectively be described as ineffective responses by stakeholders to a changing macroenvironment and decline in destination quality. Five main reasons are proposed. First, there was an unpreparedness by stakeholders for a different future. Hall (2005) has suggested in tourism there exists a tendency to assume the unthinkable will not happen. This implies the future will continue to evolve as per the past. A state of 'marketing dependence' manifested in Rotorua, where the destination was used to the NTO taking responsibility for promotion. There was a lengthy delay in the

recognition of the need to be proactive in infrastructure maintenance and promotion, at levels commensurate with the value of tourism to the local economy. Second, there was an over reliance on central government funding and support. The failure of the sanatorium concept was a major catalyst in the withdrawal of central government support between the 1950s and 1990s, during which time Rotorua stagnated. Third, the lack of forward planning and infrastructure maintenance led to a tired and run down cityscape, which became the topic of much negative national media attention. Fourth, the fortress mentality that existed among key decision makers delayed the necessary recovery efforts. Fifth, there was an inability by the local tourism community to become organised in a collaborative way.

In terms of a conceptual framework to better understand the case, Butler's (1980) destination life cycle can be linked to the changes in Rotorua's tourism development. The examination of Rotorua's history supports Butler's proposal that destinations are dynamic and evolve over time, as well as Plog's (1974) assertion that the evolution of destinations can change or obliterate the nature of attractions responsible for the area's popularity: "Destination areas carry with them the potential seeds of their own destruction, as they allow themselves to become more commercialised and lose their qualities which originally attracted tourists" (Plog, 1974, p. 58). The Rotorua case is an example of a destination that progressed through the development and growth stages, before stagnating without forward planning. A more recent example of potential stagnation is the Australian state of New South Wales, where tourism groups have called for a recovery plan to regain business lost since the 2000 Olympics, with tourism employment growth well behind the national average (Jones, 2006).

Russell and Faulkner's (1999) analysis of the development of the Australian Gold Coast suggested while destinations do evolve through the life cycle in a similar pattern, the instigators of change can be quite different. They introduced chaos theory to the model, to demonstrate the significance of the contributions of a few individual entrepreneurs. Each was responsible for an innovation that stimulated a sequence of changes, resulting in a major shift in the structure of tourism at the destination. In Rotorua however, it is argued that while entrepreneurs have played an important role in tourism development, it has been the initiatives of central and local government that have shaped the destination's fortunes. There have been three phases in Rotorua's competitiveness as a tourism destination. From the 1880s until at least the 1950s, Rotorua was managed by central government, with levels of infrastructure development and destination promotion unparalleled in New Zealand. A gradual withdrawal of government resources saw Rotorua neglect both destination promotion and city beautification between the 1950s and the 1980s, a period when Rotorua's destination image declined to such a point that local government, the public, tourism operators and travel trade intermediaries ultimately acknowledged that at crisis point had been reached. The period since 1988 has seen a gradual turnaround in destination competitiveness as a result of RDC's increased commitment to destination marketing, product development and cityscape rejuvenation. RDC's philosophical and financial commitment led to a new spirit of cooperation among the private sector and between industry and local government. The turnaround has been such that few visitors to Rotorua today would be aware of the negative images of the 1960s, 1970s and 1980s.

Although "the intensity of the moment during a crisis is clearly not the time to commence such planning" (Litvin & Alderson, 2003), this was the reality in Rotorua, and will be the case in the future for other destinations without contingency plans. In Turkey for example, neither the government nor the private sector had in place any plans to deal with that country's 2001 economic crisis (Okumus & Karamustafa, 2005). Texts have existed for at least two decades to guide organisations' preparation of planning for potential crises (see for example Finks, 1986). The diversity of disasters and crises impacting on destinations in every continent in recent years implies all DMOs must be prepared for a future of continuous discontinuous change. This should be based on the view that while it is impossible to predict the exact source of a future tourism crisis, it is entirely feasible to expect one will occur...one day.

REFERENCES

Ahmed, Z.U. (1991). The dark side of image marketing. *The Tourist Review*. 4: 36-37.

Ateljevic, I., & Doorne, S. (2000). Local government and tourism development: issues and constraints of public sector entrepreneurship. *New Zealand Geographer*. 56(2): 25-31.

Beirman, D. (2003). *Restoring Destinations in Crisis*. Crows Nest, NSW: Allen & Unwin.

Braynart Group. (1980). *100 Years of Rotorua*. Rotorua

Buckley, P. J., & Witt, S. F. (1985). Tourism in difficult areas: case studies of Bradford, Bristol, Glasgow and Hamm. *Tourism Management*. September: 205-213.

Butler, R.W. (1980). The concept of a tourist area cycle of evolution: implications for management of resources. *Canadian Geographer*. 24 (1): 5-12.

Christine, B. (1995). Disaster management: lessons learned. *Risk Management*. October: 19-34.

Conlin, M.V. (1995) Rejuvenation planning for island tourism: the Bermuda example. In Conlin, M.V., & Baum, T. (Eds). *Island Tourism: Management Principles and Practice*. Chichester: John Wiley & Sons.

Coventry, N. (2001). *Inside Tourism*. 340. February 01.

Coventry, N. (2006). Council pulls plug on RTO funding: concern others may follow. *Inside Tourism*. 592. May 12.

Cowan, J. (1935). *A Trader in Cannibal Land*. Dunedin: A & A Reed.

Curtis, J. (2001). Branding a State: the evolution of Brand Oregon. *Journal of Vacation Marketing*. 7(1): 75-81.

Cushman, G. (1990). Tourism in New Zealand. (1990). *World Leisure and Recreation*. 32 (1): 12-16.

Dahles, H. (1998). Redefining Amsterdam as a tourist destination. *Annals of Tourism Research*. 25(1): 55-69.

Doering, T.R. (1979). Geographical aspects of State travel marketing in the USA. *Annals of Tourism Research*. July/Sept: 307-317.

Donnelly, M.P., & Vaske, J.J. (1997). Factors affecting membership in a tourism promotion authority. *Journal of Travel Research*. Spring: 50-55.

Faulkner, B. (1999). *Tourism Disasters: Towards a Generic Model*. Gold Coast: CRC Sustainable Tourism.

Faulkner, B., & Vikulov, S. (2001). Katherine, washed out one day, back on track the next: a post-mortem of a tourism disaster. *Tourism Management*. 22(4): 331-344.

Fink, S. (1986). *Crisis Management–Planning for the Inevitable*. NY: American Management Association.

Frisby, E. (2002). Communicating in a crisis: the British Tourist Authority's responses to the foot-and-mouth outbreak and 11th September, 2001. *Journal of Vacation Marketing*. 9(1): 89-100

Gatty, B., & Blalock, C. (1997). New organization brings new energy to marketing the U.S. *Hotel & Motel Management*. 17 (17 Feb).

Go, F. (1987). Selling Canada. *Travel & Tourism Analyst*. Dec: 17-29.

Hall, C. M. (1999). Rethinking collaboration and partnership: a public policy perspective. *Journal of Sustainable Tourism.* 7(3/4): 274-289.

Hall. C.M. (2005). The future of tourism research. In Ritchie, B.W., Burns, P., & Palmer, C. (Eds). *Tourism Research Methods–Integrating Theory with Practise.* Wallingford, Oxfordshire: CABI Publishing.

Herbert, A. S. (1921). *The Hot Springs of New Zealand.* London: H. K. Lewis & Co. Ltd.

Hindley, D. (1989). *New Zealand Guides: Rotorua/Bay of Plenty.* Wellington: Government Printing Office.

Hopper, P. (2002). Marketing London in a difficult climate. *Journal of Vacation Marketing.* 9(1): 81-88.

Jones, S. (2006). NSW takes another pounding. *Travel Today.* Oct 19. p. 3.

Leslie, D. (1999). Terrorism and tourism: the Northern Ireland situation–a look behind the veil of certainty. *Journal of Travel Research.* 38: 37-40.

Litvin, S.W., & Alderson, L.L. (2003). How Charleston got her groove back: a convention and visitors bureau's response to 9/11. *Journal of Vacation Marketing.* 9(2): 188-197.

Mansfield, Y. (1999) Cycles of war, terror, and peace: determinants and management of crisis and recovery of the Israeli tourism industry. *Journal of Travel Research.* 38: 30-36.

Marshall, J. (2006). Rotorua among the regions doing the business. http://www.rotoruanz.com/news/news_detail.asp?ID=288 accessed 18/7/06.

Morgan, M. (1991). Dressing up to survive–marketing Majorca anew. *Tourism Management.* March: 15-20.

NZTB. (1992). *A Review of Rotorua's Tourism Infrastructure.* Wellington: Policy Planning and Investment Division, New Zealand Tourism Board. July.

NZTP. (1989/2). *The Economic Determinants of Domestic Travel in New Zealand.* Wellington: New Zealand Tourist & Publicity Department.

Okumus, F., & Karamustafa, K. (2005). Impact of an economic crisis–evidence from Turkey. *Annals of Tourism Research.* 32(4): 942-961.

PA Hotels and tourism. (1987). *Rotorua Promotions and Development Society: Development of a Marketing Strategy.* Auckland.

Pearce, D. G. (1990). Tourism, the regions and restructuring in New Zealand. *The Journal of Tourism Studies.* 1 (2): 33-42.

Pike, S. (2002). *Positioning as a Source of Competitive Advantage–Benchmarking Rotorua's Position as a Domestic Short Break Holiday Destination.* University of Waikato.

Pike, S. (2004). *Destination Marketing Organisations.* Oxford: Pergamon.

Plog, S.T. (1974). Why destination areas rise and fall in popularity. *The Cornell HRA Quarterly.* 14(4): 55-58.

Reggett, R. S. (1972). *The Tarawera Eruption: its effects on the Tourist Industry.* Unpublished MA Thesis. Dunedin: University of Otago.

Rockel, I. (1980a). Rotorua's spa background. In Stafford, D., Steele, R., & Boyd, J. (Eds). *Rotorua: 1880-1980.* Rotorua and District Historical Society.

Rockel, I. (1980b). Cutting the cord: Government control of Rotorua. In Stafford, D., Steele, R., & Boyd, J. (Eds). *Rotorua: 1880-1980.* Rotorua and District Historical Society.

Rotorua District Council. (1992). *So, you want to be a Spa City!!* Rotorua: Economic Development Section. December.

Russell, R., & Faulkner, B. (1999). Movers and shakers: chaos makers in Tourism development. *Tourism Management.* 20(4): 411-423.

Savage, P. (1980). *The Government Gardens.* Rotorua District Council.

Savage, P. (1986). In the shadow of the mountain. In: Rotorua District Council (Eds). *Tarawera Eruption Centennial.* Rotorua District Council.

Stafford, D. (1977). *The Romantic Past of Rotorua.* Wellington: Reed.

Stafford, D. (1986). *The Founding Years in Rotorua: A History of Events to 1900.* Auckland: Ray Richards.

Stafford, D. (1988). *The New Century in Rotorua.* Auckland: Ray Richards.

Steele, R. (1980). Tourism. In Stafford, D., Steele, R., & Boyd, J. (Eds). *Rotorua: 1880-1980.* Rotorua and District Historical Society.

Tapsell, E. (1972). *A History of Rotorua.* Published by the author.

WTO. (2002). *Thinktank.* World Tourism Organisation. Accessed on-line: http://www.world-tourism.org/education/menu.html

Communicating Tourism Crises Through Destination Websites

Serena Volo

SUMMARY. The present paper addresses the issue of communicating tourism crises, with a special focus on the role of the destination marketing organization's Web sites. The risks and impact of the avian flu on the mobility of people, and consequently therefore, on tourism has been addressed. Selected tourism destinations crisis communication strategies were investigated through their Web sites. The findings should (a) bring to the attention of tourism authorities the potential role that destinations' Web sites have in helping to prevent worldwide diseases and to compare different approaches adopted by different types of destinations, and (b) help governments, destinations and other stakeholders to understand the conditions necessary for communicating tourism crises and outbreaks by using their Web sites as effective tools to better share information among them.

INTRODUCTION

Tourism is a significant contributor, and in some cases the main contributor, to many national or regional economies. In many countries, and in an even greater number of regions, tourism contributes significantly to GDP, employment, economic growth, infrastructure development, and in some countries and regions, even to social development. The UNWTO's (World Tourism Organization) *Tourism 2020 Vision* forecasts that international arrivals will exceed 1.56 billion by the year 2020 and of these arrivals 1.18 billion will be intraregional and 377 million will be "long-haul" travelers. The total tourist arrivals by region shows that by 2020 the top three receiving regions will be Europe, East Asia and the Pacific and the Americas. An exceptional increase is expected in East Asia and the Pacific, South Asia, the Middle East and Africa where growth will be at rates of over 5 per cent per year, compared to the world average of 4.1 per cent. Tourism demand, and therefore its likely contribution to the economic health of these regions, as can be seen from the UNWTO statistics, is likely to remain strong for the foreseeable future.

Tourism demand will depend above all on the economic conditions in major generating markets, but among the factors influencing demand at the tourist destination area, safety and security, broadly conceived, are the most sig-

Serena Volo (E-mail: serenavolo@unipa.it) is a Researcher in the Department of Quantitative Methods for the Human Sciences at Universita di Palermo, Italy (StudioVolo, Via Pacinotti 34, 90145 Palermo, Italy).

nificant. More than any other economic activity, the success or failure of a tourism destination depends on its ability to provide a safe and secure environment for visitors, safe from all forms of controllable risks including both natural disasters and human-induced disasters such as disease, political unrest, armed conflict, and terrorism.

Any major disruption to tourism, especially if it is for a sustained period of time, can be devastating to a nation's or a region's economy. In addition to the usual transient economic disruptions of recession, depression, and loss of global competitiveness, recent history has witnessed several natural and human-induced disasters, such as the tsunami in the Indian Ocean or the Hurricane Rita that devastated New Orleans, major (e.g., 9/11) and minor (e.g., Sharm al-Sheikh) terrorist attacks, international hostilities in the middle east, and the feared spread of SARS and avian flu to places with high volume international travel. In addition to the threat these disruptions pose to a region's economy, is the equally troublesome threat these potential disasters poses to the tourists themselves, which, if not abated can lead to larger regional economic threats. Managing the risks of these threats to the economy is the responsibility of the national and regional governmental and political personnel including tourism authorities. On the other hand however, managing the risks to the tourists, whose patronage contributes to the economy, is the responsibility of both tourism authorities and tourism marketers, especially the responsibility of communicating the risk, its nature and its magnitude to the tourists.

This paper addresses primarily the risks that accrue to tourists from the threat of natural or human-induced disasters, and how these risks can be effectively communicated to the affected tourist population. In particular, it addresses how the Internet, through its potential for effective and flexible communication, can be an essential element in disaster avoidance, management and recovery for both tourism authorities and tourism marketers. In addressing how the Internet can be employed to manage the impact of disasters on tourists however, it also addresses indirectly its potential for dampening the consequences of such disasters to a region's economy.

Both tourism authorities and tourism marketers must necessarily participate collaboratively in the communication of disaster-relevant information to tourists. The Internet, because of it reach, speed and flexibility is an ideal communication channel in times of actual or potential disasters. The threat of natural and human-induced disasters to tourists however, is likely to be viewed differently by tourism authorities and tourism marketers. Consequently, their attitudes about what should be communicated to tourists in the face of a disaster threat, and how it should be communicated, are also likely to differ, although it is primarily the tourism authorities who provide, and therefore control, both the raw information as well as its interpretation. This fact is important for several reasons: (a) risk assessment will be shaded by point of view; (b) the Internet is widely accessible to anyone wanting to send, receive or post messages ("message" as distinct from "information" which has a formal uncertainty-related mathematical definition) so the opportunity for misinformation is considerable; (c) disaster-related information is often rapidly changing and the time available for quality controlling the message often short; and (d) differing versions of the same story can lead to confusion-induced panic among the tourists.

Perhaps most importantly, tourists themselves require clear, concise, and effectively communicated information so they can exercise informed decisions about their travel. However, as the research very clearly shows, a decision maker's assessment of risk is very much effected by many conscious considerations–e.g., their economic stake in the decision's outcome–as well as many unconscious factors–e.g., concern for others, regret avoidance, etc. (Bazerman, 2002). Consequently, what is communicated will depend to some degree upon who communicates it. In the case of communicating disaster related information to a tourist population however, there is little or no room for such self-interested interpretations if the tourists' welfare (and consequently the destination's long-term interests) are to be responsibly served.

The purpose of this exploratory study is to propose and explore a framework for understanding the tourists' "*information search process*" during the "pre-event" stage of a tourism disaster, and to investigate how affected countries can communicate crisis related information effectively through their websites. The Internet, because of its reach and flexibility, carries simultaneously the risk of exploitation from self-interested parties as well as the promise of an effective tool in tourism-related disaster management. The balance of this report takes up the question of how to achieve the latter in the face of the former, using the specific case of avian flu to illustrate the main issues underlying disaster management in the tourism industry. In the course of the following research questions will also be addressed:

1. What are national tourism organization doing in the area of prevention and planning?
2. How likely are tourist to be able to obtain information concerning the risk of avian flu at their intended destinations?
3. To what extent are national tourism organizations communicating basic avian flu risks to tourists?
4. How common are "crises communication centers" among national tourism organization?
5. To what extent is there clear and reliable information available to tourists on the risk of avian flu?

LITERATURE REVIEW

Recent catastrophic global events have, tragically, exposed the tourism industry's vulnerability to disasters and crises, and the vulnerability of all the industry's destinations has been rendered undeniable. Consequently an increasing amount of attention has been paid to the issues surrounding disaster risk management in the tourism industry, and the academic world has begun addressing these issues in earnest (Glaeßer, 2005; Ritchie, 2004; Beirman, 2002; Pizam, 2002; Faulkner, 2001; Santana, 2001; Soñmez, Apostolopoulos, and Tarlow, 1999; Barton, 1994; Durocher, 1994). While certain disasters and crisis are limited in their spread, others have the potentiality to become global threats and affect several destinations in a short timeframe, Further, as Ritchie (2004) has argued, regardless of the efforts made by the industry, managing crises and disasters is as unpredictable as their nature.

Defining the nature and the scope of such events is the essential first step in the process that is required to address the risks systematically and to prepare effective recovery strategies. Faulkner's study (2001) on tourism disaster management suggested that the origin of events comprising crises and disasters lie on a continuum between internally caused and externally imposed events. Faulkner defined crises as having "origins in planning and management deficiencies, and in this sense they are self-inflicted" and disasters as "triggered by events over which the victim has little control, and their impact is, therefore, to some degree unavoidable" (Faulkner, 2001, p. 146).

Strategies for dealing with crises and disasters, it has been contended, have to be carefully planned. Faulkner (2001) and Ritchie's (2004) proposed frameworks undoubtedly represent good insights into the requirements for moving in this direction. Faulkner described the phases of a community response to a disaster, and Ritchie made a parallel with strategic management steps that agree with Faulkner in that for each essential stage of a disaster or crisis there is an immediate managerial action to be taken. The essential stages, Faulkner asserts, are: (a) pre-crisis, (b) crisis, and (c) post-crisis. These, both Faulkner and Ritchie have broken down into "pre-event, prodromal (brewing), emergency, intermediate, long-term (recovery) and resolution" stages. Appropriate managerial responses and strategies are defined that span all stages, from proactive planning to evaluation of the restored initial situation. In addition, Page et al. (2006) has emphasized the importance of, and has contributed to, creating best practice cases on crisis management. In their recent work, Page et al. use scenario planning to illustrate Visit Scotland's response to the influenza pandemic and concluded that with careful communication among the different constituents involved and appropriate response strategies of the industry players, the tourism sector is likely to endure to the disaster.

Complicating the management of crisis and disasters is the need to communicate the risk and its implications to often widely dispersed audiences, and oftentimes, with widely differing concerns–e.g., in the case of the risk of avian flu, one tourist may be concerned about the likelihood of contracting the disease if they travel to a particular destination, while another may be mostly concerned about the adequacy of local treatment facilities at the destination should they contract the disease. Thus managing crises and disasters becomes a risk reduction art for both the industry (Fink, 1986) and the tourists who, to this extent, seeks accurate and updated information. What must be communicated, and the tone with which, and the context within which, it is communicated, will depend on a number of factors. Primary among these factors are: (a) the nature of the risk, (b) the magnitude of the risk, (c) the specific consequences should the risk materialize, and (d) what are the effective avoidance, response and recovery measures. If tourists have this information, they will generally feel comfortable judging whether or not the risk of travel to a destination exceeds their risk tolerance. However, the media often fails to adequately communicate to their audience, or they exaggerate the magnitude of events, creating long-term damage for individual businesses and tourism destinations (Zerman, 1995; Marra, 1998; Young and Montgomery, 1998).

Of course for the tourist, the valence of each of the aforementioned factors, and therefore the urgency of the information they seek, will depend upon the temporal relationship of the occurrence of the disaster (actual or potential) and the decision he or she must take. The information sought by a tourist deciding say, whether or not to travel to China in the face of the risk of contracting avian flu is likely to be very different from the information sought by a tourist who finds him or her self in a city in which an outbreak of the disease has just occurred. Faulkner (2001) noticed that some destinations are more used to natural disasters than others and therefore deal with them in a different way. In general the information the tourists will seek, and therefore the information that both tourism authorities and tourism marketers will need to communicate, will depend upon the magnitude of the risk–i.e., the remote or eminent nature of the risk. However, the complication arises between these two extremes, where the risk is very uncertain, such as the risk of infection of avian flu if one travels to, say, the inner provinces of China. The formulation of the risk in these types of scenarios is much more complicated: it is characterized by greater uncertainty, based upon a wider range of considerations and points of view, and requires greater involvement of the tourists to properly interpret the risk-indicating information and its implications. It is this kind of information sharing that the Internet facilitates particularly well.

Burnett (1998), in his strategic approach to managing crisis, proposed a classification of events according to the level of threat, the response options, the time pressure and the degree of control over the response. Burnett proposed appropriate managerial responses to different levels of crisis as measured on these dimensions. Recently, Page et al. (2006) noticed how the intensity and significance of crises define the impact on the tourism industry, thus creating global or more restricted local consequences. Crisis management researchers have emphasized the need of strategic planning and response preparation that is effectively communicated to, and is commonly understood by, both the tourism authorities and the tourism marketers. In addition, disaster preparedness and disaster responses must be well communicated to the population of actual and potential tourists if their interests, and therefore the region's long term economic interests, are to be effectively and responsibly served. Consequently, the threat of disruption of tourism has to be addressed collaboratively in an effective and proactive, even pre-emptive, way by both tourism authorities and tourism marketers worldwide. However, as Ray (1999, cited by Henderson, 2003) noticed, organizational responses can vary between denying any responsibilities to eliciting sympathy. In particular, the challenge of accomplishing effective collaboration between public and private tourism sector constituents can be considerable. However, because the interests of these two groups are often asymmetrical, and because disaster prediction and risk assessment are very imperfect sciences, the industry's response to a disaster can be ineffectual. Country or regional authorities, that have responsibility for the area's economic health, may have very different risk tolerances than tourism marketers, or the tourists themselves. As is commonly understood in both marketing and in politics, the perception can often be more influential than the reality.

Politicians, economic planners and tourism authorities are likely to resist premature assessments that will "spook" the tourism market and visit economic hardship, even ruin, upon their region or country. Tourism marketers on the other hand, are not likely to encourage their clients to visit destinations where there is a real or perceived threat of disaster. The perceived threat can influence the tourists' experience if they elect the destination in spite of the threat, or it can lead to a kind of "reverse buyer's remorse" if they rule out the destination but the threat does not materialize into a disaster, i.e., a false alarm. If the tourism marketers encourage tourists to a destination and a potential disaster does materialize, they could be at legal risk if it is shown they knew, or should have known, that the risk existed.

Nevertheless, in time of crisis and disasters the theme, as well as the reality, of collaboration among different constituents is a vital and a substantial part of inter-governmental agencies' efforts, as is the dedication to collaborative work among the governmental and tourism bodies. To this extent, it is important to acknowledge the World Tourism Organization (UNWTO) efforts to prepare destinations to face and prepare for, response to and recovery from, the eventual spread of the avian flu and the mutation of the disease into a pandemic influenza. To this end, the UNWTO is working closely other organizations–including the United Nations System Influenza Coordinator, the World Health Organization (WHO) and the Food and Agriculture Organization (FAO).

Moreover, collaboration and planning actions designed to give adequate information to the public on the avian flu status is also a concern of the Tourism Emergency Response Network (TERN), and with which the following organizations are involved: UNWTO, International Hotel & Restaurant Association (IHRA), Pacific Asia Travel Association (PATA), International Federation of Tour Operators (IFTO), United Federation of Travel Agents Associations (UFTAA) Airports Council International (ACI) and the International Air Transport Association (IATA). Clearly, although the effect of the avian flu on tourism would currently appear to be low, the international community recognizes the societal risks that could derive from a mutation of the virus H5N1 into possible

human pandemic. Current advisories are indeed limited to simple admonishments to avoid contact with live birds of any variety when traveling to avian-flu infected destinations. Some of the actions taken form UNWTO are: (a) the creation of an Avian Flu Support Team, (b) the designation of an Avian Flu Response Coordinator and Spokesperson, (c) the enrichment of the Crisis Management Guidelines with dedicated Guidelines for Tourism Destinations on Preparation & Response to Avian flu, (d) the creation of a Multi Stakeholder Industry Forum, and (e) the commitment to an intensified web based communication among international agencies and UNWTO member states facilitated by the development of a web portal by the UNWTO.

CONCEPTUAL FRAMEWORK

To facilitate the conceptualization of the full constellation of relevant factors involved in disaster management in the tourism industry, a conceptual framework that addresses the interests of all stakeholders and how their particular risk-reward consequences affect and are affected by the generation and flow of disaster-related information is required. The main stakeholders, at least the stakeholders whose interests are most directly affected by tourism related disasters, are the tourists, the tourism marketers, the local tourism service operators and members of their supply chain, the tourism authorities economic planners, and the political officials. Each of these stakeholders will have a cluster of stakeholders around them, but for the purpose of conceptualizing the system and the information flow that drives its behavior, these stakeholder clusters can be considered as a single entity. For example, the employees of local tourism operators will likely suffer if a destination experiences a disaster-driven loss of tourism; similarly, family members of a stricken tourist will suffer; the losses or gains of tourism authorities and the political officials in a region will most typically be linked if not perfectly dependent; governing bodies such as the WHO, the UNWTO, and NTOs typically have common if not identical risk-reward equations. In all of these cases, the interests of members of the stakeholder clusters are essentially identical and do not need to be considered separately.

Further, each stakeholder (or stakeholder cluster) will be either primarily an information provider or an information consumer. On the basis of the risk-reward profile of a stakeholder cluster–that is, what does it have at stake–its members would be predicted to be risk averse, risk neutral or risk taking with respect to a potential disaster. For example, tourist and their families can be expected to risk averse to traveling in an area where there is the risk of avian flu because they can suffer directly the consequences of serious illness or even death, and hence will tend to exaggerate the risk. The WHO, UNWTO would be predicted to be risk neutral. That is, their obligation is to keep their constituencies properly and reliably informed or the risk, not so much to control it. Thus, they would be predicted to be indifferent as to what the risk really is, though very much concerned that they properly scale the risk whatever it may be. NTOs however, because their interests are frequently tied to the political interests of the region or country, and because the political interests will have responsibility for the region's economic health, might be expected to be slightly risk-taking. Local operators on the other hand would be predicted to be significantly more risk-taking, since their livelihood depends on the existence of a tourist clientele and hence they will tend to understate the risk. All of this variation in risk assessment is predicted by utility theory and is perfectly consistent with empirical observations. The question of course is how do you take these differing tendencies into account when building an early warning system? If the system is to reliably and accurately signal the risk to all stakeholders, to whom should the responsibility for assessing the risk be assigned? And with whom should the responsibility for communicating the risk be assigned?

The main objectives of NTOs are prevention and planning. With respect to an avian flu pandemic, most world health experts declare with near total confidence that there is no question of whether a pandemic will occur, only a question of when it will occur. We are therefore already in the pre-disaster stage and would expect therefore, that UNWTO and the NTOs would have at least begun the prevention and planning

needed to counter the adverse effects of the avian flu to the tourism industry and its stakeholders. But is there evidence that this has commenced? And are the players engaged in the effort well suited by their risk-return profile the optimal ones for the job? Theory would predict, and the reality showed in the previous section, that the UNWTO would show evidence of having started to address the pending disaster, and maybe even having made substantial progress in this regard. Theory would also predict that NTOs would be lagging behind the UNWTO, even, and maybe especially, in those countries where avian flu has already been detected.

On the basis of the risk-reward profiles, the UNWTO is the best candidate to be the evaluator of risk since they are indifferent as the magnitude of the risk, but not to the reliability of the scaling of the risk. They are not necessarily the best communicators of the risk however, since the most important consumers of the risk assessment, the tourists, are more likely to seek their information form some source closer to the NTO. These facts argue for a UNWTO regulation that all NTOs be required to maintain a standardized link on their Websites to the UNWTO where all disaster related risk assessments and all emergency-related information can be accessed. All NTOs should also be required to have fully and clearly documented emergency policies and procedures that have been tested and which are periodically tested in simulations. This allocation scheme optimally pairs disaster management responsibility with the stakeholders' risk-reward profile. More importantly, pairing responsibility for risk management in a way that offsets the stakeholders' inherent interests and thereby overcomes the stakeholders' inherent risk biases, will engender confidence among the tourist and tourism marketer populations and thereby in fact serve the economic interests of all parties more fully.

METHODOLOGY

The present study is both developmental and descriptive research and therefore employs a qualitative research methodology. That is, no preconceived hypotheses guided the data collection, data analysis or data interpretation. Rather, a defined segment of reality was explored so as to better understand its composition, its state and its possible future courses of development. The approach sought to understand what the tourism authorities understand to be the nature and magnitude of the risk of avian flu to the tourism industry in their country by examining what they had posted on their web sites–i.e., what they had said through their official electronic information distribution. These data were then examined subjectively for patterns that might reveal, or give clues about, what the tourism authorities in these countries consider to be the risk of avian flu to tourism and tourists as well as their attitudes toward communicating that risk to stakeholders. In this sense the methodology uses only inductive reasoning. It is essentially an investigative report similar in approach to that which might be taken by a journalist, except that the information objective in the present case is both more defined and more constrained, and the place where to dig for the necessary information more obvious from the start, and the depth of the dig necessary to obtain the sought information easily specifiable in advance.

Some attempt has been made to understand the factors that have accounted for and shaped the development of disaster management strategies and practices in the tourism industry, how they have interacted, and how they might expect to interact and behave in general and in the future. In this sense the research might be described as "grounded theory" research, but the exploratory nature of the investigation may be even too germinal to deserve this degree of implied structure.

Essentially, what was done consisted of asking informed sources about actions that they or their organizations have or have not taken with respect to identifying and managing a particular risk (a potential disaster) to the tourists and the tourism industry, namely an avian flu pandemic. The methodology consisted of the following six steps:

Step 1–Population under investigation was defined as those countries in which there have been confirmed human cases of avian influenza A/(H5N1) reported to the WHO (World Health Organization).

Step 2–Those countries identified in Step 1 were confirmed to be UNWTO (World Tourism Organization) members and therefore obliged to follow UNWTO guidelines.

Step 3–The official Website of the National Tourism Organization (NTO) of each of these countries was identified and verified through the UNWTO Website (10 Websites identified).

Step 4–Two advanced tourism science students where instructed to search each of the Websites of these NTO's for the information listed below and to were told to indicate, on the basis of the information they had found on the Website, whether or not they believed the country had experienced some human cases of avian flu.

(a) Does there exist on the home page a link to a page that refers to tourists' safety and emergency information?

(b) If a link exists, is the reference general or does it specifically refer to avian flu?

(c) Does there exist a page or partial page in the site dedicated to avian flu though not linked to the home page (e.g., included "tourists travel tips")?

(d) Does there exist a page or partial page in the site dedicated to general health?

(e) Does the Website provide emergency phone numbers–e.g., medical, etc.?

(f) Does there exist a link to the national health organization or department of health?

(g) Does there exist a link to the WHO (World Health Organization)?

(h) Does there exist a link to the UNWTO?

(i) Using the "search" function on the Websites, verify the existence of any document referring to the "avian flu" or "bird flu" and if pages are found read them and render a belief whether or not there is avian flu on humans in the country.

Step 5–As a reliability check, within days of the students' evaluation of the Websites (June 2006), the author performed the same evaluation of the sites to evaluate the accuracy of the students' evaluation.

Step 6–The author, in the month of July 2006, revisited the websites for updates and essentially performed the same evaluation again to see if new information had been added or old information updated.

These data from the students' observations and those of the author were summarized and served as the only empirical basis of the study.

FINDING

High inter-judge reliability of the Website evaluations was observed. In only one out of ten cases was there any inconsistency across judges as to whether the country had experienced human cases of avian flu, and this inconsistency was merely in the degree of confidence of the determination, not the conclusion itself. Further, while it was observed that not many of the Websites provided very extensive information concerning the risk of avian flu, a few did (most notably Thailand) and that a few of the Websites provided much information about the risk of avian flu. In most cases general health information would be provided.

Table 1 below summarizes the relevant tourism and avian flu statistics for each of the countries studied. All countries hold membership in the WTO and all countries have experienced

human cases of avian flu, the majority of which have resulted in death.

Table 2 below shows that it was possible, from the information accessible through the countries' Websites or from links they provided, the very basic determination of whether or not there have been cases of human contracted avian flu. However, as Table 3 shows, most Websites (the exception being Thailand) provide little information concerning the risk of avian flu to tourists visiting their countries and even less information concerning where and how to obtain such information

An examination of Table 3 reveals that only Thailand provides an easily accessible and dedicated page that provides information on the risk to tourists accruing from avian flu. There is an almost complete absence of information concerning how to evaluate and manage the risk before it is encountered. The potential tourist has virtually no means to discover, through the NTOs' Websites the existence of avian flu on that particular country. In short, the information available on the Websites of these countries address the risk of avian flu in a minimal and not standardized way, and does not provide adequate guidance for evaluating the risk of avian flu or what to do should a tourist encounter the risk first hand.

TABLE 1. WTO Status, Tourist Arrivals and Avian Flu Statistics 2003-2006

Country	First yr. in WTO	Yrs in WTO	Tourist Arrivals in 2001[1]	Avian Flu[2] Cases	Deaths	Pct Deaths	Website of National Tourism Organization
Azerbaijan	2001	5	767	8	5	62.5	http://azerbaijan.tourism.az
Cambodia	1975	31	605	6	6	100.0	http://www.mot.gov.kh/default.asp
China	1983	23	33,167	19	12	63.2	http://old.cnta.gov.cn/lyen/index.asp http://www.cnta.gov.cn/
Djibouti	1997	9	-	1	0	0.0	http://www.office-tourisme.dj/ in French
Egypt	1975	31	4,357	14	6	42.9	www.visitegypt.gov.eg old http://egypt.travel/ new as of march 29, 2006 http://www.egypttourism.org/ official Website for the Americas
Indonesia	1975	31	5,153	54	42	77.8	www.budpar.go.id
Iraq[3]	1975	31	-	2	2	100.0	www.tourism-iq.net
Thailand[4]	1996	25	10,133	23	15	65.2	www.tourismthailand.org
Turkey	1975	31	10,783	12	4	33.3	www.turizm.gov.tr
Viet Nam	1981	25	1,599	93	42	45.2	www.vietnamtourism.com
Total				232	134	57.8	

[1] In thousands (compiled from UNWTO). [2] Source: WHO. [3] Not further analyzed. [4] Previously member 1975-1990

TABLE 2. Investigators Assessment of Likelihood Countries Have Experienced Human Cases of Avian Flu

Country	Investigator 1	Investigator 2	Agreement
Azerbaijan	No	No	Yes
Cambodia	Likely[1]	No	No
China	Very likely	Yes	Near
Djibouti	No	No	Yes
Egypt	No	No	Yes
Indonesia	Yes	Yes	Yes
Thailand	Yes	Yes	Yes
Turkey	No	No	Yes
Viet Nam	No	No	Yes

[1]These assessment was based on the article read by investigator on the Chinese tourism Website.

TABLE 3. Avian Flu Related Content on Websites

Country	Dedicated link from home page	Dedicated link or dedicated page	General health pages	Emergency phone nos.	Links to	Avian flu page document, link
Azerbaijan	no	No	no	yes	none	no
Cambodia	no	No	link yes, page no	yes	Cambodian Ministry of health, WTO	no
China[1]	no	No	Yes	no	none	yes
Djibouti	no	No	yes, partial page	yes	none	no
Egypt	no	No	brief, precaution	no	none	no
Indonesia[1]	no	No	no	yes	UN, WTO, WHO	yes
Thailand[1]	no	Yes, extensive: crisis communication center, with updates	Health and vaccination	yes	Thailand Bureau of Epidemiology, Dept of Diseases Control, Ministry of Public Health, WHO	yes
Turkey	no	No	Yes but page empty	yes	none	no
Viet Nam	no	No	Page dedicated to hospitals	yes	Ministry of Health phone numbers only	no

[1] China, Indonesia and Thailand were found to have pages on avian flu; Thailand even has an update on Asian flu.

The purpose of this exploratory study was to propose and explore a framework for understanding the tourists' "*information search process*" during the "pre-event" stage of a tourism disaster, and to investigate how affected countries can communicate crisis related information effectively through their Websites to relevant stakeholders. It has been argued that the Internet, because of its reach and flexibility, carries simultaneously the risk of exploitation from self-interested parties as well as the promise of an effective tool in tourism-related disaster management. However the data suggest that this is not the case currently.

We can now give very succinct and validated answers posed in the introduction of this paper: (a) What are national tourism organization doing in the area of prevention and planning? Very little. (b) How likely are tourist to be able to obtain information concerning the risk of avian flu at their intended destinations? Very unlikely. (c) "To what extent are national tourism organizations communicating basic avian flu risks to tourists?" Practically none. (d) How common are "crises communication centers" among national tourism organization? Very uncommon with the possible exception of Thailand. (e) To what extent is there clear and reliable information available to tourists on the risk of avian flu? Very little.

DISCUSSION

Judged against the ideal disaster preparedness and communication conditions, it must be concluded that the reality is woefully inadequate to manage the risks of the various stakeholders as described in the introduction to this report. For certain, the information on these websites is inadequate for tourists wishing to visit these countries, and this argues for reconfiguring the responsibility structure for providing the information. In particular it argues for relocating responsibility for the reliability of the information and its provision to UNWTO, since it has the mechanism to easily set, communicate and enforce standards through its "parent organization" status. The NTOs may be reluctant to relinquish control over the provision of the information since they are likely to view the information as proprietary and its dissemination significant to its economic interests. Such a view however, fails to take into account the fact that there will probably be more to be gained, especially form tourists contemplating a visit, by removing uncertainty (i.e., reducing the perceived risk) than by withholding it and casting doubt in the tourists' mind. All of this of course begs the question of the NTOs' responsibility to their tourism clientele.

As was pointed out in the introduction, East Asia and Pacific South Asia are among the countries forecasted to experience record growth over the next 15 years. However, countries in these regions are among the highest risk regions for avian flu, and if the health experts who assert that a pandemic is a foregone conclusion, then their economic growth will almost for certain be degraded as a result. It would seem that proactive, even pre-emptive strategies are necessary to protect not just the tourists' and tourism marketers' interests, but the economic interests of the countries themselves. It is also argued that the UNWTO will need to enforce the necessary changes and in making the risk assessment information available in an easily accessed and very clear and reliable way. The Internet, for all of the reasons previously cited is recommended as an effective supporting distribution infrastructure. It is a very powerful and democratizing force in achieving a fair and equitable distribution of information. Almost all tourists will know how to access the Internet, but most will not use it as a risk management tool if the effort required to search for, and obtain, the information is significant or the probability of finding the information that is needed is low. The content must include an updated assessment of the (a) the nature of the risk, (b) the magnitude of the risk, (c) the specific consequences should the risk materialize, and (d) what are the effective avoidance, response and recovery measures, in the specific localities where the tourist is likely to find him or her self. Also, as stated previously, the strategic planning, risk management and response preparation for disaster management must be well understood, and commonly understood by both the tourism authorities and the tourism marketers. Centralizing and standardizing the information infrastructure is a good first step toward achieving this, however tourists information search process may be limited to destinations' Websites creating therefore a stronger need for UNWTO to reinforce the presence of a link to UNWTO or WHO on NTOs' Websites.

REFERENCES

Barton, L., (1994) "Crisis management: Preparing for and managing disasters" *Cornell Hotel and Restaurant Administration Quarterly* pp. 59-65.

Bazerman, M. H. (2002). *Judgment in managerial decision making*. (5th ed.) New York: John Wiley & Sons.

Beirman, D., (2002) "Marketing of tourism destinations during a prolonged crisis: Israel and the Middle East" *Journal of Vacation Marketing* pp. 167-176.

Burnett, J.J., (1998) "A strategic approach to managing crises" *Public Relations Review* pp. 475-488.

Durocher, J. (1994). Recovery marketing: What to do after a natural disaster. *The Cornell Hotel and Restaurant Association Quarterly*, April, 66-71.

Faulkner, B. (2001). Towards a framework for tourism disaster management. *Tourism Management*, 22(2), 135-147.

Fink, S., (1986) *Crisis management*, New York: American Association of Management.

Glaeßer, D. (2005). *Crisis management in the tourism industry*. (2nd ed.) Oxford: Butterworth Heinemann.

Henderson, J. C. (2003). Communicating in a crisis: flight SQ 006. *Tourism Management*, 24(3), 279-287.

Marra, F., (1998) "Crisis communication plans: Poor predictors of excellent crisis public relations" *Public Relations Review* pp. 461-474.

Page, S., Yeoman, I., Munro, C., Connell, J., & Walker, L. (2006). A case study of best practice- Visit Scotland's prepared response to an influenza pandemic. *Tourism Management*, 27(3), 361-393.

Pizam, A., (2002) "Tourism and terrorism" *International Journal of Hospitality Management* pp. 1-3.

Ritchie, B. (2004). Chaos, crises and disasters: A strategic approach to crisis management in the tourism industry. *Tourism Management*, 25(6), 669-683.

Santana, G., (2001) Global safety and national security. In Wahab, S.; Cooper, C., Editors, *Tourism in the age of globalization*. London: Routledge.

Soñmez, S.F.; Apostolopoulos, Y.; Tarlow, P., (1999) "Tourism in crisis: Managing the effects of terrorism" *Journal of Travel Research* pp. 13-18.

WTO (2002). *Tourism 2020 Vision*. Madrid: World Tourism Organization.

WTO (1996). *Tourist safety and security: Practical measures for destinations*. Madrid: World Tourism Organization.

WTO (1998). *Handbook on natural disaster reduction in tourist areas*. Madrid: World Tourism Organization.

WTO (2002). *Tourism after 11 September 2001: Analysis, remedial actions and prospects*. Madrid: World Tourism Organization.

Young, W.B.; Montgomery, R.J., (1998) "Crisis management and its impact on destination marketing. A guide to convention and visitors bureaus" *Journal of Convention and Exhibition Management* pp. 3-18.

Zerman, D., (1995) "Crisis communication: Managing the mass media" *Information and Computer Security* pp. 25-28.

London Tourism:
A 'Post-Disaster' Marketing Response

Adele Ladkin
Alan Fyall
John Fletcher
Richard Shipway

SUMMARY. Global tourism demand has been subject to fluctuation in recent years, and London as a tourist destination has recently had to cope with both the significant forces at play in the wider environment and radical change in the way that tourism is to be managed across the UK. The purpose of this paper is to review the post-disaster destination marketing activity conducted by London in its attempt to regain its position as a premier destination for domestic and international visitors, set within the wider context of the devolution of tourism across the country. A number of the issues arising from London's post-disaster marketing campaign are identified, and a set of guiding principles for any future such action are discussed. The paper concludes that diversification of both the product and market is necessary if London is to retain its position as one of the world's leading 'iconic' city destinations.

Adele Ladkin (E-mail: aladkin@bournemouth.ac.uk) is Professor of Tourism Employment and Head of the Centre for Event and Sports Research, International Centre for Tourism and Hospitality Research, School of Services Management, Bournemouth University (P. O. Box 2816, Poole. Dorset. BH12 5YT). Alan Fyall (E-mail: afyall@bournemouth.ac.uk) is Reader in Tourism Management, International Centre for Tourism & Hospitality Research and Head of Research, School of Services Management, Bournemouth University (P. O. Box 2816, Poole. Dorset. BH12 5YT). John Fletcher (E-mail: jefletch@bournemouth.ac.uk) is Professor of Tourism Economics and Head, International Centre for Tourism and Hospitality Research, School of Services Management, Bournemouth University (P. O. Box 2816, Poole. Dorset. BH12 5YT). Richard Shipway (E-mail: rshipway@bournemouth.ac.uk) is a Lecturer in Sports Management, The Centre for Event and Sports Research, School of Services Management, Bournemouth University (PO Box 2816, Poole. Dorset. BH12 5YT).

The authors are grateful to the many individuals who kindly gave their time by contributing to the numerous interviews that were conducted in order to complete this study.

INTRODUCTION

All tourist destinations are at risk of disasters and crisis, and London is no exception. The effect on tourism of disasters and crisis has received increasing attention within the tourism literature (see Beirman, 2003; Blake and Sinclair, 2003; de Sausmarez, 2004; Fall, 2004; Faulkner, 2001; Frisby, 2002; Glaesser, 2003; Henderson, 2003; Ritchie and Crouch, 2003; Laws, Prideaux and Chon, 2007). In particular, Beirman (2003) provides many examples of destinations in crisis as a result of terrorism, natural disasters, epidemics, crime, war and a combination of crises. Although definitions and terms vary, the World Tourism Organization (WTO) has defined a crisis or emergency as:

> Any unexpected event that affects traveller confidence in a destination and interferes with the ability to operate normally.' (WTO, 2003)

Along with most destinations, London has been subject to many of the same forces and external events that have impacted demand for tourism and led to changing patterns of visitor behaviour across the world in recent times. For London, a combination of the war in Iraq, the outbreak of SARS, a weak US and world economy and the previous problems caused by the Foot and Mouth outbreak in the UK have all to varying degrees impacted on London's popularity as an iconic 'global city' destination; this before the terrorist attacks in Central London on 7 July 2005. In 2001 it was estimated to have lost £1.1 billion in tourist receipts due to the combined effect of Foot and Mouth Disease (FMD) and 911 (GLA Economics, 2003a). With the launch of a second war in Iraq early in 2003, initial estimates were that London was to lose a further £0.5 billion. Although considerable, this projection excluded the threat of a direct terrorist attack on London itself, which unfortunately became a reality on 7 July 2005. As a consequence London has been faced with the problem of how to win back visitors from both the international and domestic markets. Set against this background, this paper reviews the post-disaster destination marketing activity conducted by London (prior to the 7 July 05 at-

tack) in its attempt to regain its position as a premier destination. The paper explores a number of the issues arising from London's post-disaster marketing campaign and identifies a set of guiding principles for any future such action. It is hoped that other destinations can learn from the issues arising in the London context. Although a global problem, London's efforts are set in the national context of the devolution of tourism regionally within the UK and the specific role played by the Mayor of London in the development of tourism within the city.

In order to achieve the above, the paper is organised in the following way. Following an initial discussion of tourism disaster and crisis frameworks, tourism in London in its wider context is introduced, incorporating an overview of the regional 'devolution' of tourism in the UK and the re-structuring of tourism within London. Next, an outline of the methodology is given, followed by an examination of London's 'post-disaster' marketing response with specific attention being paid to the key lessons learned from its experience to date. The paper then proposes a framework for future action in the form of a set of guiding principles to be adopted when, rather than if future disasters occur. Although the research was undertaken prior to the terrorist atrocities committed in Central London on 7 July 2005, the conclusion makes reference to the more recent events affecting tourism in London. Furthermore it provides a summary overview of how the strategies adopted by London over the past 18 months have strengthened its ability to cope with man-made disasters of such magnitude.

TOURISM DISASTER FRAMEWORKS

The nature and definitions of crisis and disasters, and the debate concerning whether or not we are living in a more disaster or crisis prone world has been well documented (Blaikie et al., 1994; Horlick-Jones et al., 1991), and according to Richardson (1994), the increasingly complex world that we live in has contributed to making disasters more common. The outcomes of these debates notwithstanding, what is certain is that tourism destinations are at risk from crisis and disaster, and there is no shortage of recent examples of catastrophic events, both natural and those induced by human action that have beset international tourism destinations.

Despite the often devastating effect disasters and crisis can have on tourism, few organisations have in place strategies for coping with them (Faulkner, 2001). However, although the subject is still in its infancy from both an academic and practitioner perspective, in recent years, advice on how to manage emergencies in the context of tourism and hospitality has been considered (see Mitroff, 1988; Mitroff and Anagnos, 2001). Post-911, the tourism sector globally has come to hear of 'risk management,' 'destination recovery' and 'crisis management' as a matter of course. Some events are turbulent, intense and potentially relatively short-lived and adverse impacts can be, to some extent, managed and controlled by a crisis management system. However, all too often a tourism crisis can be self-perpetuating especially where authorities are slow to respond to an initial problem. Media coverage also often exaggerates the situation (Young and Montgomery, 1998). The lack of a credible response creates a media frenzy that provides an additional story behind initial inactivity–this being particularly true of the UK Government's position with Foot and Mouth Disease (FMD) in early 2001. The implications were profound, as were the outcomes.

A discussion of crisis management and its theory is beyond the scope of this paper, and have been discussed fully elsewhere (Laws et al., 2007). However, research into tourism disaster plans is worthy of mention to set the context of the present research. A number of authors have provided models for tourism disaster plans (for example, Young and Montgomery, 1998; Murphy and Bayley, 1989; Glaesser, 2003; Cassedy, 1991; Drabek, 1995). As identified by Laws et al. (2007), one of the most extensive disaster management frameworks was developed by Faulkner (2001). This six-phase approach comprises of a pre-event phase, prodromol phase, the emergency phase, the intermediate phase, long term recovery, and finally the resolution phase (Faulkner, 1991). Faulkner also identified the prerequisites for and the ingredients of effective disaster management strategies. The prerequisites are:

- A co-ordinated team approach;
- Consultation; and
- Commitment.

The ingredients and its outcomes should include:

- A risk assessment;
- Prioritisation;
- Protocols;
- A community capability audit;
- A disaster management command centre;
- Media and monitoring activities;
- Warning systems;
- Flexibility; and
- Involvement and review.

This framework provides a useful basis for examining tourism disaster responses as it highlights the key areas for consideration. Set against this background, the research presented here examines the effectiveness of a post-disaster destination marketing campaign undertaken by the various stakeholders involved in the management of an international tourist destination.

TOURISM IN LONDON

Internationally, demand for tourism generally was affected by a series of unusual events in 2003. A combination of the Iraqi war, SARS and a weak US and world economy depressed tourism activity in all major generating markets. The problems in Iraq continue to suppress demand from a number of key source markets, particularly North America, and this has impacted on London particularly. A relatively weak US economy continues to keep US visitors at home, while those that make the trip are less likely to spend because of the unfavourable Dollar to Sterling and Dollar to Euro exchange rates.

Within Europe, from a generating perspective London and the UK remain an attractive series of destinations. London has retained its status against other European capitals primarily through a mixture of relative speed and accessibility. Tourist flows from Europe to London have also remained robust despite the Euro being weak against Sterling. From a domestic perspective London has benefited from its unique position as the central driver to the UK economy. However, in recent times the economy has sent mixed messages and the UK domestic tourism industry has had to adjust to a period of uncertainty. London has not escaped its reputation as an expensive city and price sensitivity towards London has been experienced in the home market. In order to capture domestic tourism business, London must constantly seek to re-engineer its product otherwise face increased competition both at home and abroad.

London is also in the midst of a peculiar paradox in that while at the same time now receiving record high levels of visitors its overall share of international tourism is declining. For example, inbound UK tourism set a record for early summer, with visitor numbers up 11% year on year. In the three month period from May to July 2004, 7.6 million overseas visitors came to the UK, with 4.6 million of them originating from Western Europe. Visitors from North America posted an increase of 13%, while numbers from the rest of the world increased by 17% over the same time period (Visit London, 2004). Thus, while on the surface and in the context of the emergency scenario, this is encouraging, London's declining share of international tourism demonstrates the importance of issues such as the distribution of the world economy, the continual development of new destinations around the world, and longstanding negative perceptions of London as an 'expensive' destination are for tourism in London.

However, there is little doubt that tourism provides a considerable injection into the London economy. It accounts for approximately 7% of London's GDP while supporting up to 8% of London's workforce (Visit London, 2002). London serves as a major 'gateway' destination to the UK with 59% of all visitors arriving via one of London's airports. Over 50% of all overseas visitors spend at least one night in the capital while 45% come only to London. London is unusual, however, in that although business visitors contribute significantly to the tourist economy, it is largely reliant on high-value overseas leisure markets. With regard to tourist expenditure per trip, it is estimated that London requires 3.5 domestic visitors and 2 near-European visitors to compensate for the loss of one American visitor (GLA Economics, 2003b). This quite stark projection is clear evidence of the structural weakness of London's tourism position and its over

reliance on individual markets. London is disproportionately reliant on overseas tourism and is, therefore, particularly vulnerable to unpredictable external events. Bed occupancy figures of on average 52% and 47% for February and March 2003 respectively, demonstrate London's susceptibility to visitor reaction to external events–in this instance the commencement of hostilities in Iraq (GLA Economics, 2003b).

In London, running parallel to the significant forces at play in the wider environment, radical change was taking place in the way in which tourism was to be managed across the UK. The establishment of nine English Regional Development Agencies (RDAs) in 1999 and the publication by the Department of Culture, Media and Sport of 'Tomorrow's Tourism–a Growth Industry for the New Millennium' encapsulated the initial changes. This document laid down a framework to take domestic and in-bound tourism to a higher level of consciousness and within a wider scope of UK economic activity (DCMS, 2004). This period also coincided with the transfer of responsibility of some activities of Government under devolution in Scotland (1998 Scotland Act) and Wales (1998 Government of Wales Act) to the Scottish Parliament and Welsh Assembly respectively.

While devolution in Scotland and Wales brought about changes to the administration of government in those two home nations, a form of devolution also occurred in England in 2003 when greater responsibility for regional tourism strategies was devolved by Government to the RDAs. The funding, delivery, management and responsibility for sectoral performance of tourism now resided with the nine English regions who are now key players with the Government in the strategic leadership of tourism, working both individually and with one another, as well as with regional and local partners (DCMS, 2004).

With regard to how tourism is organised, in the case of London it is the Mayor of London who has the statutory responsibility for the promotion of tourism growth in London and of London as a 'gateway' to the rest of the UK. The Mayor's Office delegates the responsibility for the development and promotion of tourism in London to the London Development Agency (LDA) using resources devolved to the Mayor by the DCMS. The strategic direction for the development of tourism in London remains with the Mayor who has already taken a number of steps to encourage domestic market demand and develop new sustainable niche markets for London's tourism product with a coherent marketing and promotion strategy. In addition to providing suitable direction to overcome London's traditional dependence on volatile overseas markets, *Visit London: The Mayor's Plan for Tourism in London* serves as the necessary strategic platform for London's development as a world-class tourist destination in that it represents a single co-ordinated tourism plan for London. Launched in September 2002, *Visit London: The Mayor's Plan for Tourism in London* and the accompanying *London Tourism Action Plan 2003/4-2005/6*, together represent the first real strategic thrust for tourism in London for over a decade and serve as the essential catalyst to re-energise tourism in London.

The LDA is therefore accountable (on behalf of the Mayor) for the delivery of the *Action Plan* with it being responsible directly for the delivery of product development, infrastructure and tourism research activities identified within the plan. With regard to its implementation, the selected delivery agent for the plan is the London Tourist Board and Convention Bureau which in 2003 became Visit London (VL). In providing a suitable delivery structure, the Mayor's Plan advocated a structure that was to be fast and flexible, one that would instigate a step change in marketing performance, represent a mix between the public and private sectors and establish a broader industry and borough engagement across London. In addition it was deemed that there would exist a clear distinction between policy/strategy (LDA) and delivery (VL) with a desirable consistent approach to branding for London.

METHODS

The justifications for using a case study as a research approach are well documented (Creswell, 1998; Robson, 1993; Yin, 1994). Case studies are in fact used extensively in tourism research, making the justification for using the approach hardly necessary (Beeton, 2005), with many examples of case studies being used in the area of crisis management in tourism (Laws, Prideaux and Chon, (2007). This paper takes the case of London, and is based on research undertaken for the London Development Agency to evaluate the post-disaster marketing activity delivered by Visit London. Undertaken between March 2004 and April 2005, the study involved two methods of data collection. First, an extensive secondary audit of all evaluation reports conducted by a variety of market research agencies at various stages of London's marketing campaign was undertaken. These secondary sources comprised of studies for individual stages of the TIRP, and also those that attempted to evaluate the effectiveness of certain aspects of the plan. The secondary data sources were used both at the beginning of the research, and as they became available throughout the duration of the project. The second method of data collection comprised of interviews conducted with key players and stakeholders across London's tourism industry. A total of 12 face-to-face interviews were undertaken with representatives from the London Development Agency, Visit London, Visit Britain, The Society of London Theatres, The Association of Train Operating Companies, and a number of independent companies. Typically interviews lasted between 40 to 50 minutes. Due to the importance attached to TIRP, the research team were given unique access to the various stakeholders involved. As a condition, however, and in accord with the wishes of the client, all comments presented in this paper are in aggregate form, with no specific comments attributed to any one individual. Finally, the use of both secondary sources and interviews for this evaluation of the TIRP was an on-going process as the material became available and lasted for the full duration of the project.

DISCUSSION– LONDONS' 'POST CRISIS' MARKETING PLAN

To limit the damage caused to London's tourism economy from the succession of negative external threats, the Mayor's Office (MO) instigated the launch of the London Tourism Recovery Group (LTRG) in the first quarter of

2003. Establishing LTRG represented a permanent contingency framework designed to support the tourism and hospitality sector in London in times of emergency. Membership of the LTRG included individuals from the London Development Agency (LDA), the Greater London Authority (GLA), MO, Visit Britain (VB), Visit London (VL), the Mayor's Advisory Group, an independent member, and a member from the Tourism Alliance. With the intention of being the principal 'emergency' group of its type, LTRG concluded that the problems facing tourism in London required a market-led response and as such formed a Special Marketing Steering Group early in March 2003. One of its first actions was to identify lessons to be learned from London's previous emergency initiative for the recovery of tourism back in 2001: the London Tourism Action Group (LTAG).

Financed to the value of £4 million, the establishment of LTAG represented a temporary, short-term recovery initiative developed and implemented in an extremely tight timescale. LTAG was not linked specifically to a wider tourism strategy for London and was dominated by discount and value-driven offers. The activities of LTAG were the first significant evidence of co-operation between the key agencies supporting tourism in London, as it was implemented in a strategic vacuum that was predominantly 'bottom-up' in nature. Although LTAG achieved much in its brief life, a number of criticisms arose from the audit. One key criticism was the supply-bias of the campaign and the lack of a truly consumer-driven marketing initiative. There was also the criticism that where research was undertaken it had limited objectivity especially regarding issues of additionality and displacement, and the fragmented nature of the evaluation and monitoring of funded projects. A

significant outcome of the audit of LTAG was the proposal for a Disaster Marketing Toolkit. The Toolkit consisted of a set of guiding principles which to varying degrees underpinned the later recovery initiative. Overall, however, a number of key lessons arose from the LTAG initiative: First, a market-led response was deemed preferable to fragmented, small-scale assistance to suppliers with limited guarantees of success while it was believed that greater effectiveness could be derived if a single organisation could serve as the delivery vehicle. Significant funds were also deemed necessary for a 'step change' in marketing to take place while there was clearly a need for the establishment of a framework for co-ordination of key parties in the event of a crisis by consultation with the interested parties. Finally, there was a need to standardise the set up and procurement for an emergency response team that would expedite and simplify the response as was there a need to establish a dedicated tourism team for the development of tourism within the LDA.

In view of the above lessons, the Special Marketing Steering Group advocated a Tourism Industry Recovery Plan (TIRP) for London in response to the indicators identifying extreme negative impacts on London tourism if no emergency action were to be undertaken. TIRP provided the strategic backbone to emergency action and served as a guiding framework to facilitate the choice of marketing strategies and actions to stabilise London's tourism economy in a time of considerable unease and market turbulence. Building on the experience of LTAG, TIRP was designed as a fully-integrated marketing programme that adopted five separate but related phases, as evidenced in Figure 1. An outline of the phases and an assessment of their effectiveness follow.

FIGURE 1. Tourism Industry Recovery Plan (TIRP)

Phase 1: Domestic Short-Term Promotional Campaign	**Phase 2**: Domestic Promotional Campaigns	**Phase 3**: Domestic and near-Europe Campaigns	**Phase 4**: Domestic and near-Europe Campaigns	**Phase 5**: Events Campaign

Phase 1: The Association of Train Operating Companies (ATOC) Campaign

This was a "2-for-1" campaign run by ATOC that was already in place. The TIRP agreed for an extension to the scheme. This consisted of "2-for-1" entrance offers on London attractions, and "2-for-1" offers on London theatre in terms of either ticket sales or discounted meals, 40% of participating London hotels. The campaign was supported by 15 train operating companies. In support of the campaign a number of factors were deemed significant:

- The speed with which the campaign could be extended was of paramount;
- The campaign demonstrated 'good practice' vis-à-vis the effectiveness of collaborative marketing campaigns;
- The previous incarnation of TIRP, the London Tourism Action Group (LTAG) concluded that the ATOC "2-for-1" campaign was an effective vehicle to deliver significant return on investment to the value of 50:1;
- The campaign was in receipt of significant private sector support;
- More than one sector was represented in the campaign, i.e., transport, attractions, theatres, and hotels;
- Transport and sustainability benefits were likely as were economic benefits through increased booking levels in the low season, most notably via enhanced booking levels in serviced accommodation in the capital;
- In granting an extension to the ATOC "2-for-1" campaign, agreement was reached for the need to ensure that a high standard of information for disabled tourists be provided, that disabled people were not excluded from taking up the offers made in the campaign and that ATOC fulfilled its commitment to assisting disabled travellers. In view of ATOC's previous history in their support of disabled travellers this target was deemed achievable.

The overriding feedback from those key individuals interviewed is that the campaign was a considerable success, especially with regard to the speed with which it was initiated. Clear

Benefits and Drawbacks of Phase 1:
Benefits:
• Simplicity of format and speed of implementation
• Multi-sector collaborative marketing
• High return on investment
• Private sector backing
• Off-season bookings
Drawbacks:
• Promotional campaign fatigue
• Discount dependency culture among visitors
• 'Top-down' choice of campaign
• Weak contribution to serviced-accommodation

benefits to train operating companies were evident, as were there clear benefits to attractions in the capital. Issues of campaign fatigue and campaign competition due to events in Iraq were raised but the overwhelming view from those interviewed was one of success. However, there was a criticism which was evidence to suggest a 'top-down' bias in the choice of campaign and a sense of limited 'strategic' involvement by partner organisations. Although the emergency context necessitates a sense of urgency the need for genuine involvement and participation by industry partners can be achieved more effectively if there exists greater understanding of the longer-term direction of tourism in London. Decisions were not always possible with a long term strategic objective.

In view of the speed in which this campaign was initiated and implemented, the success of the ATOC "2-for-1" concept is to be commended, especially in the context of emergency action. The Association of Train Operating Companies demonstrate considerable experience and expertise in the organisation of such campaigns and demonstrate a track record of achievement. The previous LTAG initiative also concluded that ATOC was a highly suitable partner in the capital to energise the domestic market. The format is simple and well understood by the market and appears to have acquired a strong following. The fact that the campaign performs well in non-emergency conditions suggests that more long-term commitment should be considered by tourism bodies in London in that it represents a highly effective vehicle to attract domestic tourists to London. Although the "2-for-1" concept has not traditionally driven huge increases in service accommodation a broadening of its geographic reach across the UK is likely to contribute to higher levels of occupancy in many of London's hotels.

The success of this phase of TIRP suggests that much greater use should be made of the train operating companies in future discount-related campaigns. In the context of TIRP phases two (all components) and five could have benefited from a closer working relationship with ATOC and benefit from its experience of running such campaigns. It does however highlight the fact that although the dissection of the campaign into five phases was believed to benefit each phase by them being able to learn from preceding phases, the speed with which one phase followed another resulted in very little time at all (if any) to amend the initial plans for each. For example, phase two was launched in mid-May prior to the completion of the ATOC campaign. The involvement of ATOC in some form, in addition to their experience, would have been a considerable asset to the implantation of the second phase of TIRP.

Phase 2: Totally London Month, Totally London Tour and 'GILT'

Totally London Month (TLM) was designed to encourage Londoners and those living within the M25 to use the tourism facilities in London by offering discounts on attractions, restaurants, and theatres. A number of partners were included from across the hospitality and restaurant, retailing, and media sectors. The aim of the campaign was to generate more visits to London and support the economic recovery of the important tourism and leisure sector. It was the first ever campaign to be aimed at the local market: targeting Londoners and visitors to London, to encourage them to get out and about, and enjoy the best of the capital.

Given the size and importance of Phase 2, the LDA put in place a number of measures to monitor and evaluate the impact of TLM. These included studies on consumer awareness, participation and expenditure, media coverage, business income, and the economic ben-

> Benefits and Drawbacks of Phase 2:
>
> Benefits:
> * Multi-sector collaborative marketing generating positive incremental secondary spend
> * High media profile with strong 'local' focus
> * Strong vehicle to underpin future campaigns
> * Contribution to development of civic pride and belief in the London product
> * Visitor dispersal and use of local transport
> * Diversity of product
>
> Drawbacks:
> * Poor levels of match funding
> * Impact hindered by speed of implementation
> * Weak contribution to serviced-accommodation

efits to the tourism and leisure sector. The GLA, the LDA and VL all agree that evaluation is an important aspect of TIRP. Five core measures were agreed at the outset which VL was to monitor and evaluate the impact of the campaign:

* Additional usage of public transport over the promotion weekends;
* Actual business to London tourism-related businesses as a direct result of the campaign;
* Levels of civic pride within London pre, during and post-campaign;
* Dispersal of visitors throughout London, i.e. visitor numbers to both attractions within and outside central London; and
* Expenditure by London residents in the tourism and leisure area.

In addition, press coverage achieved from press and PR activity related to the campaign; hits to the Visit London Website; levels of public sector investment in the campaign in direct financial contribution, in kind support and adoption of the campaign creative work for use in their own marketing; awareness of the Totally London identity; and numbers of consumers participating in offers, including competitions were also measured.

The fact that it was the first ever campaign to be aimed at the local market is significant and represents a foundation for future like-minded campaigns. Although elements of the campaign (timing, funding, and lines of authority) with the benefit of hindsight may have been done differently, it has to be remembered that the campaign was initiated, developed and implemented in a considerably short period of time. This clearly had an impact on gaining partners and match funding. If one were to focus on the encouragement of industry involvement rather than meeting ambitious match-funding targets with no precedent metrics to base targets on then TLM was deemed to be a success.

Totally London Tour (TLT) was designed to promote geographically and culturally diverse aspects of London by highlighting key festivals and events such as the Trafalgar Square concert, Regent Street Festival and Covent Garden Week. These gave the areas an opportunity to showcase themselves to London as a whole. Visit London created a specific micro-site to support this activity. Some of the events were existing annual events, some were substantially changed and expanded by the support of Totally London, and others were completely new. Visit London provided the marketing support across all of the events. Activities included:

- 31 August free concert in Trafalgar Square
- 4-7 September Regent Street Festival
- 7 Brick Lane Festival
- 7-14 Covent Garden Week
- 14 Chinatown–Mid Autumn Festival
- 13-14 Mayor's Thames Festival
- 20-21 Open House Weekend
- 20-21 Greenwich Festival
- 22-26 City Showcase
- 27-28 South Bank and Bankside Weekend

The scheme was promoted by Visit London through leaflets, radio, press and poster advertising and by the promoters of individual events. Visit London was responsible for the largest marketing budget by far for these events through the Totally London Tour brand. It is important to note that some events were in fact already planned prior to the adoption of the Totally London Tour brand.

With its core objective of promoting geographically and culturally diverse aspects of London by highlighting key festivals and events Totally London Tour to some degree can be deemed to have met it objectives. In a particularly tight period of time a 'package' of events

was developed and marketed to the domestic market with good levels of awareness and participation. The overall appropriateness of such a campaign in a wider emergency-oriented campaign is, however, open to question. A positive outcome is that it helps to promote the fact that the capital remains open for business and offers a real diversity of events to accommodate all tastes and fashions. A less positive outcome is that TLT served as a vehicle to support a number of events that would have taken place anyway irrespective of grant aid. The opportunity cost of such action is what could perhaps have been achieved with monies invested elsewhere. In conclusion, that issue of principal concern evident in this stage of the wider TIRP campaign is the ability, and willingness, of organisations to work unilaterally even when advised against it by its partner organisations.

The *'Get into London Theatre Campaign'* *(GILT)* was a promotional campaign based around a discount theatre ticket offer with associated rail travel, hotel and/or restaurant involvement. This was designed to encourage economic activity via theatre going and related spend (accommodation, meals, etc.), among Londoners, and in particular the domestic audience around the UK.

The objectives of GILT were to:

- Stimulate economic activity in a key sector of the visitor/cultural economy, i.e., theatre as well as related spend (accommodation, meals, etc), primarily amongst a domestic audience around the UK with a London audience as a secondary consideration;
- Increase the profile of London Theatre among the UK domestic audience;
- Sell a minimum of 40,000 theatre tickets split 60:40 London to UK Domestic market; and
- Generate an overnight stay for 1 in 10 domestic tickets sold.

The fact that the theatre remains such a large draw for many visitors when deciding to come to London is such that it is inevitable that any emergency action ought to include the theatre sector in some way. Not only is the theatre a catalyst for visitation, but it also serves as a major component of London's imagery, its 'icon' city status and as a key partner to most other aspects of London's, and the country's, tourism industry. The issue here, however, is the extent to which the GILT campaign is the most suitable vehicle for the theatres' inclusion in campaigns designed to inspire recovery post-emergency. In drawing visitors, enhancing incremental spend, and providing a high media profile for London's tourist industry the GILT campaign makes a positive contribution to emergency action. However, its inability to make a fundamental difference to overnight stays and its over concentration on the London market, in addition to the issue of state aid suggests that the incorporation of the theatre sector into other campaigns and so gain the benefit of critical mass, may not only generate higher ticket sales and greater return on investment (and reduced costs) but contribute to a more consistent and coherent branding of emergency action *per se* and the wider marketing of tourism in London.

Phases 3 and 4: Short-Haul Campaign

After the 'local' nature of Phase 1 and Phase 2, Phase 3 (October 2003) and Phase 4 (February 2004) represented major image-led campaigns complemented by value offers from commercial partners. Phases 3 and 4 were an attempt to combat a continued downturn in forward bookings, visitor arrivals and spend from the domestic, near Europe and international markets. Designed to counter the criticism in the original LTAG Study vis-à-vis the short-term, quick-fix nature of solutions, both campaigns were designed to build short-term business as well as to change longer-term perceptions. Both campaigns were developed in response to a variety of trends. For example:

- The commercial benefit of the domestic and near Europe market remain significantly greater than the day tripper market by 6 to 10 times;
- The downturn in US visitors is still depressing overall numbers but Western Europe represents real potential;
- Qualitative research conducted by Visit Britain and Visit London conclude that perceptions of London are outdated;
- The evident growth in short-breaks and growth of the Internet as a cost-effective channel of distribution;

- Trade involvement still remains a priority in some markets (France, Italy and Germany);
- Significant and continuing growth of low-cost airline hubs outside London and the South East is opening up cheap and easy access to competing European cities;
- Across the UK there has been ongoing increasing investment in tourism and leisure infrastructure and promotional activity which has heightened the competitive threat to London, especially with regard to the historically low levels of expenditure in promoting London to the domestic audience.

In addition to the above, the campaign launched by British Airways 'London is closer than you think' was deemed to be complementary although a slight reduction in London's 'voice' may have been impacted by the English Cities Campaign conducted by Visit Britain. During the campaign period, there were also ferry-related campaigns being conducted by DFDS Seaways for the German market, advantageous rates of exchange for overseas visitors, benefits accruing form the New Year promotion, and the combination of promotions by major carriers and no-frills airlines offering cheaper access to London from abroad.

Campaign objectives for Phases 3 and 4 were to:

- Rebuild the profile of London as the place to come for a short break;
- Drive 100,000 additional trips to London between the campaign launch and the end of March 2004; and
- Drive 200,000 additional overnight stays between the campaign launch and March 2004.

In the undertaking of Phases 3 and 4, the campaign sought to promote key drivers (such as travel and accommodation), use the 'Totally London' campaign marquee, and drive people to the Web site. The primary targets were repeat domestic visitors and both first time and repeat visitors for the European markets. In addition, the campaign was designed to address many of the current barriers to visiting London.

The desired campaign outputs were to:

- Improve perceptions of London as a world-class tourist destination within the target markets;
- Increase revenue to London's tourism businesses as a direct result of campaign activity;
- Increase the likelihood to visit London within 2 years;
- Measure the propensity and frequency of domestic visitors to visit London;
- Measure if visitors to London are more or less likely to make a repeat visit;
- Increase hits to the web site by 10% over the campaign period;
- Understand key consumer insights for domestic and major European markets; and
- Improve relationships with non-tourist sectors.

Phases 3 and 4 together represented the logical next step for TIRP following the primarily domestic value and event-led orientation of the preceding phases. The significant image-led campaigns, complemented by value offers from commercial partners were deliberate in trying to counter the continued downturn in forward bookings, visitor arrivals and spend from the domestic, near Europe and international markets by building on short-term business as well as changing longer-term perceptions.

Phase 5: Events Campaign

The gradual decline in overseas visitors coming to London in the fourth quarter and the limited profile of London as a destination to spend Christmas and the New Year together

---

Benefits and Drawbacks of Phases 3 and 4:

Benefits:
- Image-building campaigns
- Build short-term business and change longer-term perceptions
- Reach important near-Europe markets
- Reduce dependency on US visitors
- Connectivity with overseas intermediaries
- Web site and serviced-accommodation focus

Drawbacks:
- Duplication of activity with other 'competing' campaigns

---

served as the catalysts for Phase 5 of TIRP. Chronologically following Phases 3 and 4 and preceding a major campaign planned for February 2004 (One Amazing Week in London), Phase 5 ran from October 2003 to January 2004 with a particular focus on the period December 26-January 4.

With target markets identified as London and the UK, France, Germany and the Republic of Ireland the principal objectives were to drive business into the hotels sector, to present London in an interesting and "surprising" manner, and to help overcome negative perceptions of London's ability to stage large public scale events by generating positive coverage in the UK and internationally. To meet the above, a two-pronged strategy was deemed appropriate. The first aspect was to enhance the quality of information available to prospective travellers throughout this period and to reinforce the reasons to come to London in conjunction with a call to action featuring strong value-led accommodation offers. The second aspect was the organisation of a New Years Eve event to raise the profile of London as a world class destination in support of the London 2012 Olympic bid. Although funded and managed separately, the event was a core component of Phase 5.

In delivering the above, the first aspect of Phase 5, similar to the TLT campaign in Phase 2, was to create new and enhance existing events so that visitors could experience London in a new and innovative way. The development of an events-led package with key travel and accommodation partners was, therefore, viewed as an essential vehicle to:

- Build a short-term improvement in the hotels business;
- Deliver secondary benefit to bars and restaurants, and possibly attractions; and
- Enhance customer perceptions of London in the longer term(and address concerns/barriers raised in earlier research).

Similar to the preceding phases of TIRP, the audience was established as a combination of domestic, near European and international markets. In a proposal submitted to the LDA on 17 September 2003, and which was subsequently approved on 24 September, the rationale for an events-based approach was as follows:

- A 9 day-long programme allowing for increased participation;
- The encompassing of two weekends and a mid week giving flexibility to the accommodation sector in the creation of specific packages;
- Building upon existing events (such as the New Years Day Parade) allowing the marketing budget to be used efficiently;
- A tele-visual spectacle which will help reduce the health and safety concerns associated with a location-specific event;
- A tele-visual spectacle that will allow for maximum inclusion as all can see it;
- The fact that London needs to be seen that it can stage world-class events effectively. In the run up to the Olympic bid it is essential that London not only raises its profile but that it does it in a manner befitting a first class destination city.

Specific objectives of the campaign were to:

- Create a unique visual event on New Years Eve which will be covered by the international media (press and television);
- Maximise consumer participation in the programme activity to run either side of 31 December;
- Maximise commercial sector participation in the programme activity to run either side of 31 December; and
- Drive business into the hotel sector.

To meet the above, the proposed strategy was to create a stunt, which "only London can do" designed to raise London's profile, package and market all the activities under the Totally London marquee, leverage collective spend of the preceding phases of TIRP to gain greater awareness of the programme, liaise with all key commercial sectors specifically restaurants/bars to encourage participation, and communicate plans to hotel and travel sector in advance so they could build offers. The principal thrust was print and online communication with the additional remit that all communication was to carry a call to action to visitlondon.com which benefited from an extensive redevelopment to capitalise on this particular campaign. Activity included an online

banner advertising, pay per click and email based activity and a New Years micro-site which was launched 1 December and was updated daily. Fifteen thousand listings were recorded in total: 386 comedy events; 751 gigs; 463 visual arts; 160 opera and classical musical events; 1189 clubs; 424 special events; 995 places to visit; nearly 10,000 shops and 2000 restaurants. Printed materials (16-page insert) appeared in the UK, Ireland, France and Germany–5.7 million copies in total. A variety of categories were produced including a section on 'suggested itineraries.'

Phase 5 represents an innovative aspect of TIRP in that it was designed to boost visitors, particularly from overseas, coming to London in the fourth quarter and raise the profile of London as a destination to spend Christmas and the New Year. Through a combination of an events-led package with key travel and accommodation partners, and the organisation of a New Years Eve event to raise the profile of London as a world class destination in support of the London 2012 Olympic bid, Phase 5 brought the emergency action to a close. Although many aspects were deemed to be successful, particularly in the former activity, a number of organisational issues arose around the planning of the New Years Eve event that requires reflection prior to the launching of a similar event/campaign. There is also a need to reflect upon how 'essential' this component was to emergency action and how more suited the phase would be in the future to more traditional aspects of annual marketing activity. However, in the reported "Evaluation of the Impact of New Activity September 2003-January 2004" dated March 2005, Visit London identified the following successes:

- The tourism industry in London welcomed the campaign being wider than just New Year's Eve where there was the opportunity to attract longer stay and higher yield visitors rather than those coming for just one day;
- Both anecdotal and statistical evidence proves a greater number of visitor the period and a good start in terms of a shift in some of the more ingrained negative perceptions of London;

- The activity showed the positive impact that insets can have in providing additional material for visitors to stimulate immediate travel whilst also overcoming outdated perceptions of the city; and
- The positive feedback from both consumers and trade partners on the inset has led to this communication tool being developed and used in other activities subsequently.

Future issues for consideration were, as with other phases of the Tourism Industry Recovery Programme, the short lead time provides a challenge to deliver a high impact campaign with little planning time, whilst welcoming the initiative, the industry also expressed a desire for a longer lead time to allow for greater packaging through the travel trade and for them to leverage the VL promotion to achieve greater impact; and the campaign could achieve greater impact also by the inclusion of key transport providers at an early stage, e.g., Eurostar, airlines–both low cost and full service. This could have the dual function of providing offers to stimulate travel and using the distribution channels by these partners.

There was little doubt that the Mayor's *Plan for Tourism* provided the necessary strategic and operational background for all aspects of tourism in London. Although it was never the intention of TIRP to adhere to the Mayor's Plan, in many instances the actions fed back into the wider structures and benefits were considerable with regard to evaluation, studies and/or reports conducted as part of TIRP that could be used outside of the emergency context.

Benefits and Drawbacks of Phase 5:

Benefits:
- Image-building campaigns
- Build and enhance London's profile as an event destination
- Change visitor perceptions of London
- Multi-sector collaborative marketing

Drawbacks:
- Primarily a television spectacle
- Non-crisis strategy

In evaluating the overall effectiveness of TIRP a number of phase-specific and generic issues were identified. Overall, the emergency nature of TIRP along with the increase in funding and status and consequent growth in confidence contributed towards the evolution of relationships among the various organisations with a responsibility for the management of tourism in London. The imposition of the Mayor's Plan for tourism did much to provide a strategic framework for the development of tourism within London and clearly facilitated strategy-setting and decision-making to the extent that an integrated marketing outcome was achieved. In addition, the significant public investment in and ambition of TIRP was such that it warranted considerable adherence to transparent processes and procedures in delivering an effective campaign. Despite the arrangements agreed between the various tourism bodies in implementing TIRP, in some instances an isolationist approach was taken, particularly with regard to the organisation of events. With regard to strategic direction, the initial decision that emergency action was to be market-led represented a significant learning experience from the previous LTAG initiative which was primarily supplier-driven. However, although there is a strong argument for a 'top down' approach in the context of emergency, this approach will often work only when genuine relationships and agreement exists with partner organisations and the wider industry, especially the private sector, under more normal market conditions.

Throughout TIRP one question that could be asked of each phase irrespective of its markets was what would the consequence have been if none or limited funds were made available? For Visit London, overseas budgets would have been cut to accommodate campaigns targeted at the domestic market. Another issue is that of match funding. Obtaining match funding was a problem for all phases of TIRP. Originally requested by the MO, match funding in the context of emergency action proved to be unavailable at the target levels set with it widely being believed to be unsustainable in the longer term. Poor cash flow and over ambitious targets were given as reasons for such low take up. In effect, emergency action was always meant to be a pump-primer to the industry rather than one generating substantial match funding. With regard to timescale, two elements are worthy of note: the balance between long and short-term objectives in the context of an emergency, and the speed with which the entire TIRP was initiated and implemented. With regard to the former, a balance is needed between long and short-term initiatives with emergency plans requiring evaluation against longer-term objectives as well as short-term requirements. Throughout TIRP there is a delicate balance to be achieved between generating short-term 'value-led' business, and at the same time changing longer-term 'brand-building' perceptions of London as a tourist destination. TIRP appears to have prevented a significant loss of demand and has provided a suitable platform for longer-term development. However, the ability to generate short-term business and change perceptions at the same time is a considerable challenge for emergency action alone. Discount fatigue is already now evident across much of London's tourism industry. This represents a considerable challenge as perceptions within the domestic market are fairly entrenched and are likely to require sustained marketing effort to break down some quite considerable barriers. Agreement is universal in that future marketing activity needs to migrate away from value-driven campaigns.

In many ways, the devolution of tourism in England has resulted in London being the recipient of quite considerable sums of money in response to events of an emergency nature. Clearly, such large-scale investment is unsustainable in the longer term. The extent to which genuine diversity and dispersal was achieved through the implementation of TIRP is, however, a cause for concern. Across all phases of TIRP the principal beneficiaries were believed to be located in and around Central London with very few benefits believed to be accruing to businesses outside of the tourist hot spots. This raises the question as to whether emergency action should solely be concentrated on the tourist hot spots in Central London anyway, and in turn maximise return on investment levels, rather than meeting wider diversity ambitions. Finally, there is a suspicion that some of the activities included among the five phases were primarily budget-led and were, therefore, opportunistic in orientation. Although an acceptable and realistic course of action, future emergency action needs to adopt a more proactive 'objective' approach with regard to pricing.

LESSONS LEARNED– A PLAN FOR FUTURE ACTION

With regard to the six-phase approach advocated by Faulkner (1991), much of the activity undertaken in London centred on the immediate short-term emergency phase and attempts to change visitor perceptions in the longer-term, the need of which can not be attributed to disaster recovery alone. For the most part, TIRP proved to be a co-ordinated team approach with consultation and commitment significant in the context of the time available and the scale of the economic shortfall precipitated by the disaster setting. It is, however, fair to say that Faulkner's proposed prerequisites for, and the ingredients of effective disaster management strategies, were less rigidly adhered to at the time.

Notwithstanding, prior to the more recent events of 7 July 2005, adherence to a set of guiding principles similar to those proposed by Faulkner (1991) was deemed to be instrumental in helping London to come to terms with any future disasters. In particular, the guiding principles were proposed by the authors to help nurture an effective culture open to collaboration whereby effective preparation and the timeliness with which such 'preparation' can be implemented will not be hindered by disharmony across the wider industry. Throughout emergency action it is essential that attention to processes, procedures and all round probity with the management of the emergency strategy is open and transparent as this will help further the degree of 'togetherness' among the industry and bode well for the need for emergency action in the future. Finally, it is important to note that all emergency actions will impact on the marketing of the destination post-emergency, this again emphasising the need for long-term, sustainable partnership activity for the destination to prosper. Although it is beyond the scope of this paper to examine in depth the guidelines proposed, a number of the key recommendations are highlighted below. Prior to any future crisis it is recommended that those organisations and individuals responsible for the future development, management and marketing of London (i.e., VisitBritain, VisitLondon, London Development Agency, Mayor's Office and the Greater London Authority) as an international 'iconic' destination:

- Be proactive and be able to anticipate rather than react to events in the external environment by establishing clear procedural guidance for future emergency funding as part of a planned public-sector response;
- Establish a framework for co-ordination of key parties in the event of a crisis–which has the authority to make quick decisions–by consultation with the interested parties;
- Develop an accountable, transparent and suitably flexible process of project approval;
- Be responsive to events by drawing up a range of contingency plans to meet a variety of needs while demonstrating strategic direction and working towards a long-term solution;
- Have adequate funds in order to implement the necessary actions in the short-to-mid-term;
- Identify a single delivery vehicle for emergency action and avoid overlap of delivery;
- Be fully aware of, and integrated with, related campaigns in the capital as well as campaigns being conducted by competing destinations around the world;
- Be research ready by developing an economic impact model of tourism in London that would enable a more informed response to future 'tourism crises'–benchmark data;
- Identify the principal catalysts that drive visitation to the destination and understand fully the behavioural and booking patterns of the key markets and their propensity to change existing patterns of behaviour in the context of emergency;
- Determine the exact relationship between emergency recovery and long-standing destination marketing strategies. To what extent should the former adhere to the latter, i.e., diversity, social inclusion and dispersal?

- Be aware of the 'tactical' orientation which often follows match funding against the longer-term 'strategic' outcomes that may be desired; and
- Identify and nurture the appropriate skill sets necessary to accommodate emergency action.

During the crisis, it is particularly important that those organisations and individuals responsible for the future development, management and marketing of London:

- Avoid an overly 'top down' approach to emergency action;
- Establish the degree to which emergency recovery is to be market (demand) led or supplier led;
- Identify and target campaigns to those markets able to return a quick return on investment while identifying and planning longer-term recovery for established markets;
- Communicate from the front line by rebuilding the destination brand through the private/public/consumer sectors.
- Communicate a consistent message to the media;
- Develop campaigns with suitable degrees of flexibility to accommodate changing circumstances as the emergency worsens, improves or takes a new direction;
- Evaluate and monitor consistently throughout the emergency period;
- Avoid the temptation to take individual corrective action in preference to collective partnership activity;
- Allow suitable flexibility between campaigns to facilitate corrective action if needed;
- Maintain the longer-term effectiveness of inter-organisational relationships;
- Maintain informal networks with other destination marketing organisations to monitor comparative campaigns; and
- Manage the media effectively at all times. Be proactive in your relationship with the media.

Once the crisis is deemed to be over, it is of paramount importance that continuous efforts are made to recover tourist confidence. In particular, the appropriate authorities ought to be in a position to:

- Communicate confidence in the destination;
- Evaluate security measures;
- Evaluate the success or otherwise of emergency action;
- Evaluate fully the organisational and structural arrangements for emergency action;
- Evaluate the longer-term implications of the emergency on the existing destination marketing strategy;
- Evaluate the longer-term implications of discount and value-led campaigns to the future marketing of the destination;
- Incorporate the experiences and views of the industry at large in developing a cohesive, inclusive tourism strategy for London post-emergency; and
- Re-visit the 'before the crisis' preparations.

CONCLUSION

Thursday 7 July 2005 saw an act of terrorism in the UK. With the activities of four suicide bombers occurring in Central London, 56 people were killed with over 700 sustaining injuries. In addition to the further failed bombing attack on Thursday 21 July 2005 London remains in a state of nervousness regarding level of security. As with all acts of terror, tourism is always impacted negatively and the challenge is for the authorities to minimise the negative impacts of such actions in the short, medium and longer term. According to Visit London's Visitor Attraction Monitor, visits to London museums during July declined on average by 17.8% while initial indications for August were that overall visits were projected to fall by 20-25% (Visit Britain, 2005). However, building on the success of TIRP as discussed throughout this paper and adherence to many of the guiding principles outlined in the preceding section, London is projected to record inbound tourism figures ahead of those recorded in 2004 with foreign visitor numbers and spending in the UK and London still expected to end at 3.5-4% higher than in 2004.

On the assumption that no further shocks occur, many of the collaborative marketing activities put in place as a consequence of the wider devolution of tourism in England and as a response to previous disasters, growth in inbound tourism is projected to increase (Visit Britain, 2005). Recent indicators from Visit London (2007) are positive in that overall visits from overseas are set to increase by 2.8% in 2007 while foreign visitor spending is set to increase by 3.4%. This is especially encouraging in view of the growth of 4.1% and 7.8% in 2006 with regard to overseas visitor arrivals and foreign visitor spend. Although not all of this success can be attributed to TIRP, a combination of each of the phases of activity, the original strategic framework developed in 2002, and more recent and continued investment in the 'destination' have all played their part in enhancing the appeal of London in the face of increasingly fierce competition from around the world.

Most importantly, however, to maintain and to build on its position in the world as a leading 'iconic' city destination London needs to continually develop its market and diversify its proposition. The theme of market development represents one of the four pillars of the Mayor of London's Tourism Strategy and has at its core four principal targets: the need to develop markets and reduce dependency on any one market; the need to explore and develop markets that will promote diverse and dispersed tourism business and expand the portfolio of London's offer; increase the appeal of London as a tourist destination while managing the costs of tourism and spreading the benefits to all London's communities; and, promote, support and actively develop London's role as the principal 'gateway' to the UK. If these four targets can be achieved then London stands an excellent chance of long-term, sustainable, recovery.

REFERENCES

Beirman, D. (2003). *Restoring Tourism Destinations in Crisis: A Strategic Marketing Approach*. Oxford: CABI Publishing.

Beeton, S. (2005). *The case study in tourism research: a multi-method case study approach*. In. B.W. Ritchie, P. Byrns, and C. Palmer. Tourism Research Methods: Integrating theory with practice. CABI Publishing. Wallingford.

Brent Ritchie, J.R. & Crouch, G.I. (2003). *The Competitive Destination: A Sustainable Tourism Perspective.* Oxford: CABI Publishing.

Blake, A. & Sinclair, M.T. (2003). Tourism crisis management: US response to September 11. *Annals of Tourism Research*, 30(4), 813-832.

Cassedy, K. (1991). *Crisis management planning in the travel and tourism industry: A study of three destinations and a crisis management planning manual.* San Francisco. PATA.

Creswell, J.W. (1998). *Qualitative inquiry and research design: Choosing among five traditions.* London. Sage Publications.

DCMS (2004). *Tomorrow's Tourism Today.* London: Department for Culture, Media and Sport.

Drabek, T.E. (1995). Disaster responses within the tourism industry. *International Journal of Mass Emergencies and Disasters*, 13(1), 7-23.

Fall, L.T. (2004). The increasing role of public relations as a crisis management function: An empirical examination of communication restrategising efforts among destination organisation managers in the wake of 11th September 2001. *Journal of Vacation Marketing*, 10(3), 238-252.

Faulkner, B. (2001). Towards a framework for tourism disaster management. *Tourism Management*, 22(2), 135-147.

Frisby, E. (2002). Communicating in a crisis. The British Tourist Authority's responses to the foot-and-mouth outbreak and 11th September, 2001. *Journal of Vacation Marketing*, 9(1), 89-100.

GLA Economics (2003a). *London's Economy Today.* Issue 9: May 2003. London: GLA Economics.

GLA Economics (2003b). *Impact of Gulf War or Terrorist Attack on London's Economy.* London: GLA Economics.

Glaesser, D. (2003). *Crisis Management in the Tourism Industry.* Oxford: Butterworth Heinemann.

Henderson, J. (2003). Communicating in a crisis: Flight SQ 006. *Tourism Management*, 24(3), 279-287.

Horlick-Jones, T., Fortune, J., and Peters, G. (1991). Measuring disaster trends part two: Statistics and underlying processes. *Disaster Management*, 4(1), 41-44.

Laws, E., Prideaux, B., and Chon, K. (2007). (Eds). Crisis management in tourism. CABI Publishing. Wallingford.

Mitroff, I.I. (1988). Crisis management: Cutting through the confusion. *Sloan Management Review* (Winter).

Mitroff, I.I. & Anagnos, G. (2001). *Managing Crises Before They Happen: What Every Executive and Manager Needs to Know about Crisis Management.* New York: Amacon.

Murphy, P.E., and Bayley, R. (1989). Tourism and disaster planning. *Geographical Review*, 79(1), 36-46.

Richardson, B. (1994). Crisis management and the management strategy; Time to 'loop the loop.' *Disaster Prevention and Management,* 5(5). 5-10.

Robson, C. (1993). *Real World Research.* Oxford. Blackwell.

de Sausmarez, N. (2004). Crisis management for the tourism sector: Preliminary considerations in policy development. *Tourism and Hospitality: Planning & Development*, 1(2), 157-172.

Visit Britain (2005). *Update from the Tourism Industry Emergency Response Group, 9 September 2005.* London: Visit Britain.

Visit London (2002). *The Mayor's Plan for Tourism in London.* London: Visit London.

Visit London (2004). *London Visitor Index, September 2004.* London: Visit London.

Visit London (2007). *Visit London: Prospects for 2006/07.* London: Visit London.

WTO (2003). *Crisis Guidelines for the Tourism Industry.* Madrid: World Tourism Organization.

Yin, R.K (1994). *Case study research: design and methods.* 2nd edition, Sage Publications, Thousand Oaks, California.

Young, W.B., and Montgomery, R.J. (1998). Crisis management and its impact of destination marketing: A guide to convention and visitors bureaus. *Journal of Convention and Exhibition Management*, 1(1), 3-18.

Understanding the Potential Impact on the Image of Canada as a Weekend Travel Destination as a Result of Western Hemisphere Travel Initiative Passport Requirements

Wayne W. Smith

Barbara A. Carmichael

Nicole M. Batovsky

SUMMARY. On April 5th, 2005 the US Departments of State and Homeland Security announced the Western Hemisphere Travel Initiative (WHTI) which will require Americans traveling to Canada to present a passport for re-entry into the USA. The Conference Board of Canada estimates that this legislation (for the years 2005-2008) will result in a loss of nearly 7.7 million trips and cost the Canadian tourism industry approximately $1.6 billion in lost revenues. The purpose of this study was to investigate how this change in legislation will affect southwestern Pennsylvania residents' perceptions and image of Canada and their propensity to visit Canada. A series of three focus groups designed to measure these impressions was conducted. The results indicate that successful mitigation strategy could reverse potential image issues as a result of the USA legislation.

INTRODUCTION

The events of September 11, 2001 and their repercussions on the travel industry of the United States and global travel patterns are yet to be fully analyzed (Beirman, 2003, p. 66) and continue to unfold. One major consequence was the increasing level of security measures along US borders in an attempt to more tightly control access by international travelers and re-

Wayne W. Smith (E-mail: smithww@cofc.edu) is Assistant Professor in the Department of Hospitality and Tourism Management at College of Charleston (Charleston, SC 29424-001, USA). Barbara A. Carmichael (E-mail: bcarmich@wlu.ca) is Associate Professor in the Department of Geography and Environmental Studies at Wilfrid Laurier University (Waterloo, ON, N2L3C5, Canada). Nicole M. Batovsky (E-mail: BAT7181@cup.edu) is Research Assistant at California University of Pennsylvania.

The authors would like to thank the Canadian Embassy and the Government of Canada for sponsoring this research.

turning residents. On April 5th 2005 the US Departments of State and Homeland Security announced the Western Hemisphere Travel Initiative (WHTI) which will require Americans traveling to Canada to present a passport for re-entry into the USA. The Conference Board of Canada (2005) estimates that this legislation (for the years 2005-2008) will result in a loss of nearly 7.7 million trips and cost the Canadian tourism industry approximately $1.6 billion in lost revenues (readers desiring more detailed background information on the Canadian Conference Board study are referred to the citation in the references). Beyond the fiscal damages, there could be a change in perception regarding Canada's position in relation to the United States. While this legislation is being enacted with safety in mind, it also presents tourism marketers with a new challenge. Tourism marketers are now presented with the challenge of how to inform potential visitors to Canada of the new legislation while still presenting the country as a safe, easily accessible destination.

In 2001, residents of Pennsylvania took over 705,000 trips to Canada staying over three million nights and spending approximately $393 million while visiting (Canadian Tourism Commission, 2002). The southwest portion of the state includes the Pittsburgh metropolitan area which has been identified by the Canadian Tourism Commission as one of their key United States market places. This area of Pennsylvania could be considered especially important given its relative distance to Canada. The region is considered by many to be outside the day trip zone (more than 500 Km) but close enough to travel to for a weekend or get-away trip. Will the enactment of the WHTI affect the travel decision-making process in regards to booking a weekend get-away in Niagara Falls given the added difficulty of having to possess passports?

The purpose of this study is to investigate how this change in legislation will affect southwestern Pennsylvania residents' perception of Canada (in relation to image and risk). The results of this study will not only provide insights into southwestern Pennsylvania's residents' perceptions and image of Canada as a leisure travel destination but also present recommendations as to ways to circumvent potential neg-

ative responses to visiting the country with the enactment of the WHTI.

DESTINATION CHOICE

Moutinho (1987) developed a model of tourism decision-making that is divided into three stages (pre-decision and decision process; post-purchase evaluation; future decision making). The first stage is based on the pre-purchase influences. Moutinho (1987), and later Teare (1994), defined the pre-decision process as 'the flow of events, from the tourist stimuli to the purchase decisions' (Moutinho, 1987, p. 39). In the case of the new passport legislation, the ability to choose Canada for weekend getaways by residents of southwestern Pennsylvania could be affected in two ways: (1) the legislation could provide a negative image of Canada as a less safe and secure destination for Americans; and (2) it could make a weekend getaway trip to Canada be perceived as being more difficult. The additional paperwork and expense may influence the potential traveler to make easier and cheaper choices. In total, the new legislation creates an image problem whereby choosing Canada as a weekend getaway destination becomes less attractive. Potential visitors have to negotiate through more cost and structural constraints, as well as being reminded about increased security measures at the border.

Decrop (2000), in an interpretation of Moutinho's (1987) model, argues that the preference structure can be split into three sub-fields (*stimulus filtration, attention and learning, choice criteria*). The first two sub-fields were labeled as *stimulus filtration* and *attention and learning* whereby individuals examine both internal and external information sources. *Choice criteria*, according to Decrop (2000), are then developed based on the alternatives that comprise the individual's evoked set. The evoked set as defined by Moutinho (1987), and later by Teare (1994), consists of the factors decided upon based on decisions made at the earliest levels pertaining to motives, perceived risk, environmental influences and personal inhibitors and are influenced by personality, lifestyle, attitude and family. They argue that the evoked set, combined with the learning conducted in the first two sub-fields, work in conjunction, creating the cognitive structure that allows for a decision to be made. Can a strategy whereby education about the WHTI legislation and incentives to address the potential concerns raised by it be used at this point to mitigate potential issues related to choosing Canada as a destination?

In 2001, Woodside and King presented a model where they explicitly state that travelers use heuristics or a decision-set to state priorities in their decisions related to trip taking. The model they developed however focuses on motivations as a primary driver in the creation of the heuristic or decision-set. Is this the case with international travel? In the context of this study, would those who have visited Canada previously, be less likely to develop a negative image or be more willing to obtain a passport based on their previous experiences visiting the country? Woodside and King (2001) while explicitly stating the process is hierarchical in nature, find that the hierarchy is not based on individual categorizations but groupings of categorizations. This is similar to Moutinho's (1987) concept of the 'evoked set.' Woodside and King (2001) go on to state that between categorizations, a hierarchy is taking place but within each a non-linear process is taking place. For instance, in Woodside and King's (2001) model demographics, reference group and marketing influences affect problem framing, information search strategies, heuristic frame working and

intentions. Where does the new legislation fit into the travel decision-making process? Is the fear of being hassled at the border or losing a passport and not being allowed to re-enter the United States a major component of the travel decision-making process? Is the expense in terms of both time and money a strong detriment to choosing a Canadian destination for a weekend get-away when one has a large base of choices among American destinations that do not require this outlay of resources?

In essence, where do the new requirements of the WHTI fall into the decision-making process? What are the interpretations of the legislation by potential visitors from the USA and how will these interpretations affect the decision-making process? Will this legislation cause American visitors to switch to destinations in the United States? These are the questions that will be addressed in this study.

IMAGE AND ITS RELATION TO DESTINATION CHOICE

As was described above, how decisions are made may be conceptualized using a series of hierarchical linkages and relationships. If a decision is illustrated in a conceptual framework, several linkages may be identified. In the case of this study, a linkage in which government policy affects existing destination image is possible (Figure 1). Both the government policy

FIGURE 1. Model of Government Policy Effects on Image

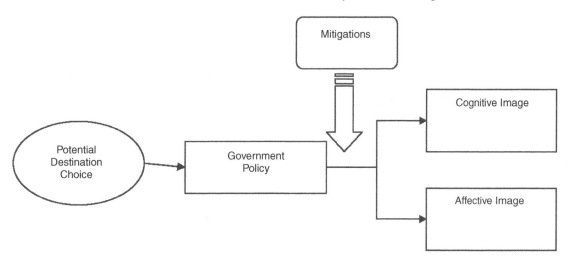

that is implemented as well as mitigation strategies as a reaction to that policy may affect tourist destination image. Image has tremendous power and it is often the image of a place rather than its actual characteristics that affects tourist decision-making (Carmichael, 1992). Ryan and Cave (2005) suggest that " the cognitive and affective skills possessed by humans impute values and feelings to images, so images are not always perceived as either neutral or devoid of evocative power" (p. 143).

Cognitive image can be described as being the logical perspective one develops regarding a potential product based on a variety of criteria (Schlosser & Shavitt, 1999). In a tourism context cognitive image typically relates to the resources needed to attract visitors to a destination (Echtner & Ritchie, 1991; Stabler, 1995; Beerrli & Martin, 2004). This view is focused on the motivations aspect of travel. There is however, a constraint component such as: price, accommodation availably, ease of access and time availability must also be considered. In the case of this study, the WHTI legislation may for instance increase the price accumulation of visiting Canada thus creating a negative cognitive image of the destination.

Affective image refers to emotional perspective one has related to image (Beerli & Martin, 2004). Typically, affective image research that delves into the emotional state is understudied in the tourism literature because it does not easily lend itself to quantitative analysis. This may be the result of the difficulty of modeling emotion and its resultant non-logical state of decision-making. For instance, Baloglu and McCleary (1999) attempted to quantify affective image

using factor and path analyses; however, their study results may have missed the undercurrents and the sometimes irrational nature of emotion-based decision-making. For instance, in this study does the new legislation create a sense of fear that Canada is a dangerous or unfriendly country to the USA? This perception is not necessarily based on fact but rather innuendo based on USA legislation.

In this study there is a need to understand what the possible image impacts are as a result of the changes in legislation. If as expected, there are negative image issues, the question that needs to be addressed is: what are the most effective ways to deal with these issues? What type of strategies could be put into place in order to address these issues early in the decision-making process and re-create a positive image or reverse one that is negative?

METHODOLOGY

To address the issue of how the WHTI passport initiative is perceived and affects the travel decision-making process, an in-depth research approach using three focus groups was used. These groups were stratified by those who have visited Canada and those who have considered Canada but those who have not visited Canada. Further, the groups were also stratified by age and gender (Table 1).

Recruitment for the focus groups was done using a randomized approach (please see the Appendix to view the screening questions). The recruiters began with a random letter in the 2006 southwestern Pennsylvania phone book.

TABLE 1. Proposed Stratification of Focus Groups

Focus Group	Number of Participants	Vacation Intentions	Gender	Age
One	10	5 had visited Canada	5 male	5 > 45 years
		5 had not visited Canada	5 female	5 < 45 years
Two	10	5 had visited Canada	5 male	5 > 45 years
		5 had not visited Canada	5 female	5 < 45 years
Three	10	5 had visited Canada	5 male	5 > 45 years
		5 had not visited Canada	5 female	5 < 45 years
Totals		**15 Have Visited**	**15 Males**	**15 > 45 years**
	30	**15 Have Not Visited**	**15 Females**	**15 < 45 years**

They were instructed to call the 10th name in that letter. After that phone contact, they were instructed to call a name in the next 'phone book' letter. They then called the 20th name on the page. Once this process was exhausted they began again with another randomized letter in the phone book. This process was continued until the focus groups were filled as closely to the stratification requirements as possible. The recruiters began each phone call with a series of screening questions. If the respondent met the screening requirements, they were invited to participate in the focus group. As an incentive for participating, $50.00 USD was offered. 12 participants were recruited for each focus group. If all 12 participants attended they were all used as part of the study. This methodological approach was designed to randomize the participants as much as possible within the proposed stratas.

The focus groups were held in three locales across southwestern Pennsylvania in May 2006. The focus groups were both audio taped as well as video recorded. All participants were made aware of this and of the confidentiality processes which were followed (i.e., that they were not be personally identified in anyway and that any direct quotes was only cited as a participant "letter"). Participants were required to sign a letter outlining that they have read and understand their confidentiality rights. The three focus groups lasted on average 53 minutes per focus group. The participants were asked a series of questions from an interview guide.

The focus group interview guide was designed using a 'systems theory' approach. Systems theory, according to Patton (1990), is concerned with how and why factors interact to form behaviour. He states that a systems approach requires 'synthetic' thinking in the design, implementation and analysis of the research questions. Synthetic thinking was defined by Gharajedaghi and Ackhoff (1985) as the process of revealing why a systems works as it does but not necessarily how it does. Synthetic thinking takes a system and disaggregates it in an attempt to reveal each elements role or function in the system as a whole (Gharajedaghi & Ackhoff, 1985). By using this approach, analysis and synthesis are complimentary.

The focus group guide was divided into three sections. In section one the groups were asked the following questions:

Q1. Say for instance you have a chance to go away for a weekend. What is the first thing you look for when choosing a destination?
Q2. What features do you look for in a weekend get-a-way destination?
Q3. How would you rank these from most important to least important?
    Q3a. Ask why people feel certain items are more of less important.

These questions were designed to gain an overall understanding of the participants' weekend getaway preferences. Probing questions, when appropriate, were asked in order to gain greater detail.

Section two of the focus group then shifted to questions regarding Canada and the participants' perceptions of the country.

Q4. How many of you have been to Canada?
Q5. For those of you who have not been to Canada, what do you think of when it is mentioned?
Q6. For those of you who have been to Canada, how would you describe it to your friends?
Q7. How would you describe Canada in relation to the United States?

Finally, in section three questions related specifically to the WHTI initiative were asked.

Q8. What forms of ID are required to enter Canada from the United States?
Q9. How many of you know that the USA government is putting stricter regulations on the ID requirements for Americans re-entering the USA from Canada?
Q10. Do you know that those requirements will be?
    Q10a. Does this change in legislation change your perception of Canada at all?
    Q10b. How likely would these new requirements lead to you choose a destination within the USA?

Q11.   How do you feel Canadian tourism officials should inform Americans about the new ID requirements?

Q12.   How many of you possess a passport?

Q12a. For those of you who do not, would needing a passport or another special form of ID affect your ability to choose Canada for a weekend get-a-way?

Q12b. For those of you who said yes, what kind of incentive would you need to overcome this perspective?

Q13.   Does anyone have any thoughts that they would like to add to this discussion regarding how the new ID requirements are going to affect residents of the areas willingness to travel to Canada?

These questions were designed to get an overall impression of the legislation and what the participants felt the impact that this legislation would be upon their ability to choose Canada as a weekend getaway destination.

After the focus groups were conducted, a transcription of the proceedings was developed. The data was then coded through the in-vivo process as described by Huberman and Miles (1994). In this process the research began by open coding whereby the researcher examined the field notes and transcripts for each interview looking for 'fractures' in the data which identified key categories. The process then went into a 2nd phase where more in-vivo coding took place where specific words and phrases are identified as being part of a categorization. Finally, core categorizations were developed so that themes may be explored. This purpose of this phase was to examine the system in a manner that reduces it to an understandable set, while retaining the depth of qualitative inquiry (Huberman & Miles, 1994).

RESULTS

Thirty-one respondents participated in the focus groups (Table 2). Additionally to the initial quotas of the 31 respondents, 9 currently possessed passports while 22 did not. As of May 2006, focus group members generally had a positive image of Canada. In all of the focus groups, Canada was described as a destination that is clean, has friendly people and is multi-cultural. When asked about the destination they would most like to visit in Canada, 26 of the 31 focus group participants stated Niagara Falls. This response was expected due to the geographical proximity to Niagara Falls and the marketing focus the destination has on the region.

In general, the focus group participants when planning a weekend getaway considered a balance of experiences available at the destination versus that of price. It must be noted however, that due to rising gas prices the majority of focus group members are becoming increasingly price sensitive. As illustrated in this selection of quotes from focus group three, cost is becoming increasingly important:

> Moderator: . . . So if you're going through and you're trying to pick a weekend place, what would be the top three things you would look for in a place?. . .
>
> J: Expenses. Yeah, gas prices, how far I have to travel, if I have the gas money.
>
> K: Cost would be the first thing, if I could afford it. Second would be location, how close by it was. If we decide to go further would we have the time?
>
> A: I think cost would be my first concern, and then the quality of the experience. Someplace that I really want to go.
>
> D: Kind of the same thing, making the best choice for your money's worth. If it has enough entertainment that you're going to enjoy yourself for the money you are putting out.

Overall, the groups felt that this legislation would affect their ability to choose Canada as a destination. In each group it was asked how many individuals would think twice about visiting Canada and 23 stated that it would have a negative effect. All those who did not currently have a passport stated that this would be an issue especially for a weekend getaway trip. For instance in group two, the following group discussion arose:

> Moderator: Ok. Think about your friends and people in the southwestern Pennsyl-

TABLE 2. Stratification of Focus Groups

Focus Group	Number of Participants	Vacation Intentions	Gender	Age
One	8	5 had visited Canada	3 male	6 > 45 years
		3 had not visited Canada	5 female	2 < 45 years
Two	10	5 had visited Canada	7 male	6 > 45 years
		5 had not visited Canada	3 female	4 < 45 years
Three	13	5 had visited Canada	4 male	4 > 45 years
		7 had not visited Canada	9 female	9 < 45 years
Totals		**15 Have Visited**	**14 Males**	**16 > 45 years**
	31	**16 Have Not Visited**	**17 Females**	**15 < 45 years**

vania area. The requirement to have a passport, do you think that it will stop a lot of people from going to visit Canada?

B: I think that it would. I think that people are going to be more likely to stay in the United States.

T: The money that you would have to spend on a passport would be extra money to spend in another place.

R: My family doesn't always know what we're going to do, and since we don't have passports, that would eliminate Canada as an option.

P: Between the added expense of a passport and the gas prices, I think that it will really hurt them.

These findings are consistent with of the Conference Board of Canada (2005) whose research indicated that USA overnight pleasure travelers traveling to by car were the most likely of all types of travelers to choose other destinations if the legislation was enacted. As is illustrated in that discussion, this is a complex issue and affects the decision-making process in many ways. It is also not necessarily considered in isolation but adds a perceived layer of complexity to the decision that many consumers do not want to have to consider. This in turn, can be described as creating a negative image of the destination.

Image as described previously can be divided into two theoretical bases: (1) affective, and (2) cognitive. The results of these focus groups revealed that both types of image could be negative affected by the proposed legislation. In terms of affective image, perceptions related to increased hassle, a perceived diminishing ability to travel spontaneously and the perception of having to accommodate others all were illustrated clearly during the focus group sessions. Hassle was illustrated in two ways during the focus groups. The first was related to anxiety over crossing the border itself:

G: . . . Every time I go they get stricter and stricter. The last time I went, I needed more identification than I did before . . . It's almost like the U.S. is using Canada as a threat.

D: I remember though we did get stopped, and they searched our vehicles. I know we showed them [my] driver's license. It was very uncomfortable.

Second, there was the issue related to getting the passport itself and the fact that it reduces the ability for spontaneity in travel. Concerns were raised about the paper work and the time needed to get the passport as illustrated in these quotations from the focus groups.

D: It would bother me. I'd have to take time out to get a passport and wait for a passport and all that crap. It's just a hassle.

A: I think that it would be the majority probably won't bother to get them. We like to be spontaneous, and if we need a passport, something like that takes 4-6 weeks to get.

M: It's just a hassle. You're going to have to have more advanced planning to leave time to apply for a passport.

Finally, concerns were raised about related to travel partners' needs.

J: Well, I have a passport, but it's still going to affect me because a lot of my friends don't have passports, and there's going to be no one to go with.

If the legislation is to be enacted there will need to be policies that create the perception that the passport process is easy and timely. There is also going to be the need to educate Americans on how passports make border-crossings easier and protects both the country of origin and the destination country. Finally, there is going to be a need to develop a program where American travelers who have passports encourage those who do not to get one.

As for affects on cognitive image, the most ready examples include factors related to increased cost and time requirements. In terms of cost, the increased expenditure is not perceived as an investment by the members of the groups but rather an add-on price to the trip as illustrated in this exchange from focus group three:

Moderator: Ok, with this new requiring of a passport, it has been raised to about $80. It is good for 10 years. How many of you would say that this new legislation would impact your decision to go ahead and go to Canada for a weekend? Just a show of hands quickly. 1, 2, 3, 4, 5, 6, 7, 8. Ok. Why would you say so?

A: Money issues, especially with children.

J: Money

P2: I was just gonna say if you go there once or twice, you have to spend $80 just for a couple days. People who go on bus trips usually go for a couple of days, so that's $80 for about three days.

P1: It's just another added expense to the gas prices and everything else.

D: If you're talking about a family of four, that's a big chunk of change right up front.

The effects of cost were further illustrated during group one in this exchange:

Moderator: So basically, if you think about these new requirements, do you think that would affect people's desire to go to Canada? Would having to pay the extra money for a passport affect your decision about whether or not to go to Canada?

A: You can go somewhere else and have a similar experience without having to pay all that extra money for a passport.

T: The money that you would have to spend on a passport would be extra money to spend in another place.

In terms of time requirements, it is not just related to spontaneity which is an emotional response but also to the actual time required to fill out the paper work required in order to apply for a passport. This was illustrated in the following quote from group two:

T: Buying for yourself is one thing, but it's different to buy for a whole family. Buy it before and not spend that much on one trip. Plus it is the hassle of getting the whole family together to get pictures taken, finding everyone's ID and then filling out all the forms for each person. It is very time consuming and quite annoying to have to pay that much for that much hassle.

With the increasing costs of travel (gas prices, etc.) adding another perceived large expense to the cost of a trip will leave Canada at a disadvantage over the competition. Added to that the time requirements of filling out the paper work and getting pictures taken and the process itself can become a constraint to choosing Canada as a destination. As will be discussed later on however, if these image issues can be addressed, the effects this legislation could be mitigated.

In each focus group a series of questions related to mitigation strategies were posed. The results of the focus groups indicate in terms of mitigations that first the new travel requirements under the WHTI legislation has to be communicated to the traveling public in a manner that is non-threatening. Secondly, a mitigation strategy in which incentives are offered to offset the cost (in both relation to time and resources) has to be put into place.

In addressing the issue relating to communicating the new legislation to the public, those who participated in the focus group were mixed as to whose responsibility it was. In focus group one, this exchange illustrated the typical response:

> Moderator: Do you think it's Canada's responsibility to tell American's about this new legislation?

> M: Yeah, I think just something little like yeah, we want you to come, but just so you know, you're going to need a passport to get back in.

> F: No, I don't agree with that. I feel if it's America's legislation, then it's their responsibility.

There was agreement however, that the Canadian tourism industry has to address the issue. This quote from focus group two best illustrates the need for education related to the legislation by the Canadian tourism industry:

> G: I don't read fine print. I'm dumb like that. It gets me into trouble. Before you register for a hotel or something, if you click on something for Canada, you should get something that comes up before you can even go there. How many Americans go to Canada and European countries?

How to approach the message can be contentious as illustrated by this exchange from focus group two:

> Moderator: Alright. In terms of getting a passport and working through it, do you see anything in terms of what the Cana-

dian tourism industry can do to really encourage people to come to Canada and maybe choose Canada over another destination? Should it be on the TV commercials that are playing in this area?

> T: Maybe advertise a package deal, stating that the new passport is in effect.

> G: I go with comedy. If I saw a commercial that says come to Canada, we're not in Iraq it'd make me laugh.

> P: It shouldn't be serious.

> B: Humor is good.

> T: I don't think so. It's a new law. If you use humor, people won't know if it's a serious thing or a joke.

The approach to the message in almost all of the groups was divided by gender. Males typically wanted a more humorous approach while females tended to believe that a more serious approach was warranted. However, there was general agreement the currently there is a lot of confusion around what was going on with the legislation in general as outlined in the following quote from focus group one:

> D: Canadian tourism officials can ease the mind of travelers by having a task bar addressing the issue on their Websites. There's a lot of confusion about the time frame and when this is going to be in effect.

In terms of which medium to use to get the message out, all of the traditional media were mentioned. Of special note however, was the role the Internet was deemed to have. In all three groups, it was generally agreed that the Internet was the best way to inform potential visitors of the legislation. Of the 31 focus group participants, 29 of them used the Web as part of their trip planning. What was disagreed upon, however, was what the best method to present the information was, best illustrated in the following exchange from group two:

> T: It should definitely be on there somewhere saying important message you now

need a passport. Maybe somewhere at the bottom.

B: It should be on the first page. You may have to click on it to read it, but it should be right on the first page.

R: There should be a link somewhere on the page.

G: Yeah, on the homepage.

P: There should be a link on there about where you can get a passport.

Of the 31 focus group participants 30 of them felt that Canada should develop an incentive for Americans to get passports. Generally, the groups agreed that this was not really a security issue. There was general agreement that this is the way the United States was post 9-11 and they did not see Canada as being any more of a threat as a result of the WHTI legislation. This exchange from focus group three was typically of the feeling towards the legislation:

Moderator: . . . Now does this regulation change your perception of Canada at all? Does it make it seem unsafe? Does it change at all?

Group: No.

Moderator: No? So why would you say this law needs to be enacted?

A1: 9-11

A2: We have that kid of mind set right now.

H: It's kind of a knee jerk reaction; I think you know you got to protect the borders. You can come from the south all you want.

Generally the groups agreed that this was more of an economic issue that may prevent them from visiting Canada. As was eloquently stated by a focus group two member:

M: It is a financial issue; therefore, discount packages would be an incentive to travel to Canada or getting a passport cheaper.

In total, 30 of the 31 focus group participants felt that Canada should offer some sort of incentive to get Americans to get their passports and visit the country. What the incentive should entail however, was debated thoroughly in all three groups. An example of this debate came from group two:

Moderator: . . . Ok, so what kind of incentive do you think the Canadian tourism could use to get you to get a passport?

T: Buy a room for a night and get one free.

G: I used to work for a ski lift, and if you showed them your airline ticket, you got a free ski lift ticket. The first time you come there and show them your passport, they scan it, and there needs to be some kind of incentive for like a park or a hotel.

P: Everyone is different though so you can't make it just one thing.

N: Yeah, just something that acknowledges and says thank you.

S: I agree.

P: Well, it has to be something worth it, not a little souvenir.

G: It shouldn't break the Canadian tourism industry because America changed their legislation either. Just something little like a $50 ski lift.

Recommendations from the groups also included: coupon books (which was mentioned in two groups); casino chips (for Niagara Falls); discount travel packages (get a percentage off if you show your passport receipt); and cash back options. For instance, at present USA visitors can apply to get a Canadian Goods and Services Tax rebate at the border; this program could be extended to include a passport rebate. While these incentives do seem like an expensive proposition, focus group participants in all groups stated that if they were to get a passport, they would use it more frequently to 'get their monies worth' and that having a passport would keep visiting Canada as a 'top of mind' option.

DISCUSSION

Image and Decision Making

This research focused on the pre-decision phase and the influence of the external political environment on the image of the destination of Canada for potential travelers from the nearby U.S. state of Pennsylvania. As the focus groups occurred, ideas emerged about the importance of the WHTI legislation to Canada's image and the propensity to travel to Canada. While the responses were mixed, many concerns were expressed related to the additional cost of travel and the uncertainty over the implementation and timing of the new legislation. The model presented in Figure 1 illustrated an opportunity to correct a negative image through presenting alternative mitigation strategies. In order to do so however, there needs to be a clear understanding of what the negative image issues are in order to create and implement successful mitigation strategies. In this study, the focus groups revealed that this legislation is not necessarily viewed as a security concern related to Canada but rather is viewed as an issue related to additional expense and hassle in terms of getting a passport. Given this, any mitigation strategy employed should focus upon alleviating those financial and inconvenience issues. Suggestions from the focus groups suggest that the participants would welcome different forms of discount incentives or rebates. From what seems to be a negative situation for the Canadian tourism industry, there may be an unrealized opportunity to use this legislation as a catalyst to develop a loyalty program.

Canadian Marketing Competitiveness

Canadian tourism marketing response to the WHTI could change its destination marketing competitiveness relative to other markets affected by WHTI. By the time the legislation is fully implemented on December 31 2007, the WHTI will require that all travelers between

United States, Canada, Mexico, the Caribbean and Bermuda carry passports. The response by the Caribbean nations is ready to be announced in an Internet based incentive that enhances the Caribbean image and eases the costs for travel. Already there is an awareness campaign in place in which Caribbean advertisements are stamped in the corner with a message that says passports will soon be required. Campaign details are Web accessible at http://www.onecaribbean. org/information/categorybrowse.php?categoryid= 759. (accessed July 27th 2006). Passports will be paid for by the Caribbean countries when American book trips to these locations (as yet restricted information on the Web resource but revealed by Wallace, 2006, keynote speaker). Approximately 30% of Americans currently possess passports and costs per passport are likely to be about $100. The initiative of paying for passports would amount to merely giving a $100 discount per first time visit with a passport but would bring much in the way of customer relations benefits. As yet, the Canadian Tourism Commission has not announced a similar policy.

The Canadian market from the U.S. in 2005 suffered a decline, especially in the short haul market (Shifflet & Associates, 2006 p.1), This may be the result of the cumulative effects of multiple barriers (exchange rate, border hassles, document requirements, price of gas) and may be giving rise to an "is it worth it" perception (p. 3). For the non previous visitors to Canada, "cost" was cited as a factor in four of the five barriers to travel to Canada: cost of air transportation, cost of hotels, while be perceived as not being good value for money, while also having an unfavorable exchange rate (p. 3). Adding the additional cost of passport purchase will only reinforce this perception, suggesting the urgent need for the implementation of mitigation strategies. Research on the American market by Roper Reports 2004, indicates that while 55% of respondents were budget conscious, 43% said they were willing to pay for quality (Roper Report, 2004 cited in Canadian Tourism Commission, 2005). Canadians are responding by focusing their marketing efforts on quality experiences for the elite market (skiing, fly-in fishing, gay-lesbian friendly destinations), while tending to ignore the "cost" concerns of some of the traditional short haul market. As was revealed during the focus group sessions, some were very price sensitive citing "cost" as a barrier to travel. For others there was a perception that the money paid for a passport would be better spent on the trip itself. Also, given the spontaneous nature of a weekend getaway, most focus group participants stated they would just choose another destination in the United States.

What should not be forgotten, however, was that if the focus group participants who did not have a passport did follow through and get them, they would be more likely to travel to Canada in order to 'get their money's worth.' This indicates that a potentially negative situation, if addressed properly could lead to an opportunity to develop customer loyalty.

CONCLUSION

Terrorist attacks with the magnitude and directness of those that took place on September 11, 2001 are disasters that have far reaching effects. According to Prideaux et al. (2003), "disaster are unpredictable catastrophic change that can normally only be responded to after the event, either by deploying contingency plans already in place or through a reactive response." The WHTI is an example of a far reaching "reactive response" that is part of what Turner refers to as the sixth stage of a crisis labeled "full cultural readjustment." In this stage, "an inquiry or assessment is carried out and beliefs and precautionary norms are adjusted to fit the newly gained understanding of the world" (Turner, 1976, p. 381).

When such new understandings lead to changes in legislation, the tourism industry must continue to adjust to new market realities in the tourism system. Indeed, market turbulence as a result of legislative change influences existing patterns and creates new barriers and opportunities. As observed by Scott and Laws (2005), focusing on a system perspective is useful because it includes the idea of system resilience, changes of system states, and the fact that disasters are one way for a system to change. The outcome of a disaster does not necessarily mean a return to a "normal state" as experienced before a disaster, rather there is likely to be a change of state to reflect the new realities in terms of perceived risks, barriers and opportunities to travel.

One negative effect of changes and dislocations in a political legislative environment is uncertainty. Implementing the change in WHTI legislation using a three stage phased-in approach is already leading to visitor confusion and uncertainty and may curtail cross border travel (Canadian Tourism Commission, 2005). As was stated by several participants in the focus groups, there is confusion related to the legislation in terms of what ID will now be required, when it is to be implemented and how it will affect their visitor experience. Perhaps most telling, focus group members did not perceive this legislation as something that would enhance border security but rather viewed this as an additional expense and barrier in relation to visiting Canada.

Overall, the results of these focus groups revealed that potential visitors will view this legislation as a serious barrier to visiting Canada. While the WHTI is American legislation, the responsibility for its 'fall out' rests on the Canadian government and tourism industry. If the Canadian tourism industry in conjunction with the Canadian government does not develop and employ successful mediation strategies in response to this legislation, a negative image of visiting Canada will be perceived and preclude many from choosing it as a destination. It seems, however, that at least as of November 2006, the Canadian response is merely to focus on the potential of the high-end U.S. market (Tourism Staff, 2006). Members of this group tend to already have passports, so the passport issue can be effectively ignored for this target group. Nevertheless, this group is difficult to attract and retain for repeat business, unlike the more easily accessible and perhaps more consistent rubber tire market from nearby border-states.

REFERENCES

Balogu, S. & McCleary, K.W. (1999). A model of destination image formation. *Annals of Tourism Research, 26(4),* 868-897.

Beerli, A. & Martin, J.D. (2004). Tourists' characteristics and the perceived image of tourist destinations:

A quantitative analysis–a case study of Lanzarote, Spain. *Tourism Management, 25 (4),* 623-636.

Beirman, D. (2003). *Restoring Tourism Destinations in Crisis A Strategic Marketing Approach* Wallingford Oxon: CABI International.

Canadian Tourism Commission (2002). *Canadian Tourism Fact & Figures 2001.* [Available Online: Last Retrieved: September 2005] http://www.canadatourism.com/ctx/files/Research_Files/F_F_Brochure2001.pdf.

Canadian Tourism Commission (2005). The Long Road from Surviving to Thriving. *CTC Tourism Intelligence Bulletin*–Issue 27, May, 19 pages.

Carmichael, B.A. (1992). Using conjoint modeling to measure tourist image and analyze ski resort choice. In P. Johnson and B. Thomas (eds.) *Choice and Demand in Tourism.* 93-106, Mansell Press: Harlow, UK.

Conference Board of Canada (2005). *The Potential Impact of the Western Hemisphere Travel Initiative Passport Requirement on Canada's Tourism Industry.* Ottawa: Canadian Tourism Commission.

Decrop, A. (2000). Tourists' decision-making and behavior processes. In. A Pizam and Y. Mansfeld Eds. *Consumer Behavior in Travel and Tourism.* New York: The Haworth Hospitality Press. 56-75.

Echtner, C.M. & Ritchie, J.R.B. (1991). The meaning and measurement of tourist image. *The Journal of Tourism Studies, 2(2),* 2-12.

Goodale, T.L. & Witt, P.A. (1989). Recreation non-participation and barriers to leisure. In E.L. Jackson and T.L. Burton Eds. *Understanding Leisure and Recreation: Mapping the Past, Charting the Future,* 421-449. State College PA: Venture.

Gharajedaghi, J & Ackoff, R.L. (1985). Toward systemic education of system scientists. *Systems Research, 2,* 21-27.

Huberman, A.M. & Miles, M.B. (1994). Data management and analysis methods. In N.K. Dezen and Y.S. Lincon Eds. *Handbook of Qualitative Research,* 428-444. Thousand Oaks CA: Sage.

Moutinho, L. (1987). Consumer behaviour in tourism. *European Journal of Marketing, 21,* 2-44.

Patton M.Q. (1990). *Qualitative Evaluation and Research Methods 3rd Edition.* London: Sage.

Prideaux, B., Laws, E. & Faulkner, B. (2003). Events in Indonesia: exploring the limits to formal tourism trends forecasting methods in complex crisis situations. *Tourism Management, 24*(4), 511-520.

Ryan, C., & Cave, J. (2005). Structuring destination image: A qualitative approach. *Journal of Travel Research, 44,* 143-150.

Schlosser, A., & Shavitt, S. (1999). Effects of an approaching group discussion on product responses. *Journal of Consumer Psychology, 8*(4), 377-406.

Scott, N. & Laws, E. (2005). Tourism crises and disasters: enhancing understanding of systems effects. *Journal of Travel and Tourism Marketing, 19* (2/3), 149-158.

Shifflet, D.K. & Associates (2006). Changing US Travel Trends to Canada Executive Summary of the US Task Force Research. Ottawa, Canada: Canadian Tourism Commission.

Stabler, M.J. (1995). The image of destination regions: Theoretical and empirical aspects. In B.Goodall & G. Ashworth (Eds). *Marketing in the Tourism Industry: The Promotion of Destination Regions.* 133-159. London: Sage.

Teare, R. (1994). Consumer decision-making. In R. Teare, J.A. Mazanec, S. Crawford-Welsh and S. Calver. Eds. *Marketing in Hospitality and Tourism: A Consumer Focus* 1-96. London: Cassell.

Tourism Staff. (2006). WHTI will change how we do business. *Tourism Magazine, 3*(11) [Available Online: Last Retrieved: December 2006] http://www.canadatourism.com/ctx/app/en/ca/magazine/article.do?path=templatedata\ctx\magArticle\data\en\2006\issue11\news_and_opinion\whti

Turner, B.A. (1976). The organizational and inter-organizational development of disasters. *Administrative Science Quarterly, 21,* 378-397.

Wallace, Vincent Vanderpool, (2006), Secretary General of The Caribbean Tourism Organization, Keynote Speaker at TTRA International Conference, Dublin, Ireland, June 18-20th 2006.

Woodside, A.G. & King, R.I. (2001). An updated version of travel and tourism purchase-consumption systems. *Journal of Travel and Tourism Marketing, 10,* 3-27.

APPENDIX. Recruiting Script and Screener

Script for Pre-screen Telephone Interview
Canada Border Vacation Focus Group

Good morning/afternoon/evening, My name is _____ and I am a student at California University of Pennsylvania. As part of some research that the Tourism Program is conducting, we are looking for people who would be interested in helping us by participating in a focus group. It will only take one hour of your time, and you will receive $40.00 honorarium for participating.

The sessions are taking place at _____ on _____ and are about travel.

Would you be interested in finding out if you qualify to participate?

I have __ questions that I need to ask you because we are trying to ensure that we have a wide variety of people from all walks of life attending our sessions.

1. Have you traveled for business or pleasure in the past 2 years or plan to travel in the next 2 years?
    Y   N (Thank and terminate)

2. Have you traveled outside of the United States?   Y   N

3. Have you traveled to Canada?   Y   N
    (watch Quotas for groups)

4. Are you considering a trip to Canada in the next 2 years? Y   N
    (watch Quotas for groups)

5. May I ask your age? _____ (Watch quotas for age ranges)

6. Are you single or in a committed relationship?   single   relationship
    (watch quotos)

7. May I ask your occupation? _____

8. May I ask your spouse's occupation? _____

    For 7 & 8, thank and terminate if occupation is related to Travel, Hospitality, Marketing, Market Research, Advertising, Public Relations

If they qualify, read the following:

You are eligible to participate in our research study, being conducted on _____ from ____ to ____ at _____.

Branding Post-Conflict Destinations: Recreating Montenegro After the Disintegration of Yugoslavia

Andriela Vitic
Greg Ringer

SUMMARY. This paper examines the challenges and opportunities of promoting Montenegro as a destination for sustainable tourism in the post-civil war era of the former Yugoslavia, given the country's unique status as the world's only self-proclaimed "ecological state." There is no denying the recent history of ethnic violence and turmoil that divided the Balkans in the 1990s. Consequently, the incremental return of foreign and domestic visitors to Montenegro, as well as Serbia, Croatia, Slovenia, Macedonia, and Bosnia-Herzegovina, represents a significant return to stability almost ten years after the fighting stopped. And the particular interest of many tourists in the biology and cultural geography of the region makes clear the potential usefulness of "green" branding for Montenegro to distinguish itself from its competitors in the Mediterranean, and to resurrect the country's political image and visitor appeal through targeted environmental practices and promotions.

The ability to embellish its "eco" credentials and image through complementary partnerships and policies that sustain both tourism and the nation's economy would allow Montenegro to strategically and successfully position itself in the Adriatic travel market over the long term. Collaborative management and branding of World Heritage sites and transboundary parks for sustainable tourism will also enable Montenegro, and its former allies and foes, to restore the social and biological integrity and connectivity of a shared landscape severely degraded by a decade of war. In this manner, tourism can be a critical catalyst in overcoming the negative imagery and distrust which still impedes the Balkans' ability to achieve greater political integration and prosperity in an increasingly unified Europe.

INTRODUCTION

Among the many roles that tourism plays, perhaps the most important are the opportunity for visitors to experience significant change in their beliefs as a result of direct interaction with people from other places and cultures, and the ability to effectuate meaningful societal change,

Andriela Vitic is affiliated with the Faculty of Tourism & Hotel Management, Kotor University of Montenegro. Greg Ringer is affiliated with the International Studies Program University of Oregon, USA and Resource Recreation & Tourism Program University of Northern British Columbia, Canada.

by de-constructing social stereotypes that often mislead residents and visitors. Whether these transitions occur–and the extent to which they are meaningful for participants–depends on a number of factors applied by tourists when selecting a destination, including the range of available entertainment and leisure activities; the comfort and quality of existing accommodations and transportation; the adequacy of the visual scenery and the authenticity of local cultural practices and history; the level of personal risk from disease or threats of terrorism; and the accuracy of information provided visitors beforehand.

In spite of the probable challenges, or perhaps because of them, tourism has reputedly become one of the world's largest–and perhaps the most significant–industries in the post-World War II period, in terms of total employment, land use, and socioeconomic spending. Spurred by increases in personal income levels, more flexible working hours and greater leisure time, along with greater access to affordable transportation and information technology options (such as budget airlines, multi-country train passes, and the Internet), more people now travel both domestically and internationally. Credited by its proponents with poverty alleviation and long-term job creation, an ever-growing list of countries and communities now market themselves worldwide as tourist destinations in hopes of sharing in the profits of global travel, while offering a growing array of options for the travel consumer in activities and facilities (Louillet, 2005).

To help the visitor choose from among the many recreational choices, destination branding has become a strategic marketing component with considerable importance in promoting the (re)discovery of tourism destinations severely impacted by global crises, including war, genocide, ethnic and political conflict, disease, poverty, and international terrorism in the post-9/11 world. In these communities, it is a critical tool in resurrecting international travel to countries that seek social security and economic recovery through tourism, and must rely upon a uniquely identifiable brand attraction and targeted visitor niche in the initial stages of market development and recovery.

The importance of this marketing tool is especially apparent to the former republics of the Soviet Union and those of Yugoslavia (Figure 1). While significant challenges admittedly confront the foreign traveler in any newly independent state, perhaps the most pervasive–and disruptive to tourism's revival in the Balkan states–are the dated, and often inaccurate, misperceptions and images of the civil wars and ethnic barriers that prevailed throughout the 1980s and early 1990s, yet still define the region for many international visitors and tour operators (Prentice, 2003).

> Positive brand images have helped several economies boost their exports and attract investments, businesses, factories, visitors, residents and talented people. On the other hand, an uncountable number of places are unfamiliar to consumers or suffer image problems that impair their ability to compete in the marketplace. In some cases, these images are based on inaccurate information or widespread stereotypes recurrently reinforced by the media and the entertainment industry. In other instances, these images are founded on past episodes of political unrest, natural disasters, violence, and economic downturns. Place images may be clouded by these occurrences much longer than it would take to overcome or correct the problems.
>
> Brand management seems to be particularly challenging for emerging, newly industrialized, and transitional nations, including those that have shifted from socialist to free market economic systems. Unfortunately, these experiences are pervasive and afflict myriad places spanning the various regions of the world, such as Latin America, Eastern Europe, Africa, and Asia. While a few places have succeeded in overcoming their image problems and enhancing the equity of their brand names, others still struggle to do so. (Gertner, 2007: 4)

Whether the newly independent countries of the Balkans will effectively move beyond their histories of violence and succeed in es-

FIGURE 1. Montenegro and the Balkans (Source: Greg Ringer, 2006).

tablishing successful, sustainable tourism industries, depends greatly on the degree to which all participants are fully and collaboratively engaged in the branding process–an option that remains problematic for economies and political systems still in transition from socialism and the terrorism of war to tourism. Nonetheless, the Republic of Montenegro has made tourism its priority for social and economic recovery in the post-conflct period, and a strong destination brand is critical if Montenegro is to successfully reposition itself in the world travel market (Ringer, 2004).

DESTINATION BRANDING: THEORY AND PRACTICE IN THE BALKANS

Simply defined, a brand is "a name, term, sign, symbol, or design, or combination of them intended to identify the goods and services of one seller or group of sellers and to differentiate them from those of the competition" (Kotler and Gertner, 2002: 4-5). When applied to a geographic place, a destination brand may therefore comprise a specific recreational image intended to influence visitor perceptions, and an identity that arguably reflects the prevailing views and values of local users and inhabitants. Whatever its individual features, a destination brand is considered one of the most important tools in international travel when differentiating locally available tourism products and services–and a process increasingly complicated by globalization and the Internet (Graburn, 1995; Anholt, 2006).

The proliferation and intensity of these promotional efforts at the local and national levels, as well as the dissimilar results witnessed by competing attractions in visitor totals and investments in the necessary infrastructure and training, reflect the influential role that destination branding can play in differentiating–and profiting–select emergent tourism venues. No longer only an option for local businesses to consider as they search for a global market and recognizable identity, it is now a fundamental requirement for countries who seek to move beyond the conflicts of previous decades through improved communication, trade, and the promotion of international travel.

The creation of a national icon is particularly useful in reinforcing legitimate social practices in the state, and in fostering support for targeted investment policies, such as the establishment of appropriate markets, partners, services, and standards for tourism. In this context, a destination brand is intended to generate greater visitation in terms of numbers or specific visitor segments by highlighting proximate leisure activities through descriptive themes and identities. By so doing, adjacent tourist locations are distinguished through social construction and recognition of each place, its people, and its associated attractions.

> The development of themed (or branded) environments ... generally goes beyond [the] de-differentiation of spaces, functions, styles and symbolisms and the deliberate blurring of the real with the artificial and the imaginary. It rests on the effectiveness of the idea of 'invented' landscapes and places and aims at creating contemporary wonderlands of selective nostalgia and pseudo-idealistic visionary. (Terkenli, 2006: 11).

Thus, the U.S. state of Hawaii aggressively promotes itself as a tropical "paradise" for Pacific tourists willing to incur the additional expense to fly to the islands, while Ireland emphasizes its reputation as a "country of honest people" for visitors concerned about crime and terror threats elsewhere in Europe. Even Bosnia-Herzegovina promotes the sale of souvenirs from the Yugoslavian civil war to capitalize on its own history of ethnic conflict (Kotler & Armstrong, 2001). Through similar brand identities, destinations worldwide seek to reassure consumers that they will experience the promised quality, value, and security, should they select the preferred facility or location.

The equity of this brand–blending a country's traditions, history, and physiography–is perhaps best determined, however, by the extent to which travelers are cognizant of the trademark and share a sense of loyalty, and a willingness to financially support their preferred attractions through travel. This degree of motivation depends, in part, on access to specific recreational resources. But perhaps more critical for newly (re)developing destinations, these personal choices are deeply affected by the recommendations and preferences of family and friends, and by social perceptions and stereotypes that may be more "dispositional rather than situational" (Renwick and Renwick, 1991: 167). When the images and advice are erroneous or simplistic, they form the basis of inappropriate visitor behavior and attitudes, and remain overly difficult to correct.

> Once an image or stereotype of a culture, country, foreign nationals, or their products have been developed, these beliefs will partially determine an individual's affective orientation and may be the main determinant of intended and subsequent behaviors. (Fishbein and Ajzen, 1975, cited in Renwick and Renwick, 1991: 168)

The successful resurrection of Montenegro's tourism industry, whose government proclaimed it the nation's highest priority in late 2005, therefore depends largely on its ability to reshape the beliefs of international visitors (especially North American), who have yet to clearly distinguish the Balkans' history of conflict from the serenity of Montenegro. The former Yugoslavia was a popular destination for visitors from Europe and the U.S. prior to its dissolution in 1991, when Montenegro was promoted as a cheap destination for mass tourism and Hollywood film stars who flocked to the privacy and privileges of resorts, such as Sveti Stefan (once an island village). Others traveled to the Balkans for therapeutic medical treatments and physical exercise at facilities specializing in health, wellness, and medical tourism, such as the renown Igalo spa in Montenegro. Yet, foreign visitors and their economic contributions declined dramatically during the civil war, when much of Yugoslavia's recreational landscape and infrastructure were decimated, and tourists avoided the area (Figure 2).

The ethnic cleansing and social disruption that ensued also left the new countries, upon independence, with few national traditions or symbols to reunite their remaining populations. Nevertheless, Yugoslavians everywhere expressed a strong desire to disconnect from the post-socialistic images that had defined their communal behavior and beliefs since the end of

World War II. As a result, after a decade of armed conflict and geopolitical isolation, the former republics of Yugoslavia now find themselves competing with each other for their place in the global tourism market, not with guns and militias, but with newly created brands that recall the pre-war attractions and ambiance, as well as the wider range of educational and volunteer opportunities available for today's independent, eco-oriented traveler (Antunac, Mihoviloviæ, and Navratil, 1979; Jordan, 2000; Hall, 2002; Martinoviæ, 2002).

"WILD BEAUTY"–
VISIT CRNA GORA

A creative and effective marketing campaign requires an intimate knowledge of the destination, the highly personalized linkages and personal interactions that delineate it social landscape, and the product attributes as perceived by its potential users (including quality, availability, and affordability). This is particularly true in the Balkans, where a decade of civil

FIGURE 2. Civil war and Yugoslavia tourism, 1990-1991 (Source: Montenegro Ministry of Tourism, 2006).

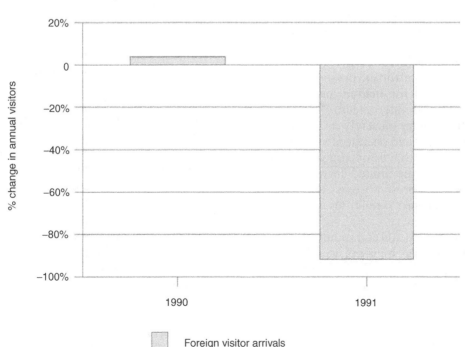

Foreign visitor arrivals

war in Croatia and Bosnia-Herzegovina, the bombing of Serbia by the United Nations, and the ongoing strife in Kosovo continue to dominate visitors' opinions, and make the task of re-imaging and rebranding Montenegro as an "ecologically sustainable destination" especially challenging for national tourism authorities. Although more Europeans, particularly from Ireland and the United Kingdom, are attracted by Montenegro's ease of entry, affordable services, historic heritage, and proximity to the Adriatic coast, many tourists still choose competing destinations in nearby Croatia and Slovenia, which they erroneously perceive to be more secure from ethnic conflict than their neighbor (Morgan, Pritchard and Pride, 2003; Floyd and Pennington-Gray, 2004).

Efforts to rebuild Montenegro's international appeal have long been impeded by its political association with Serbia (which were finally dissolved with the union's breakup and Montenegro's independence in May 2006), and the country's lack of arable land or extractive natural resources. Nevertheless, Montenegro does possess considerable advantages for a resumption and expansion of tourism activities that respond to the growing worldwide demand for outdoor recreation and nature activities, visits to historic ruins and religious sites, and marine exploration.

The growing discontent with high costs and summer crowds in nearby Dubrovnik, and the proliferation of low-cost European and U.S. airline routes in the Mediterranean, further support Montenegro's efforts to position itself as a model destination for marine and mountain tourism in the Mediterranean. To succeed, however, the country must rely on the capacity of travel providers and operators to entice, and satisfactorily cater to, visitors drawn in spite of the challenges by the limited crowds and low travel costs which presently exist, and the richness of Montenegro's religious history and physical landscapes.

Already, political and community leaders in Montenegro are reaching out to all affected stakeholders, including private and non-governmental agencies, learning institutions, and social organizations, to develop a consensus on the preferred direction and discourse of tourism development in the country. With the input provided from this participatory process, authorities plan to designate core themes or "eco-brands" that best highlight the diverse nature, culture, history, and industry available in Montenegro. They also hope to identify specific market segments for each set of attractions, and to dramatize these niches for specific audiences, with specialized itineraries and promotional events constructed around cultural performances, accommodations, transportation networks, and entertainment and leisure alternatives (Ritchie & Crouch, 2000).

As part of the process, the Montenegro Ministry of Tourism recently released its updated destination brand, "Wild Beauty." Part of a newly developed marketing and management strategy to replace its previous logo, "Enjoy Difference" (which lacked specificity), the new brand includes an identifying logo, official website (www.visit-montenegro.com), and participating venues for potential visitors and investors. Each unit of the brand is designed to reflect and reinforce for viewers Montenegro's:

1. Geographic location in the Mediterranean region and the physiographic diversity it offers tourists, from rugged mountains and canyons in the interior to the sandy beaches and headlands of the coast;
2. Relative safety and low level of personal risk for tourists from crime, terrorism, or disease; and the
3. Education, skills, and professional capabilities of Montenegro's tourism industry for greater numbers of visitors.

In thematically embracing Montenegro's natural scenery and rugged environment, the brand makes three implicit promises to visitors. First, it offers a sense of discovery, in a manner that is simultaneously wild, romantic, and personally challenging, yet simple. Second is the experience of entering a country slowly reopening to outside visitors, where residents still outnumber foreign tourists. The third assures each participant of the personal enrichment and learning environment that only travel provides. Though admittedly vague, these symbolic promises help define visitor expectations and beliefs about Montenegro as a safe and attractive alternative to other locations in the eastern Mediterranean (Graburn, 1995).

Montenegro's local tour operators were initially reluctant to join in the branding process, widely believing until recently that the country's natural geography and human history were too complex to define through slogans or icons, a challenge compounded by the number of involved stakeholders and sites, and the lack of agreement in interpreting and promoting the country's diverse attractions to foreign visitors. However, growing numbers of government officials and providers now acknowledge that distinctive brands can be a strategic management and marketing tool to successfully promote Montenegro's attractions and visitor services.

To assist the national government in inventorying and marketing its visitor attractions, the Investment and Development Company (DEG), a German company specializing in long-term project and corporate financing, prepared a master tourism plan in collaboration with MOT. The *Tourism Master Plan for Montenegro* outlines specific steps to be undertaken in support of the priority role assigned nature-based tourism in the country by the government through the year 2020.

As part of the assessment, a SWOT analysis (strengths, weaknesses, opportunities, threats), was prepared, which identified a number of advantages for Montenegro in pursuing visitors who were environmentally and culturally aware. Among the more significant strengths named were the country's biological diversity (despite its relatively small size), the moderate climate, and the physical terrain, stretching from sandy beaches along the Adriatic to Skadar Lake in central Montenegro (an internationally protected, migratory bird stopover), and the mountains and deep ravines of the north. Indeed, these physiographic features inspired the "Wild Beauty" brand. Also ranked as "visitor worthy" was the cultural heritage evident in the numerous castles, military forts, and Orthodox monasteries dating to the Roman Empire, and found throughout Montenegro.

Equally positive in Montenegro's desire to gain more visitors were the country's experience with international tourists prior to the 1991 civil war, its proximity and direct flights to the main European travel markets, the adoption of the Euro as the national currency, the availability and ease of obtaining no-cost tourist visas upon arrival, and the diverse outdoor recreation options available for ecotourists and "extreme" adventure travelers, such as SCUBA diving, snow skiing, mountain climbing, and whitewater rafting. At the same time, visitors to Montenegro are plagued by antiquated transport systems and inadequate accommodations, the absence of low-cost airlines at the country's two international airports, Podgorica and Tivat (as well as the lack of critical communications and radar facilities at Tivat), and a sense that other destinations in the former Yugoslavia offer better "value for the money."

Other perceived negatives include the perceptions of political instability and ethnic conflict in the region, the absence of interpretative material in languages other than Montenegrin, and the inferior quality of Montenegro's tourist accommodations and infrastructure, after years of isolation and economic sanctions imposed for its alliance with Serbia. These problems were particularly acute along the coast, where water shortages in Kotor are a recurring issue in local hotels each summer during the height of the tourism season, due to aging pipes, growing populations, and little money for routine maintenance.

The country is further weakened by an exodus of university graduates in search of professional employment elsewhere, and rising competition from Croatia and Slovenia for European, Asian, and American visitors. Successful and sustainable tourism growth for Montenegro will, therefore, require the country to concentrate on a few key factors, or indicators, that are achievable. It will also entail the formation of key branding processes that help establish the desired quality and perceived value, and reassure potential customers that their experience will be satisfactory (Henley Centre, 1998; Roberts and Hall, 2001; MacNulty, 2002; Crouch, 2006; d'Hauteserre, 2006).

CONCLUSION

There is certainly greater emphasis in Montenegro today on promoting brands that highlight the multiple attractions which exist for leisure tourists and ecotourists, who view Montenegro as an undervisited or relatively undeveloped, yet highly complex and unique destination on the Mediterranean coast. Recent market analyses suggest that the ideal visitor is interested in summer bathing, and most likely from either Serbia, the Ukraine, Hungary, Ireland, Germany, or the United Kingdom. Health-oriented tourists and spa visitors are also considered a potentially lucrative market, given the therapeutic role that sanitariums and allegoric treatments have long played in eastern Europe, Russia, and the Balkans. And there is considerable potential for adventure and nature-based ecotourism (especially bird-watching), religious-themed tours, and heritage travel, given the heightened awareness exhibited by residents in the former Yugoslavian, post-communist countries of their evolving national identity (Figure 3).

The public-private sector processes and partnerships already underway in Montenegro will certainly play an important role in Montenegro's branding efforts, as they facilitate the gathering of critical data and viewpoints from every important stakeholder and thus, encourage broader acceptance and use of the national brand by the different users. Co-branding with Croatia and the other former Yugoslavian countries is also considered critical for the country's success. When properly coordinated, this marketing approach would allow the member states to articulate their common history and physiography to a broader audience, while simultaneously expounding upon their distinctive identities and abilities. For rural residents, co-branding may also prove beneficial in drawing attention to potential new attractions in the Balkan hinterlands, along with the tourism enterprises historically concen-

FIGURE 3. Primary Montenegro Attractions for European Visitors (Source: Greg Ringer and the Montenegro Ministry of Tourism, 2006).

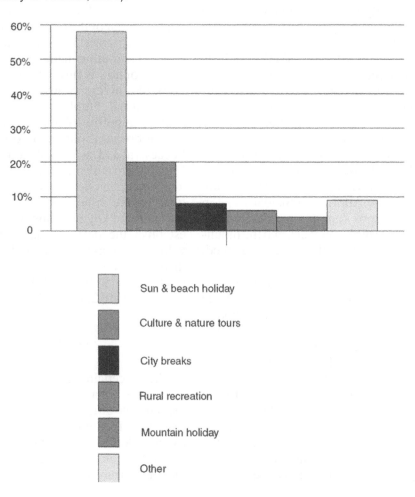

trated along the coast (Tomic, 2006). Whether implemented alone or in partnership with its Balkan neighbors, these brands should build upon the legislature's proclamation of Montenegro as an ecological state. With more than 40% of all international visitors now self-labeled as eco- tourists, it is apparent that more tourists worldwide now seek attractions that are environmentally sensitive and supportive of indigenous communities. Though their numbers may not yet constitute a majority of all travelers, their disproportionate impact is perhaps best illustrated in surveys undertaken by the World Wildlife Fund (2005). This data notes that tourists, for whom nature or culture are the primary motivators of their trip, spend approximately US$ 143 per day on location, in contrast to the US$ 117 in daily spending by tourists unconcerned with either.

As a result, an eco-destination may earn an equivalent income by focusing on the environmental quality of the visitor experience, rather than the quantity of visitors alone. Consequently, there is considerable potential for Montenegro to capture a larger share of this market and the related earnings, by constructing "green" facilities and implementing "ecofriendly" practices that reduce environmental degradation, pollution, and waste. In this manner, Montenegro can reinforce its legislated mantle as an environmental leader in the Mediterranean, and thereby further distinguish the country from similar destinations in the remainder of the Balkans (Weber and Teliman-Kosuta, 1991; Popesku and Maric, 2005; U.S. Agency for International Development, 2005; Stoddard, 2006).

Greater participation by tourism stakeholders in Montenegro is also needed in developing a core message that simultaneously satisfies the four dimensions of state branding (public diplomacy, tourism, export promotion, and FDI, or foreign development investments), and emphasizes anew the peace and tolerance that prevail in Montenegro, as well as its strategic location in the Mediterranean. In this sense, "Wild Beauty" may indeed aptly describe the diversity of attractions that currently await the visitor to Crna Gora ("Black Mountain" in Montenegrin). But the brand should not further construe as "wild," a country that has already experienced too much conflict amidst such

beauty. To do so would only perpetuate the lack of appreciation expressed by many tourists for Montenegro's attractions and history, in a world that appears increasingly determined to benefit from travel to destinations for enjoyment and recreation, as well as conservation and education (Allcock and Counihan, 1989; Renwick and Renwick, 1991; Graburn, 1995; Terkenli, 2006).

Should these recommendations enable potential visitors to become better educated about the country's status, then tourism will have socially and economically profited both Montenegro and the Balkans, by affording greater access to investments in transboundary attractions, and in raising the perceived quality of the available tourism product through shared experiences and more meaningful social linkages between contiguous countries. Only in such a manner will visitors discover the Balkans in a manner that benefits both them personally and the region as well, as it recovers from the war. Though the long-term success of Montenegro's efforts to rebrand itself as a destination for conservation, rather than conflict, will ultimately be determined by regulatory practices and sustained levels of public awareness and acceptance, the authors hope that the analysis presented in this paper will stimulate additional efforts to reconnect the former Yugoslavia through travel attractions and brands that fully acknowledge their shared ecology, history, and politics.

REFERENCES

Ahmed, Akbar and Cris Shore (eds)(1995) *The Future of Anthropology: Its Relevance to the Contemporary World*, London & Atlantic Highlands, NJ: Athlone.

Allcock, John and Joan Counihan (1989) *The Studies in the History of Tourism in Yugoslavia*, Bradford Studies on Yugoslavia, No. 14, Bradford, U.K.: Research Unit in Yugoslav Studies, University of Bradford.

Anholt, Simon (2006) "Nation branding: Introduction," *Journal of Brand Management* March: 1.

Antunac, I.; M.A. Mihoviloviæ; and J. Navratil (1979) *Economic and Social Problems of Tourism in Europe, Yugoslavia: Desk Research*, Studies and Reports, Zagreb, Croatia: Center for Social Research, University of Zagreb.

Commission of the European Communities, D.G. XXIII-Tourism Unit (1993) *Tourism Customers in Central and Eastern Europe: Perspectives of Development,*

Luxembourg: Office for Official Publications of the European Communities and I.P.K.-Institut für Planungskybernetik, Marktforschung, Marketinplanung und Erfolgskontrolle im Tourismus..

Crouch, David (2006) "Embodiment and performance in the making of contemporary cultural economies," in *Landscapes of a New Cultural Economy of Space,* Landscape Series, Dordrecht, The Netherlands: Spring, pp. 19-40.

d'Hauteserre, Marie (2006) "Landscapes of the Tropics: tourism and the new cultural economy in the third world," in *Landscapes of a New Cultural Economy of Space,* Landscape Series, Dordrecht, The Netherlands: Spring, pp. 149-170.

DEG Investment & Development Company (2001) *Master Plan: Strategy of Tourism Development Till 2020,* Podgorica: Montenegro Ministry of Tourism.

Floyd, Myron F. and Lori Pennington-Gray (2004) "Profiling risk perceptions of tourists," *Annals of Tourism Research* 31(4): 1051-1054.

Freire, Joao R. (2005) "'Other tourists': a critical factor for a geo-brand-building process," *Place Branding* 2(1): 68-83.

Gertner, David (2007) "Editorial: Place branding: Dilemma or reconciliation between political ideology and economic pragmatism? Place Branding 3, 3-7.

Graburn, Nelson H.H. (1995) "Tourism, modernity and nostalgia," in *The Future of Anthropology: Its Relevance to the Contemporary World,* (eds) Akbar S. Ahmed & Cris N. Shore, London & Atlantic Highlands, NJ: Athlone, pp. 158-178.

Hall, D. (2002) "Brand development, tourism and national identity: The re-imaging of former Yugoslavia," *The Journal of Brand Management* 9(4-5): 323-334.

Henley Centre (1998) *Planning for Consumer Change: Issues,* London: Henley Centre for Forecasting.

Jordan, Peter (2000) "Restructuring Croatia's coastal resorts: Change, sustainable development and the incorporation of rural hinterlands," *Journal of Sustainable Tourism* 8(6): 525-539.

Kaynak, Erdener (ed.)(1991) *Sociopolitical Aspects of International Marketing,* London: The Haworth Press, Inc.

Kotler, P. and G. Armstrong (2001) *Principles of Marketing,* 9th ed., New York: Prentice Hall.

Kotler, P. and D. Gertner (2002) "Country as a brand, product and beyond: A place marketing and brand management perspective," *Journal of Brand Management* April (9): 4-5.

Locum Destination Review (2000) *Analysis: Benchmarking Attractions* 1: 53-55.

Louillet, Marie Claire (2005) Proposal for a success model for destination management systems. Unpublished Ph.D. dissertation, Faculty of Business Administration, Sherbrooke University, Canada.

MacNulty, Peter (2002) *Conclusions.* Paper presented to the World Tourism Organization's Rural Tourism in Europe: Experiences and Perspectives Seminar,

24-25 June, Belgrade, Serbia and Montenegro, pp. 1-10.

Martinoviæ, Stijepo (2002) "Branding Hrvatska–A mixed blessing that might succeed: the advantage of being unrecognizable," *Journal of Brand Management* April (9): 4-5.

Milosavljeviæ, Gordana (1988) *Tourism for Health Purposes: The Resources of Yugoslavia,* Belgrade, Serbia: Joint EFTA-Yugoslavia Committee, European Free Trade Association.

Morgan, N.; A. Pritchard; and R. Pride (2003) *Destination Branding: Creating the Unique Destination Proposition,* Oxford, UK: Butterworth-Heinemann.

Popesku, Jovan and Rajko Maric (2005) *Ecotourism development as a tool for repositioning of Serbia as a tourism destination,* paper presented to the Institute for Economic Sciences, Belgrade, Serbia.

Prentice, Eve-Ann (2003) "Why I love battered Belgrade," *The (London) Observer,* 10 August, pp. 4-5.

Renwick, Frank and Rebecca M. Renwick (1991) "Country of origin stereotyping: The social linkage effect upon foreign product attributes," in *Sociopolitical Aspects of International Marketing,* (ed.) Erdener Kaynak, New York & London: The Haworth Press, pp. 165-185.

Ringer, Greg (ed.)(1998) *Destinations: Cultural Landscapes of Tourism,* London & New York: Routledge.

Ringer, Greg (2004) "Montenegro sustainable tourism assessment," in *Household Survey Report #10,* (ed.) P. Ivanovic, Podgorica: Institute for Strategic Studies and Prognoses and the Center for Entrepreneurship & Economic Development, pp. 23-30.

Ritchie, B.J.R. and Crouch G.I. (2000) "The competitive destination: a sustainable perspective," *Tourism Management* 21(1): 1-7.

Roberts, Lesley and Derek Hall (eds)(2001) *Rural Tourism and Recreation: Principles to Practice,* London: CABI Publishing.

Stoddard, Ed (2006) "African countries brand themselves with eco-labels," *Reuters,* 12 June, pp. 1-4.

Terkenli, Theano S. (2006) "Landscapes of a new cultural economy of space: an introduction," in *Landscapes of a New Cultural Economy of Space,* Landscape Series, Dordrecht, The Netherlands: Springer Publishers, pp. 1-18.

Terkenli, Theano S. and Anne-Marie d'Hauteserre (eds) (2006) *Landscapes of a New Cultural Economy of Space,* Landscape Series, Dordrecht, The Netherlands: Springer Publishers.

Tomic, Borka (2006) *Rebranding Serbia: A Hobby Shortly to Become a Full-time Job?!* Brussels: Invest-in-Serbia and the Institute for Serbia and Montenegro.

U.S. Agency for International Development (2005) *Supporting tourism entrepreneurship along Serbia's Corridor X–One of Serbia's 10 'Perfect Places',* Washington, D.C.: U.S. Government Printing Office.

Weber, Sandra and Neda Telišman-Košuta (1991) "The possibilities of foreign tourism market segmentation and the evaluation of the tourism supply of SR

Croatia (Yugoslavia)," in *Sociopolitical Aspects of International Marketing*, (ed.) Erdener Kaynak, New York & London: The Haworth Press, pp. 347-365.

World Wildlife Fund (2005) *W orld Ecotourism Survey*. Geneva, Switzerland: The World Wide Fund for Nature.

Tourism Market Recovery in the Maldives After the 2004 Indian Ocean Tsunami

Jack C Carlsen

Michael Hughes

SUMMARY. This paper will use a range of tourism data and a case study to examine the rates of recovery of ten source markets for the Maldives in the wake of the 2004 Indian Ocean tsunami. The market response and recovery rates for these ten markets varied significantly and the reasons for this will be explored. It is evident that a 'one size fits all' marketing strategy will not in itself be sufficient to achieve acceptable rates of recovery following a disaster. The strategies, opportunities and rates of market recovery experienced in the Maldives will provide useful insights for the marketing and monitoring of other destinations that have experienced a crisis or disaster.

INTRODUCTION

The immediate question after a crisis or disaster in a tourism destination is always "how long before visitor numbers will be back to normal?" The lives and livelihood of a great number of people depend on viable visitor arrival numbers, especially in destinations where dependency on tourism is high. Often the ongoing economic hardship caused by a crisis or disaster that has a more severe impact than the physical damage of the initial event. This was certainly the case in the Maldives, that suffered a severe downturn in bookings and arrivals following the 2004 Indian Ocean tsunami, (herein 'the tsunami'), where potential operating losses were estimated to be more than the costs of repairing the limited number of damaged resorts (Carlsen 2005, 2006).

For these reasons it is imperative that strategies be implemented to assist with market recovery immediately following a crisis. Such strategies developed for Bali post after the Octo-

Jack C Carlsen (E-mail: jack.carlsen@cbs.curtin.edu.au) is Professor in the Curtin Sustainable Tourism Centre at Curtin University Western Australia (P. O. Box U1987, Perth, Western Australia, 6845). Michael Hughes (E-mail: Michael.Hughes@cbs.curtin.edu.au) is Lecturer in the Curtin Sustainable Tourism Centre at Curtin University Western Australia (P. O. Box U1987, Perth, Western Australia, 6845).

The authors wish to thank Dr. Mahmood Shougee, Minister of Tourism and Civil Aviation, Dr. Abdulla Mausoom, Director, Maldives Tourism Promotion Board, Mr. Mohamed Umar Maniku, Chairman and Mr. Shoumo Mukherjee, General Manager-Sales and Marketing, Universal Resorts and also Mr. Sim Mohamed, CEO and Secretary General, Maldives Association of Tourism Industry for their input and assistance. Thanks also to Dr. Janne J Liburd, Chair of BEST EN for her valuable comments.

ber 2002 bombings in Kuta Beach and the more recent SARS threat in Asia (Beirman 2003, PATA n.d, Lynch 2004) provide models for developing public relations, marketing and communication strategies that will aid in market recovery. Likewise in the Maldives, crisis communications and tourism recovery strategies were developed and implemented in the course of 2005, requiring significant input from industry and government (Carlsen 2005, 2006).

The immediate tourism impacts and strategic response to the tsunami have been documented elsewhere (Carlsen 2005, 2006, Cohen 2005, UNWTO 2005, de Sausmarez, 2005) but the market response and recovery rates of main tourism markets are less well understood. In effect, it was a 'double disaster' (WEF/UNWTO 2005) for the countries affected, with the initial loss of lives and infrastructure compounded by the ongoing losses associated with declining tourism arrivals.

For many of the countries impacted, tourism was the main source of income, especially for the small businesses that that populated the coastal tourism resorts around the Indian Ocean and Andaman Sea. Whilst an immediate and extensive global effort was mounted to recover lives and essential infrastructure, the recovery of livelihoods of those directly and indirectly employed in tourism took longer. In the post-disaster environment, disaster recovery and crisis marketing assume an important place in the process of return to normalcy (de Sausmarez 2005), which is the tacit goal of all those affected. Indeed, WEF/UNWTO (2005: iv) suggest that:

A very important point is that rapidly putting tourism infrastructure back into service quickly provides the tax and general economic base to fund the general regional recovery (e.g., hotel tax and income taxes on wages of employees). That is, the recovery of the tourism sector is a major driver of the funds and economic activity needed to support the general recovery of the entire affected regional economy. Effective crisis management can result in the tourism sector becoming a catalyst for general economic and social recovery.

The Government organization responsible for marketing the Maldives, the Maldives Tourism Promotion Board [MTPB] was quick to recognize the importance of tourism recovery and released the following statement on January 5, 2005, two weeks after the disaster (MTPB 2006):

While Maldivians strive hard to bring back normalcy to their everyday lives, they are more than eager to welcome international tourists from around the world in a bid to save the economic well-being of the island communities that exist within one of the world's most fragile yet beautiful natural environments.

This article will examine in detail the strategies, actions and market response in the case of the Maldives and identify trends and issues in specific markets following tourism disasters. In this way the links between tourism impacts, market responses and destination recovery are analyzed and lessons for marketing destinations following disasters and crises are elucidated. The notion of market resilience will also be explored, with the contention that some markets are more so than others.

LITERATURE REVIEW

Santana (2003) commented that crisis management research has had a relatively low profile relative to other areas in tourism development and management research. This is significant given that tourism is recognised as being highly vulnerable to crisis, as demonstrated by tourism downturns after the 2001 terrorist attacks on the United States, the bombings in Bali, SARS outbreaks in Asia and the tsunami.

Beirman (2003) recommended a number of marketing and communications strategies for destinations recovering from crises. Also, the UNWTO (2005) recommended marketing and communications steps for recovering tourist confidence and addressing than many misperceptions that can follow disasters. More specifically, the PATA Bali Recovery Taskforce (n.d.) recommended market strategies following the 2002 bombings (Table 1).

However, market recovery following the 2002 Bali bombings was less than optimal.

Growth was mainly Asia Pacific markets (Japan, Australia, Taiwan, South Korea), creating dependence on four main countries which accounted for almost 60 percent of arrivals in 2004. These visitors had a shorter stay and lower spending compared with pre-bombing visitors from long-haul destination such as USA and U.K. Bali continued to suffer from a shortfall in visitor nights and revenues. However, whilst Malaysian arrivals grew substantially due to increased air access resulting from partnerships developed between Indonesian tourism authorities and Malaysian Airlines, USA and U.K. market recovery was slow.

Henderson (2003) documents the responses of tourism and marketing agencies to the 2002 Bali bombings, although no analysis of the rates of market recovery was undertaken. The main marketing response by tourism authorities was through the media in an attempt to limit the damage to the destination image which was exposed as vulnerable to terrorist attack. Mea-

TABLE 1. Recovery Marketing Strategies

Beirman (2003)	UNWTO (2005)	PATA (n.d.)
• Project primary messages	• Be pro-active in communications	• Bring all disparate elements together and follow a common agenda
• Build solidarity messages	• Look for positive news	• Create an environment for careful planning
• Set out the facts	• Increase familiarization trips for journalists	• Establish an integrated Crisis Management Plan
• Restore confidence	• Remember anniversaries	• Recognise importance of aviation sector
• Protect branding	• Anticipate legal actions	• Rebuild the Bali brand
• Offer incentives	• Create your own news outlet on the destination website	• Broaden the brand to include culture and heritage
• Publicise positives	• Join the global communications campaign for tourism	• Introduce contemporary marketing platforms
• Report and monitor progress	• Create new niche market products	• Increase brand awareness through partnership marketing
	• Target experienced and special interest travelers	
	• Create special price offers	
	• Quickly shift promotion to most promising markets	
	• Step up promotion to domestic market	
	• Increase familiarization trips for tour operators and special events	
	• Take travel advisories seriously	
	• Intensify co-operation	
	• Survey generating markets on perceptions of your destination	

Sources: Compiled from Beirman (2003), UN WTO (2005) and PATA (n.d.)

sures included establishment of media centres in Jakarta and Kuta, calls by the Ministry of Tourism and Culture for foreign governments to revoke travel warnings (which had been issued in many Asian and Western countries) and scheduling of meetings and workshops in Bali to demonstrate confidence in the safety of the destination. Marketing emphasis changes dramatically, with road shows replaced by sympathy visits to home countries of the bombing casualties and advertising messages replaced with broadcasts of memorial and purification ceremonies. Tourism authorities sought sympathy and solidarity by expressing remorse for victims and offering reassurance that Bali was really a safe destination (although subsequent bombings in Jakarta and Kuta would cast doubt on this claim). Domestic tourists and near country markets in Asia were targeted through discounting and partnerships with national airlines. The contagion effect was also evident, with countries such as Singapore and Malaysia National Tourism Organisations moving to reassure long-haul travelers by making safety and security central marketing themes in attempt to project positive images of the South East Asian region.

de Sausmarez (2005) suggested that the speed of recovery for countries affected by the tsunami not only depends on the time taken to repair the initial damage, but also on 'an effective marketing message announcing that the destination is open again' (p. 56). Santana (2003) also observed that, in tourism, 'perception is reality' (p. 318) and repairing to infrastructure will not itself restore confidence in a destination, a process that requires a parallel campaign to change public perceptions. Recommended responses include increased cooperation between all stakeholders (public and private) and marketing that focuses on developing of new markets in addition to expansion of existing ones. However, there has been virtually no detailed analysis of the effectiveness of these strategies and actions, in terms of the market response apart from reporting of visitor arrival statistics in the countries affected.

METHODS

A combination of qualitative case study material and quantitative visitor data analysis was used to identify the strategies employed in the Maldives and their effectiveness is restoring visitor arrivals from established and emerging markets in 2005. Case study materials identified specific actions by (i) the Ministry of Tourism and Civil Aviation (MTCA) and the Marketing Section, the Maldives Tourism Promotion Board (MTPB) and (ii) Universal Resorts, the largest resort company in the Maldives. Interviews and written correspondence with both organizations provided indications of the adoption of specific strategies and corresponding marketing actions and outcomes. Analysis of actual arrivals data from six main markets and four emerging markets that comprised the top ten sources of visitor arrivals provides insights into the varying market responses to the tsunami and subsequent marketing by the public and private tourism organizations in 2005. In this way analysis of the effectiveness of the crisis marketing strategies in the Maldives is presented. The next section describes the tourism situation and response to the tsunami, followed by the case study and analysis of arrivals data.

MALDIVES TOURISM

Tourism contributed about 30 per cent of Maldives Gross Domestic Product (GDP) between 1999 and 2003 and about 40 percent of total taxation revenue (Ministry of Tourism 2004). Inbound tourism has been responsible for gradual improvement in Maldivian foreign exchange earnings since 1983 when the value was US$13.4 million compared to the same figures in 2003 when earnings had increased ten-fold in value to US$149 million (Ministry of Tourism, 2004). Tourism accommodation capacity had an annualized average compound growth rate of 11.65 percent between the years of 1972 and 2004 and the 87 resort islands currently have bed capacity of about 17,000 (Ministry of Tourism 2004). The volume of international visitors or tourist arrivals has risen from around 42,000 in 1980 to almost 600,000 in 2004; more than a ten-fold increase over the 23 year period, with an annual growth rate of above 9 percent. In 2004, 71.3 percent of visitors were from six main markets–Italy (21.2 percent), United Kingdom (18.5 percent), Germany (11.8 percent), Japan (7.6 percent), France (7.5 percent) and Switzerland (4.7 percent)–indicating a high degree of dependence on a small number of markets for tourism. For some markets, such as Italy and Switzerland, negative growth rates were experienced in 2004 compared with 2003, while other major markets, such as Germany remained relatively flat. On the other hand, markets such as the UK and Japan demonstrated substantial growth in 2004 (Ministry of Tourism 2004), until the tsunami waves hit the islands at around 9:00 am on December 26th, 2004.

IMPACT OF THE TSUNAMI

Maldives tourism sustained significant damage from the tsunami with 19 of the 87 resorts closed due to minor or major damage. This included six that were badly damaged and expected to take at least six months to be back in operation. The remaining 13 damaged resorts were operational within a shorter time span. The 'One Island-One Resort' concept of resort development in the Maldives requires that all resorts are essentially self-sufficient within their designated island location. Each resort has its own infrastructure including the island's own power supply, sewerage system, water supply and other support facilities. Resort staff took responsibility for rapid restoration of infrastructure and most was operational again within hours of the passing waves. Also, the impacts in other Indian Ocean destinations such as power outages, water contamination, diseases and epidemics were negligible in the Maldives compared with other nations affected by the tsunami.

MARKET RECOVERY STRATEGIES

One month after the tsunami, Carlsen (2005, 2006) developed a tourism market recovery strategy for the Maldives, which included marketing strategies for the short-, medium- and long-term. The principle aim in the short-term was to stop cancellations and use the media to correct the mis-perception that the Maldives was severely impacted by the tsunami. This was not the case, although the media coverage of the

disaster tended to group together severely affected countries such as Thailand and Sri Lanka with the Maldives, in a typical case of the contagion effect.

Stopping cancellations would require a concerted effort of communication with travel agents and tour operators in major markets to re-assure their clients that had already booked holidays that there was no need to cancel. Tour operators had allowed clients to cancel or change bookings at no cost until the end of January 2005. This strategy was effective in some markets, but in others there was some market resistance. Also, some 20 percent of arrivals are by charter flight and some airlines chose to suspend charter flights until April 2005.

A communications strategy to address the concerns of consumers through solidarity messages as well as delivering primary messages through travel agents, tour operators and airlines was needed immediately. This supports the return of visitors that have already booked, as well as generating new bookings in the short-term. A communications strategy aimed at the travel trade, consumers, media, airlines and foreign governments was proposed. These strategies were aimed at re-building confidence in travel to the Maldives and reducing risk and uncertainty. Perceptions of conditions in the Maldives suffered from the negative media coverage of devastation in other destinations such as Thailand and Sri Lanka, where damage and loss of life was much more severe. There was an immediate need to inform potential visitors that most Maldives resorts remained fully operational in 2005. Considerable effort was made to isolate the Maldives from these other destinations through direct contact with the travel trade, hosting of media representatives, negotiation with scheduled and charter airlines to maintain services and lifting of foreign government travel warnings about travel to the Maldives. The primary message to all these groups was that Maldives tourism was operational and most resorts were unaffected. The solidarity message was that by visiting, tourists would be assisting in the recovery of the Maldives. This message was designed to capitalize on the enormous outpouring of sympathy for the people affected, as evidenced by unprecedented levels of foreign aid and charity. One month after the tsunami, Maldives Tourism

Promotion Board [MTPB] announced the allocation of US$1.5 million to fund initiatives aimed at stopping cancellations and joint marketing and promotions (de Sausmarez 2005).

It is evident from the Maldives experience that a co-ordinated and well-funded marketing strategy can indeed mitigate the short-, medium- and long-term effects on tourism. It is not always necessary to immediately offer discounts, as this can result in shortfalls in revenue, compounding the losses from cancellations and locking the industry into lower margins and rates. In any case, as was demonstrated in the Maldives, it is pointless to offer discounts to visitors who have already expressed a propensity to purchase packages in the high season at full price. What is required is prevention of cancellations in the short-term, so that existing bookings are honored and sales are maintained.

Reflecting the high level of dependence on travel wholesalers and intermediaries for selling all-inclusive package holidays to Maldives, the MTPB and resorts companies increased their presence at 14 international tourism trade shows and promotional fairs in 12 countries during 2005. This enabled them to market the Maldives to the major travel agencies in the traditional markets in Western Europe and Japan as well as the emerging markets in Russia and China. The Ministry undertook other actions and achieved certain outcomes in 2005 to expand new markets and maintain confidence in existing markets (Table 2).

CASE STUDY: UNIVERSAL RESORTS

Universal Resorts owns and operates eight resorts in the Maldives as well as two cruise ships, the Atoll Explorer and the Island Explorer. Of these, none were severely impacted by the tsunami and most were operational again with a few days of the disaster. The official

TABLE 2. Maldives Marketing Actions and Outcomes 2005

Action	Outcome
Familiarization trips for media from all major markets	350 familiarization trips, including 195 organized by MTPB
Status of the tourism industry reporting on local media, especially television and radio	Resort 'operating status' uploaded to the MTPB site
Attend international trade shows and promotional fairs	14 International Trade Fairs in 12 countries attended by MTPB and Industry
Road shows and promotional workshops in major markets	Promotional events in India, France, Germany, Spain, Portugal
Advertising on international television and other media	Aggressive TV campaigns in Europe. Advertorials in 37 international magazines. Billboards in major cities, airports and trains
High level delegation to meet operators and government authorities in all major markets	Ministerial delegations in conjunction with trade shows in major markets. Also sent delegations to China and Korea
Welcome banner at the airport	Banner and visitor information centre established
Bi-monthly electronic newsletter to be distributed by MTPB	www.visitmaldives.com launched in 8 languages
Joint destination promotion with major tour operators and airlines	Joint advertising campaigns with Thomas Cook and Kuoni
Research tourist's perceptions of the Maldives	Monitored tourism related internet communications
	Interviewed arriving and departing guests to gain their feedback and to reinforce solidarity and primary messages

Sources: Compiled from Carlsen (2005, 2006), Ministry of Tourism and Civil Aviation (2006)

Website of the Maldives Tourism Promotion Board reported that 63 resorts (including all eight Universal Resorts) were operational as at January 16th, 2005.

On December 29th, 2004, General Manager of Sales and Marketing for Universal Resorts and his team finalized a recovery plan for the UK market together with their leading partner agencies in the UK. The recovery plan was implemented immediately based on the following actions (Shoumo Mukherjee *personal communication*):

1. Media–get real story of Maldives out. Universal Resorts arranged for over fifty journalists to visit their resorts, see the status for themselves and produce stories and other media on their impressions.
2. Travel Agents–Re-familiarize travel agents and intermediaries with Universal Resorts.
3. Specific promotion around Valentine's Day (February 14th). A promotional campaign for the Maldives as 'the most romantic destination on earth' was produced for multiple media outlets.

As a result, business recovered to 70% of its 2004 levels by 15 April 2005, representing a three-month recovery period. This was an incredible effort by the sales and marketing team and ensured losses and cancellations were minimized. Use of the media through visiting journalists and also guest testimonials provided timely and independent accounts of operational status in the weeks and months following the tsunami, a factor that mitigated against cancellations and restored confidence in the resorts and the destination. An example of a guest testimonial from the March 2005 Newsletter of Universal Resorts is shown in Box 1.

New markets in Russia in alliance with travel trade partners and airlines were also targeted with the same strategies and actions and the Russian market grew by 10 per cent above its 2004 levels for Universal Resorts, in spite of an overall decline for the Maldives in 2005. Visits to China and presentations to travel agents and coverage in the media generated over 25 rooms a day in the critical summer period after the tsunami. The Chinese were one of only two markets to produce positive growth rates in 2005.

Box 1. Guest Testimonial from Universal Resort March 2005 Newsletter

> A Postcard from Full Moon
>
> My wife and I arrived on Full Moon on 14th January for a seven-night stay, after which we have booked for four nights on Kurumba. This was a long-standing booking and, once the tsunami occurred, we worried as to whether or not we should travel. Kuoni Travel was extremely fair offering us the alternatives of a refund, or a change of venue, or a delayed holiday to the same venue. We emailed the resort, and were reassured, so decided to travel in any event.
>
> We are having a marvellous time, but concerned for the resort because there are so few guests here. It seems that numbers are cancelling, because they are told that there are building works going on and are naturally concerned that this will be a problem. Whilst it is right that there are building works, these are on only one side of the island and the good news is that the accommodation, the bars and the restaurants are on the other side of the island. We have not heard any noise from building works.
>
> In summary, if you want a unique experience to sample a first class resort island without ever needing to reserve a sunbed, and with a guaranteed best table at every restaurant–then come! I'm now going back to my sunbed......David Mitchell

Source: Adapted from http://www.universalresorts.com/newsletter/2005 march.pdf

Consequently, the markets that turned around the quickest were UK, Russia and China for Universal Resorts.

The recovery plan was also implemented in Germany, Italy, and France. By mid 2006, the Germany market was back at 2004 levels and France had grown by over 20 percent on 2004. However, the Italian market continued to languish below 2004 levels, perhaps due as much due to domestic economic conditions in Italy, rather than any lack of response to marketing efforts of Universal.

The importance of strong partnerships with tourism intermediaries, airlines and the media cannot be over-estimated. Universal's strategies were driven in alliance with tour operator and airline partners and focused consumer campaigns through media and travel agents directly. The experience of Universal Resorts exemplified all Maldives Resorts with regards to the concerted marketing effort and market response, and this is borne out in the following analysis.

ANALYSIS OF VISITOR ARRIVALS

The Maldives had been experiencing a steady growth in arrivals for most of the main six markets from 2001 to 2003, despite global disasters such as the September 11th terrorist attacks in the USA, Bali bombings and SARS outbreak (Figure 1). Four of the six main markets exhibited growth from 2001 to 2003 with Japan and Switzerland remaining on a plateau. The UK in particular displayed very rapid growth during this period. Arrivals from the four key emerging markets were generally growing strongly through the four years 2001 to 2004, especially China and Russia (Figure 2). Examination of the change in arrivals between 2004 and 2005 from key and emerging markets indicate some interesting variations. Figure 3 shows the percentage change in Maldives arrivals from the six main source markets and indicates large declines in arrivals from France, Japan, Italy, China and Switzerland after the tsunami, with lesser declines in the remaining markets. All of these markets, except Italy, had been either growing or steady up to 2004, despite SARS, the terrorist attacks on the US and Iraq Wars. Thus it would appear that the tsunami had precipitated or accellerated decline, and had a direct and tangible impact on Maldives tourism arrivals in 2005.

Interestingly, data for the first nine months of 2006 (Department of Immigration and Emigration 2006) indicate a return to growth in all markets when compared with the same period for 2005, with France (165.8 percent), Italy (92 percent) and Japan (80.7 percent) showing the highest growth in 2006, after having the highest

rates of decline in 2005. Growth in three of the emerging markets in the first three quarters of 2006 was also strong, with China (150.9 percent), Austria (71.7 percent) and Russia (57.2 percent) showing signs of a return to trend, whilst India (19.3 percent) remained steady after having the lowest rate of decline in 2005 (Figures 2 and 3). India arrivals in 2005 remain an anomaly as many came in on business and other matters related to the tsunami recovery effort so were not typically tourist arrivals. A 90 day visa is granted to Indians, which allows them to conduct business and engage in short-term employment without having to apply for a work permit. Arrivals with work permits are not counted in the tourism arrivals data for the Maldives.

LIMITATIONS

The tsunami and subsequent damage reduced bed capacity in the Maldives by 3,554 beds or 22 percent of the pre-disaster level of 16,400 beds (Maldives Tourism Promotion Board n.d.) in the critical first four months of 2005. Reduced accommodation capacity would necessarily mean that total arrivals will be less in 2005, when compared with 2004. It should be noted here that December to April is the peak tourism season for the Maldives as it corresponds with the European winter. Occupancy rates are typically more than 80 percent with some resorts overbooked for the entire five month period. However, with renovations and repairs, as well as the construction of five new resorts, accommodation capacity was expected

FIGURE 1. Maldives Arrival Trends for Six Major Markets 2001 to 2005

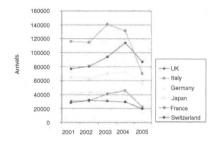

Source: Adapted from Ministry of Tourism and Civil Aviation (2006)

FIGURE 2. Maldives Arrivals Trends for Top Four Emerging Markets 2001-2005

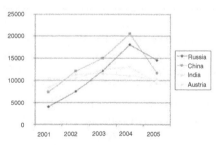

Source: Adapted from Ministry of Tourism and Civil Aviation (2006)

FIGURE 3. Percentage Change in Top Ten Maldives Arrivals 2005/2004

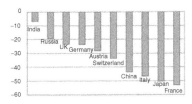

Source: Adapted from Ministry of Tourism and Civil Aviation (2006)

to return to 2004 levels by the end of 2005. In addition to the resorts there are 1700 beds on charter boats and 360 beds in guest houses. The changing accommodation capacity means that average occupancy rates are not a good indicator of overall tourism market recovery (although useful for individual resorts) during 2005, so the use of monthly visitor arrivals is advisable following a disaster that impacts on accommodation capacity and infrastructure.

There are also limitations to using visitor arrival data in the Maldives because it is based on immigration data cards that request the nationality, but not the country of residence of arriving tourists. The extent to which expatriate populations of say, UK passport holders, are resident in other countries (such as the Middle East) is not known, but may affect the accuracy of market recovery analysis. Obviously any marketing strategy mounted in the UK will not be viewed by non-residents, who may independently decide to visit the Maldives.

Perhaps a more appropriate indicator of tourism recovery is not visitor origin or arrivals but resumption of industry investment and by this measure the Maldives had certainly made a full recovery within 12 months of the disaster. This is demonstrated by the allocation in 2005 and 2006 of an additional 35 islands over a two to five year period, which will facilitate significant expansion of resort capacity and an additional 5000 to 7000 beds by 2010.

CONCLUSION

The direct, though relatively minor, impact of the tsunami on the Maldives appeared to re-

sult in a considerable decline in arrivals in 2005. By the end of 2005, there were indications of recovery, with occupancy rates for the high season of December 2005 to February 2006 returning to 2004 pre-tsunami levels. Average occupancy rate was 64.4 percent for 2005, but reached as high as 85.2 percent in November 2005 and 74.5 percent in December, equivalent to 2004. Also by the end of 2005, bed capacity had been restored to 2004 levels, mainly through existing resorts developing additional rooms (Abdulla 2006).

Research into the impacts of crises and disasters and their effects in tourism destinations has accelerated in the wake of increased incidents over the last decade. Numerous prescriptive strategies and case studies have provided examples, templates and checklists for NTOs and tourism agencies to formulate marketing responses. These responses usually emphasize the importance of marketing in the recovery process and most recognize that a prompt, co-ordinated and collaborative effort is required on the part of all stakeholders in the destination.

However, it is evident from the limited amount of post-crisis analysis that has been undertaken that a 'one size fits all' approach is inadequate. Crises and disasters are variable in duration and scale. The flow-on and contagion effects depend very much upon the nature of the disaster (natural or man-made) and the corresponding change in public perception in response to media coverage and crisis communication. It is also becoming evident that marketing strategies that are ill-informed or hastily prepared can prolong the adverse impacts on the destination, as was the case in Bali. Projecting safety and security as marketing themes renders a destination vulnerable to loss of destination image, should subsequent disasters or crises occur. It could be argued that very few destinations are now safe from the threat of war or terrorism, as contagion effects reverberate around the globe and erode the confidence of international tourists.

The response by public and private sector tourism organizations in the Maldives have been instrumental in returning tourism arrivals and capacity to 2004 levels within 12 to 18 months of the tsunami. There are obvious benefits in generating tourism income, employment and investment in countries with such high dependency on tourism, as well as from new opportunities that emerge from disasters. One such opportunity was to focus marketing efforts into new markets such as China, India and Russia, based on formation of new travel trade partners and airline alliances. The market response to the public and private marketing, promotion and communication initiatives was generally positive for the Maldives. The effectiveness of travel trade shows and promotional events, familiarization programs, timely communication of primary and solidarity messages and other measures that restore market, trade and investor confidence in the destination was clearly demonstrated.

Analysis of market trends before disasters and crises should be undertaken as part the market recovery process to provide a reality check on the prospects for discrete markets. For various reasons, markets will recover at vastly different rates following disasters and crises, and market-specific strategies and actions need to be formulated based on comprehensive analysis of the precursors and prospects for incremental growth in discrete markets and possibly even market segments. As the rates of market response and recovery become better analysed and understood, corresponding marketing strategies can be modified and monitored to ensure maximum effectiveness.

Crises and disasters by their nature can cause wholesale changes to all aspects of tourism destination management, including the means by which tourism is monitored. Existing metrics may need to be revised for accurate indicators of recovery rates and market conditions to be developed. Government and private sector initiatives that lead to expansion of capacity when re-building destinations will also pose considerable marketing challenges if high occupancy rates, revenue and margins are to be maintained at viable levels. Historical indicators of tourism performance such as occupancy rates may become redundant in an environment of reduced overall capacity (at least at the macro-economic level), and visitor arrivals, preferably by country of residence rather than nationality is a better overall indicator of

market recovery and trends. At the level of firm, rapid restoration of capacity, resumption to operational status and a concerted and focused marketing effort can ensure that business losses are minimized.

REFERENCES

Beirman, D (2003) Restoring Tourism Destinations in Crisis. CABI Publishing: Cambridge

Carlsen, J (2005) 'Crisis Communication and Tourism Recovery Strategies for the Maldives'. BEST Education Network Think Tank V, University of West Indies, Jamaica, June 16-19. University of Western Sydney: Sydney. ISBN 1741080843

Carlsen, J (2006) Post-Tsunami Tourism Strategies for the Maldives. *Tourism Review International*, Volume 10, Number 1, pp. 69-79 (11).

Cohen, E. (2005) 'Tourism and Disaster: the tsunami waves in Southern Thailand'. In Alejziak and R. Winiarski (Eds.) *Tourism in Scientific Research.* Academy of Physical Education in Krakow: Poland, pp. 81-114.

Department of Immigration and Emigration (2006) Tourist Arrivals by Nationality, January-September 2006, unpublished report.

de Sausmarez, N. (2005)'The Indian Ocean Tsunami.' *Tourism and Hospitality Planning and Development*, 2 (1) pp 55-59.

Henderson, J. C. (2003) 'Terrorism and Tourism: Managing the Consequences of the Bali Bombings.' *Journal of Travel and Tourism marketing*, 15 (1), pp 41-58.

Lynch, M. (2004) *Weathering the Storm. A Crisis Management Guide for Tourism Businesses.* Matador: Leicester.

Maldives Tourism Promotion Board [MTPB] (n.d.) http://www.visitmaldives.com.mv/mu/latest/update_situation_assessment.php accessed 20/1/ 2005.

MTPB (2006) http://www.visitmaldives.com/mu/latest/update.php?subaction=showfull&id=1104940019&archive=&start_from=&ucat=& accessed 13/6/06.

Ministry of Tourism (2004) *Tourism Statistics.* Statistics Section-Ministry of Tourism: Maldives.

Abdulla, M [Editor] (2006) *Tourism Yearbook 2006.* Planning and Research Section, Ministry of Tourism and Civil Aviation: Maldives.

PATA (n.d.) The Project Phoenix Story, CD-ROM, PATA: Bangkok.

PATA Bali Recovery Taskforce (n.d.) *Report and Recommendations* (unpublished).

Santana, G. (2003) 'Crisis Management and Tourism: Beyond the Rhetoric. *Journal of Travel & Tourism Marketing*, 15, (4), pp 299-321.

World Economic Forum/World Tourism Organization [WEF/UNWTO] (2005) Disaster Response: The Tourism Dimension, Volume 1. http://www.world-tourism. org/risk/index.htm accessed 12/6/2006.

United Nations World Tourism Organization [UNWTO] (2005) 'Evolution of tourism in the tsunami-affected destinations' TF2/MKT Report: Madrid.

Market Segmentation in Time of Crisis: A Case Study of the MICE Sector in Thailand

Kom Campiranon
Charles Arcodia

SUMMARY. The MICE sector (meetings, incentives, conventions, and exhibitions), has generated high foreign exchange revenue for the economy worldwide. In Thailand, MICE tourists are recognized as 'quality' visitors, mainly because of their high-spending potential. Nonetheless, Thailand's MICE sector has been influenced by a number of crises in the past since September 11, 2001. While a number of researchers have discussed the tourism market segmentation strategies during a crisis situation, less effort has focused on the MICE sector. Using Thailand as a case study, this research has adopted Seaton and Bennett's (1996, p. 31) concept of tourism market segmentation in order to understand the market segmentation strategy implemented by organizations in the MICE sector in time of crisis.

INTRODUCTION

As part of the tourism industry, the MICE (meetings, incentives, conventions, and exhibitions) sector increasingly generates significant revenue worldwide (e.g., Hing et al., 1998, p. 3; Mistilis & Dwyer, 1999) and is considered to generate a wide array of benefits to host countries and regional economies (Dwyer & Forsyth, 1997, p. 35). The Asian region has been taking advantage of this interest from the traditional markets such as Europe and North America. Thailand, in particular has been no exception (Rogers, 2003, p. 276).

Although tourists in the MICE sector contribute only three per cent of the overall tourist arrivals to Thailand each year, the spending of tourists in this sector is three times higher than spending of tourists in other sectors (Tourism Authority of Thailand, 2004). MICE delegates are therefore recognized as the most desirable category of 'quality' visitors, mainly because of their high-spending potential (Bangkok Post, 2003b) which generates strong foreign exchange revenue for the Thai economy (Tourism Authority of Thailand, 2001). The Tourism Authority of Thailand is consequently putting major emphasis on the promotion of the coun-

Kom Campiranon (E-mail: s4085712@student.uq.edu.au), is a PhD student in the School of Tourism at The University of Queensland (11 Salisbury Road, Ipswich Qld 4305, Australia). Charles Arcodia (E-mail: c.arcodia@uq.edu.au) is a Senior Lecturer in the School of Tourism at The University of Queensland (11 Salisbury Road, Ipswich Qld 4305, Australia).

try's MICE business as it is considered as a major high-yield target market with strong growth (Tourism Authority of Thailand, 2000).

Thailand's tourism, however, has been influenced by a series of external crises in recent years (Srikatanyoo & Campiranon, 2005b), such as September 11, Bali Bombing, SARS, Iraq War, Bird Flu, and the tsunami (Pacific Asia Travel Association, 2004). An external crisis can be defined as a crisis that is beyond the destination (or company's) control and therefore inherently provides a greater degree of risk and uncertainty (Evans & Elphick, 2005, p. 135). These recent crises and their adverse impacts have shifted the tourism industry into an entirely new paradigm, emphasizing the need for strong crisis management and rapid response mechanisms in order to retain the confidence of travelers (Bangkok Post, 2003a; World Tourism Organization, 2005).

In a world of growing political and environmental instability, tourism marketing plays a key role in crisis management (Hannam, 2004, p. 259). Understanding market segments is a critical element of marketing (Ranchhod, 2004, p. 35) and as a result segmentation is the most extensively researched area in tourism marketing (Seaton & Bennett, 1996, p. 31). While the utilization of market segmentation in time of crisis has been found in a series of tourism studies (e.g., Beirman, 2002; Hopper, 2002; Stafford, Yu & Armoo, 2002), less attention has been focused in the MICE sector. Therefore, it is an aim of this research to examine the market segmentation strategy implemented by the MICE sector in the time of crisis. It is envisaged that results from this research will contribute to the tourism marketing and the crisis management bodies of knowledge.

Having established a research gap and an aim of this research, the following sections will firstly provide an analysis of the most relevant academic contributions in this field. Then, the methodology and data collection techniques utilized in this research will be explained, followed by a conclusion and recommendations for future research.

LITERATURE REVIEW

In order to achieve an aim of this research, the literatures of the MICE sector, market seg-

mentation, and crisis management will be examined.

The MICE Sector

The MICE sector comprises one of the fastest growing sectors of the tourism industry worldwide (Dwyer & Forsyth 1997, p. 21; Hing et al., 1998). In addition, the MICE sector has long been recognized as a sector that draws lucrative direct and indirect revenue for host destinations (Lawrence & McCabe, 2001). It consists of various components, including: conventions, conferences, meetings, seminars, trade shows, exhibitions, and incentive travel. Its activities require many different players, including transport (international and domestic), accommodation, pre- and post-conference touring, purpose-built convention centers, exhibition facilities and hotels and catering and audiovisual services (Dwyer et al., 2001).

Having said that, there is a lack of an accepted and properly defined terminology for aspects of the MICE sector. Whilst the acronym 'MICE' is in widespread use around the world, 'business tourism' is widely used in Europe as the accepted generic term. In Australia, the industry has adopted the term 'business events' to describe its focus. Canada, on the other hand, uses MC&IT: meetings, conventions, and incentive travel (Rogers, 2003). Having acknowledged these differences, the term 'MICE' will be employed in this research as it has been widely used by key authorities in Thailand including the Tourism Authority of Thailand (TAT) and the Thailand Incentive and Convention Association (TICA). Each component of the MICE sector is now explained below.

Meetings are a crucial element of business with millions of meetings being held all over the world everyday. Whilst meetings can be held for different reasons (Hindle, 1998), one of the most common reasons is to solve problems and make decisions (Hayes, 1998). Basically, a meeting is an event usually involving relatively few executives discussing business around a boardroom table. However, the word 'meetings' is also used in a wider sense to describe conferences, meetings, and seminars, in a collective manner (Seekings & Farrer, 1999). It can also be defined as an event where the primary activity of the attendee is to attend educational sessions, participate in meetings and discussions, socialize, or attend other organized events. There is no exhibit component to this event (Fenich, 2005).

Incentives can be defined as all-expense-paid travel (Rogers, 2003, p. 52) which organizations mostly use to motivate and reward their employees or business partners (Fenich, 2005; Rogers, 2003, p. 52; Seekings & Farrer, 1999). Incentives may also include an educational element, team-building activities, and a conference-type session. It is however more susceptible to the ups and downs of the economies and political situations than most other components of MICE. The Gulf War in 1990, for example, virtually wiped out the American incentive travel market. Similarly, the impact of 'September 11th' on the American travel industry was huge and it will take some time to recover (Rogers, 2003, p. 54).

When meetings are combined with exhibitions, the event is called a 'convention' (Montgomery & Strick, 1995). Whilst this term is mostly used in America, the term 'congress' is the usual English equivalent in continental Europe (Seekings & Farrer, 1999). A convention can be defined as an event where the primary activity of the attendees is to attend educational sessions, participate in meetings/discussions, socialize, or attend other organized events (Convention Industry Council, 2005). It is also globally recognized for its valuable economic contribution in terms of employment and income. Other contributions include associated social and cultural benefits to the destination, the exchange of ideas, the cultivation of business contacts, the provision of forums for continuing education and training, and the facilitation of technology transfer (Dwyer, 2002).

An exhibition is an event at which the primary activity of the attendees is to visit exhibits on the show floor. These events focus primarily on business-to-business (B2B) relationships (Fenich, 2005) particularly to gain new clients (Jurisevic, 2002). The practice of holding exhibitions alongside conferences has also grown significantly in recent years. Part of the reason is because an exhibition can be invaluable to the delegates. For instance, it can give the delegates the opportunity of viewing the latest developments in technology, comparing the offerings of various suppliers, checking prices, obtaining

technical information, and discussing their particular needs with the exhibitors. Exhibitions can therefore 'add value' to the event, being seen by the delegates as something offering benefit over and above a basic conference (Seekings & Farrer, 1999).

Market Segmentation

As market segmentation is part of an organization's marketing strategies, it is therefore crucial for one to understand the concept of marketing. Ranchhod (2004, p. 19) defined marketing as the process of planning and executing activities that satisfy individual, ecological and social needs ethically and sincerely while also satisfying organizational objectives. An organization also needs to match its corporate and marketing capabilities to the opportunities or threats that exist within the marketplace. Pride et al. (2006, p. 5) added that the essence of marketing is to develop satisfying exchanges from which both customers and marketers benefit. The customer expects to gain a reward or benefit in excess of the costs incurred in the marketing transaction. The marketer expects to gain something of value in return, generally the price charged for the product or service.

Understanding segmentation is a critical element of marketing (Ranchhod 2004, p. 35) for many reasons. Kim and Jogaratnam (2003) explain that segments can be described as customer groups that share a similar problem and respond to market stimulus in an identical way. Kotler, Adam, Brown, and Armstrong (2006, p. 216) add that buyers are too numerous, too widely scattered, and too varied in their needs and that different organizations vary greatly in their abilities to serve different segments of the market. Rather than trying to compete in an entire market, sometimes against superior competitors, it is recommended that each organization identify the parts of the market that it can serve best. Therefore, target marketing has been implemented to help companies to find their marketing opportunity more efficiently.

Interestingly, segmentation is the most extensively researched area in tourism marketing (Seaton & Bennett 1996, p. 31). For practitioners, the underlying logic and the possible rewards that market segmentation can offer are well established in the travel and hospitality industry (Yuksel & Yuksel, 2002). Moreover, segmentation also helps effective control of how advertising budget can be allocated to maximize positive impacts to the economic base. As a result, segmentation strategy has become increasingly important for successful marketing planning in the tourism industry (Hu, 1996).

Whilst tourists have been segmented using a broad range of criteria (Littrell, Paige & Song, 2004), there is no single way to identify and analyze the market segments (Kotler et al., 2006, p. 218; Ranchhod, 2004, p. 37; Sarabia, 1996). After reviewing several studies in tourism market segmentation, it appears that the one proposed by Seaton and Bennett (1996, p. 31) appears to be suitable for this research. According to Seaton and Bennett (1996, p. 31), tourism market segmentation can be categorized into two broad categories of 'trip descriptors' and 'tourist descriptors.' 'Trip descriptors' break down the total tourism market by different types of trips. It concentrates not on describing the person but the kind of trip taken. Examples of tourist market in this category are recreational/pleasure, visiting friends and relatives (VFR), business, and others. 'Tourist descriptors,' on the other hand, focuses not on the trip but the person making it. These categorize a market segment by socio-demography, customer demand, time, geography, and frequency (Seaton & Bennett, 1996, p. 34).

Crisis Management

A crisis can be defined as an adverse incident with an unpredictable outcome (Bland, 1998; Campbell, 1999; Coombs, T. & Holladay, 2002; Coombs, W., 1999; Ruff & Aziz, 2003). In order to cope with crises, crisis management is needed. Many scholars have made an attempt to define crisis management. Fundamentally, crisis management is a systematic effort by organizational members to avert crises or to effectively manage those that do occur (King III, 2002). As an extension of risk management, crisis management is perceived as an established management decision-making aid applied to finance, business development, and new project feasibility studies. It is also used for proactive decision-making

that continuously assesses potential risks, prioritizes the risks, and implements strategies to cope with those risks (Pacific Asia Travel Association, 2003).

O'Tool and Mikolaitis (2002) add that crisis management does not only involve identifying and controlling risks, but also identifying the context and communicating the risks in order to minimize losses while maximizing the opportunities. Coombs (1999) suggests that crisis management involves a set of factors which specifically aim to cope with crises and lessen the actual damage inflicted by the crisis. Moreover, crisis management also seeks to prevent or lessen the negative outcomes of a crisis and thereby protect the organization, stakeholders, and industry from damage.

A series of studies (e.g., Fall & Massey, 2005, p. 77; Peters & Pikkemaat, 2005, p. 9; Pine & McKercher, 2004; Srikatanyoo & Campiranon, 2005a; Stafford, Yu & Armoo, 2002; Yu, Stafford & Armoo, 2005) have examined the crisis management process in the tourism context and findings revealed that tourism is susceptible to crises. As a result, Glaesser (2006, p. xi) suggested that tourism organizations not only need to implement measurements to minimize risk, but they also need to analyze negative events from every angle, to systematically identify critical success factors, to integrate them, and take them into account when considering the strategic corporate orientation. Glaesser (2006, p. xi) also noted that marketing in this perspective is vital. As many crises in tourism are causing impacts on companies and destinations, it is important to understand marketing when coping with crises.

METHODOLOGY AND DATA COLLECTION

This research adopted a qualitative approach as it is suitable when a concept or phenomenon needs to be understood because little research has been done on it (Creswell 2003, p. 18). The sampling design implemented in this research has been guided by a sampling design process proposed by Malhotra (2004) and Aaker, Kumar, and Day (2004, p. 374) which emphasizes the need for the researcher to define the target population, determine the sampling frame, and select a sampling technique.

In this research, the target population is defined as organizations offering MICE services in Thailand. The sampling frame has been obtained from a cd-rom directory of organizations in Thailand offering MICE services (Thailand Incentive and Convention Association, 2003). Having determined the second sampling frame, this research then adopted a convenience sampling technique as it allows the respondent to be deliberately selected to reflect particular features of or groups within the sampled population (Ritchie, Lewis & Elam, 2003, p. 78).

With all these considerations, in-depth interviews using semi-structured interviews technique have been undertaken in Thailand with the high-level executives of 37 organizations that offer MICE services. The position titles of these interviewees were director, general manager, and president of their organization. Each interview took about 30-45 minutes. The interviews were conducted in 10 weeks starting in the middle of November 2005 and finished in the end of January 2006.

Prior to an interview, the interviewees were given a consent form explaining that their participations in the interview are voluntarily. The form also explains the objective of this research and provides the university contact details of the researcher and his advisor. As suggested by Malhotra (2004), the researcher started the interview by asking a general question and then encouraged the subject to talk freely about their attitudes toward an issue. Following the general discussion, the interviews were guided by questions used in Srikatanyoo and Campiranon's (2005b) study by asking the respondents how they coped with crises that have happened since September 11, 2001. Interviews were recorded for later transcription.

DATA ANALYSIS AND FINDINGS

This research employed N6 software as a tool to categorize and simplify the qualitative data. N6 is a computer package designed to assist the researcher in managing non-numerical and unstructured data, such as data from interviews. The program provides tools to assist in-

terpretation and coding, or Indexing, Searching text or patterns of coding and theorizing about what has been identified and understood as the patterns become clearer (QSR International 2004).

Having discussed the data analysis tool used in this research, it is important to consider the underpinning concept that will provide a lens for the researcher in order to understand the phenomenon, in this case 'market segmentation in time of crises.' Tourism researchers (e.g., Hu, 1996; Hudson & Ritchie, 2002; Kim & Jogaratnam, 2003; Yuksel & Yuksel, 2002) have adopted different means by which to segment a market.

Market Segmentation–Tourist Descriptors

The concept of 'Tourist Descriptors' (Seaton & Bennett, 1996, p. 34) has been used by interviewees to cope with a crisis situation by targeting different geographical regions. Segmenting the tourism market by using geographical area has been implemented in tourism and Seaton and Bennett (1996, p. 38) emphasized that in fact one of the first tasks of segmentation for any tourism organization is that of examining the geographic origins of its customers or potential customers. Kotler et al. (2006, p. 218) further explained that geographical segmentation calls for identifying and analyzing the different geographical unit such as nations, regions, states, municipalities, cities, or neighborhood which make up a market. A company may decide to operate in one or a few geographical areas, or to operate in all areas but pay attention to geographical differences in needs and wants.

In this research, interviewees agreed that crises did affect their business and they need to change the strategy and the way they marketed. Therefore, organizations offering MICE services have to look at market segments that are willing to come to organize a MICE activity during this difficult time of the destination. It is crucial that those organizations constantly determine a potential market segment and be quick enough to switch to that market once the crisis happens, as interviewee #33 supported that:

> Business will continue as long as the money has been made. It is shortsighted

for MICE companies to say that their business has been wiped out because of the crisis. The reality is that the market has been wiped out, not their business, therefore they need to look ahead and seek other target market.

According to the data analysis, long haul markets appear to be the mainstream of revenue for a number of organizations offering MICE services due to their high spending. However, attracting these markets in time of crisis appears to be problematic. First of all, long haul markets tend not to have a good geographical understanding which is why they are quite vulnerable to crises. For example, SARS happened in Singapore and Hong Kong but tourists in Europe had an impression that those countries are close to Thailand therefore they have decided not to come to have their MICE event in Thailand. Interviewee #12 added that long haul market is more vulnerable to crisis than regional market by saying that:

> Foreigners often assume that a crisis that happened in Indonesia might affect the whole Asia Pacific region. The fact is that Thailand is very far from Indonesia. However they perceive that Thailand has been negatively affected from Bali bombing and even bird flu in Vietnam. They are too sensitive! The first groups of tourist that return to Asia are Asian tourists. This is because they know that the situation is not that bad.

Results from the data analysis also explained that the overseas MICE markets, especially the long haul market, are susceptible to crises due to two major factors, which are news and travel advisory notice issued by the government or reliable association. Firstly, overseas tourists rely heavily on news which is normally overwhelmed with the crisis situation. Sometimes the news depicts a very negative image of the situation and repeats those images again and again when the situation is not as bad as it was. Secondly, travel advisory issued by the government or reliable association also causes MICE to be vulnerable because the tourist would listen to those advisories. If the government or the World Health Organization (WHO) issues a travel advisory concerning a risk in traveling to Bali, for example, few organizations would ignore this advisory.

These two dominant factors significantly influence the decision making process of the MICE tourists. As a consequence, any life-threatening situation will make the MICE tourists hesitate to come. This is mainly because they feel that the crisis, e.g., the tsunami, might happen again. They also feel that the destination might be unattractive or the essential infrastructure may be negatively affected by the crisis. Some say that they feel that it is inappropriate to enjoy their activities while other local people are suffering from the aftermath of the crisis. These reasons clearly indicated that long haul markets are generally vulnerable to crises. This finding also support Kim and Jogaratnam's (2003) argument that customers in the same segment share a similar problem, in this case 'crisis vulnerability,' and respond to market stimulus in an identical way, by avoiding the crisis-affected destination.

As long haul markets are the main customer base for many organizations offering MICE services, those organizations must look at alternative or replacement markets that are resilient to the current situation. While many interviewees agreed with Hudson and Ritchie's (2002) statement that the return on marketing activities in local market is normally lower than those in overseas market, they did put their marketing efforts at local market in time of crisis. Interviewees explain that local market tends to be more resilient to crises than long haul markets. Moreover, there is also a demand of MICE services from local customers as their business must go on and therefore meetings, incentives, conventions, and exhibitions are still needed. Interviewee #26 noted an example of this strategy from an exhibition perspective that:

> In time of crisis, everyone would probably need to attract more domestic market. Instead of relying on overseas exhibitors, exhibition businesses in Thailand need to put a marketing effort to focus more in a domestic market. The reason is because domestic business still needs to do a marketing activities and exhibition is one of the available marketing tools.

Apart from a local market, short-to-medium haul market (regional market) has also been targeted in time of crisis rather than long haul market as regional market has better understanding of the crisis situation. Interviewee #27 stated that the September 11 crisis has resulted in a sharp decline in incentive tourists from the United States. Therefore, his company has changed target market to Asian markets such as Philippines or Malaysia. Fortunately, his company has made a timely decision and the strategy of targeting regional market has proved to be a successful one.

Having determined the vulnerable and resilient markets, organizations also need to understand the concept of 'different points in time.' According to Glaesser (2006, p. 180), one needs to understand an issue of 'different points in time' when applying a marketing strategy to crisis management. Even under normal circumstances, the effect of the marketing instruments differs depending on the time factor. The onset of a negative event strongly influences the different points in time when the marketing strategies are to be employed. This external influence is a very important difference compared to the normal situation, when time plays a far less important role.

In this research, interviewees have implemented a strategy similar to Glaesser's (2006, p. 180) concept of 'different points in time' by determining different market segmentation in different crisis period. When asked whether there is any difference between the marketing segmentation in different crisis period, interviewee #35 replied:

> Yes, there is a difference and we have to be quite aggressive in time of crisis. We have a timeframe for 1, 2, and 3 months... which is short, medium, and long term planning. Short term strategy aims to acquire an immediate business.

According to the data analysis, interviewees classify the different points in time into three major periods, which are short, medium, and long term. A 'short-term' strategy has been implemented during crisis by targeting particular resilient markets, mostly local market, in order to temporarily replace other major markets that have been declined. The local market is often

targeted as a short term strategy as they are quite resilient to crises due to the good understanding of the situation. After targeting local market as a short-term strategy, a 'medium-term' strategy should then target at regional countries within three hours flight. If organizations can successfully stimulate these markets then there is a high chance that the demand for MICE services from long-haul market will be increased.

A 'long-term strategy' should be implemented when the crisis situation has been resolved. In this stage, it is recommended that organizations resume a marketing strategy to lure back overseas market that has been targeted prior to a crisis situation. Revenue from overseas MICE tourists is crucial to many organizations, such as hotels and event planners, as the overseas market often required more services than local market. For example, a meeting requested by customers from overseas not only required a meeting room but also a hotel room, pre/post city tour, and other activities for the meeting participants from overseas, whereas a large number of meeting booked by local customers only require a meeting room as the majority of their meeting participants are from local area.

In brief, organizations offering MICE services have to decide on where their potential source market can be in that particular crisis. Once they have decided 'where,' then they can tailor a call for action by using marketing strategies to attract that market. It should be pointed however that crisis and consumer behavior are complex systems and therefore local and regional market are not always the right market to target in time of crisis. The reason is because each crisis is different which is why a local and regional market can be vulnerable to certain crises too, as interviewee #36 stated that:

> I think you also have to look at what your crisis is. And from there, you will see that some markets will be more resilient than others. Some markets will be less affected by one crisis . . . and more affected by another type of crisis. So I think culture and people are different . . . so they respond differently. From the tsunami lesson in Phuket, the Asians are the hard market to get back because the Asians are incredibly superstitious and incredibly uncomfortable about being around spirits that

have not been properly buried. Whereas the European they would say it's no big deal and they might come to Phuket if there is a good deal.

Consequently, it is not all about distance and the easiest market to get back, but also about an issue of psychology and cultural difference. Crises are all different and they all have different implications to crisis management. It is essential that marketers take these issues into consideration before planning a short, medium, and long term marketing strategy.

Market Segmentation–Trip Descriptors

The second market segmentation strategy found in this research is similar to the concept of 'Trip descriptors.' 'Trip descriptors' have been described by Seaton and Bennett (1996, p. 31) who consider that market segmentation can be classified by different types of trips. In this research, some interviewees reported that the MICE market is too vulnerable in time of crisis and therefore they need to find substitute revenue by attracting non-MICE markets, such as leisure or group tour. Before discussing such a strategy, it is important however for one to understand the reason why MICE is more susceptible to crises than other tourism sectors.

Generally, a MICE trip is sponsored by a company. And most of the time, high level executives will be joining the MICE event and traveling on a corporate insurance plan. Due to this liability issue, the decision makers at the company will be very careful before requesting their staff to attend any MICE event in a crisis-affected area. Interviewee #12 also emphasized that MICE is more vulnerable to crises than other tourism sectors by saying that:

> FIT tourists are now returning to Thailand after the tsunami crisis, but not MICE. Normally, MICE requires long-term planning about 1 or 1.5 year, while a large conference may require 2 years of planning. So the planner will have to defend why the conference should be held in that destination. Therefore, if there is bad news about the destination then it is unlikely that the conference will be held there.

For that reason, organizations that largely focus on the MICE market would experience difficulty during crises. Therefore, those organizations need to come up with other strategies. According to the data analysis, a majority of organizations involved in the in-depth interview reported that they have focused at other non-MICE market in time of crisis. As each tourist market has different characteristic, therefore organizations offering MICE services need to have a good mix of business in order to survive the crisis. Interviewee #1 suggested that organization can hardly survive by focusing only on MICE business because:

> MICE has been affected by crises significantly. During SARS, I think companies that provide incentive or MICE business had lost 60% of their business. However, if you have a good mix of business . . . for instance between MICE and leisure . . . then you should be able to sustain your business.

Therefore, when possible, a good mix of various tourism services such as MICE, leisure, collective, FIT, and group tour market is needed to compensate the loss of business and to achieve the profitability of an organization, as Interviewee #17 supported that:

> We have many types of business . . . and MICE is only one of them . . . so if the MICE business is bad then we will have to earn more revenue from other business segment . . . instead of keep focusing in the problematic MICE business.

Organizations such as hotels appears to be flexible enough that they can cater their service to suit the need of different customer types such as MICE, leisure, and group tour market. Having said that, it should be pointed that this strategy can be difficult for some organizations to implement as those organizations have resources specifically designed to suite the need of MICE activities. An exhibition center provides a clear example that its facilities are suitable for a large trade or consumer exhibition. Therefore, the management of those organizations needs to evaluate its potential revenue opportunity.

CONCLUSION

To sum up, the tourism industry, particularly the MICE sector, is sensitive to crises and market segmentation plays a key role here to lure back MICE tourists. In this research, Seaton and Bennett's (1996, p. 31) concept of 'tourist descriptors' and 'trip descriptors' have been adopted as a framework in order to understand the use of tourism market segmentation among organizations in the MICE sector during crisis situation. Results from this research support Kim and Jogaratnam's (2003) argument that customers in the same segment share a similar problem, in this case 'crisis vulnerability,' and respond to market stimulus in an identical way.

As crises are unpredictable (Bland, 1998; Campbell, 1999; Coombs, T. & Holladay, 2002; Coombs, W., 1999; Ruff & Aziz, 2003), organizations also have to take an issue of 'different points in time' (Glaesser, 2006, p. 180) into consideration as marketing strategy can be shaped by different period of crisis situation. Organizations in the MICE sector showed that they have recognized the importance of different point in time by classifying their crisis marketing activities into three major phases, which are short, medium, and long term strategies.

By targeting the resilient market segments as a short term strategy, organizations will be able to temporarily compensate the loss of revenue while it is recommended that a medium-term and long-term strategies are to target regional and long haul markets respectively. It is also noted that, where possible, organizations cannot survive in time of crisis by targeting only MICE customers as MICE can be very sensitive to crises due to its unique characteristics. Therefore, organizations should not 'put all their eggs in one basket' and broaden their customer base to other types of tourists such as leisure and group tours.

It is also important that organizations take an issue of culture differences into account and be able to adapt their marketing strategy accordingly (Kotler et al., 2006, p. 163). In different crises, certain markets may be more vulnerable than other markets according to cultural differences. The recent tsunami provides a clear example of this issue. During the tsunami, Asian tourists, who are normally resilient to crises within Asia, appeared to be vulnerable and decided not to choose Phuket, and even Thailand, for their MICE activities as they were afraid of ghosts as a large number of people lost their lives there due to this disaster. Hence, organizations should be aware that local and regional market may not always be an ideal market segment for short-term strategy.

Thus far, this paper has made an attempt to achieve its objective by examining the use of tourism market segmentation in the crisis situation. Results from the data analysis have been discussed. In conclusion, recommendations for future study will be presented.

RECOMMENDATIONS FOR FUTURE STUDY

There are a few limitations in this paper. Firstly, this paper only examines one of many marketing aspects, which is market segmentation. It is envisaged that research in other marketing aspects, such as marketing mix and pricing, will greatly help researchers and practitioners to have a better understanding of marketing as a crisis recovery strategy. Secondly, this paper does not aim to identify factors that play an important role to the decision of MICE customers in time of crisis. It is recommended, however, that future studies need to investigate those factors, such as the notion of 'pull factors' and 'push factors,' in crisis situations in order to develop the most cost-effective marketing activities.

REFERENCES

Aaker, D., Kumar, V. & Day, G. 2004, *Marketing Research*, 8th edn, John Wiley & Sons, Inc., New York.

Bangkok Post 2003a, *2003 Review: What A Year!*, Bangkok Post, Available at: < http://www.bangkokpost.com/tourism2003/year.html>.

— 2003b, *Business Events in Thailand*, Bangkok Post, Available at: < http://www.bangkokpost.net/tourism2003/business.html>.

Beirman, D. 2002, 'Marketing of tourism destinations during a prolonged crisis: Israel and the Middle East,' *Journal of Vacation Marketing*, vol. 8, no. 2, pp. 167-77.

Bland, M. 1998, *Communicating out of a Crisis*, Macmillan Press, London.

Campbell, R. 1999, *Crisis Control: Preventing & Managing Corporate Crises*, Prentice Hall, Australia.

Convention Industry Council 2005, *APEX Industry Glossary*, Convention Industry Council, Available at: <http://glossary.conventionindustry.org/>.

Coombs, T. & Holladay, S. 2002, 'Helping crisis managers protect reputational assets: Initial tests of the situational crisis communication theory,' *Management Communication Quarterly*, vol. 16, no. 2, pp. 165-87.

Coombs, W. 1999, *Ongoing Crisis Communication: Planning, Managing, and Responding*, Sage Publications, London.

Creswell, J. 2003, *Research Design: Qualitative, Quantitative, and Mix Methods Approaches*, 2nd edn, Sage Publications, California.

Dwyer, L. 2002, 'Economic Contribution of Convention Tourism: Conceptual and Empirical Issues', in *Convention Tourism: International Research and Industry Perspectives*, eds K. Weber & K. Chon, Haworth Hospitality Press, New York.

Dwyer, L. & Forsyth, P. 1997, 'Impacts and benefits of MICE Tourism: A framework for Analysis,' *Tourism Economics*, vol. 3, no. 1, pp. 21-38.

Dwyer, L., Mistilis, N., Forsyth, P. & Rao, P. 2001, 'International price competitiveness of Australia's MICE industry,' *International Journal of Tourism Research*, vol. 3, no. 2, pp. 123-39.

Evans, N. & Elphick, S. 2005, 'Models of crisis management: an evaluation of their value for strategic planning in the international travel industry,' *The International Journal of Tourism Research*, vol. 7, no. 3, pp. 135-51.

Fall, L. & Massey, J. 2005, 'The Significance of Crisis Communication in the Aftermath of 9/11: A National Investigation of How Tourism Managers Have Re-Tooled Their Promotional Campaigns,' *Journal of Travel & Tourism Marketing*, vol. 19, no. 2/3, pp. 77-90.

Fenich, G. 2005, *Meetings, Expositions, Events, and Conventions: An Introduction to the Industry*, Pearson Education, New Jersey.

Glaesser, D. 2006, *Crisis Management in the Tourism Industry*, 2nd edn, Butterworth-Heinemann, Oxford.

Hannam, K. 2004, 'Tourism and development II: marketing destinations, experiences and crises,' *Progress in Development Studies*, vol. 4, no. 3, pp. 256-65.

Hayes, C. 1998, *Meetings*, Eastern House, Victoria.

Hindle, T. 1998, *Managing Meetings*, Dorling Kindersley Limited, UK.

Hing, N., McCabe, V., Lewis, P. & Leiper, N. 1998, 'Hospitality trends in the Asia-Pacific: a discussion of five key sectors,' *International Journal of Contemporary Hospitality Management*, vol. 10, no. 7, pp. 264-71.

Hopper, P. 2002, 'Marketing London in a difficult climate,' *Journal of Vacation Marketing*, vol. 9, no. 1, pp. 81-9.

Hu, C. 1996, 'Diverse developments in travel and tourism marketing: a thematic approach,' *International Journal of Contemporary Hospitality Management*, vol. 8, no. 7, pp. 33-43.

Hudson, S. & Ritchie, B. 2002, 'Understanding the domestic market using cluster analysis: A case study of the marketing efforts of Travel Alberta.' *Journal of Vacation Marketing*, vol. 8, no. 3, pp. 263-77.

Jurisevic, S. 2002, *Exhibitions and Trade Shows*, Pearson Education Australia, New South Wales.

Kim, K. & Jogaratnam, G. 2003, 'Activity preferences of Asian international and domestic American university students: An alternate basis for segmentation,' *Journal of Vacation Marketing*, vol. 9, no. 3, pp. 260-70.

King III, G. 2002, 'Crisis management & team effectiveness: A closer examination,' *Journal of Business Ethics*, vol. 41, no. 3, pp. 235-50.

Kotler, P., Adam, S., Brown, L. & Armstrong, G. 2006, *Principles of Marketing*, 3rd edn, Pearson Education, New South Wales.

Lawrence, M. & McCabe, V. 2001, 'Managing conferences in regional areas: A practical evaluation in conference management,' *International Journal of Contemporary Hospitality Management*, vol. 13, no. 4/5, pp. 204-8.

Littrell, M., Paige, R. & Song, K. 2004, 'Senior travellers: Tourism activities and shopping behaviours,' *Journal of Vacation Marketing*, vol. 10, no. 4, pp. 348-63.

Malhotra, N. 2004, *Marketing Research: An Applied Orientation*, Pearson Education, New Jersey.

Mistilis, N. & Dwyer, L. 1999, 'Tourism Gateways and Regional Economies: the Distributional Impacts of MICE,' *International Journal of Tourism Research*, vol. 1, no. 6, pp. 441-57.

Montgomery, R. & Strick, S. 1995, *Meetings, Conventions, and Exhibitions: An Introduction to the Industry*, John Wiley & Sons, New York.

O'Tool, W. & Mikolaitis, P. 2002, *Corporate Event Project Management*, John Wiley & Sons, Inc., New York.

Pacific Asia Travel Association 2003, *Crisis: It Won't Happen to Us*, Pacific Asia Travel Association, Bangkok.

— 2004, *Tsunami Recovery Travel Facts*, Pacific Asia Travel Association, Available at: <http://www. pata.org/patasite/index.php?id=1137#3>.

Peters, M. & Pikkemaat, B. 2005, 'Crisis Management in Alpine Winter Sports Resorts: The 1999 Avalanche Disaster in Tyrol,' *Journal of Travel & Tourism Marketing*, vol. 19, no. 2/3, pp. 9-20.

Pine, R. & McKercher, B. 2004, 'The impact of SARS on Hong Kong's tourism industry,' *International Journal of Contemporary Hospitality Management*, vol. 16, no. 2, pp. 139-45.

Pride, W., Elliott, G., Rundle-Thiele, S., Waller, D. & Paladino, A. 2006, *Marketing: Core Concepts & Applications*, John Wiley & Sons Australia, Milton.

QSR International 2004, *Getting Started in N6*, QSR International.

Ranchhod, A. 2004, *Marketing Strategies: A twenty-first century approach*, Pearson Education Limited, England.

Ritchie, J., Lewis, J. & Elam, G. 2003, 'Designing and Selecting Samples,' in *Qualitative Research Practice: A Guide for Social Sciences Students and Researchers*, eds J. Ritchie & J. Lewis, Sage Publications, London.

Rogers, T. 2003, *Conferences and Conventions: A Global Industry*, Butterworth-Heinemann, Oxford.

Ruff, P. & Aziz, K. 2003, *Managing Communications in a Crisis*, Gower Publishing Limited, England.

Sarabia, J. 1996, 'Model for market segments evaluation and selection,' *European Journal of Marketing*, vol. 30, no. 4, pp. 58-74.

Seaton, A. & Bennett, M. 1996, *Marketing Tourism Products: Concepts, Issues, Cases*, Thomson Learning, London.

Seekings, D. & Farrer, J. 1999, *How to Organize Effective Conferences and Meetings*, 7th edn, Kogan Page, UK.

Srikatanyoo, N. & Campiranon, K. 2005a, 'Crisis Management of Hotels in Phuket: Compare and Contrast between Thai and Foreign Hotel Management Style,' *ASAIHL-Thailand Journal*, vol. 8, no. 2, pp. 165-76.

— 2005b, Crisis Management of Hotels in Phuket: Compare and Contrast between Thai and Foreign Hotel Management Style (Refereed Paper), paper presented to The 15th Inter-University Conference, Bangkok, Thailand, Sukhothai Thammathirath Open University and ASAIHL Thailand.

Stafford, G., Yu, L. & Armoo, A. 2002, 'Crisis management and recovery: How Washington, D.C., hotels responded to terrorism,' *Cornell Hotel and Restaurant Administration Quarterly*, vol. 43, no. 5, pp. 27-41.

Thailand Incentive and Convention Association 2003, *Thailand MICE Planning Guide 2003-2004 (cd-rom)*, Thailand Incentive and Convention Association.

Tourism Authority of Thailand 2000, *Organizational restructure, boost MICE industry become TAT's main policies*, Tourism Authority of Thailand, Available at: < http://www.tatnews.org/tat_release/765.asp>.

— 2001, *Thai MICE Industry gets another big boost*, Tourism Authority of Thailand, Available at: < http://www.tatnews.org/tat_news/detail.asp?id=977>.

— 2004, *MICE Business in Thailand*, Tourism Authority of Thailand, Available at: <http://www2.tat.or.th/tat/e-journal/>.

World Tourism Organization 2005, *Crisis Guidelines for the Tourism Industry*, World Tourism Organization, Available at: <http://www.world-tourism.org/tsunami/eng.html>.

Yu, L., Stafford, G. & Armoo, a. 2005, 'A Study of Crisis Management Strategies of Hotel Managers in the Washington, D.C. Metro Area,' *Journal of Travel & Tourism Marketing*, vol. 19, no. 2/3, pp. 91-105.

Yuksel, A. & Yuksel, F. 2002, 'Measurement of tourist satisfaction with restaurant services: A segment-based approach,' *Journal of Vacation Marketing*, vol. 9, no. 1, pp. 52-69.

Post Crisis Recovery:
The Case of After Cyclone Larry

Bruce Prideaux

Alexandra Coghlan

Fay Falco-Mammone

SUMMARY. In recent years a growing number of disasters have affected the tourism industry on scales that range from regional to global. Although there have been a number of significant disasters including SARS, the September 11 attack on the US in 2001, coups in Fiji and the Asian Financial Crisis of 1997/98 the impacts on the tourism industry in the affected regions and/or countries have been surprisingly short-term. There is still much to learn from how crisis events were managed by the various industry and government authorities involved. This paper focuses on aspects of the impact of Cyclone Larry on the North Queensland tourism industry by examining the impact on visitor flows in the short term and recording the views of visitors who had travelled to the region several months after the event. The research identifies aspects of visitor behaviours and expectations that may be of use to industry and government to better inform managers and policy makers in their planning and management functions.

As previous research has shown (Fall and Massey 2005), it is essential for destinations to begin the task of recovery from a crisis or disaster at the earliest possible opportunity. Immediately after a crisis event has occurred the affected area can expect to receive considerable media attention. The degree and form of coverage will largely depend on the severity of the

Bruce Prideaux is affiliated with the Tourism Program–School of Business James Cook University, P.O. Box 6811, Cairns, QLD 4870, Australia (E-mail: bruce.prideaux@jcu.edu.au). Alexandra Coghlan is affiliated with the Tourism Program–School of Business, James Cook University, P.O. Box 6811, Cairns, QLD 4870, Australia (E-mail: alexandra. coghlan@jcu.edu.au). Fay Falco-Mammone is affiliated with the Tourism Program–School of Business, James Cook University, P.O. Box 6811, Cairns, QLD 4870, Australia (E-mail: fay.falco@jcu.edu.au).

Funding for this project was provided by the JCU/CSIRO Tropical Landscapes Joint Venture and the Skyrail Foundation. The authors of this research report would like to acknowledge the following for their valuable assistance and support for this research project: Scotty's Beach House, Lake Barrine Teahouse, Mission Beach Visitor Information Centre, Tully Visitor Information Centre, Beachcomber Coconut Caravan Village, Cairns Coconut Caravan Resort, Tourism Tropical North Queensland, andTourism Queensland.

crisis and its impact on people and property. Large scale disasters such as the 2004 Tsunami that struck in Indonesia and other nations bordering the Indian ocean generated considerable media attention and for areas such as Phuket in Thailand the impact was to some degree sensationalised by the media coverage that focused on death and destruction. In many crisis situations good news stories rarely receive attention at least until the reporting of death and destruction has run its course.

As Peters and Pikkemaat (2005) point out, crisis management is essential and rebuilding confidence in destinations is a key recovery strategy. Rapid restoration of infrastructure is essential and once underway steps can be taken to restore a positive image in the recovery phase. Faulkner's (2001) paper on recovery from severe flooding in the small outback town of Katherine in Australia both illustrated the type of steps that were required to effect recovery and set the scene for further academic enquiry in this area. In an examination of the crisis recovery communications used by Convention and Visitors Bureaus, Fall and Massey (2005) note the need for managers to consider the significance of crisis communications in post crisis rebuilding strategies.

The large number of crises and disasters that have affected parts of the global tourism industry in recent years has generated considerable interest in academic circles. Since the observation by Faulkner (2001:136) that "relatively little systematic research has been carried out on disaster phenomena in tourism," there has been a significant growth of interest in the impacts on the tourism industry of crises and disasters. Recent contributions by Hall, Timothy and Duval (2003), a recent special issue of the *Journal of Tourism & Travel Marketing* (Vol 19:2/3) edited by Laws and Prideaux and a forthcoming book on tourism crisis management edited by Laws and Prideaux illustrate the growing interest in this area of research.

In 2003 Prideaux, Laws and Faulkner (2003:512) observed that while the future is impossible to predict, "What is known of the future is that there are a number of circumstances that may exert influence on the course of events in following years." These circumstances included trends, crises, disasters and change in the structure of government, social organiza-

tion or economic structure. Many such events are unpredictable in respect to timing, severity and précis location but are predictable in a broader sense of inevitability. For example, Hurricane Katrina was one of numerous Hurricanes that develop in the Caribbean and which annually cause significance damage. The possibility that a Hurricane could hit New Orleans had been long recognized by the authorities who had erected numerous defenses but the severity of this expected event was larger than predicted and caused enormous damage. While it is possible to predict events based on observable trends such as weather patterns the extent of the impact on industries such as tourism can only be guessed at and responded to on the basis of what actually occurs. One way to build a learning frame that can be used to educate managers who have to respond to crises is to record the responses to crisis situations as case studies. While each crisis is different the impacts on the tourism industry are more predictable.

The research reported in this paper examines the impact of a cyclone on a number of popular tourism locations in North Queensland, Australia. The significance of this study is that it records the views of tourists who visited the affected regions several months after the event. What is interesting to the researchers is that the respondents were not particularly worried about the event and still found much to interest them in their visit to the area. Research of this nature is important because if gives tourism managers insights to the reactions of visitors to the visual effects of cyclone damage and indicates the best mix of media to use when undertaking post event marketing.

TROPICAL CYCLONE LARRY

Tropical Cyclone Larry (TC Larry), a category 5 severe cyclone, struck the Queensland coast near Innisfail early on the morning of March 20, 2006. As it made landfall, wind gusts of over 294km/hour were recorded near Innisfail (Bureau of Meteorology, 2006b). The immediate impacts of the cyclone were felt on communities from the coastal zone to the hinterland region of the Atherton Tablelands. Significant damage occurred to houses, businesses and industry, utilities, infrastructure (including road, rail and air transport systems, schools, hospitals and communications), crops and state forests (Bureau of Meteorology, 2006a). An aerial assessment undertaken on 23 March (Bureau of Meteorology, 2006) indicated that in Innisfail, a provincial city of 20,000 residents, 50% of homes, 35% of commercial structures and 25% of government buildings were damaged. In the popular coastal tourism area of Mission Beach, 30% of homes, 20% of commercial premises and 45% of the area's caravan park accommodation were damaged. Crop losses were extensive particularly in the Banana industry which supplies up to 90% of the nation's banana crop.

Immediately after the passing of the cyclone the region's counter disaster plan was implemented and local resources were mobilised to initiate rescue and recovery based on a previously rehearsed cyclone disaster plan. The enormity of the damage was such that the Federal Government deployed a large military contingent on the day of the disaster to assist with clean-up operations. External resources were also mobilized to assist in restoration of electricity, communications and other essential services. Several days after the event the State Government appointed a popular former Chief of the Defence Force, General Peter Cosgrave, to head the organisation tasked with rebuilding the affected area. Despite suffering a category 5 cyclone, the same category as Hurricane Katrina in New Orleans, no lives were lost because of effective pre-cyclone preparations taken by residents and the authorities during the night before the cyclone struck.

The study region has two distant geographic and climatic regimes. In the east, the region is coastal and tropical while to the west on the Atherton Tablelands the affected region is rural and has milder temperatures particularly in summer. In both parts of the study region the tourism industry has a strong focus on natural resources including the rainforest. Innisfail, Mission Beach and Tully are located in a coastal zone that strides the main road and rail corridors that connect Cairns with the southern state capital cities of Brisbane and Sydney. Innisfail, Tully and Mission Beach benefit from this location and are frequent stopover points for international backpackers and domestic tourists travelling along the East Coast tourist route. The main attractions in the coastal part of the study region include beaches in the Mission Beach area, the meeting of the rainforest and reef World Heritage Areas, outdoor activities such as bush walking, wildlife spotting, fishing, parachuting, swimming and snorkelling. For a growing number of international backpackers the opportunity to work in the banana industry as well in service jobs particularly in the food and beverage sector is also a major attractor. Tully is well know for its white water rafting industry while the remnant population of Cassowary, in addition to other bird species, is a major attraction in the Mission Beach area. Off shore, Dunk Island attracts significant numbers of day tourists as well as overnight visitors.

The Atherton Tablelands located to the west of the Great Dividing Range and away from the East Coast tourist transit route attracts a different group of visitors. In this region, which has a diversified agricultural economy and a relatively small tourism sector, the majority of visitors are day trippers from Cairns. A smaller overnight sector draws visitors from the region centred on Townsville to the south and from the grey nomads sector. The attraction of the region is built around its proximity to Cairns, peaceful rural countryside, country towns and attractions that include Lake Tinaroo, the Crater lakes, weekend country markets, waterfalls, botanical and rainforest walks and a wide range of accommodation. According to a study of the local tourism industry's view of the Atherton Tablelands, the image is based on waterfalls and lakes, rainforest, wildlife, scenery and the hospitality of the locals in this rural environment (Williams, 2004).

Tourists visiting the study region include both domestics and internationals who are able to be further categorised into sectors that include backpackers (including those who are on working holidays), fly/drive, free independent travellers of all ages, grey nomads, day trippers and package tourists. In some cases there groupings may not be mutually exclusive. Much of what is known about the Tropical North Queensland (TNQ) tourism market comes from studies carried out in Cairns. Queensland attracts well over half (62%) of Australia's international backpacker visitors with the North, including Cairns, attracts the highest percentage of backpackers (68%) on a state wide basis. A study by Prideaux, Falco-Mammone, Thompson (2006) found that the majority of these backpackers were under 30 years of age, British or European, students and on incomes of less than $20,000 per year. Previous research (Prideaux and Shiga 2006) suggested that there are a growing number of Asian backpackers many of whom have a poor command of English making them potentially more vulnerable to tourism disasters such as tropical cyclones (Measham, 1999).

THE STATE OF TOURISM
IN THE REGION AFTER THE CYCLONE

TC Larry caused considerable damage to the rainforest substantially reducing the rainforest canopy cover from as high as 100% in some areas to under 30% in the most heavily damaged areas. Physical damage to property and other infrastructure including roads, bridges and electricity grids was severe. In the national park estate the Environmental Protection Agency (EPA) reported that up to 73 of the region's parks and forests were affected, with an estimated cost of $10 million in damage to infrastructure and resources (Environmental Protection Agency, 2006). Additionally, many heritage buildings were severely damaged, the majority of walking tracks were closed, roads were damaged, and road signage was destroyed. This damage to the region's natural resources and infrastructure was widely reported in the national and international media causing the cancellation of a large number of forward bookings and a significant down turn in visitor numbers in the affected area. The destruction of the region's banana industry had a further impact on visitor numbers as backpackers sort alterative destinations for rural work.

Cairns to the north suffered little physical damage and while there was a small fall in arrivals by air immediately after the cyclone domestic arrivals at the Cairns airport were higher in the months after the cyclone then for comparable months in the preceding year. The same pattern was observed with international arrivals. However, it appears that arrivals by road did decline based on visitor numbers at Visitor Information Centres. The impact of Cyclone Monica which struck an extensive area of Cape York Peninsula several weeks after Cyclone Larry may have also have had an adverse impact, however, the lack of significant and widespread damage to buildings may have mitigated the impact of this cyclone on intensions to visit the north. There has been no research to indicate the extent of the possible impact of Cyclone Monica on intentions to travel and visitor perceptions.

Tropical Cyclone Larry is one of seven cyclones to have hit the North Queensland region in the last 10 years. The other six included: Cyclone Justin (Category 2) in 1997, Cyclone Rona (Category 2) in 1999, Cyclone Tessi (Category 2) and Cyclone Steve (Category 2) in 2000, Cyclone Fritz (Category 1) in 2004 and several weeks after Cyclone Larry, Cyclone Monica (Category 5) struck parts of Cape York Peninsular. Each cyclone had some impact on the region between Townsville and Cape York including destruction of crops, homes, severe flooding, road closures and loss of power. Only in the case of Cyclone Steve, however, was there a report of the loss of tourism revenue due to cancellations and loss of infrastructure.

According to the Handbook on Natural Disaster Reduction in Tourist Areas (WTO, 1998) the main post-cyclone concerns for the tourism industry are the restoration of normal activities and repair or reconstruction of damaged tourism plant and infrastructures. Relaunching and revitalising tourism are critically dependent on how well the tourism site is portrayed in the media and how well the tourism industry develops and spreads positive messages about the site as a suitable destination.

After Cyclone Larry, considerable energy was put into a media recovery program as part of the Tourism Crisis Management Plan developed by Tourism Queensland (TQ). The State Government pledged $250,000 to boost promotion of the region (TTF, 2006) while Tourism Tropical North Queensland (TTNQ) and Tourism Queensland developed a staged media campaign to restore confidence in the region. TQ developed a 5 stage response campaign with stage one covering the period immediately after the cyclone hit. The plan was time based and paralleled the activities undertaken to effect the physical recovery of the area such as restoration of essential services and reopening damaged roads and bridges. In stage two, *Threat of Continuing Bad Weather* and Stage three, *Clean-Up and Repairs*, the plan focused on updates and PR activities with an estimation that the response to the campaign would be very low. By stage four of the plan, *Roads Open Repairs Completed,* it was envisaged that the response to campaign activities would be moderate and that PR activities would be increased. In this stage specific advertising bookings were also made. In the final stage of the plan, *Operations Nearly Back to Normal,* consumer promotional activities were increased and tactical marketing activities commenced based on the theme *Never Better.* The regional tourism organisation, Tourism Tropical North Queensland (TTNQ) contributed by running special promotions in conjunction with the local tourism industry. A TTF (TTF, 2006) media release issued shortly after the passing of the cyclone encouraged tourists to visit the area suggesting that Cyclone Larry was expected to have only a short-term effect due to the resilience of the domestic tourism market and the passion that Australians have for North Queensland. The Federal Government also funded several projects to investigate the impacts of Cyclone Larry on the tourism industry and assist the industry to recover in a short period of time.

METHODOLOGY

The objective of this study is to investigate the perceptions of tourists visiting the region a short time after the event to ascertain their reactions to the damage and identify any media sources which may have influenced their decisions. After completing a visual inspection of the area and conducting informal discussions the study team decided that the most appropriate method of undertaking the research was to conduct a visitor's survey designed to gather information on a range of visitor attitudes towards the cyclone. The instrument was constructed to include a comprehensive range of questions that included demographics, trip planning and routes, information sources, budget and expenditure, activities and satisfaction. The questions were structured using 3-point and 5-point Likert scales for pre-determined

variables. A number of open-ended questions were also included.

A convenience sampling approach was taken on the survey collection days. Interviewing was conducted on weekdays and weekends during June 2006, approximately 3 months after the event. Only English-speaking, domestic and international visitors to the region were given the self-administered questionnaire to complete. Experienced interviewers approached visitors at several different locations in the cyclone-affected region. A total valid sample of 276 surveys was collected. Survey sites in Mission Beach, Tully and the Atherton Tablelands were selected on the basis of their ability to capture responses from people who had travelled through the cyclone affected region.

There are several limitations to this study that need to be considered whilst reviewing the results and discussion. First, it should be noted that the ability to generalise the data collected in this study to other regions affected by disaster should be regarded with caution as the survey was specifically designed to test visitor reaction to Cyclone Larry. In addition, the interviewing period represented only a snapshot of the entire tourism season, and no allowances have been made for seasonality within the data set. Finally, the data presented in this research does not include the views of visitors who cancelled their holiday to the affected region. It is obvious that for this group, the possibility of experiencing a less than optimum holiday was high and in many cases a substitute location would have been sort.

To identify the immediate impact on visitor trends, visitor numbers collected by accredited Visitor Information Centres (VICs) were analysed. Visitor numbers for the January to May period (2006) were at a level that was only 61.5% of the previous year's visitors. For the months during and immediately after TC Larry the visitor numbers were down 56% on the previous year's visitor numbers for the same period.

The sample consisted of 53.5% females and 46.5% males and the age of visitors was spread across the age groups, with the 20-29 year old group representing the highest percentage (21.3%) with similar percentages in age groups between 30 and 65 years old. The main occupations for visitors were retired/semi-retired (25.1%), professionals (21.8%), students (12.9%), and self-employed people (9.2%). Sixty-eight percent of visitors were domestic with the remaining 32.5% being international. The origins of domestic visitors were Victoria (23.5%), other Queensland (14.9%), and New South Wales/ACT (14.2%). International visitors originated from the United Kingdom (14.3%), USA/Canada (6.0%), and other Europe (7.1%).

Slightly more than half of the respondents were repeat visitors to the region (50.4%), with the remaining visitors (49.6%) travelling in the region for the first time. Domestic visitors were much more likely than international visitors to have visited Tropical North Queensland previously and of the figures given for repeat visitors, 90% were domestic visitors. Visitors mainly travelled as couples (45.8%), with family (22.9%), with friends (16.6%) or alone (10.3%). Whilst the majority of respondents (54%) were planning on staying in TNQ for four to 14 days, many were also planning longer holidays. Further analysis shows that of the 14% of respondents who were staying for more than one month and 6% of respondents were staying for two months or more.

The main type of accommodation used by visitors was caravan parks/cabins (36.7%). Other visitors stayed in backpacker hostels (17.0%) and holiday apartments/units/houses (13.0%). A chi-squared statistical analysis revealed differences in accommodation preferences based on nationality: 70% of Queensland respondents used caravan parks, stayed with friends or relatives, or used holiday apartments; 67% of interstate visitors stayed in caravan parks or in holiday apartments; 55% of respondents from New Zealand stayed in caravan parks or resorts; 63% of respondents from the UK stayed in backpacker hostels; 84% of European respondents stayed in backpackers or caravans parks; and 62% of North American respondents stayed in hotels/motels or backpackers.

Visitors were asked to indicate their main form of travel to TNQ. Private/rented vehicles (53.1%) was the dominant mode of travel while a further 25.6% used a fly/drive combination. In the fly/drive group domestic visitors were significantly more likely than international visitors to fly/drive or use a private or rented car to get to the region. In comparison, British and North American visitors were the most likely to be participating in package tours or using inter-

city coaches as their primary form of transport ($\chi^2 = 89.524$, p = 0.00).

In terms of travel planning and information sources, the most popular sources of information for respondents were tourist guide books (31.3%), friends/family (23.9%), visitor information centres (18.0%), and the internet (15.6%). In this case there was no significant difference in how domestic and international visitors used the different information sources. Making plans on a day to day basis was the most frequently cited approach to trip planning followed by a high degree of pre-trip planning. Organising an itinerary around a package tour was the least popular approach. First time, international and younger visitors were significantly more likely to visit TNQ on package tours, whereas repeat visitors (mainly the domestic visitors) were more likely to plan some or all of their itinerary before starting the trip ($\chi^2 = 16.36$, p = 0.03). Respondents who were between the ages of 20 and 29 were the most likely to plan their trips on a day to day basis.

MAIN SOURCES OF INFORMATION REGARDING THE IMPACTS OF CYCLONE LARRY

Visitors were asked where they had mainly heard about the impacts of TC Larry. The responses, shown in Table 1, indicate that the most important source of information was TV news program (43.2%). This was followed by other information sources namely newspapers (19.9%), friends/relatives in North Queensland (13.0%), and radio (9.3%).

Information sources for TC Larry's impacts were crosstabulated with visitors' place of origin. The results revealed that the main sources for domestic visitors were TV news (92.1%), newspapers (44.2%), friends/relatives in TNQ (26.1%), and radio (23.6%). International visitors mainly heard about the cyclone's impacts from TV news (63.8%), newspapers (19.1%), and the internet (17.0%). Visitors were asked if they had seen post-Larry tourism promotions advertised by various organisations in TNQ. Only 16.6% of visitors (n = 44) said they had seen these promotions, and of these, 27.7% (n = 12) indicated

TABLE 1. Information Sources for TC Larry Impacts

Information Source	Frequency	Percentage
		(n = 276)
TV News program	219	43.2
Newspapers	101	19.9
Friends/Relatives living in North Queensland	66	13.0
Radio	47	9.3
Friends/Relatives elsewhere	22	4.3
Internet	21	4.1
TV Other programs	16	3.2
Other Sources (locals in region n = 3)	13	2.6
Travel Agent	2	0.4
Total	507	100.0

that these promotions had encouraged them to visit the region. The older, domestic market were much likely to be aware of the post-Larry promotion, whereas the younger, international market who made their plans on a day to day basis were the least likely to be aware of the post-Larry promotional campaign.

VISITOR MOTIVATIONS AND REGIONAL ATTRACTIONS

Visitors were asked to indicate the three main features of TNQ that had attracted them to the region, despite the potential effects of TC Larry. An analysis of the responses revealed that the weather (20.9%) was the most popular attraction, followed by the rainforests (17.4%), the Great Barrier Reef (12.4%) and beaches (8.3%). As a comparison, motivations for travel to TNQ were examined with factors being rated as on a 5 point Likert scale where 1 = most important and 5 = least important. The results revealed that rest and relaxation was the most important motivation across all respondents with an average score of 1.68 (very important to important). The climate was also important with a score of 1.83, and experiencing the natural environment (1.89), visiting the islands and beaches (2.00), seeing Australian wildlife (2.10) and visiting the Great Barrier Reef (2.17) were all rated as important by most respondents. Table 2 displays the mean ratings for these features, and

for comparison, the features that visitors rated as least important are also listed in the table. These results support the main features that visitors said attracted them to holiday in the TNQ region.

PERCEIVED IMPACTS OF CYCLONE LARRY

Respondents were asked to indicate to what extent they thought that TC Larry might have impacted on tourism in the area, using a three point Likert scale where 1 = very much, 2 = a little, and 3 = not at all. The results showed that 54.9% of the respondents thought that TC Larry impacted "a little," while 27.5% believed that there was "no impact," and 17.6% said the cyclone had strongly impacted on the region's tourism industry.

To provide additional details on the form of impacts that Cyclone Larry might have had on the local tourism industry, visitors were also asked in an open-ended question to indicate what they thought the three greatest impacts were. A total of 543 responses were received from 234 visitors. The results revealed that the main individual impacts visitors (N = 543) perceived were:

- Damaged rainforest/vegetation (12%)
- Accommodation/caravan park damage (9%)
- Access–damage/closure (8%)
- Facilities–lack of/loss of/damage to (7%)

- Attractions–destroyed/closed (6%)
- Fewer tourists (5%)
- Infrastructure/buildings–damaged (4.7%)

Interestingly, 26 respondents did not respond to the question or indicated that there were "no impacts/didn't think of any" while considering this trip.

The individual responses were grouped for ease of understanding. The grouped impacts with the highest responses (N = 543) were:

- Natural landscape (27.6%)
- Access (20%)
- Accommodation/Food & Beverage (17%)
- Infrastructure/Facilities (13%)
- Local community (5%)
- People (5%)
- Activities (3.7%)
- Safety (1.5%)

Visitors were asked to indicate the extent of visible damage that the cyclone had made on the rainforest in TNQ using a three point Likert scale where, 1 = some visible damage, 2 = little visible damage, and 3 = no visible damage. Over a quarter of the visitors (78.5%) indicated there was some visible damage to the rainforests, while a further 16.5% indicated there was little visible damage. Only 5.0% said there was no damage visible damage at all. There was some slight difference in damage perception between visitors who had visited the region previously and those who had not: specifically more repeat visitors (n = 106) than first time visitors (n = 97) felt that there was some damage, and the reverse for those visitors who felt that there was no damage.

Visitors were asked if the impacts of TC Larry had influenced their travel itinerary for this trip. Only 42 (15.7%) visitors indicated that the cyclone influenced their itinerary, with the main changes being that they couldn't travel to Dunk Island (n = 7). Other visitors shortened their trip or moved to other regions (n = 10) earlier than anticipated due to the impacts in the cyclone-affected region.

SATISFACTION WITH TRAVEL EXPERIENCE IN TNQ

Overall satisfaction of visitors' holiday in TNQ was measured using a 4 point Likert scale with 1 = very satisfied. Visitors reported that they were very satisfied (46.9%) and satisfied (49.6%) with their holiday. Visitors were also asked how much they thought the impacts of TC Larry had affected their satisfaction with their holiday in TNQ using a 3 point Likert scale, where 1 = very much, 2 = a little bit, and 3 = not at all. The majority said that the cyclone had not impacted (57.9%) or had impacted very little (33.5%) on their satisfaction. Only 8.6% indicated that the cyclone had a strong impact on their satisfaction. These respondents were more likely to be first time visitors to the region than repeat visitors. The direction of travel did not seem to have much of an impact on visitor satisfaction levels (see Table 3).

TABLE 2. Features in Decision to Travel to TNQ

Most Important Features	Mean	Least Important Features	Mean
Rest & relax	1.68	Meet new people	2.55
Climate	1.74	Snorkelling & diving	2.73
Visit the rainforest	1.83	Experience the outback	2.77
Natural environment	1.89	Spend time with my family	2.96
Visit islands & beaches	2.00	Experience Aboriginal culture	3.00
See Australian wildlife	2.10	Visit friends & relatives	3.04
Visit the Great Barrier Reef	2.17	Shopping	3.37
The price matched my budget	2.30	Special event	3.78
		Business/Conference/Meeting	4.39

When asked in what ways TC Larry had influenced their holiday satisfaction, visitors indicated a number of impacts as shown in Table 4 (only results with a frequency greater than 5 are listed). Interestingly, 20.2% of visitors said that there were no impacts on their holiday satisfaction. Of those who indicated particular impacts, the weather (12.2%) and effects on the visible landscape (16.4%) were the most common influences on holiday satisfaction. The effects of the weather was understandable, considering there was persistent rain at the time the survey was conducted.

Visitors were also asked to respond to a scenario question, stating "if there were no rainforests anywhere within TNQ, would you still visit the region?" The responses to this question were that an overwhelming 71.4% of visitors said they would still visit the region, with a further 19.0% saying they were unsure. Finally, visitors were asked if they would recommend the TNQ region to prospective visitors, even after a cyclone had impacted the region. The majority (89.9%) said that they would recommend TNQ.

DISCUSSION

Initially, the results suggest that there are two distinct markets that were visiting Tropical North Queensland three months after Cyclone Larry. The major visitor sector identified was the domestic drive and fly/drive visitors who, although significantly aware of TC Larry's devastation, travelled to the region anyway. This sector can be characterised as repeat visitors to the region who appear to be travelling to locations in and around Mission Beach as well as the Atherton Tablelands. The second major market comprised international backpackers who indicated that they were largely unaware of the cyclone's impacts. While these results suggest there is still a visitor market servicing the region, the Mission Beach VIC statistics indicate that this is only a small percentage of the usual visitation to these regions.

Domestic Market

The older market were predominantly retired or professionals, resident in Victoria, Queensland and New South Wales/ACT and had travelled to the region previously. They were staying in caravan parks and cabins, as well as with friends and relatives or in holiday units. Interstate visitors were usually staying in the region for one week to one month while Queenslanders and short-stays (one to three nights) were more likely to drive to the region or fly in and rent a car. They used similar sources of information to plan their trips to the region as international visitors, i.e., guide books, friends and family, visitor information centres and the Internet, but tended to organise most of their trip before they arrived in the region.

The domestic market was more aware of the impacts of Cyclone Larry, and had become aware of the cyclone through television programs and news, newspapers, friends and relatives in Tropical North Queensland and the radio. The influence of word of mouth from friends and relatives in TNQ may therefore play an important role in perceptions of the cyclone's impacts and the decision to visit the area. Further, the domestic market was more likely to be aware of post-cyclone Larry tour-

TABLE 3. The Impact of Cyclone Larry on Visitor Satisfaction

Direction of Travel	Very Much	A little	Not at all	Total
North	2.0	12.0	14.2	28.5
South	5.5	17.5	38.0	61.0
East	0.0	0.5	3.0	3.5
West	0.5	3.0	4.0	7.5
Total	8.0	33.0	59.0	100.0

TABLE 4. Ways in Which TC Larry influenced Satisfaction

Impacts	Frequency	Percentage
		(n = 174)
None	53	20.2
Weather/still raining/climate change	32	12.2
Devastation to trees/rainforest damaged	27	10.3
Damage/visible differences/scenery/sights	16	6.1
Walking tracks–wet/muddy/damaged/closed	15	5.7
Dunk Island–closed/couldn't travel to	12	4.6
No bananas/price of bananas	8	3.1
Tourism outlets not available/attractions closed	7	2.7
Accessibility/areas closed	7	2.7
Environ./landscape–changed/damaged	6	2.3
Beaches–dirty, state of, damaged	6	2.3
Lack of people/no social life	6	2.3

ism promotions in the area. As many of the domestic respondents had previously visited the region, it is not surprising that they were more likely to have noticed some impacts of Cyclone Larry. These visitors were also more likely to say that Cyclone Larry had has some impact on their satisfaction with their trip to TNQ.

The Younger International Market

The other main segment visiting the area was the younger (20-30s), international market. These tourists were more likely to be students and professionals, from New Zealand, North America, Europe and the UK and Ireland. This was usually their first trip to Tropical North Queensland and they tended to stay for at least a week, generally in backpacker accommodation. New Zealand and North American respondents were more likely to stay in resorts and hotels. These visitors were the most likely to visit TNQ by coach, and therefore to either plan their trip on a day to day basis or have it pre-organised. Within this group there was a smaller subgroup who were travelling on package tours.

The international market had less knowledge of Cyclone Larry and their main sources of information regarding the cyclone were TV news programmes, newspapers, and the Internet. They had very little awareness of the post-Cyclone Larry promotional campaign. They were also likely less likely to have considered the im-

pacts that Cyclone Larry might have had on the region and generally had not noticed the actual impacts of the cyclone on the region. They were also more likely to say that Cyclone Larry had not affected their satisfaction with their trip to Tropical North Queensland.

A significant factor characterising these two visitor markets is that they were largely independent travellers. There is insufficient information to establish whether this was a factor based on the sample of visitors surveyed or this represents evidence of the lack of this visitor market in the region. Nevertheless, this is a characteristic that requires further investigation in future research.

The visitors' travel patterns within the cyclone-affected region included locations surrounding Mission Beach and the central and Southern Atherton Tablelands. Therefore, these visitors were in a position to have directly experienced and seen the evidence of the cyclone's impacts but did not recognise it, most likely because they had no previsit knowledge of issues such as canopy cover rates.

Additionally, the majority of both domestic and international visitors had been informed of the cyclone through various forms of media, including television news, newspapers and radio. However, it is interesting that very few of these visitors were exposed to the post-Larry tourism promotions on television, the Internet, radio and newspapers. This result may be understandable, considering the main information sources that visitors used were not those where the tourism promotions were mainly used–that is, these visitors used tourists guide books, friends/relatives, visitor information centres and the Internet. This is an important characteristic for tourism crisis management planning, as these are not information sources that generally tend to be used to disseminate immediate updates on the state of the region. In the case of Cyclone Larry, however, Tourism Queensland utilised the Internet for regional updates and to encourage holiday bookings for the region. Additionally, information from friends/relatives appeared to be significant, yet very little research is available on the extent and type of information that is disseminated by friends/relatives following a natural disaster such as Cyclone Larry.

It is interesting that the main attractors of the region were the relaxed atmosphere, climate, rainforests and natural environments, islands and beaches, wildlife and the Great Barrier Reef. These were all features of the region that suffered varying levels of impacts from the Cyclone. The rainforests, in particular were one of the most attractive features, with high levels of visitation to the majority of sites in the Wet Tropics World Heritage Area, despite the levels of damage that occurred in most of these locations. Regardless, the visitors' travel motivations focussed on the opportunities for rest and relaxation, warm weather, as well as the natural environment (rainforest and Great Barrier Reef) and the islands and beaches.

A comparison with the region's attractions and the impacts that visitors noticed in the region shows a relatively large overlap. This is particularly true for the rainforest, natural landscape and islands and beaches, the main activities and attractions of the region. Other important impacts include "instrumental" impacts that affect the basic structure of tourism, such as the availability of accommodation and restaurants, services, access to the area and within the area, and general infrastructure. A third group of impacts can be considered to be the atmospherics of the region, which include the scarcity of other tourists, the mood of the local community and its impacts on the relaxed tropical lifestyle and the unusual weather patterns experienced (less sunshine and more rain). Not surprisingly, the suggested improvements focussed on accommodation, shopping, food and beverage, and activities.

CONCLUSION

The results presented in this study highlight some of the factors that impact on a regional tourism industry after a natural disaster such as a severe cyclone event. To provide industry and local tourism agencies with useful information to rebuild the tourism sector, this research investigated a range of characteristics of visitors who had decided to visit the region in spite of the cyclone event some 3 months earlier. It must be stated that the actual number of visitors in the affected region was significantly below the levels of previous years. It is therefore apparent that visitors who chose to cancel their trip would have given very different responses to this survey and were apparently far more concerned about the impacts of the cyclone than the respondents whose views are recorded in this research.

The finding that the majority of respondents reported no or little impact on their satisfaction with the region was significant. As soon as essential services are restored and the affected area was made safe, marketing played a major role in informing visitors that the area was again "open for business." This was clearly the focus of the region's two key tourism marketing organisations (Tourism Queensland and Tourism Tropical North Queensland). If marketing of this nature was delayed, further business would have been lost and it would have become more difficult to recover lost business.

An important finding of the research was the values or motivations (Table 2) that resulted in respondents continuing to visit the region event though it had been affected by a severe cyclone. The pull of these values and positive visitor motivations for visiting the region are strong and should form the platform on which successful post-disaster promotions should be built. Marketing should therefore provide some form of guarantee to visitors that they will continue to be able to experience the features of the region that they consider to be most valuable to them, despite any impacts from natural disasters.

In the case of Cyclone Larry, the combination of fast recovery for tourism facilities and infrastructure, and the accurate rapid delivery of information through key visitor information sources contributed to the continuation of visitor flows to the region, particularly by air. This study has shown that the data gained from post-Cyclone visitation is extremely useful in understanding the perceptions, behaviours and expectations of visitors to impacted regions. Cyclone recovery management plans, as well as other disaster recovery plans would benefit from further research on the perceptions of both on-site and potential visitors to regions that experience these disasters. Finally, the strategies developed by TQ and TTNQ fit with those advocated in the literature reviewed earlier in this paper and demonstrate the necessity for well planned recovery strategies.

REFERENCES

Bureau of Meteorology (2006a). Cyclone Larry Forum Report. Edited by Jim Davidson, Regional Director (Queensland), Australian Bureau of Meteorology, Retrieved on 15 June, from http://www.rainforest-crc.jcu.edu.au/ latestNews/ForumReport.pdf

Bureau of Meteorology (2006b). Severe Tropical Cyclone Larry. Retrieved on 15 June, from http://www.bom.gov.au/weather/qld/cyclone/tc_larry/

Environmental Protection Agency (2006). EPA Bulletin, Issue 34, April 2006. Retrieved on 3 July, from http://www.epa.qld.gov.au/about_the_epa/public_reporting/epa_bulletin/cleaning_up_after_cyclone_larry/

Faulkner, B. (2001). Towards a framework for tourism disaster management. *Tourism Management*, 22, 135-147.

Hall, Timothy and Duval (eds.) (2003), Safety and Security in Tourism; Relationships, Management, and Marketing, The Haworth Hospitality Press; New York.

Kuehlbrandt, E., (2000). Tropical Cyclone Awareness and Preparedness amongst Backpacker Accommodation Providers and Backpackers in Cairns. Centre for Disaster Studies, James Cook University: Townsville, September 2000.

Laws, E. and Prideaux, B. (eds) (2005). *Journal of Travel and Tourism Marketing*, 19(2/3), 1-159.

Measham, T. (1999). Community Vulnerability to Tropical Cyclones and Associated Storm Surges: Cairns Caravan Parks Study. Centre for Disaster Studies, James Cook University.

Prideaux, B. and Laws, E. and Faulkner, B. (2003). Events in Indonesia: Exploring the Limits to Formal Tourism Trends Forecasting Methods in Complex Crisis Situations, *Tourism Management*, 24(4): 511-520.

Prideaux, B., Falco-Mammone, F., Thompson, M. (2006). Backpacking in the Tropics: A review of the backpacker market in Cairns and their travel patterns within Australia. Cairns: James Cook University.

Tourism & Transport Forum (TTF), (2006). Media Release, Retrieved on 28th July, from http://www.ttf.org.au/newsroom/pdf/MR060321_Cyclone_Larry.pdf

Williams, J. (2004). Branding of a rural destination; a case study of the Atherton Tablelands. Unpublished Masters Thesis, James Cook University, Townsville.

World Tourism Organisation(1998). Handbook on Natural Disaster Reduction in Tourist Areas. World Tourism Organisation and World Meteorological Organisation, Madrid.

The Heart Recovery Marketing Campaign:
Destination Recovery After a Major Bushfire
in Australia's National Capital

E. Kate Armstrong
Brent W. Ritchie

SUMMARY. Crisis communication plans and marketing recovery campaigns are a key component of destination recovery after crises or disasters. Despite increasing researcher and practitioner interest in crisis and disaster management, further analysis of these components of recovery is warranted. This article contributes to this growing body of research by analysing the advertising components of a recovery marketing campaign developed and implemented immediately after bushfires in the Australian Capital Territory in January 2003. The findings are drawn from relevant documents, marketing collateral and in-depth interviews with government agencies, professional associations and businesses. Despite a lack of relevant plans, the marketing campaign was an effective exercise in crisis communication under temporal and resource constraints and demonstrated application of research, rapid response, financial support, consistency of messages, honest and open communication and evaluation. Planning, training and further analytical case study research is recommended.

INTRODUCTION

A book entitled Safety and Security in Tourism: Relationships, Management and Marketing (Hall, Timothy, & Duval, 2003) may have been viewed as 'fringe reading' a decade ago (MacLaurin, 2005) but now constitutes a 'must read' for the tourism industry and especially destination management organizations (DMOs). As Beirman (2006a) states, risk management has moved from being an afterthought in tourism marketing theory to a core issue and the same can be said for disaster and crisis management with increasing researcher and practitioner interest since 2000. Why the sudden interest? As Beirman (2006a) points out, mass tourism has

E. Kate Armstrong is affiliated with the School of Business and Government, University of Canberra, ACT 2601, Australia (E-mail: kate.armstrong@canberra.edu.au). Brent W. Ritchie is affiliated with the School of Business and Government, University of Canberra, ACT 2601, Australia (E-mail: brent.ritchie@canberra.edu.au).

The authors wish to acknowledge scholarship funding for Kate Armstrong from the Federal Department of Education, Science and Training and the Sustainable Tourism Co-operative Research Centre.

been impacted by crises and disasters for almost 50 years. The recent globalisation of media and information dissemination, however, has meant that negative perceptions of a destination can rapidly erode its marketability. Therefore, destinations need to prepare themselves with strategic, effective and up-to-date plans for handling crises and disasters (Federal Department of Industry Tourism and Resources, 2005b; Gonzalez-Herrero & Pratt, 1998; Ritchie, 2004; Young & Montgomery, 1998) and a key component is the crisis communication plan. Communication is an important ingredient in destination recovery during and/or after a crisis or disaster and a comprehensive communication strategy ensures that DMOs can be proactive and effective rather than reactive and ad hoc (Ritchie, 2004). Providing timely and accurate information to key stakeholders (government bodies, tourism industry, media and consumers) can assist overall destination recovery by limiting the impact of the incident while safeguarding a valuable image and reputation (Ritchie, Dorrell, Miller, & Miller, 2003).

A key role of the crisis communication plan is to monitor and manage media reporting. Exaggerated and sensationalised reporting of crises or disasters is commonplace and the impact on the market is frequently out of proportion to the nature and extent of the actual damage (Beirman, 2006a; Cassedy, 1991; Murphy & Bayley, 1989). As Young and Montgomery (1998, p. 4) state, 'a crisis has the potential to be detrimental to the marketability of any tourism destination, particularly if it is dramatised and distorted through rumours and the media.' Misleading reports exaggerating the extent of 1993 bushfires in Sydney, Australia, were noted by Christine (1995) and, as Faulkner (1999) points out, lingering negative images may cause recovery to take longer than the restoration of services and facilities. A communication plan that is well integrated into the disaster or crisis management plan can lead to rapid dissipation of negative images and a quicker recovery (Faulkner, 1999, 2001).

A key component of a crisis communication plan is a recovery marketing campaign which is frequently used in the short to medium term to counteract negative media coverage, inform consumers and other stakeholders of the desti-

nation's status and regain consumer confidence (Ritchie et al., 2003). Marketing recovery campaigns aimed at encouraging continuation of travel or formation of new travel plans are a significant feature of recovery, particularly if the economy is relatively dependent on tourism, and the description and analysis of recovery marketing is receiving considerable researcher and practitioner attention (see, for example, Beirman, 2002, 2003, 2006a, 2006b; Faulkner & Vikulov, 2001; Frisby, 2002; Ritchie et al., 2003).

Key issues in an effective and ethical crisis communication strategy have been summarised by Coombs (1999) and Berry (1999) as:

- existence of a crisis communication plan including a recovery marketing plan;
- rapidity of development and implementation of the marketing campaign;
- access to funding for marketing activities;
- consultation with stakeholders;
- consistency of messages;
- use of messages to correct destination image perceptions; and
- honesty and openness (willingness to disclose information).

This article contributes to this growing body of research by analysing the advertising components of a recovery marketing campaign based on the key issues identified by Coombs (1999) and Berry (1999). The campaign was developed and implemented by the Australian Capital Tourism Corporation (ACTC) (formerly Canberra Tourism and Events Corporation) immediately after devastating bushfires swept through the Australian Capital Territory (ACT) in January 2003. After explaining the research design the article will briefly describe the ACT tourism industry before outlining the disaster, its impacts and the resulting marketing campaign. The results and discussion will address the issues identified by Coombs (1999) and Berry (1999) before concluding with recommendations.

RESEARCH DESIGN

This article is based on emerging findings from a doctoral study on destination recovery after natural disasters. The research design is informed by the interpretive social sciences paradigm which features a holistic-inductive approach where the whole phenomenon of destination recovery in all its complexity is being studied. This paradigm also assumes that there are multiple explanations or realities to explain a phenomenon such as recovery (Jennings, 2001). The methodology is qualitative and a case study method is being adopted. According to Beeton's (2005, p. 42) definition, a case study is 'a holistic empirical inquiry used to gain an in-depth understanding of a contemporary phenomenon in its real-life context, using multiple sources of evidence.' Document analysis, participant-observation and in-depth interviewing are the key data collection tools (Jennings, 2001; Yin, 2003). The findings for this article are drawn from relevant documents, marketing collateral and in-depth interviews conducted with industry stakeholders in January 2004. The participants included representatives of government agencies, professional associations and businesses and the 16 interviews investigated the short and medium term actions taken by organisations to assist destination recovery. The resulting interview transcripts were coded using the qualitative analysis software NVivo V2 and analysed based on the grounded theory approach using constant comparative analysis and successive approximation (Jennings, 2001; Wimmer & Dominick, 1997).

THE ACT TOURISM INDUSTRY

Canberra, the capital of the ACT and the national capital of Australia, is a tourist destination of local, national and international significance with a unique position in the Australian tourism landscape. It is the seat of Federal Government and hence features national attractions which present the history, future and values of the nation (Australian Capital Tourism Corporation, 2004a). The ACT has a broad range of tourist and visitor infrastructure and a diverse range of special interest products and services although in the early 2000s the industry tended to focus on five product areas: cultural, nature-based, sport and wine tourism and festivals and events (Canberra Tourism and Events Corporation & Tourism Industry Council, c. 2000). Domestic tourism accounts for the majority of overnight visitors to the ACT with numbers sitting around 2 million per annum. The main interstate markets in 2002 were New South Wales (66%), Victoria (19%) and Queensland (7%) and the average duration of stay was 2.7 nights. The purpose of trip was evenly divided among holiday/leisure (31%), visiting friends and relatives (33%) and business (32%) (Australian Capital Tourism Corporation, 2004a). In 2002, 195,000 international tourists visited the ACT, a decline from a peak of 230 000 in 2000, the year that Sydney hosted the Olympic Games. The key source markets in 2002 were the United Kingdom and Europe (39%), China (12%) and USA (11%) (Australian Capital Tourism Corporation, 2004a).

As the national capital of Australia, Canberra contains numerous national institutions and monuments, represents national values and is the seat of Federal Government. Like other national capitals, however, it has experienced some negative perceptions by tourists because of its association with politics and central government. Research suggests that national capitals can be 'both beneficiaries and victims of their position in their nation' (Campbell, 2003, p. 27), where political and administrative importance is also often cited as their downfall for tourism (Hall, 2002). Canberra is often derided as a pretentious 'fat cat public service city' or as the source of unpopular political decisions which influence destination perceptions negatively. Peirce and Ritchie (forthcoming 2007) indicate that it 'has been described as 'cool,' 'stuffy,' 'reserved' and 'closed' 'and the planned nature of Canberra with deliberate zoning and separation of residential, commercial, parliamentary and light industrial areas has led to the common epithet of 'the city without a soul.' Studies such as Ritchie and Leon-Marillanca (2006) have gauged perceptions of Canberra and these have guided marketing and product development activities. Recent marketing campaigns have primarily centred around the See Yourself in the National Capital brand which, rather than denying the political dimension of the destination, celebrates nationhood and national values, institutions and attractions while addressing the less positive perceptions.

THE BUSHFIRE

On 8 January 2003 electrical storms in the ACT resulted in a series of lightning strikes and consequent ignition of bushfires. Exacerbating conditions included dry fuel due to prolonged and severe drought, high fuel loads and difficult weather conditions. The separate bushfires gradually spread eastwards and became a single fire front. A total fire ban was declared from midnight 16 January to midnight 21 January 2003, a duration unprecedented in ACT history. Day 11 of the fire event (Saturday 18 January 2003) is recognized as the day of the 'Canberra firestorm' despite the bushfires having already wrought critical impacts on reserve, forestry and rural lands by that time. Locally, this date has gained 'iconic' status because of the extensive damage to the suburbs of Canberra, the national capital of Australia, and the mass evacuation of residents. For the first time in the ACT's history a state of emergency was declared underlining the extreme seriousness of the situation. On Sunday 19 January 2003 (Day 12) the ACT community was in a state of shock as the widespread and severe impacts of the fire became known. The bushfires continued to threaten but recovery actions commenced in an atmosphere of ongoing preparedness. The state of emergency was eventually lifted on Tuesday 28 January 2003 (McLeod, 2003).

IMPACTS ON THE TOURISM INDUSTRY

Almost immediately after the disaster the Tourism Industry Council ACT and Region Ltd (2003b) (TIC) conducted a questionnaire survey to provide credible information to local and federal government about the impacts of the bushfires and found that they had 'significant impacts upon the ACT and region tourism industry' (p. 1). Businesses reported on average a 50 per cent decline in visitation with the impact of the fires continuing much longer than expected (Tourism Industry Council ACT and Region Ltd, 2003a). In-depth interviews with stakeholders revealed general agreement with the TIC findings and a representative of the National Capital Attractions Association indi-

cated that 'even businesses that were not physically affected, fire affected, were affected in other ways,' referring to a typical ripple effect.

Two significant issues affected the whole industry–sensationalised reporting and the subsequent impact on destination image and a decrease in visitor activity. Numerous interviewees received reports from friends, relatives and colleagues throughout Australia and the world that the mainstream media was portraying Canberra as burnt to the ground with sewage running through the streets. Media reporting implied that Canberra was inaccessible by road with no essential services such as water, sewerage and electricity (Canberra Tourism and Events Corporation, 2003c). These sensationalised messages gave the inaccurate impression that central Canberra with its attractions of national significance had been damaged if not completely destroyed. An immediate decrease in visitor numbers was reported by the Canberra and Queanbeyan Visitor Centres (Tourism Industry Council ACT and Region Ltd, 2003b); a decrease probably caused by (a) complete cancellation of planned travel, (b) postponement of planned travel, (c) cancellation of planned travel and switching to another destination (if possible) and (d) prospective visitors not seeing the ACT as a potential destination. Tour operators, attractions and accommodation reported significant cancellations and door counts for the Canberra and Region Visitors Centre compared with 2002 illustrate a downturn in visitor activity over a 6 month period until July 2003 (Figure 1). Decreased visitor activity throughout 2004 and 2005 as part of an overall downward trend in domestic tourism which has been attributed to rising fuel prices and the availability of cheaper international air fares (Federal Department of Industry Tourism and Resources, 2005a).

Natural attractions in the western part of the ACT including national parks, nature reserves, river corridors and forestry plantations were severely and directly impacted by the bushfires. In addition to loss of visual amenity, ecological communities and built and cultural heritage (notably historic huts and aboriginal rock art), visitor facilities and infrastructure such as car parks, camping areas, barbeques, fireplaces, outdoor furniture, amenity blocks, signage and fencing were extensively damaged. Mt Strom-

FIGURE 1. Monthly Door Count Data from the Canberra and Region Visitors Centre, 2002-2005 (raw data provided by G. Wang of ACTC on 17 July 2006).

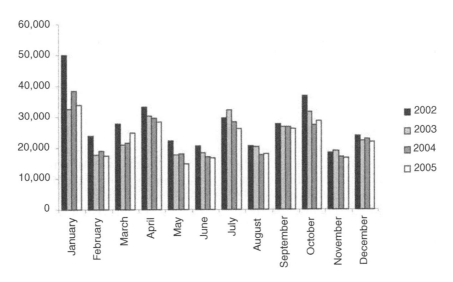

lo Observatory, an astronomical research and education facility featuring heritage-listed telescopes and buildings, was also very extensively damaged. Several tour operators that featured these natural and cultural attractions in their itineraries were highly impacted by closures and the long-term damage to sites. These predominantly small and micro businesses were seen by an ACTC representative as the hardest hit tourism businesses with both loss of bookings and tour product.

Food and beverage outlets were affected by both the downturn in visitor activity and the disinclination of locals to dine out during and for several weeks after the disaster. The ACT and Region Chamber of Commerce and Industry commented that '. . . quite a few restaurants came to the brink–it nearly sent them broke and of course they received no community or government support because they weren't burnt out.' Four outlets were directly impacted due to being located in fire-damaged areas which were closed in the short to medium term or were affected in the medium term by a decrease in traffic on a tourist driving route (Tourism Industry Council ACT and Region Ltd, 2003b).

Impacts on accommodation were mixed. In the ACT Bushfire Impacts questionnaire hoteliers reported substantial cancellations (Tourism Industry Council ACT and Region Ltd,

2003b) whereas the Canberra Accommodation Association indicated there was demand for temporary accommodation for homeless residents, volunteers, fire fighters and emergency services personnel. Much of that, however, was donated or heavily discounted so overall there was a short term loss. More directly, a range of campgrounds, cabins and lodge-style accommodation located in western ACT and run by educational, charity and religious groups were significantly fire damaged as were campgrounds run by protected area managers.

THE HEART RECOVERY MARKETING CAMPAIGN

Given these impacts ACTC recognised the need to implement a recovery campaign that would remind Australians of the importance of their national capital and inform potential visitors that the ACT was still operating as a tourism destination (Canberra Tourism and Events Corporation, 2003a). The campaign was also designed to 'combat reports that attractions/tourism is under threat or unavailable at the moment' (Canberra Tourism and Events Corporation, 2003b). The regular Autumn campaign brochure had been developed prior to the disaster and text and images were rapidly adjusted before printing to suit the new situation (Canberra Tourism and Events Corporation, 2003d). A recovery campaign featuring the brochure and print and television advertising was devised by ACTC and Grey Worldwide, an international communications company, based on research commissioned by ACTC to gauge perceptions of Canberra post-bushfires amongst residents of the eastern and north shore suburbs of Sydney (Australian Capital Tourism Corporation, 2004b). Sydney is recognised as a key part of the significant New South Wales market for the ACT. The research comprised a short telephone survey with a random sample of residents (N = 100) and found that 53 per cent of respondents agreed with the statement 'the recent bushfires have made me see the human side to Canberra in a way I didn't before' and 25 per cent with 'the recent bushfires in Canberra have made me realise the importance of Canberra as the national capital of Australia' and 'has given me a stronger sense of ownership and identification with Canberra as a national capital.' These findings contributed to the format and creative direction of the print and television campaign in February and March 2003.

The *print campaign* comprised eight full colour advertisements carrying the line 'Our heart's still going strong' which appeared in Sydney metropolitan and NSW regional press between 2 and 10 February 2003.

A similar advertisement was placed in the March 2003 edition of the TNT Backpackers Magazine in response to a drop in backpackers. There were five clear messages (Table 1).

An ACTC representative mentioned that the print advertising served as a public thank you for the support the ACT had received from other jurisdictions in addition to letting people know that 'we are still going, open for business and this is when we really need support, so if you were coming to Canberra really think about it before you cancel your holiday.'

The *television campaign* ran for three weeks in Metropolitan Sydney, Northern and Southern NSW and Canberra from 30 March to 19 April 2003. Three advertisements were prepared: 60 and 30 second advertisements for interstate audiences and a 60 second advertisement for local audiences. The advertisements commenced with images of fire fighters followed by ACT attractions and hospitality venues and concluded

with the free call telephone number and web address for Canberra Getaways.

The overall message of the television commercials was 'This heart's still going strong' from a song composed for the campaign by Jimmy Barnes, a well known Australian singer (Table 2).

Both the print and television advertising spend were directed to media outlets in New South Wales in recognition of this markets 66 per cent share in ACT interstate tourism and its reputation as a traditional and reliable market.

Rather eerily the Autumn seasonal brochure made no mention of the bushfires and did not feature any of the messages communicated in the print and television advertising. That said, it also did not refer to or picture any of the damaged attractions or facilities and without viewing the original version it is not possible to comment on the amount and type of editing undertaken. All forms of advertising were examples of isolation marketing where the 'trouble spot' is separated from the rest of the intact destination and the focus is on the latter (Beirman, 2002, 2003). It was also recognised that Canberra, as a regional tourism hub, has a role to play in feeding visitors to regional areas that had also been affected by bushfires (Tourism Industry Council ACT and Region Ltd, 2003b).

In May 2003 the campaign impact was gauged via a telephone survey (N = 200) with a random sample of residents from the same areas of Sydney that featured in the pre-campaign research. Twenty-four per cent of the sample were aware of the campaign and the key messages they received are summarised in Table 3.

From those respondents who saw the advertising, 68 per cent expressed an interest in visiting Canberra for a short break holiday and 70 per cent in visiting for cultural events or exhibitions (compared with 49 per cent and 54 per cent respectively for those who did not see the advertising). ACTC (2004b) believe these results indicate that the campaign was 'successful in delivering their key message objectives in the Sydney marketplace.' This approach confirms that proposed by Zerman (1995) who suggests research should precede any action and Britton (2003) who outlined the significant research American Airlines conducted prior to releasing marketing campaigns after the terrorist bombings on 11 September 2001. Gauging

TABLE 1. Messages in the Print Campaign

Direct quote from advertisement	Implied message
Our heart's still going strong.	The heart of Canberra (central Canberra) which contains the national attractions (for example, National Gallery, High Court, Old Parliament House, Parliament House, National Museum, National Library) was not damaged by the bushfires. They are still open.
	Canberra is still healthy-it's heart is still beating.
Maybe it took the heartbreak of Canberra's bushfires to remind us of all the things we treasure about our national capital.	With disaster comes reflection on what we value about Australian society and community.
	The capital contains many nationally significant monuments, museums and collections and the true value of these was not acknowledged until Australians were in danger of losing them.
Fortunately, our unique attractions that teach us so much about Australia's past, present and future remain unscathed.	The unique national capital attractions in Canberra were not damaged in the bushfires.
And now Canberra's people have an even stronger sense of mateship, community and pride in our city.	Canberra is often derided as the 'city without a soul' but the bushfires have shown that the city does have a strong sense of community as evident in the cooperative recovery effort.
It's something we're keen to share with others–so why not book now and visit a place where the Aussie spirit is very much alive.	When interacting with locals, visitors will encounter this Canberra spirit.
	Visit Canberra to experience the Aussie (slang for Australian) spirit.

perceptions of potential consumers is vital in preparing a suitable recovery marketing campaign and part of a broader process in using information to develop more effective responses.

RESULTS AND DISCUSSION

Existence of a Crisis Communication Plan Including a Recovery Marketing Plan

ACTC didn't have a disaster or crisis management plan, a crisis communication plan or recovery marketing plan and this is not an uncommon situation as noted by Ritchie et al. (2003) and Young and Montgomery (1998). However, as Burnett (1998) notes, crises are difficult to resolve due to the pressure on time, limited control and high uncertainty. To address this time pressure and lack of preparedness, ACTC staff contacted the Blue Mountains and Illawarra-South Coast tourism regions who had experienced bushfires in 2002 for advice (Canberra Tourism and Events Corporation, 2003e). ACTC obtained their marketing plans

and help in quantifying impacts and received advice on lobbying for Federal Government assistance and handling the media. Although the plans were from different destinations they stimulated thinking and ideas and described processes–an outcome that lends weight to the usefulness of generic recovery models. That said, a senior manager at ACTC conceded that it 'would have been really lovely to have [a disaster plan] to refer to even if it was basic, it would have been a bit of a structure that helps when things were going completely wrong–you can pull something out that you've planned when you've got the head space and the time to do it properly.' Another manager at ACTC also supported more disaster management planning 'I believe that if you get your planning right then you've got a range of disaster scenarios which follow a templated sort of response that says that at event plus six hours you should have a media release stating what the things are in respect to tourism.'

Tourism and practitioner literature strongly recommends that tourism industry stakeholders and particularly DMOs have crisis or

TABLE 2. Messages from the Broadcast Campaign

Direct quote from advertisement	Implied message
Voice over–Maybe it took the heartbreak of the bushfires to remind us of the things we treasure about our national capital.	With disaster comes reflection on what we value about Australian society and community. The national capital contains many nationally significant monuments, museums and collections and the true value of these was not acknowledged until Australians were in danger of losing them.
Lyrics sung by Jimmy Barnes There is brightness in our future and spirits from our past, There are times we will treasure and memories will last, There is beauty around us and laughter in our soul, Right here's where you'll find us, This heart's still going strong. We got something here for the young and old, This heart's still going strong.	The ACT and Canberra offers a range of attractions that look to the future and the past and it is an attractive and interesting place for the whole family to visit. The heart of Canberra was not damaged by the bushfires and is still here to visit.
Alternative endings	
Voice over for interstate audiences–Book your Capital Autumn package now because our heart is still going strong.	A call to action to purchase.
Voice over for local audiences–One of the best ways to rebuild our community is to invite visitors to rediscover those treasures and support our local businesses, so encourage people you know to come and enjoy autumn in the capital and show them our heart's still going strong.	Calling on residents to encourage friends and relatives to visit as we need the visitors at this time.

disaster plans and Cassedy (1991) argues further that a crisis communication plan needs to be properly integrated into the crisis management plan. However, this is not always the case with Lee and Harrald (1999) finding in a study of Fortune 1000 companies in the United States that 71 per cent of companies had a crisis management plan, with 82 per cent noting crisis communication as part of that plan. In 1991 PATA discovered that only four National Tourist Offices in the region has a crisis management strategy (Henderson, 1999). Nowadays there are numerous examples of crisis and disaster management plans for a range of contingencies and stakeholders (for example Cassedy, 1991; World Tourism Organization, 2005; Young & Montgomery, 1998) so there is no excuse for non-preparation other than the typical lack of resources and the belief that a crisis or disaster will not occur. A crisis communication plan should ideally be in place at all times as much can be done or organised before a crisis such as nomination of membership of the crisis management team and appointment of a spokesperson (Gonzalez-Herrero & Pratt, 1998). This, however, relies on regular updating to ensure the information is current. This ideal situation is not infallible however as there is often a gap between planning and actual response to a major disaster (Quarantelli, 1988).

Rapidity of Development and Implementation of the Marketing Campaign

In the weeks following the bushfires many ACTC staff members were on leave during the traditional Australian summer holiday period and others, including the Chief Executive Officer, were taking leave to handle often substantial personal losses from the bushfires. Still more staff were based at home on alert for the continuing bushfire threat. It could be argued that lack of staff would make it difficult to effectively implement any plan and the situation was further complicated by the continuing threat of bushfires as a senior manager at ACTC explained:

> We couldn't put things out and say 'everything's fine keep coming to Canberra' especially while there was still a major threat that the fires were going to blow

TABLE 3. Messages Received in the Sydney Market from the Heart Recovery Marketing Campaign

Messages received from campaign materials	Percentage
specific features of Canberra	28
nation's capital or the national capital experience	11
specific locations or places to stay	11
help Canberra recover/return to Canberra	11

Source: Adapted from Australian Capital Tourism Corporation (2004b)

back into town and barbeque another few hundred houses.

The lifting of the state of emergency on 28 January marked an official end to the disaster and this expedited the rapid development of the campaign unlike situations where crises or disasters tend to linger with no clear ending such as political conflict (Beirman, 2002) and diseases (Ritchie et al., 2003). The rapidity of the campaign development and implementation was also governed by the extent of damage. As Young and Montgomery (1998) indicate, crises or disasters that damage essential infrastructure, services and facilities necessarily delay marketing recovery campaigns as the priority is on restoring those parts of the destination. The fact that the ACT was largely intact meant that the campaign could proceed reasonably rapidly. In analysing the response of the Alaskan cruise operator, Holland America, to the Exxon oil spill, Cassedy (1991, p. 59) argues 'timing and honest communication are foremost elements for effective crisis management' and Holland America made proactive decisions to quickly disseminate accurate information before negative perceptions had settled in the public's mind. This was the practice of ACTC with editing of the already developed Autumn campaign brochure a priority. In this process ACTC wanted to ensure that the Heart Recovery Marketing Campaign was smoothly integrated into the existing Autumn campaign in order to convey stability and a 'getting on with it' ethos (Canberra Tourism and Events Corporation, 2003b).

Under these circumstances the print advertising was developed and implemented rapidly. A brief indicating ACTC's commitment to a promotional/advertising campaign and outlining the main themes and target market segments was prepared by 28 January (Canberra Tourism and Events Corporation, 2003b) and the first press advertisement appeared on 2 February 2006–just five days after lifting of the state of emergency. The television campaign took longer to develop with the first advertisements aired on 30 March (61 days after the state of emergency was lifted). Putting together television commercials is a more complicated process but some planning may have helped achieve this goal more rapidly. A representative of the National Capital Attractions Association conceded that it was a 'difficult brief, probably the impossible brief' but indicated that it was a bit too late 'It was right on the margins of that emotional tug which would have been the call to action . . . [it] started running about six to seven weeks after the fires and it really was, we thought, just a wee bit too late and that was possibly because the CEO was personally affected.' The Canberra Convention Bureau, which was largely unaffected, was more supportive saying 'in fairness I think they did a very good job in getting the money and getting the campaign out on air. I think it was a good campaign and getting someone like Jimmy Barnes was a real coup. I am not sure that a lot of people recognise the work that went into producing that so quickly and so effectively.'

Access to Funding for the Marketing Campaign

Following advice from the Blue Mountains and Illawarra-South Coast tourism regions, TIC and the ACT Government lobbied the Federal Government for $500 000 for recovery marketing and the Bushfire Impacts Survey served as important 'ammunition' for this exercise (Tourism Industry Council ACT and Region Ltd, 2003a, 2003b). At the time TIC envisioned a $1.3 to $1.5 million campaign and eventually about $1 million was raised with approximately $200,000 from industry, $500,000 from the Federal Government and $300,000 from local government.

A key budgetary issue was the incremental amount of funding. Early documentation indicated budgets of $100,000 and $260,000 (Canberra Tourism and Events Corporation, 2003b, 2003e) and as a senior manager at ACTC explained:

> What would have been ideal at the time was knowledge of the resources in terms of dollars that we had to spend. When we went into the recovery campaign we started off with a $50,000 budget which grew to $60,000, it grew to $80,000, it grew to a couple of hundred thousand and ended up being a million. If we knew we had that million dollars from the start we probably could have done a much more effective campaign.

In hindsight, a better option may have been an agreed budget outlined in an established disaster or crisis management plan or, as the manager indicated 'some money stashed away somewhere that treasury doesn't find out about.'

Consultation with Stakeholders

ACTC did not appear to consult extensively with stakeholders in preparing the Heart Recovery Marketing Campaign although under the circumstances this may have been appropriate. Stakeholder consultation is a necessarily long and involved process and the aforementioned lack of staff and time did not lend itself to comprehensive consultation. It could be argued that DMOs with their integral role in crisis communication and marketing recovery need to act rapidly and on behalf of the industry as argued by Henderson (1999, p. 108): 'National Tourist Organisations with their responsibility for general destination marketing, research and development have an important role to play in the process of travel and tourism crisis management, representing and acting on behalf of the industry as a whole.'

The campaign received a mixed response from industry. From the perspective of the Canberra Convention Bureau it was positive–'The messages that got out through the ACTC television campaign were very good and indirectly spoke to our market [business travellers].' Similarly the Canberra Accommodation Association expressed: 'I think that what Canberra Tourism did at the time was pretty good–I mean they got the message out that the city was open for business' and TIC (2003a) indicated in mid May 2003 that recovery had been assisted by the campaign. Others felt that the campaign did not address all the messages and issues of a diverse industry and less high profile players may have felt unconsulted–'The Heart [campaign] was ... probably the impossible brief. To try to give all these messages was very difficult and there was a fairly disparate range of views throughout the [National Capital Attractions Association] members about its success or otherwise.' In this situation greater dissemination of the pre- and post-campaign research may have addressed these criticisms.

Beirman (2003) notes that the strength and effectiveness of relationships with private and public stakeholders who depend on destination marketing is often tested in times of crisis and that destinations demonstrating shorter recovery periods and better post-disaster growth are grounded in the establishment of a formal recovery stakeholder alliance (Beirman, 2006a). The existence of such a group may have resulted in greater levels of consultation and satisfaction in this instance but may have had implications for the timing of the response.

Consistency of Messages Within the Marketing Campaign

A comparison of Tables 1 and 2 indicate that the messages delivered in the print and broadcast components of the campaign are consistent and uniform with a common thread of survival, national pride, local spirit and recovery woven through the text, images and lyrics. The brochure did not feature any of these messages and was inconsistent with these mediums. This was a lost opportunity as even a short introductory paragraph acknowledging the bushfires and their impacts would have complemented the other campaign tools and presented the three as a complete package.

The print and television messages were further supported by the staff of the Canberra and Region Visitors Centre (operated by ACTC) who were instructed to communicate clearly to potential and actual visitors that Canberra was operating as a city, the major attractions and tourist facilities were 'open for business' and exactly which attractions or facilities were closed while still acknowledging the disaster and its impacts (Canberra Tourism and Events Corporation, 2003e). This was a fine balancing act. The manager of the Centre indicated 'It was a regular briefing to our staff to be positive. Not to put a really negative slant on the bushfires ... we were sympathetic to the situation but also Canberra is still alive and the industry, the attractions were still open.'

However, developing consistent messages in the recovery period is difficult in some instances (Ritchie et al., 2003) and this may be in part due to the scale of a crisis or disaster and the number of stakeholders communicating messages to various publics. The Foot and Mouth outbreak in the United Kingdom was geographically spread so that some destinations were in the immediate phase of the crisis while simultaneously others were in recovery or totally unaffected (Miller & Ritchie, 2003; Ritchie et al., 2003). This confusing situation was exacerbated by the number of stakeholders speaking out about the crisis and early communication failures between local, regional and national level agencies as the situation changed rapidly. In the case of the ACT bushfires the geographical concentration of the disaster, rapid progression to the recovery phase and smaller number of stakeholders meant that it was easier to develop consistent messages through crisis communication strategies.

Use of Messages to Correct Destination Image Perception

Inaccurate media reporting is a particular issue for the tourism industry due to its reliance on image perception to generate visitors (Cioccio & Michael, 2007). The ACT suffered both a disaster and a 'perceptual' crisis (Beirman, 2006a). The disaster left the majority of tourism assets intact, however, so the recovery marketing campaign was largely about perception management, correcting distorted perceptions and inaccurate reporting rather than spin doctoring.

The formal pre-campaign research and informal analysis of the images and stories being broadcast resulted in the campaign messages being carefully crafted around correcting perceptions about Canberra as a destination. As explained, many inaccurate and sensational stories had been broadcast and a key objective and achievement of the campaign was to correct possible misconceptions (Figure 2). In this way the ACT was in a similar situation to that faced by Katherine after the 1998 floods where the perception by both consumers and industry was that the town had been 'washed off the map' (Faulkner & Vikulov, 2001).

The bushfires and subsequent marketing campaign may have also contributed to changing perceptions of Canberra as a destination. The images and stories about Canberrans as ordinary Australians and real people coping with a disaster were seen by many industry and government representatives as helping change perceptions and 'humanising' the city. As a representative of the Canberra and Region Visitors Centre commented 'we are real people and we do have feelings and we're like any other ordinary community. ...we are just ordinary people doing the same things that other families, other people do in other states.' This humanising of the city was seen as helpful for promoting the ACT. The Canberra Convention Bureau indicated 'there is probably a lot more empathy with the Canberra community now and that is not a bad thing when you are selling a destination because every city, every place has a heart and soul and Canberra does, you know.'

Honesty and Openness

A key strategy in building confidence in a destination is contextualizing the disaster by accurately communicating the extent and nature of the problems for the tourism industry and through that the parts of the destination that are unaffected (Beirman, 2006a). Misleading tourists about the state of a destination is unethical and likely to backfire in the long term. As Beirman (2003, p. 15) noted the information released by the British Tourist Authority about foot and mouth

FIGURE 2. Campaign Messages Developed in Response to Possible Misconceptions

Possible misconceptions   **Campaign messages**

Physical environment

| Canberra is burnt to the ground and major infrastructure is not working. Attractions have been damaged or destroyed and Canberra is no longer an attractive or feasible tourism destination. | | The fires did occur but the majority of Canberra was not damaged. The tourism industry is still functioning and the previous nationally significant attractions are open for business. |

Emotional environment

| The people of Canberra and the tourism industry do not have the time or energy for tourists.
Visiting at this time is insensitive to Canberra's loss. | | Although Canberra has sustained a loss, tourists are critical for revaluing our national assets and for economic and business recovery and hence are very welcome. |

disease was a good example of 'short term pain for long term gain' and these ethical and honest confidence-building measures help establish a reputation for reliability and trust (Beirman, 2006a). Although this article concentrates on the marketing campaign it is worth noting that a media release from ACTC before the campaign stated that, despite the bushfires, it was 'business as usual' in the tourism industry and then went on to clearly list attractions that were open and closed and talk openly and without dissembling about the importance of tourism to Canberra's economy (Canberra Tourism and Events Corporation, 2003c).

The messages communicated in the print and television campaign (see Tables 1 and 2) were honest and open about the general state of the destination although were noticeably silent about the areas that suffered damage. The only reference to the seriousness of the fires were the evocative images of fire fighters at the beginning of the commercials and the use of terms such as 'heartbreak' and 'rebuild.' It could be argued, however, that featuring or mentioning damaged sites or facilities was counterproductive to communicating the main message. This agrees with another of Beirman's (2006a) key strategies for building confidence by not deviating from honest communication but still trying to keep the messages positive. The brochure was completely silent on the bushfire and in a sense did not continue the practice of honesty

and openness established by the other campaign components.

CONCLUSION

Despite the lack of a disaster or crisis management plan, crisis communication plan or marketing recovery plan ACTC achieved a strategic response in the Heart Recovery Marketing Campaign. Under difficult resource and temporal constraints, the campaign was grounded in a modest but formal research exercise, demonstrated a rapid response, was supported by reasonable levels of funding from industry and government, contained consistent messages that addressed the 'perceptual' crisis, was generally honest and open in its communication and was partially evaluated. The main issue in the campaign was the level of stakeholder consultation and this could have been addressed at least partially through adequate planning. In hindsight, the preparation of crisis communication and marketing recovery plans may have ensured that a range of communication issues and decisions were discussed, debated and resolved before the disaster. Such an exercise may have included the planning of the membership of a recovery alliance which could have rapidly formed immediately after the bushfires and served as an instant forum for ideas, advice,

TABLE 4. Crisis Communication Training for Tourism Organisations

Theoretical training	Defining crisis and disaster and forming the skeleton of the crisis or disaster management plan.
Brainstorming	Thinking about the various types of crises and disasters that could occur and how staff could respond. Asking questions about who the audience would be and how would they react? How do we communicate most effectively with the audience?
Planning	Written plans are incorporated into a crisis and disaster manual.
Media training	Training of spokespeople in handling the media and interview techniques.
Simulations	Conducting crisis and disaster simulations to assess the strengths and weaknesses of the team and keep them crisis-aware.
Audits	A crisis and disaster auditor can check individual awareness of procedures and ensure data and manuals are kept up to date.

Source: Adapted from Bland (1995)

consultation and assistance. This may have led to clearer roles and responsibilities and the confidence for ACTC to work on behalf of the industry rather than, as one participant put it, 'asking forgiveness later.'

As indicated previously, there are numerous models of disaster and crisis management plans and crisis communication plans available to destination managers so there is no reason to 'reinvent the wheel.' Tailoring an existing plan to the nature, scope and scale of a particular destination is clearly useful but much of what is prescribed as good practice is fundamentally similar. As Sonmez, Apostolopoulos and Tarlow (1999) point out, the cost of preparing a crisis communication plan and associated marketing recovery plan is likely to be much less than the impacts of decreased visitor activity and flagging consumer confidence due to a slow response to a crisis or disaster. Training and preparation for crises and disasters is also critical. Bland (1995) presents six components of crisis management training for organisations which provides a useful framework for training for DMOs (Table 4).

Barton (1994) also argues that traditional training methods such as seminars, books and videos do not prepare a marketing manager and advocates interactive simulated scenarios and role playing. Maybe training software that focuses on destination management during and after disasters and crises is a profitable development for the tourism industry in the 21st century.

Finally, from the perspective of destination recovery, effective crisis communication and marketing recovery campaigns are a vital role for DMOs. Further case studies on destination recovery and how crisis communication is achieved, both good and poor practice, will ensure that disaster and crisis management ceases to be an afterthought for the tourism industry.

REFERENCES

Australian Capital Tourism Corporation. (2004a). *Fact sheets–2002 domestic and international visitor profiles.* Retrieved 3 March 2004, from www.tourism. act.gov.au

Australian Capital Tourism Corporation. (2004b). *Market research–Autumn/post-bushfire campaign evaluation,* 15 December 2004, from www.tourism.act. gov.au

Barton, L. (1994). Preparing the marketing manager for crisis: The use and application of new strategic tools. *Marketing Intelligence and Planning, 12*(11): 41-46.

Beeton, S. (2005). The case study in tourism research: A multi-method case study approach. In B. W. Ritchie, P. Burns & C. Palmer (Eds.), *Tourism research methods: Integrating theory with practice* (pp. 37-48). UK: CABI Publishing.

Beirman, D. (2002). Marketing of tourism destinations during a prolonged crisis: Israel and the Middle East. *Journal of Vacation Marketing, 8*(2): 167-176.

Beirman, D. (2003). *Restoring tourism destinations in crisis: A strategic marketing approach.* UK and USA: CABI Publishing.

Beirman, D. (2006a). BEST Education Network Think Tank V Keynote Address: Marketing tourism destinations from crisis to recovery. *Tourism Review International: An interdisciplinary journal, 10*(1/2): 7-16.

Beirman, D. (2006b). A comparative assessment of three southeast Asian tourism recovery campaigns: Singapore Roars: Post SARS 2003, Bali post the October 12, 2002 bombing, and WOW Philippines 2003. In Y. Mansfeld & A. Pizam (Eds.), *Tourism, security and safety: From theory to practice* (pp. 251-269). USA: Elsevier.

Berry, S. (1999). We have a problem. call the press! (crisis management plan). *Public Management, 81*(4): 4-15.

Bland, M. (1995). Training managers to handle a crisis. *Industrial and Commercial Training, 27*(2): 28-31.

Britton, R. (2003). *Keynote presentation–Rebuilding credibility after a crisis*. Paper presented at the Tourism and Travel Research Association (TTRA) Conference, 15 June, St Louis, Missouri, USA.

Burnett, J. J. (1998). A strategic approach to managing crises. *Public Relations Review, 24*(4): 475-488.

Campbell, S. (2003). *The enduring importance of national capital cities in the global era*. University of Michigan: Urban and Regional Planning Program.

Canberra Tourism and Events Corporation. (2003a). 2003 Post-bushfire advertising campaign. Canberra, ACT: Canberra Tourism and Events Corporation.

Canberra Tourism and Events Corporation. (2003b). Briefing document–CTEC Canberra campaign January 2003, unpublished document.

Canberra Tourism and Events Corporation. (2003c). Canberra opens its heart to visitors [media release, version 1, 23 January]. ACT: Canberra Tourism and Events Corporation.

Canberra Tourism and Events Corporation. (2003d). *A capital autumn (seasonal marketing brochure)*. Canberra: Canberra Tourism and Events Corporation (CTEC).

Canberra Tourism and Events Corporation. (2003e). CTEC response to bushfire crisis, unpublished document.

Canberra Tourism and Events Corporation, & Tourism Industry Council. (c. 2000). *ACT Tourism Masterplan 2001-2005*. Canberra, ACT: Canberra Tourism and Events Corporation and Tourism Industry Council.

Cassedy, K. (1991). *Crisis management planning in the travel and tourism industry: A study of three destination cases and a crisis management planning manual*. San Francisco: Pacific Asia Travel Association.

Christine, B. (1995). Disaster management: Lessons learned. *Risk Management, 42*(10): 19-34.

Cioccio, L., & Michael, E. J. (2007). Hazard or disaster: Tourism management for the inevitable in Northeast Victoria. *Tourism Management, 28*: 1-11.

Coombs, T. (1999). *Ongoing crisis communication: Planning, managing and responding*. USA: Sage.

Faulkner, B. (1999). *Tourism disasters: Towards a generic model (Work-in-progress report 6)*. Queensland, Australia: CRC for Sustainable Tourism Pty Ltd.

Faulkner, B. (2001). Towards a framework for tourism disaster management. *Tourism Management, 22*(2): 135-147.

Faulkner, B., & Vikulov, S. (2001). Katherine, washed out one day, back on track the next: A post-mortem of a tourism disaster. *Tourism Management, 22*(4): 331-344.

Federal Department of Industry Tourism and Resources. (2005a). *Australia's tourism facts and figures at a glance*. Australia: Federal Department of Industry, Tourism and Resources.

Federal Department of Industry Tourism and Resources. (2005b). *National tourism incident response plan–An action plan for governments across Australia*. Australia: Commonwealth of Australia.

Frisby, E. (2002). Communicating in a crisis: The British Tourist Authority's response to the foot-and-mouth outbreak and 11th September, 2001. *Journal of Vacation Marketing, 9*(1): 89-100.

Gonzalez-Herrero, A., & Pratt, C. B. (1998). Marketing crises in tourism: Communication strategies in the United States and Spain. *Public Relations Review, 24*(1): 83-97.

Hall, C.M. (2002). Tourism in capital cities. *Tourism, 50*(3): 235-248.

Hall, C. M., Timothy, D. J., & Duval, D. T. (Eds.). (2003). *Safety and security in tourism: Relationships, management, and marketing*. New York: Haworth Hospitality Press.

Henderson, J. C. (1999). Tourism management and the southeast Asian economic and environmental crisis: A Singaporean perspective. *Managing Leisure, 4*: 107-120.

Jennings, G. (2001). Tourism research. Queensland: John Wiley and Sons Australia Ltd.

Lee, Y. F., & Harrald, J. R. (1999). Critical issue for business area impact analysis in business crisis management: Analytical capability. *Disaster Prevention and Management, 8*(3): 184-189.

MacLaurin, T. (2005). Book review–Safety and security in tourism: Relationships, management and marketing, edited by C. Michael Hall, Dallen J. Timothy and David Timothy Duval. *Journal of Travel Research, 43*(4): 433 - 434.

McLeod, R. (2003). *Inquiry into the operational response to the January 2003 bushfires in the ACT*. Canberra, ACT: ACT Legislative Assembly.

Miller, G. A., & Ritchie, B. W. (2003). A farming crisis or a tourism disaster? An analysis of the Foot and Mouth disease in the UK. *Current Issues in Tourism, 6*(2): 150-171.

Murphy, P. E., & Bayley, R. (1989). Tourism and disaster planning. *The Geographical Review, 79*(1): 36-46.

Peirce, S., & Ritchie, B. W. (forthcoming 2007). National capital branding: A comparative case study of Canberra, Australia and Wellington, New Zealand. *Journal of Travel and Tourism Marketing*, Vol. 22 (3/4).

Quarantelli, E. L. (1988). Disaster crisis management: A summary of research findings. *Journal of Management Studies, 25*(4): 373-385.

Ritchie, B. W. (2004). Chaos, crises and disasters: A strategic approach to crisis management in the tourism industry. *Tourism Management, 25*: 669 - 683.

Ritchie, B. W., Dorrell, H., Miller, D., & Miller, G. A. (2003). Crisis communication and recovery for the tourism industry: Lessons from the 2001 Foot and Mouth disease outbreak in the United Kingdom. *Journal of Travel & Tourism Marketing, 15*(2/3): 199-216.

Ritchie, B. W., & Leon-Marillanca, C. (2006). *Australians' perceptions of their National Capital–National Perceptions Study.* Canberra, ACT.

Sonmez, S. F., Apostolopoulos, Y., & Tarlow, P. (1999). Tourism in crisis: Managing the effects of terrorism. *Journal of Travel Research, 38*(1): 13-18.

Tourism Industry Council ACT and Region Ltd. (2003a). $500,000 Federal Government support welcome! *TIC Update, 16 May,* 3.

Tourism Industry Council ACT and Region Ltd. (2003b). The impacts of bushfires on the ACT and Region tourism industry: Survey results, unpublished document.

Wimmer, R. D., & Dominick, J. R. (1997). *Mass media research–An introduction* (5th ed.). USA: Wadsworth Publishing Company.

World Tourism Organization. (2005). *Tsunami relief for the tourism sector–Phuket action plan.* Spain: World Tourism Organization.

Yin, R. K. (2003). *Case study research: Design and methods* (3rd ed.). California: Sage Publications.

Young, W. B., & Montgomery, R. J. (1998). Crisis management and its impact on destination marketing: A guide for convention and visitors bureaus. *Journal of Convention and Exhibition Management, 1*(1): 3-18.

Zerman, D. (1995). Crisis communication: Managing the mass media. *Information and Computer Security, 3*(5): 25-28.

Crisis Management–
A Case Study from the Greek Passenger
Shipping Industry

Outi Niininen

Maria Gatsou

SUMMARY. This paper reviews the crisis preparedness of the Greek passenger shipping industry after two widely publicized crises events (Superfast III and Express Samina). As far as Greece is concerned, the travel and tourism industry is one of the most significant contributors to the country's GDP at a rate of more than 10% and the country's passenger shipping industry contributes fundamentally to this figure. Overall findings suggest that both the State as well as the passenger shipping companies encompass crisis management tools and mechanisms to protect the industry, and the whole Greek tourism sector. This paper also identifies the 'ripple effect,' the wider implications a crisis can have on the business environment. Therefore the Faulkner (2001a,b) model for tourism disaster management framework is adapted to accommodate permanent changes enforced on the whole industry as an outcome of a crisis situation.

INTRODUCTION

The tourism industry has had several acute reminders of the need for crisis preparedness in the recent past (e.g., Bird flu, Hurricane Katrina, SARS; September 11, 2001; Bali bomb attacks; London bombings; Gulf War 1991; Iraq conflict 2003; continuing political instability in Israel; Foot and Mouth in the UK; Tsunamis, Global warming) (e.g., Gundel, 2005; Pizam, 2005; Ritchie, 2004). Such international crises have demonstrated how the marketability of individual destinations, and the global tourism in general, is vulnerable to sudden changes in market perceptions. Several acts or events (whether man-made, natural or social consequences) may transform the desirability and reputation of individual companies and or-

Outi Niininen (E-mail: o.niininen@latrobe.edu.au) is a Lecturer in the Department of Management and Marketing of the School of Business at LaTrobe University (Bundoora, Victoria 3086, Australia). Maria Gatsou (E-mail: mg@vando.gr) is Account Manager at V + O COMMUNICATION (91, Michalakopoulou str., 115 28 Athens, Greece).

ganizations, as well as tourist destinations. For instance, the attacks on New York City and Washington D.C. on 11 September 2001 generated worldwide panic, compromising the safety of tourists with specific focus on the United States and Europe. Since tourism is a discretionary activity for most international travelers, many countries had to invest heavily on new campaigns in order to acquire the misplaced inbound tourists and increase demand from domestic travelers (Fall, 2004; Stanbury, Pryer and Roberts, 2005). In other words, '... it is no longer a question whether [a crisis] will arise, but when and how it will be dealt with' (Henderson and Ng, 2004, p. 411). Tourism crisis is, therefore, defined as 'events that disrupt the tourism industry at regular, though unpredictable intervals' (McKercher and Pine, 2005, p. 107). Much of the existing literature focuses on holiday destinations and the recovery strategies they have adopted. This study is therefore unique in a sense that it focuses on a specific sector of the tourism industry (passenger shipping). Furthermore, this paper discusses the 'ripple effect' a crisis situation can cause, i.e., how a single critical event can change the trading environment for the whole industry sector (McKercher and Pine, 2005).

The Greek tourism industry was chosen for case study research as it has been exposed to some recent media attention during crisis situation; hence the industry should be well versed in how to handle such sudden attention. Furthermore, the passenger shipping sector is a vital part of the whole tourism experience in Greece, a country where tourism is a major contributor to the national economy.

Finally, the tourism disaster management framework proposed by Faulkner in 2001 is adjusted to also accommodate industry wide (permanent?) changes due to crisis situations.

Background to the Greek Passenger Shipping Industry

The ferries of the Greek coastal shipping industry complement to the country's attractions with numerous and regular connections between the mainland and islands. Vessels of every type such as passenger ships, ferries, hydrofoils and catamaran crafts connect the central harbors of Attica, Piraeus and Rafina with al-most all the islands. Moreover, other harbors of mainland Greece such as Patras, Kyllini, Thessaloniki, Igoumenitsa, Alexandroupolis, Volos, etc., also have a coastal connection to the island region. These ferries also provide a vital service to the local community as on some routes they are the ONLY available form of transportation (Papadimitriou, 1996).

The transportation by passenger ships in Greece is quite different from those in other European Union countries and Greece was exempted from the European Union's Common Shipping and Transport Policies due to the unique nature of their shipping industry. This is mainly due to the long coastline (approx. 15.000 kilometres) as well as to the great number of islands served scattered in every part of the Greek sea area, established interconnecting coastal shipping lines and the impact sea tourism has on the GDP (Papadimitriou, 1996; Papageorgiou, 1999).

At the time of the interviews, the Greek passenger ships had a total carrying capacity of more than 12.000.000 people and 3.000.000 vehicles on a yearly basis (40% of the total passenger vessels of the European Union). The forecast for 2004 is approximately 20.000.000 and by 2010 to more that 25.000.000 (Kouis, 2002). This considerable increase has been mainly attributed to the increase of vessels' size and speed as well as to the improvement of the industry's safety standards. Table 1 outlines key companies in the Greek passenger shipping industry.

These vessels belong to members of the Greek Union of Coastal Passenger Ships' Owners and the Union of Domestic Ferries; some are newly built and some are recently renovated. All ships must fulfill all the requirements set forth by international agreements, community regulations and national legislation with respect to matters of fire safety, safe navigation, and the protection of marine environment (Papageorgiou, 2003).

Yet, in the past there have been incidents of accidents, wreckages, and mechanical failures that brought the industry under spotlight. In November 1999, the *Superfast III* caught fire outside the port of Patras and although all 413 passengers were rescued, 14 illegal immigrants hiding in the garage died. One year later, the *Express Samina* hit a reef a mile outside the island of Paros and sank, drowning 82 passengers. Al-

TABLE 1. Key Passenger Shipping Companies in Greece (at the time of the interviews)

Company	Key routes	Key competitors	Other interests/facts
ANEK Lines	Piraeus–Crete;	Minoan Lines;	Owns 43% of DANE lines and 20% of NEL lines
	Patra–Italy	Superfast Ferries	
ATTiKi Enterprises/	Patra–Italy;	Minoan Lines;	Relatively new company with new vessels;
Superfast Ferries	Aegean–Crete and Dodecanese	ANEK Lines	Owns a large share of Blue Star Ferries/Strintzis Lines
Blue Star Ferries/	Cyclades;		All vessels new
Strintzis Lines	Ionian Sea Patra–Sami–Ithaki;		
	Piraeus–Rhodes; Piraeus–Crete (Chania)		
DANE Lines	servicing exclusively the Dodecanese complex of islands		partially owned by ANEK Lines and GA Ferries
GA Ferries	servicing the Cyclades and the Dodecanese (South Eastern Aegean)		Hellas Flying Dolphins owns 46% of this company
Hellas Flying Dolphins–HFD (formerly known as	Piraeus–Paros–Naxos–Ios–Santorini (61% market share);	Blue Star Ferries	
Minoan Flying Dolphins):	Rafina–Andros–Mykonos (58% market share)		
Minoan Lines	servicing exclusively the island of Crete (32% market share); Patra–Italy		Hellas Flying Dolphins is major shareholder
NEL Lines	Cyclades and the North East Aegean islands complex; Pireaus–Chios–Mitilini (70% market share)		ANEK owns 20% of this company

Compiled from Anagnostou, 2003; Kouis 2002.

most 500 passengers were rescued, most of them by local fishermen, who rushed to the scene of the wreckage despite the acute weather conditions. The *Express Samina*, even though refurbished in 2000, was an old ship due to be decommissioned in 2003. Following the accident, the company faced a major crisis and the planned entry to the Greek Stock Market was abandoned (Tyler, 2000). These specific incidents, as well as others that occurred during the same period, heavily injured the shipping multiple companies,' thus served a serious blow to the image of the whole shipping industry in Greece.

CRISIS AND ISSUES MANAGEMENT IN TOURISM

The demand for tourism products and services depends on the perception the tourist holds about the destination and the degree of risk he/she is willing to bear. The higher the perceived risk, insecurity and uncertainty regarding a tourist destination, the lower will be its demand. In other words, the media is particularly powerful in communicating to the consumers whether a destination is a 'safe' place to visit. Therefore, any element that contributes to an increase in the perceived risk in using a tourism product or service will negatively affect the consumer's purchasing behavior. This consequence also applies to other business crises (Gondlez-Hmero and Pratt, 1998; Stanbury et al., 2005).

Issues management refers to the first set of activities an organization may conduct to avoid a crisis. It is based on two principles: (1) to identify potentially troublesome issues as soon as possible, and (2) to resolve such issues before they threaten the organizational objectives (Regester and Larkin, 2002). These issues include the environmental analysis, timely and effective decisions, effective communication, human relationship management, short as well as long term planning and, finally, the strategy (Gondlez-Hmero and Pratt, 1998).

Crisis management is one of the most consuming issues of the 21st Century as crisis can threaten the very existence of businesses today. Even an abundance of resources and archives of experiences cannot ensure a company's security and rapid recovery in the event of a crisis.

Only crisis management training, planned prevention, and immediate response to reduce losses can keep a company operational and productive (Mitroff, 2005; Regester and Larkin, 2002). In other words, 'any time you are not in crisis, you are instead in a pre-crisis, or prodromal mode' (Fink, 1986, 7, *as cited in* Henderson and Ng, 2004, p. 412). Crisis preparedness reduces the likeliness of total surprise regarding the type of crisis, the timing of the crisis and how to handle the situation. In other words, 'dealing with crisis means dealing with nightmares and nightmares become less of a threat if someone turns on the light' (Gundel, 2005, p. 106).

General theories of crisis management assume that events move through a series of stages where appropriate action can avert a crisis. Turner (1976) summarizes those phases into three broad positions: (a) pre-crisis, (b) crisis and (c) post-crisis. The movement is essentially cyclical, beginning with normality and eventually returning to it, although many organizations or individuals may have been deeply affected by the experience. It is human to play down the likelihood as well as the consequences of a crisis situation; hence a framework to assist crisis preparedness at each likely stage of this critical event will help in planning the crisis management approaches. This is where a disaster management framework becomes valuable (e.g., Faulkner 2001a,b; Henderson and Ng 2004). Faulkners's framework describes six disaster stages: Pre-event–Prodromal–Emergency–Intermediate–Long-term (recovery)–Resolution. Each stage in this model also outlines the minimum management responses required. The value of such framework is in detailing the steps tourism management teams should take at each stage of the crisis situation. In other words, the framework identifies necessary steps that managers need to address, and these guidelines are based on collective experience in crisis management world wide, thus offering some support to managers dealing with acute situation. A crisis situation is further amplified by pressure on managers to make immediate decisions often with incomplete data; this is where the crisis planning can be of great assistance. This time pressure further adds to the stress the situation places on managers and employees, thus resulting in anxiety (Stafford, Yu and Kobina Armoo, 2002). However, crisis can also bring out the best in people since 'a lot of negative things were forgotten in the cooperative effort between the employees and the management' (Durocher, 1994, p. 68; Faulkner 2001a, b).

Post-crisis: The impact from a crisis needs to be viewed in relation to other recent events reported in the media of the tourism generating countries since 'tourists may resume "normal" travel habits after a single [crisis] event [however] it is becoming clear that investors take longer to return to what they perceive as unreliable business climate' (Baral, Baral and Morgan, 2004, p. 186; McKercher and Pine, 2005; Sadd, 2006). The above quote illustrates two important considerations for post-crisis recovery: (1) the long term impacts on different stakeholder groups will be different, e.g., professional investors have a more rational decision-making system than the average tourists as well as the need to receive an income from their investment (here we are drawing parallels to organizational decision-making and B2B buying); (2) human nature would categorize a single crisis event as a 'fluke' (where no blame was attached to the organization), yet consecutive crisis events would be interpreted as a sign of something greater at large (e.g., violence against tourists in Florida). Furthermore, abnormal crisis events create the feeling of low/no control of the unfolding events thus resulting in even greater stigmatization of the location or organization. Human perception and memory can also distort future holiday demand as we tend to generalize, e.g., the stereotypical belief that Tsunami affected 'the most South East Asian' destinations. For example, on Phuket Island much of the essential tourism infrastructure was restored quickly after the Tsunami disaster and the local communities were hoping for the return of the tourists. However, observations in 2005 conclude that the much needed tourism cash is not yet flowing towards Phuket (Ichinosawa, 2006). Durocher (1994) cites a further reason why tourists appear reluctant to return to a destination or to use a tourism business after a very public crisis event: 'When a destination [or a tourism facility] is unavailable to tourists, they find alternative destination [or facilities]' (p. 66). Media has also been blamed for misinforming the potential tourists and increasing the duration of a crisis situation with replays of the images, even reminding the traveling public of the fragile nature of our tourism business by 'special reports' of past events during anniversaries.

A crisis situation can represent 'a turning point in the evolution of the destination' or organization (Faulkner 2001b, p. 332). After a crisis situation the destination/organization can either be reduced to a lower level of existence than before the crisis, restored to what was before the crisis or use the crisis as an opportunity to improve the facilities (i.e., negative, neutral or positive outcomes of the crisis). There are some good examples of the positive that can come out from a crisis situation, e.g., Katherine (a town badly damaged in a flood; Northern Territory, Australia). We are also likely to witness the 'even better' New Orleans once the rebuilding has been completed after Hurricane Katrina; the promotional campaign to restore the city to the tourism map is likely to be making such claims.

However, crises will inevitably result in some financial losses as well as human suffering. As a result some businesses will be closed or relocated. Some could argue that the crisis simply brought forward what was due to take place and that a 'natural process of weeding out the weak' has taken place. The Katherine example by Faulkner (2001b) suggests that the town received a much needed face lift during the rebuilding process. Yet Faulkner himself calls for testing the applicability of his model through different tourism crisis situations (p. 343). A destination with multiple stakeholders and a larger pool of resources for restoration work is likely to recover better than a private tourism enterprise or a village with over reliance on just a few tourism businesses. Furthermore, the human souls shattered by the crisis can not be healed to their pre-crisis levels and this may result in resentment of the rebuilding work. In other words, the reconstruction of a destination (or a business) damaged by a crisis situation can never fully erase the hurt felt by the community (nor should it aim to do that either) but it will help the affected people to restore some of their routines and, to some extent, their lives. However, it is important to note that in some situations the community feels it is better NOT to reconstruct the built environment but to erect a memorial instead, thus establishing a new purpose for the site/destination/company (Carr, 1997; Pardasani, 2006). Thus the possibility of a negative outcome from a crisis should be added to Faulkner's (2001a,b) tourism disaster management framework. Figure 1 adapts Faulkner's model for tourism disaster management to incorporate a permanent change in the trading environment.

How the organization's crisis communication is received by the public depends on 'the severity of the crisis, the degree to which the public attributes blame on the organization causing the crisis and the public's perception of the organization's competence (measured through past) track record of responding to similar crisis and strength of existing relationships with each audience' (Downing, 2005, p. 4). Crisis preparedness (before crisis preparation) will help organizations respond better to a crisis/ emerging issues and a disaster framework helps in structuring these plans.

The 'Ripple Effect'

A single crisis event may have far reaching consequences; even organizations not involved with the actual crisis will have to deal with a changed business environment. Ichinosawa (2006, p. 116) refers to 'secondary impacts' from major crisis as well as effects of 'risk-induced stigmatization.' Crisis that has deterred tourists away from a destination (or from a company) can be devastating for a destination (or a company). The magnitude of the crisis situation as well as the frequency of critical events also impact on the rate of recovery. Large scale disasters (e.g., the tsunamis, earthquakes and even 9/11) reduce the social capital of a community. This 'is a measure of the resilience of a community to withstand crisis and the level of interconnectedness among members. It is not just the sum of institutions which underpin a society, but the glue that holds them together . . . Social capital is, therefore, a source of strength for the community' (Pardasani 2006, pp. 84-85).

Crises perceived to be random events will not deter tourists as much as ongoing or more systematic crises like terrorism in Egypt, war in Lebanon and earthquakes in Indonesia. Yet, the economic costs of any crisis can mount up as the tourism industry has a high multipliers effect,

thus when tourists keep away the whole economy will suffer and this will further de-moralize local residents (Sadd, 2006; Smith and Carmichael, 2005; Tarlow, 2006; Stafford et al., 2002).

Moreover, when it is a large scale crisis with substantial *ripple effect* in the locality it is important to remember that tourism employees (who often live near the company/destination) will have their private lives affected as well (Faulkner, 2001b). Disney proved its true colors during the hurricanes of 2004 when it set up a special employee relief team and relief fund (approx. US$8 million distributed to 95,000 employees). Furthermore, free emergency accommodation was offered to families (and even their dogs) as well as access to hot and cold meals. To prepare for a crisis is difficult, even the best laid plans are just guidelines, but members of staff who have actually helped re-build the company/destination have valuable experience that the company should aim to keep. Therefore, 'if you are serious about business recovery, you need to be serious about investing in your employees and in the community' (Higgins, 2005, p. 46; Tarlow, 2006).

The crisis situations of today are unlikely to be limited within national or institutional borders. Consequently, with the instant multimedia focus on crisis, many events are heartfelt internationally, resulting in a 'mass-psychological' change. That is, individuals not directly affected by the crisis suddenly begin to question the risk proneness of their local environment. For example, the AIDS epidemic has changed how the public views gays and shipping incidents make tourists choose alternative modes of transport. Crisis events also often result in actions by politicians and legislators, especially if there is reasonable doubt of failure of crisis prevention or error of judgment in crisis response. Once crises become politicized they tend to have greater and more far-reaching consequences and 'crises are no longer written off as freak incidents, but become labeled increasingly as symptoms of underlying problems.' Furthermore, 'data are selected and molded to construct winning arguments in a battle for political-bureaucratic survival' ('t Hart, Heysen and Boin, 2001, p. 184). Emotional responses to suspected acts of terrorism can also result in un-reversible acts of retribution as well as rush-

FIGURE 1. Enhanced Tourism Disaster Management Framework

Phase in disaster process	Elements of the disaster management responses	Principal ingredients of the disaster management strategies
1. *Pre-event*	*Precursors*	Risk assessment
2. *Prodromal*	*Mobilisation*	*Disaster contingency plans*
3. *Emergency*	*Action*	*Disaster contingency plans*
4. *Intermediate*	*Recovery*	*Disaster contingency plans*

PARADIGM SHIFT–CHANGED TRADING ENVIRONMENT

INDUSTRY SPECIFIC	*COMPANY SPECIFIC*	
• Reduced consumer confidence	*Long-term (recovery) in changed business environment*	*Reconstruction and reassessment*
• Active consumer pressure groups	Continuation of previous phase, but items that could not be attended to quickly are attended to at this stage.	• Repair of damaged infrastructure
		• Rehabilitation of environmentally damaged areas
• Introduction of new legislation		• Counselling victims
• Restriction of business practice	• Post-mortem • Self-analysis	• Restoration of business/consumer confidence and development of investment plans
• Increased insurance premiums	• Healing	• Debriefing to promote input to revisions of disaster strategies
• Changed competition	• Discontinuation	• Closing down the business
	5. *Resolution*	*Review*
	Routine restored/ new improved state established/ New deteriorated state established	

Adapted from Faulkner 2001a, p. 144.

ing of new legislations that aims to limit the possibility of similar crises in the future (Carr, 1997).

Crisis Recovery

The recommendations for speedier recovery involve a two-tier strategy: organization/destination level and national level. Immediate reaction to a crisis is to withdraw all existing promotion and the crisis management team should focus on getting accurate facts to the media to remove the need for speculation. Once the organization/destination is ready to receive tourists again, the independent businesses should start by focusing on less-sensitive target markets, e.g., in the post 9/11 USA, domestic tourists were targeted as they could make the journey by car. Visiting friends and relatives as well as the business travel market have also proven to be less sensitive segments. Price discounts, innovative packaging, and lobbying support from major media players has also been proven to work (Litvin and Anderson, 2003; Sadd, 2006; Stafford et al., 2002).

Moreover, the management and the regulatory agencies should also provide reassurances about preventing further accidents and making traveling even safer in the future, thus emphasizing the role of strategic communication campaigns to bring travel as an activity back on the agenda for the traveling public (Fall, 2004).

Governments also play a great role in large scale crisis recovery as they should commit funds for major promotional campaign (e.g., the USA now has a nationwide strategy). The governments can also hasten the recovery with tax concessions, grants or loans and the local governments can champion tourism business coalitions to pool together available expertise and resources (Litvin and Anderson, 2003; Pratt, 2003; Sadd, 2006; Stafford et al., 2002).

METHOD

The aim of this study is to investigate the crisis preparedness of the Greek passenger shipping industry after two heavily publicized crises (*Superfast III* and *Express Samina*). Furthermore, the *ripple effect* of these crises is also investigated. Interviews with key members

from the Greek passenger shipping industry were conducted to assess industry sector's preparedness to handle potential crisis issues today. A qualitative approach and in particular the in-depth interview method was adopted in order to gather primary information (Sekaran, 2003). Due to the sensitivity of the research topic complete anonymity of responding individuals was assured.

The interview questions were organised under the following key headings: respondents views of the crisis management practice in tourism in general and with the specific focus on the Greek passenger shipping industry; pre-crisis–during crisis–after crisis policies relevant to their industry; handling journalists and media; crisis management team; most likely crisis events for this industry; specific questions about the 'Express Samina' and 'Superfast III' events; and finally, the general crisis preparedness and responsiveness of the Greek passenger shipping industry.

The Sample

Twelve interviews with executives related to the Greek passenger shipping industry were performed in order to assemble the primary data required (four interviews each segment): managers of different passenger shipping companies (please note that at the time of these interviews there were only seven companies operating in the Greek passenger shipping industry); academics as well as consultants from crises management and media relations agencies in Greece (external consultancies that have direct contact with the passenger shipping industry were given preference); and the regulatory and governmental agencies. Our interviewees were all managers from the Greek passenger shipping industry with some personal experience of handing crisis situations. They represented the following companies: Blue Star Ferries, Hellas Flying Dolphins, Minoan Lines, Superfast Ferries, Association of Greek Tourist Enterprises (AGTE), Greek National Tourism Organization (GTNO), Union of Coastal Passenger Ships' Owners, Regulatory Authority for Domestic Maritime Transportation (RAHTE), Mediaccess S.A., Pallidan Communications Specialist, Public Affairs Management, and SK Consulting.

The interviews took place during the summer months of 2003 and the interview language was Greek to ensure that the finer 'nuances' of verbal communication was captured; as expected this limited our possibility to use direct quotations from our interviewees. Back translation technique was used in question wording.

FINDINGS AND DISCUSSION

In order for a company to be ready to respond to a crisis, the management needs to get prepared ahead of time. The interviewees from the passenger shipping industry identified wreckages, collisions, fire, economical crisis, labor accidents and other issues caused by external factors, the most common issues that cause possible problems to a shipping company (Table 2). The companies interviewed classified each situation according to its severity and responded accordingly. For instance, if loss of life is involved in the incident, then this is considered of primary importance and is handled as such by the teams. In a similar way, a mechanical problem that is faced on a regular basis may not require the same mobilization.

As far as the Greek passenger shipping industry is concerned, all firms questioned stated that they embrace media relations and crisis management practices mainly at top management level to guide the specific departments on the handling of the crisis. The key aim of the interviewed organizations is to identify issues and deal with them before crisis levels emerge from such situation.

The companies interviewed used research and environmental scanning to identify issues to ensure as effective dealing with the crisis as possible. Some crises may also arise worldwide and influence the tourism industry as a whole, yet they may be handled as an opportunity by some enterprises. An example of such an occurrence was the war in Kosovo in 1999, which was regarded by *Superfast* as a chance to expand and make its routes to Italy more frequent in order to facilitate the need for transportation of passengers and vehicles during the war.

Table 3 makes a comparison between a typical crisis management team as suggested by the literature and the crisis teams used by the interviewees. As shown in Table 3, the main difference is that in the passenger shipping field the crisis teams are actually divided into three sub-categories: (a) quick response team, (b) specialists team, and (c) destination team. Depending on each crisis situation either one or several of the response teams are used to handle the incident. Additionally, since transportation of passengers is regarded a sensitive matter, the customer services department has an active role

TABLE 2. Categorization of Potential Issues and Crisis in the Shipping Industry

1. Safeties and Security	4. Internal issues (labor related)
1.1 Wreckage	4.1 Shift in the management
1.2 Grounding	4.2 Friction between stockholders
1.3 Mechanical failure	4.3 Strikes
1.4 Fire	4.4 Personnel dismissals
1.5 Passengers health	
	5. Political intervention
2. Environment	5.1 Competition regulations
2.1 Sea pollution–waste	5.2 Control of ticket prices
	5.3 Environmental regulations
3. External issues (caused by third parties)	5.4 Economic crisis
3.1 Terrorist attacks	5.5 Taxes–duties
3.2 Defamation campaigns	
3.3 Protests against the company	6. Technology
3.4 Personal Chi (i.e., suicide on board)	6.1 Loss in communications
3.5 Illegal immigrants	6.2 Computer system's malfunction
	6.3 Mechanical problem

TABLE 3. Types of Crisis Management Teams

	Recommendation from Literature	Findings from Greek Shipping Industry
Number of teams	One team	Three teams:
		a) The quick response team
		b) The specialists' team
		c) The destination team
People involved	Team Leader	The company's CEO
	The President, CEO, or Managing Director	The Marine Operations Department
	The company's spokes-representative	The Corporate Relations and Development Department (acting also as spokes-representative)
	The Research and Development Manager	The Customer Services Department
	Team coordinator–usually coming from the Human Resources	Financial Director
	The general secretary or company's receptionist	Legal Advisor

in the team to facilitate communication both with passengers and their relatives.

The 'Ripple Effect' Evident from These Case Studies

It is important to note that it is not just the organizations directly involved with a crisis situation that have to cope with the outcome of such un-planned events. In addition to the two named shipping companies, the *ripple effect* was evident throughout the national as well as the international passenger shipping industry. In the past, most members of the Greek passenger shipping industry have faced at least one of the crises identified in our interviews. The ones that are still remembered by the general public are the *Express Samina* wreckage in September 2000 and the fire on the *Superfast III* in November 1999. Both incidents negatively affected the companies' image, but also attached blame on the Greek government for not imposing more strict safety and security measures.

These case studies suggest that the *ripple effect* was felt by the other companies within the industry as these crises resulted in changes in the domestic as well as international (EU) legislation. In the Greek passenger shipping situation, it was more the interpretation of these laws that changed as the EU legislation was already in place but not yet in effect in Greece. The Greek government had found a way to delay the imposition of the EU law (cabotage) so as to

'protect' the shipping industry by implementing the changes in smaller steps (had the new law been imposed at once, more than 100 ships would have had to be withdrawn in just one year and this would have meant a catastrophe for the Greek fleet). After these crises the Government took a very pro-active (and public?) role to ensure the safety standards were now met by suspending an impressive total of 65 ferries and tour boats for failing the safety inspections in 2001.

As a further outcome, the Government finally imposed the existing legislation to create a new (safer) environment for future passenger shipping operations. This new ferry safety legislation consisted of the measures described below.

Cabotage Date Brought Forward: Greece decided to open up its coastal services to other European operators on the 1st of November 2002, rather than on the 1st of January 2004, as it was entitled to under the European Union exemption. The regulations regarding the maximum age for passenger ships has been tightened to a 30-year limit from the previous age limit of 35.

Liberalization of Ferry Route Licensing: The vested interests that blocked rivalry between companies on profitable routes are being investigated. Over the years, certain routes had become virtual monopolies, due to a mix of powerful ferry operators and ministerial patronage. However, the liberalization brought forward would mean that travelers have a wider choice of vessels on the more popular routes and that companies need to make greater effort to offer better ships and services. Additionally, the government is protecting the unpopular routes with plans to offer long-term public service franchises, in order to attract interest from ferry operators.

New Rules for Crews: As the *Express Samina* disaster is perceived as being the result of human failings, Greece has moved quickly to improve standards in this area. Survivors have reported that the vessel's crew failed to help passengers find lifejackets, board and launch lifeboats. Furthermore, the company was found responsible for the incident, since it was the management's decision to let the ship travel in such bad weather conditions. Guilty parties received prison sentences and the weakened company was taken over by 'Blue Star–Superfast Ferries.' As an outcome of this crisis event, the government has increased checks to assure that seafarers are sufficiently trained in rescue drills. There are also plans to limit the hours the crew can work, particularly in the high season. This is a good example of the politicization of the event ('t Hart et al., 2001, p. 184) as the companies will face reduced profits if these new regulations are implemented. The Greek passenger shipping industry is a good example how industry sectors should aim to 'clean up their own house.' In other words, organizations should work together towards an acceptable code of conduct with self regulation. The UK Advertising Standards Authority would be a good example of how an industry has taken a pro-active view to protect themselves against possible future crisis and the resulting tightened legislation (please see http://www.asa.org.uk/asa/ for more details).

CONCLUSIONS

To conclude, the management of crises and issues is a pro-active management practice which protects and promotes the organization in case its reputation or assets are in danger. The efficient management of any crisis is achieved through programming, preparation, and training as well as through the correct application of the decisions during the crisis. This would permit an organization to take drastic and efficient measures before and during the crisis, with the objective to maintain the equilibrium between the interests of the company or organization and those of the shareholders, the employees, the clients and the public.

Crises occur often as a result of external changes or internal incidents. Hence, it is essential for all companies, regardless of size, to have a comprehensive and well-rehearsed crisis management plan, and a continuum of services to meet the industry's response needs in emergency situations. Effective contingency plans and procedures combined with well-trained and motivated personnel are the best defense against the operational challenges during crisis. This makes good business sense and ultimately protects the image of the company, the industry as well as national/regional governments or regulatory agencies.

The three specialist crisis teams approach adopted by the Greek passenger shipping industry fits in well with the tourism context and should be adopted by other tourism businesses too.

REFERENCES

Agnastou, A. (2003) "Economic problems in the shipping industry; An unprecedented economical crisis" *Apogevmatini*, 20 July

Baral, A., Baral, S. and Morgan, N. (2004), "Marketing Nepal in an uncertain climate: Confronting perceptions of risk and insecurity," *Journal of Vacation Marketing, 10*(2), 186-192.

Carr, A. (1997), "Terrorism on the couch–a psychoanalytic reading of the Oklahoma disaster and its aftermath," *Disaster Prevention and Management, 6*(1), 22-32.

Downing, J.R. (2005), "No greater sacrifice: American Airlines Employee crisis communication response to the 9/11 attacks." *Personal communication*, 19 February 2005.

Durocher, J. (1994), "Recovery marketing: What to do after a natural disaster," *The Cornell H.R.A. Quarterly*, April, 66-70.

Fall, L.T. (2004), "The increasing role of public relations as a crisis management function: An empirical examination of communication restrategizing efforts among destination organization managers in the wake of 11th September, 2001." *Journal of Vacation Marketing, 10*(3), 238-251.

Faulkner, B. (2001a), "Towards a framework for tourism disaster management," *Tourism Management*, 22, 135-147.

Faulkner, B. (2001b), "Katherine, washed one day, back on the track next: a post-mortem of a tourism disaster," *Tourism Management, 22*, 331-344.

Gondlez-Hmero, A. and Pratt, C. (1998), "Communication marketing crises in tourism: strategies in the United States and Spain." *Public Relations Review, 24*(1), 83-97.

Gundel, S. (2005), "Towards a new typology of crisis," *Journal of Contingencies and Crisis Management,* 13(3 September), 106-115.

Henderson, J. and Ng, A. (2004), "Responding to crisis: Severe Acute Respiratory Syndrome (SARS) and hotels in Singapore," *International Journal of Tourism Research, 6*, 411-419.

Higgins, B.A. (2005), "The storms of summer–Lessons learned in the aftermath of the hurricanes of '04,' *Cornell Hotel and Restaurant Administration Quarterly,* February, 40-46.

Ichinosawa, J. (2006), "Reputational disaster in Phuket: the secondary impact of the tsunami on inbound tourism," *Disaster Prevention and Management, 15*(1), 111-113.

Kouis, L. (2002), "The Greek shipping industry's uncertain future" *Touristiki Agora,* 146 (March), 128-130.

Litvin, S.W. and Alderson, L.L. (2003), "How Charleston got her groove back: A Convention and Visitors Bureau's response to 9/11." *Journal of Vacation Marketing, 9* (2), 188-197.

McKercher, B. and Pine, R. (2005), "Privation as a stimulus to travel demand?" *Journal of Travel and Tourism Marketing, 19* (2/3), 107-116.

Mitroff, I. (2005), "From my perspective–Lessons from 9/11. Are companies better prepared today?" *Technological Forecasting and Social Change, 72,* 375-376.

Papadimitriou, C. (1996), *Service Discrimination and Quality Evaluation by Ferry Passengers.* Unpublished MSc Dissertation, Guildford: University of Surrey.

Papageorgiou, Tr. (2003), "The Passenger Shipping in Greece." *The Union of Coastal Passenger Ships' Owners,* April, 1-7.

Pardasani, M. (2006), "Tsunami reconstruction and redevelopment in the Maldives: A case study of community participation and social action," *Disaster Prevention and Management, 15*(1), 79-91.

Pizam, A. (2005), "When Mother Nature speaks, we must listen and learn," *International Journal of Hospitality Management, 24,* 473-474.

Pratt, G. (2003), "Terrorism and tourism: Bahamas and Jamaica fight back," *International Journal of Contemporary Hospitality Management, 15*(3), 192-194.

Regester, M. and Larkin, J. (2002), *Risk Issues and Crisis management: A casebook of best practice.* 2nd Edition, London: The Institute of Public Relations.

Richie, B.W. (2004), "Chaos, crisis and disaster: A strategic approach to crisis management in the tourism industry," *Tourism Management, 25,* 669-686.

Sadd, D. (2006), "Will London 2012 tourism initiatives suffer post July terrorist attacks?" *Cutting Edge Research in Tourism–New Directions, Challenges and Applications.* University of Surrey, UK, 6-9 June.

Sekaran, U. (2003), *Research Methods for Business: A Skill Building Approach,* 4th Edition. New York: Wiley Publications.

Smith, W.W. and Carmichael, B.A. (2005), "Canadian seasonality and domestic travel patterns: regularities and dislocations as a result of the events of 9/11." *Journal of Travel and Tourism Marketing, 19* (2/3), 61-76.

Stafford, G., Yu, L., and Kobina Armoo, A (2002), "Crisis management and Recovery, How Washington, DE., Hotels Responded to Terrorism." *Cornell Hotel and Restaurant Administration Quarterly,* 27-40.

Stanbury, J., Pryer, M. and Roberts, A (2005), "Heroes and Villains–Tour operator and media response to crisis: An exploration of press handling strategies by UK adventure tour operators," *Current Issues in Tourism, 8*(5), 394-434

Tarlow, P. (2006), "Issues in health, safety and security," *e-Review of Tourism Research, 4* (3). http://ertr.tamu.edu.

't Hart, P. Heysen, L. and Boin, A. (2001), "Guest editorial introduction: New trends in crisis management practice and crisis management research: setting the agenda," *Journal of Contingencies and Crisis Management, 9* (4 December), 181-188.

Turner, B. A. (1976), "The organizational and inter-organizational development of disasters." *Administrative Science Quarterly, 21,* 378-397.

Tyler, R. (2000), "Third Greek ferry accident brings death total to at least 78." News & Analysis: Europe www.wsws.org/sections/category/news (accessed 3rd March 2003)

Crisis Management Planning
to Restore Tourism After Disasters:
A Case Study from Taiwan

Yu-Chin Huang
Yung-Ping Tseng
James F. Petrick

SUMMARY. The tourism industry is vulnerable to natural and human induced incidents such as terrorist attacks, political instability, flood and earthquakes. On September 21st 1999, a devastating earthquake struck Taiwan which caused severe damage to both local people and the tourism industry. This paper proposes an innovative integrated approach that could be adopted as a crisis management plan for Taiwan to restore its tourism industry. A thorough review of the crisis management literature is introduced and examined to generate an integrated crisis management framework. It is anticipated that this framework could accelerate tourism recovery by showing secure images for tourists, and hence the competitiveness of a tourist nation could be enhanced through sound crisis management practices.

INTRODUCTION

Tourism plays an important role in enhancing a nation's business activity, income, foreign currency earnings and the creation of jobs. It is perhaps one indication of the importance of tourism that often one of the biggest effects of a natural disaster is the impact on a destination's tourism industry. Thus, the tourism industry tends to be highly sensitive to negative environmental factors such as natural disasters, serious social conflicts, war, economic crises and acts of terrorism like the Bali Bomb terrorist attack (Mansfeld, 1999). Of these events it is inevitably natural hazards such as hurricanes, earthquakes, and tsunami that are especially characterized by a low degree of control and forecast impossibility (Gee & Gain, 1986). Lee and Harrald (1999) articulated that "natural disasters can disrupt the supply and distribution chains for even the best prepared businesses . . . service businesses are increasing vulnerable to electrical, communication and other critical infrastructure failures."

Yu-Chin Huang is a Doctoral Student, Yung-Ping Tseng is a Doctoral Student, and James F. Petrick is Associate Professor, Department of Recreation, Park & Tourism Sciences, Texas A&M University, 2261 TAMU, College Station, TX 77843-2261 (E-mail: jocehuang@neo.tamu.edu).

When a disaster happens, various aspects of international tourism demand can be affected negatively including reduced visitor arrivals, a fall in employment, declines in private sector profits, a reduction in government revenues, and eventually the cessation of further investment. In recent years, the global tourism industry has experienced many crises and disasters. Thus, one of the main questions for all branches of economic activity, particularly for tourism, is to bring risk, security, and crisis management under control (Peters & Pikkemaat, 2005). Faulkner (2001) and Ritchie (2004) argue that there is a lack of research on crisis or disaster phenomena in the tourism industry, on the impacts of such events on both the industry and specific organizations, and the responses of the tourism industry to such incidents.

Background: Sequence of Events of the Unavoidable Earthquake in Taiwan

Taiwan is approximately 14,000 square miles; its size is closest to the States of Massachusetts and Connecticut, and is located 100 miles east of Mainland China (Goltz, 1999). The majority of the population of 23 million lives in cities along the western coast of the island. The island has a high mountain range, which extends from the north to the south in the central portion of the island. The epicenter of the earthquake on September 21, 1999 was located in this mountainous central region of the island near Chi-Chi in Nantou County, approximately 90 miles south of the Capital city of Taipei (Figure 1).

On September 21, 1999, the 7.3 magnitude earthquake was felt island-wide in Taiwan. Five counties in central Taiwan including the city of Taichung, in the middle of Taiwan, experienced the greatest number of casualties and most severe damage. The earthquake occurred at 1:47 a.m. local time while most of the population was asleep, thus the collapse and damage to residential structures caused a great number of the 2,405 deaths and 10,718 injuries. Additionally, in excess of 10,000 were left homeless, many buildings were destroyed, and roadways, water, sewage, gas, and power systems were cut (Goltz, 1999).

Impacts on the Travel and Tourism Industry

Taiwan's tourism industry experienced a harsh winter as a result of the September 21 Earthquake. One year before the earthquake, tourism contributed 1.3% of the GDP and brought USD 3.4 billion to Taiwan. The composition of the inbound international tourists to Taiwan contained 36.5% Japanese travelers and 15.2% American travelers. Those two countries brought most of the tourists to Taiwan (Tourism Bureau of Taiwan, 1999). The earthquake severely shook the island economy and led government officials to cut the estimated growth of the 1999 GDP in the fourth quarter to 5.3% from 5.7% (Directorate-General of Budget, Accounting and Statistics, 2000).

The post-quake rescue operations diminished many travelers' desire to visit during the initial time period following the disaster. There were also misleading reports that the earthquake had engulfed the entire island which also frightened away many potential tourists (Huang & Min 2002; Huang & Ralston, 2001). The Tourism Bureau said international news media's extensive coverage of the devastating earthquake had prompted many prospective foreign tourists to cancel their Taiwan travel plans. The quake frightened off foreign tour groups and at the same time hurt the economy in central Taiwan. International tour groups plummeted by an average of about 90% and 50% of the reserved domestic tour groups were cancelled. All in all, the tourist industry is estimated to have lost NT$ 30 billion (about US$ 1 billion) between September 21, 1999 and January 10, 2000 (Taiwan He@dlines, 2000).

The Ministry of Transportation and Communications reported nine hotels in the disaster area that depended entirely on tourist revenue had lost approximately NT$ 776 million (US$ 24 million). Meanwhile, another 70 hotels in the devastated area had lost around NT$ 2.2 billion (US$ 69.4 million) and eight privately operated recreational areas in the same area had NT$ 440 million loss (US$ 13.7 million). Financial losses did not include the government-run resorts. The room occupancy rates of hotels for international tourists plummeted by an average of about 60%. During the period of September to November 1999, these hotels lost more than NT$ 920 million (US$ 28.7 million)

FIGURE 1. Epicenter of September 21; Earthquake in Taiwan (2000, RMS Report)

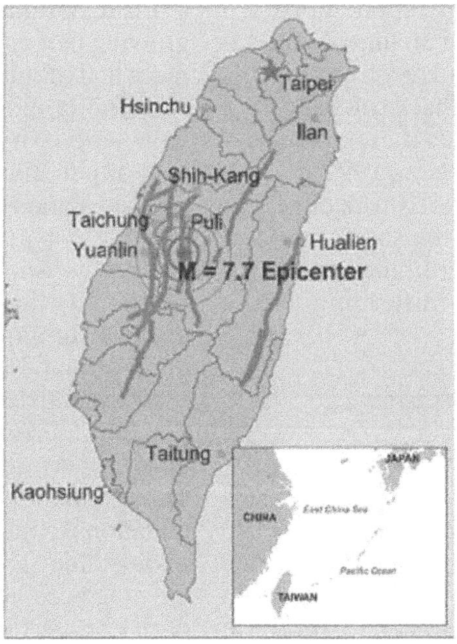

From "Risk Management Solutions, Inc, Event Report," by Chi Chi Reconnaissance Team, 2000, P.1. Retrieved November 10, 2006 from http://www.rms.com/Publications/Taiwan_Event.pdf, Copyright 2000 by Risk Management Solutions, Inc. Used with permission.

because of a high rate of room cancellation. Additionally, more than 210,000 airline reservations were cancelled between September and December 1999. According to calculations made by the Transportation Ministry's Tourism Bureau, the slowdown in tourism cost around NT$ 10 billion (US$ 313 million) each month (Taiwan He@dlines, 2000) from September to December, 1999.

According to the Tourism Bureau of Taiwan (2000), during the period of January to August 1999, visitor arrivals had increased 15% as compared to the same period of the previous year, which had been reviving as Asia recovered from the financial turmoil of 1997-1998. Notwithstanding, there was a significant decrease in tourist arrivals during the post-quake period mainly caused by the secondary impact which induced new negative media reports. The number of international tourists declined by 15% during September to December when compared to the same time period in 1998, and the number of visitors to 230 major scenic spots dropped by 27%.

It is evident that the natural disasters affected the tourism industry dramatically. Further, this kind of incident placed tourist related organizations into tough situations related to decreasing tourist visitation and revenue. Tourist destinations can fight these difficulties more effectively and efficiently if a sound crisis management plan is in place.

LITERATURE REVIEW

The purpose of this study is to investigate various crisis management models that have been developed between 1986-2006 to find the similarities and differences between the models and to conclude the most appropriate model to accommodate the unique needs for the September 21, 1999 Earthquake in Taiwan. Using this approach should be useful to further restore the tourism industry. In addition, special attention will be focused on a "secondary" impact model development for the September 21 earthquake since misleading reports impacted the entire island by creating an unrealistic impression of Taiwan. "Secondary" impact or effect refers to consequences that "extend beyond the people directly affected by the regional hazard event or report" (Kasperson, 1992, p.160). The earthquake-induced tourism decline has therefore deeply disrupted the social fabric of the area, and formulated the stigmatization of a place in Taiwan due to misleading media reports.

Definition of Crisis and Disaster

At present, there is an abundance of published articles in the tourism literature on handling crisis management. Faulkner (2001) made a clear distinction between the definition of "crisis" and "disaster" as the extent to which the situation is attributable to the organization itself. A crisis describes a situation where the root cause of an event is, to some extent, self-inflicted through such problems as inept management structures and practices or a failure to adapt to change, while a disaster can be defined as when an enterprise is confronted with sudden unpredictable catastrophic changes over which it has little control (Faulkner, 2001). Prideaux et al. (2003) distinguish between crisis and disaster, with the former being described as the possible, but unexpected result of management failures that are concerned with the future course of events set in motion by human action or inaction precipitating the event. On the other hand, they described disaster as an unpredictable catastrophic change that can normally be responded to only after the event, either via implementing contingency plans already in place or through reactive responses. Thus, for the purpose of this analysis, "disaster" will be used to refer to the earthquake situation in Taiwan where the collection of enterprises in the case of a tourist destination is confronted with sudden unpredictable catastrophic changes over which it has minimum control.

Perceived Risk and Destination Image

Tourism cannot develop in places that are perceived as dangerous (Reisinger & Mavondo,

2005). Safety and physical security are two of the primary conditions for development of a tourism destination. Unfortunately, there is a growing perception of the world as a more risky place to live and travel (Fischhoff, Nightingdale & Iannotta, 2001), and this perception could have serious implications for tourism. The concept of perceived risk in tourism has been examined in many studies (Roehl & Fesenmaier, 1992; Yavas, 1987). Risk in tourism has been defined as what is perceived and experienced by tourists during the process of purchasing and consuming traveling services and at the destination (Tsaur, Tzeng & Wang, 1997).

Perceived risk has been found to greatly affect potential tourists' intentions to travel (Reisinger & Mavondo, 2005). Crompton (1992) asserted that destinations perceived as too risky, due to situational constraints or barriers, may become undesirable. Therefore, at this moment, media coverage can greatly influence the perceptions of risk by causing one destination to appear less or more risky than others (Sonmez & Graefe, 1998). The misconception of risk, frequently exaggerated by the mass media, can cause a significant level of unwarranted anxiety among potential travelers.

The accuracy of media coverage is essential for shaping potential visitors image toward the destination during the aftermath of a disaster since tourists do not tend to thoroughly evaluate the reality behind delivered images via the public media (Mansfeld, 1999). Lepp and Gibson (2003) found that the image an individual holds of the risks at a destination may influence the likelihood of visiting it. It seems logical that marketers could improve the image of a destination by decreasing the impression of perceived risk. Therefore, it is important to counter negative images by offering timely information to make current and prospective visitors feel safe during the recovering period (Durocher, 1994). It is therefore crucial for destination marketers to understand touristic perceptions in order to tailor promotional messages accordingly. Communications need to address tourist concerns, change false perceptions, and reinforce positive perceptions.

Image based on safety may become increasingly important as the number of economies tied to tourism increases. The perception of risk associated with a destination can have dire economic consequences. However, secondary impact after a disaster may come in when news companies often exaggerate the situation to attract audiences' attention to their messages instead of reporting the truth of the incidents. As a result, media coverage not only complicates the process during the recovery stage, but also lessens the willingness of tourists, or potential tourists to visit (Milo & Yoder, 1991). Destination image plays a critical role for tourists in selecting their vacation destination (Baloglu & McCleary, 1999; Huang & Min, 2002; Huan, Beaman & Shelby, 2004). A positive image of a destination increases visitation (Gartner & Shen, 1992; Dimanche & Lepetic, 1999), but it requires long and costly marketing efforts to alter a negative image. It is imperative to reintroduce a destination via offering up-to-date information since tourists' perceptions of safety concerning a destination affects their willingness to travel (Durocher, 1994). Informing potential tourists of successful physical rehabilitation is only one element of retrieving users and getting new ones and it should be a long-term process (Huan, Beaman & Shelby, 2004).

Summarization of Crisis Management Plans (1986-2006)

Crisis management is the planning for, responding to and recovering from a crisis. It is the skill of removing much of the risk and uncertainty inherent in low-probability and high-impact events so that tourism administrators and business managers can achieve more control over management operations (Fink, 1986). Crisis management plans in tourism should deal with the recognition of crises at the destination and the recovery and rebuilding after a crisis, while aiming to restore a positive image and on prevent a decrease in tourist arrivals. In an organization or tourism destination, potential crises or disasters could be avoided with the use of active crisis management plans (Peters & Pikkemaat, 2005). Therefore, crisis management, in its most basic form, implies being prepared before the crisis strikes, effectively executing the crisis management plan during the crisis, and quickly recovering to normal after the crisis (Yu, Stafford & Armoo, 2005).

In the past twenty years (1986-2006), crisis management has emerged as a substantive focus area and a number of strategic approaches and models have appeared. By looking at the major ones, patterns of crisis management can be determined. A thorough review of the literature revealed 11 different crisis/disaster models proposed in the last twenty years. Table 1 summarizes the crisis management models chronologically, and the approaches, phases, and processes that different researchers specified in their crisis management plans.

Through vigorous examination of the 11 models the current authors were able to identify four different crisis management approaches. The reduction of these 11 models can help simplify the complex processes and thereby provide a better understanding of the problem domain. The four resultant classifications are life cycle approach, strategic crisis management approach, action-oriented crisis management approach, and an integrated approach. Descriptions will be provided as follows to explicitly explain how each of the four approaches has been specified.

The first classification of crisis management focused on the life cycle approach (Fink, 1986; Roberts, 1994; Faulkner, 2001; Luhrman, 2005). This three-phase (pre-event, emergency, post-event) crisis management approach is the early version of the life cycle framework which was later incorporated into a six-phase (pre-event, prodromal, emergency, intermediate, long-term, and resolution) crisis management plan to more comprehensively manage tourism disasters. The second classification is the strategic crisis management model that has three primary components–crisis management formation, implementation, and evaluation–which was proposed by Preble (1993, 1997).

Action-oriented crisis management (Mitroff, 1988; Pearson and Mitroff, 1993; Burnett, 1998; Wilks and Moore, 2005) is the third classification. These plans broke crisis management into four or more distinct phases including: reduction, readiness, response, and recovery. Many action-oriented crisis management frameworks used similar terminologies to achieve effective crisis control. This approach (also called the Four Rs) demonstrates the kinds of actions and activities that should be taken to restore tourism after crises and disasters.

TABLE 1. Summary of Crisis Management (CM) Framework

Author information	Type of crises	Phase of CM process	Content of elements in CM	Ingredients of CM
Fink (1986)	General	Comprehensive Audit 1. Prodromal 2. Acute stage (emergency) 3. Chronic stage(recovery) 4. Resolution		
Mitroff (1988 / Pearson and Mitroff (1993)	Management	Portfolio Planning Approach 1. Signal detection 2. Preparation/ Prevention 3. Containment/ Damage limitation 4. Recovery 5. Learning	1. Signal detection • Early warning system 2. Preparation/ Prevention • Crisis management team • Crisis training and simulation exercises 3. Containment/ Damage limitation • Damage control • Evacuation plans and procedures 4. Recovery • Short-term and long-term recovery mechanisms • Alternatives 5. Learning • Learning and reassessment • Critical examination	Strategic actions • Integrate CM into strategic planning process • Include outsiders in the CM team • Training and workshop • Diversity CM strategies Technical and structural actions • CM team • Dedicate budget expenditures for CM • Emergency policies and manuals • Backup system • Working relationship with public/private sectors Evaluation and diagnostic actions • Legal and financial audit • Insurance coverage with CM contingencies • Environmental impact audits • Tracking system for warning signal and past crisis Communication actions • Training for dealing media • Communication line with local community • Communication with intervening stakeholders Psychological and cultural actions • Increase visibility of strong top management commitment • Relationship with activist group • Improve upward/downward communication • Psychological support and training • Reinforce symbolic recall

Preble (1993)	Financial	Normative Approach
		1. Formulation (Pre-event)
		2. Implementation
		3. Evaluation (Post-event)
			1. CM Formulation
			  • Top management initiates contingency planning
			  • Risk assessment
			  • Develop alternative strategies
			2. CM Implementation
			  • Documentation of plan
			  • BOD approval
			3. CM Evaluation
			  • Recycle
				• Group formed
				• Resources allocated
				• Identity threats
				• Estimate likelihood
				• Determine impact
				• Prevention techniques
				• Backup plan
				
				• Steps
				• Responsibilities
				• Strategies
				• Procedures
				
				• Update
				• Revise
				• Retest

Roberts (1994)	Natural Disaster-Flood	1. Pre-event
		2. Emergency
		3. Intermediate
		4. Long term
			1. Pre-event
			  • Warning system
			  • Monitoring vulnerable area
			  • Liaison group
			  • Evacuation plan
			2. Emergency
			  • Mass rescue
			  • Immediate safe and care
			  • Evacuate
				3. Intermediate
				  • Short-term needs
				  • Re-establishment of utilities
				  • Essential service
				  • Accessibility
				4. Long term
				  • Re-housing
				  • Repairing
				  • Providing clear information
				  • Dealing with stress and counseling
				  • Re-investment policy
				  • Producing financial plan and aid
				  • Assessing response
				  • Learning from experience
				
				• Obtain an overview the incident(s).
				• Obtain a clear the main events.
				• Decide on priorities.
				• Insert order into
				• Build up a cohesive team.
				• Check on needs.
				• Fulfill needs.
				• Reduce duplication.
				• Ensure the most essential tasks carried out.
				• Set a program actions.
				• Instigate quality
				• Care for people better way.

TABLE 1 (continued)

Author information	Type of crises	Phase in CM process	Content of elements in CM	Ingredients of CM

Preble (1997)	General, Business Oriented	Crisis/Strategic Management Integration 1. Formulation 2. Implementation 3. Evaluation	1. Formulation
			  • Develop mission statement
			  • Perform internal and external audit
			  • Revise mission statement and establish long-term objectives
			  • Perform crisis audit
			  • Generate, evaluate, and select planned and crisis strategies
			2. Implementation
			  • Establish policies, annual objectives and crisis plans
			  • Allocate resources
			  • Crisis approval and simulations
			3. Evaluation
			  • Evaluation and control
				• SWOTs analysis
				• Conduct a crisis audit
				• Worst-case scenario
				• Environmental impact assessment
				• Outside-in/inside-out vision
				• Extensive contingency capabilities
				• Use of advanced technology
				
				• Expected crisis procedures
				• Employee and manager area of responsibility
				• Crisis management team
				• Sufficient support and authority
				• Training and education
				• Media communications for public trust
				• Simulations and rehearsals
				• Seek formal approval and commitment
				
				• Feedback and feedforward controls
				• Special alert controls
				• Extensive evaluation
				• New crisis prevention strategy

Burnett (1998)	Management	Burnett's Strategic Approach-Classification Matrix focused on crisis assessment mechanism. There are four dimensions of strategic approaches to managing crisis: 1. Time pressure 2. Control issues 3. Threat level concerns 4. Response option constraints	1. Goal formulation 2. Environmental analysis 3. Strategy formulation 4. Strategy evaluation 5. Strategy analysis 6. Strategic control	

| Faulkner (2001) | Natural Disaster-Flood | 1. Pre-event
2. Prodromal
3. Emergency
4. Intermediate
5. Long term (recovery)
6. Resolution | 1. Precursors
• Disaster management team (DMT)
• Relevant institution and department
• Communication system
• Develop strategy
• Education system
• Activation protocols
2. Mobilization
• Warning system
• Command centre
• Secure facilities
3. Action
• Rescue/Evacuation
• Daily supplies
• Medicals
• Monitoring systems
4. Recovery
• Monitoring system
• Restoration/Clean-up
• Media
5. Reconstruction and reassessment
• Repair
• Rehabilitation
• Reactivate
• Revision
• Counseling victim
• Review | Initial stage:
Risk assessment on disaster probability, impact, contingency plans

Implementation detail:
Disaster contingency plans
• Likely impact
• Community and visitor capabilities
• Minimum impact action
• Priority action
• On-going review on experience, structural change, environment |

TABLE 1 (continued)

Author information	Type of crises	Phase in CM process	Content of elements in CM	Ingredients of CM
Luhrman (2005)	General	1. Before a crisis 2. During the actual problems 3. Immediately after a crisis	1. Before a crisis-preparing for the worst • Communication strategy • Promotion planning • Reviewing security system • Research readiness 2. During the actual problems- minimizing damage in a crisis • Communication from the front line • Hard decision about promotion • Ensuring security • Quick research tactics 3. Immediately after a crisis • Image building communication • Flexibility in promotion • Security for the future • Using research effectively	• Designate spokespersons • Press and communications department • Communicate and pay attention regularly with • Maintain working relationship with public and sectors • Security training • Emergency centre • Monitoring system • Not to impose a news blackout • Media centre • Challenge untrue statement • Positive and honest • Increase promotional budget • Financial assistance • New niche market product • Experienced and special interest travele • Special price • Incentive • Post-evaluation

| Wilks and Moore (2005) | General | 1. Reduction–detecting early warning signal
2. Readiness–preparing plans and running exercises
3. Response–executing operational and communication plan in a crisis situation
4. Recovery–returning the organization to normal after a crisis | 1. Reduction
  • Crisis awareness
  • Political awareness
  • Standard operating procedures
2. Readiness
  • Crisis management plan
  • Tourism planning
  • Health and safety measures
3. Response
  • Emergency response procedures
  • Investigation
  • Family assistance
  • Communication
4. Recovery
  • Business continuity plan
  • Human resource
  • Debriefing | • SWOT analysis
• Identify risk and impact
• Secure political cooperation and involvement
• Anticipate system
• Enhance staff awareness
• Crisis management team
• Public and private sectors involvement
• Priority decision
• Contingency plan
• Training system
• Caring for visitors and involving the community
• Target marketing
• External marketing communications
• Leadership
• Victim support
• Public communication
• Domestic health services
• Disability issues
• Counseling
• Return of effects of deceased victims to next-of-kin
• Community harmony
• Community support
• Rural issues
• Inter-governmental welfare issues
• Role of airlines
• Insurance coverage
• Domestic economic issues
• International issues and interaction with other |

TABLE 1 (continued)

Author information	Type of crises	Phase in CM process	Content of elements in CM	Ingredients of CM
Moe and Pathranarakul (2006)	Natural Disaster-Tsunami	There are two approaches in crisis management. Pro-active approach 1. Initiating 2. Planning Reactive approaches 3. Executing and controlling 4. Closing	1. Prediction 2. Warning 3. Emergency relief 4. Rehabilitation 5. Reconstruction	• Mitigation and preparedness activities • Structural and non-structural measures • Impact prediction • Provision of timely and effective information • Immediately assistance • Basic subsistence needs • Life preservation • Restoring and improving the pre-disaster living c • Encouraging and facilitating necessary adjustments

Ichinosawa (2006)	Natural Disaster/ Rumors	Secondary impact of the tsunami-Reputation disaster (Risk amplification and stigmatization model)
		1. Source of stigma
		2. Stigma formation
		3. Stigma ripples and effect
		4. Stigma mitigation
			1. Source of stigma
			  • Negative events: overbooking, environmental pollution, economic turmoil, natural disaster
			  • Stigmatization of a place
			2. Stigma formation
			  • IInformation flow (TV, communication channels, mass media)
			  • Stereotypical perception
			  • Formation of public perceptions
			  • Making of the place
			  • Change of the place's identity
			3. Stigma ripples and effect
			  • Stigma rippling beyond the place itself
			  • Resulting impact on other places, things, or people.
			  • Vulnerability evaluation
			4. Stigma mitigation
			  • Long-term recovery
			  • Emergency measures
			  • Policies focused	

Finally, an integrated approach (Moe and Pathranarakul, 2006) has been developed to crisis management. The integrated approach includes both proactive and reactive strategies to assist the crisis management team in responding to a disaster before, during and after. The integrated management approach is proactive by allowing for mitigation, preparedness, and warning for disasters before they take place. It is reactive by including the assessment of impacts after a disaster. From the experience of the September 21, 1999 earthquake disaster, it is found that the lack of proactive and reactive approaches had caused chaos and social disorder. Therefore, the integrated approach is the most appropriate crisis management for Taiwan to adopt.

MODEL DEVELOPMENT

In the September 21, 1999 earthquake in Taiwan, the physical impact was indeed dreadful, but was momentary. The most important issue after the disaster is the corruption of the regional economy due to the dramatic drop of inbound tourism in Taiwan. In this study, we not only propose the use of an integrated crisis management plan as a framework, but also include a "secondary" impact approach to establish a comprehensive model (Moe and Pathranarakul, 2006; Preble, 1993 & 1997; Faulkner, 2001; Wilks and Moore, 2005; Ichinosawa, 2006) for adapting the natural disaster induced crisis. We propose that Ichinosawa's (2006) risk amplification and stigmatization model could assist in minimizing the negative social impacts of tourism decline (see Figure 2). The model consists of four fundamental phases: sources of stigma, stigma formulation, stigma ripples and effect, and stigma mitigation.

This study proposes an innovative integrated approach (Moe and Pathranarakul, 2006; Preble, 1993 & 1997; Faulkner, 2001; Wilks and Moore, 2005; Ichinosawa, 2006) that could be used as a crisis management plan in Taiwan (Figure 2). In this model, similar life cycle phases (Fink, 1986; Roberts, 1994; Faulkner, 2001; Luhrman, 2005) are compared and merged. This integrated approach includes both proactive and reactive strategies targeted for management plan before, during and after

disasters. Activities that are planned and conducted before the disaster to minimize the adverse impacts are called proactive approaches. In contrast, activities post a disaster related to responses and recovery are termed reactive approaches (Moe and Pathranarakul, 2006). Furthermore, there are three primary components within the two approaches (Preble, 1997). First, the formulation phase is concerned with determining the future direction of the management of the crisis. Second, the implementation phase focuses on the modification of organizational structures and processes to help ensure that the planned results are obtained. The third phase is evaluation, which is concerned primarily with the review and feedback after a disaster.

In this model, we used Faulkner's (2001) crisis management phases which include six generic phases in the tourism industry, namely:

1. Pre-event Phase

   In the case of the September 21 Earthquake, actions were taken to prevent disasters. At this initial phase, the Tourism Bureau of Taiwan should begin to plan for the worst-case scenarios for crisis management, this could be done by (a) scrutinizing current resources for handling a disaster and identifying responsibilities and chains of commands for decision-making; (b) establishing an emergency list which includes all the public and private tourism organizations' key contacts; and (c) after the establishment of the crisis management plan, rehearsing the procedures.

2. Prodromal Phase

   This is when it is apparent that a disaster is imminent, but has not yet struck. For an earthquake, this period of time may be very short and give no time for preparation. To help travel-related services weather their current difficulties and to assist with threats to the future tourism industry, the Tourism Bureau should form a Task Force to assist the tourism industry in recovering from the natural disaster through a sound crisis management plan.

3. Emergency Phase

   This phase refers to when the effects of

the disaster have been felt and action has to be taken to rescue people and property. In the case of an earthquake, extensive negative information may be generated by news reports. The Tourism Bureau should take the main responsibility to form this task force and inform all tourism-related sectors about how important it is to cooperate together in order to recover tourism image in Taiwan in a timely manner. The task force should include representatives from all possible industry groups (Sonmez & Backman & Allen, 1994). This is also a great opportunity for students majoring in tourism, communication, marketing, and finance to participate in this project. This would provide them a chance to devote their knowledge and efforts to serve their country through what they have learned from school. The goal of the Task Force should be to bring tourists back to Taiwan or any affected areas after an earthquake by consolidating ideas and resources in order to recover tourism business, get residents back to work, and recover the region's economy back to normal.

4. Intermediate Phase

This refers to when the short-term needs of the people affected must be dealt with–restoring utilities and essential services. In the tourism case, the objective at this point is to limit the transformation of negative impact in some specific areas and stop stigma rippling from the place itself to other places as quickly as possible. The immediate post crisis management plan should take action right after the formation of the task force is completed. This crisis management plan should have clear goals and objectives, and provide management strategies and thoroughly analyze risk to achieve tourism recovery (refers to Figure 2).

5. Long-Term (Recovery) Phase

This is a continuation of the previous phase, but items that could not be addressed quickly are attended to at this point. Special attention should also be given to bring major tourist markets back to Taiwan.

Seventy percent of the Taiwan's inbound tourists come from Japan, Hong Kong, the United States of America, Singapore and Korea (Tourism Bureau of Taiwan, 2000). Therefore, increased marketing efforts should target these countries. The media in these countries should be provided with accurate information about Taiwan's recovery status and also re-confirm their pre-booked convention or tours. The media spokesperson and communication coordinator from the Task Force should keep in close contact with the primary media coordinators from these countries.

The Tourism Bureau of Taiwan can invite the press to Taiwan to show them what has been done to restore the tourism industry. Familiarization trips should emphasize the positive media coverage to counteract the harmful effects of negative images of the disaster in the mindset of potential travelers (Luhrman, 2005). There is also a need to reduce the overall prices of taking trips to Taiwan during the recovery stage.

6. Resolution Phase

The final phase of the proposed crisis management plan is the return to normalcy or movement to an improved position based on reflection. How well Taiwan responds to the earthquake and how quickly it recovers from this disaster will have a long-term effect on visitors' perceptions of the nation (Huang & Ralston, 2001). Therefore, Taiwan must clearly and frequently explain to the international community its recovery status and also reassure the public that they are working aggressively to return to normal operations.

In the six phases of crisis management plan, four essential actions should be taken before, during and after the disaster (Wilks and Moore, 2005). They are:

1. Reduction

Reducing potential impacts is the most important issue in a crisis management plan. SWOT (strengths, weakness, opportunity, and threats) analysis is recommended to reduce the possibility of a crisis. This includes evaluating what the strengths and weakness that Taiwan possesses, and external opportunities and

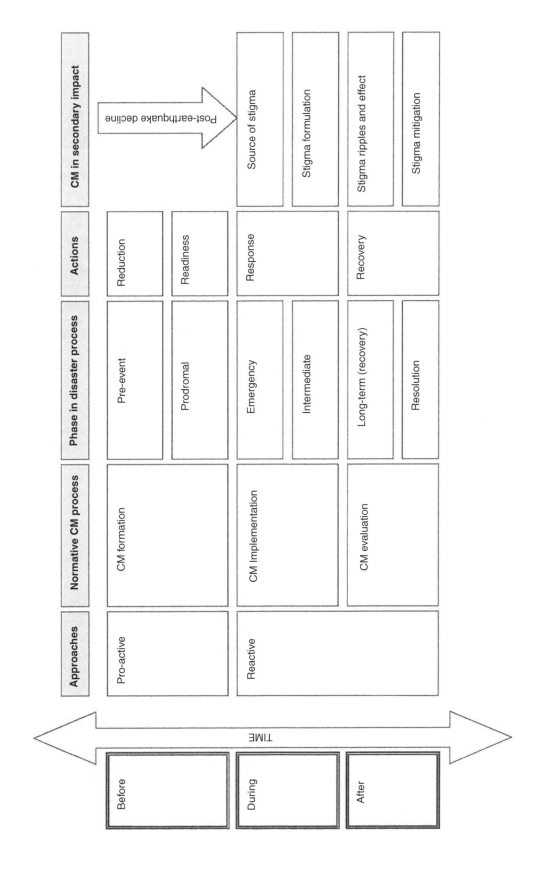

FIGURE 2. Integrated crisis management framework. Adapted from Moe and Pathranarakul (2006); Preble (1993, 1997); Faulkner (2001); W Moore (2005); Ichinosawa (2006)

217

threats that Taiwan as a tourist destination would confront after the earthquake. It may also be an opportunity for Taiwan to create new niche market products which target experienced and special interest travelers, as more experienced travelers and repeat visitors are less likely to be scared away by disasters (Luhrman, 2005). Some special interest travelers may want to come to Taiwan to experience or observe the earthquake aftermath.

2. Readiness

"Being Ready" involves more than making plans and running an occasional drill. Organizations need to evaluate their crisis exposure and develop strategic, tactical and communication plans. Managers must regularly audit crisis management plans, conduct crisis response exercises and continually acquire crisis management skills. Managers and staff need to be psychologically and physiologically prepared for the impact and stresses that crisis events may impose upon them.

3. Response

Response is dedicated to the immediate aftermath of an event when everything is at its most chaotic. It will quickly become apparent whether the reduction and readiness phases have developed continuity and contingency plans that are effective. The initial operational emphasis should be on damage control in both lives and property. The crisis communication strategy should already be in play, pre-empting and reassuring stakeholders and the public. It is imperative to designate spokespersons so the information sent to the media in a crisis can be authoritative and coordinated. A press and communication department should be established which should include staff trained in working with the media, a good contact list of both local and international media, telephone lines, and fax broadcast machines or a mass email account capable of reaching the media to update the destination recovery process in a timely manner. Furthermore, place information about the disaster on an

official Website so that potential visitors can have the ability to receive the most current and accurate information about the destination. The official Website should emphasize on areas that are affected by the disaster and which are not affected, as well as what has been done to end the disaster (Luhrman, 2005).

4. Recovery

In this case, a crisis management plan's effectiveness can be gauged in three ways: (1) The speed with which an organization resumes or continues full business operations; (2) The degree to which business recovers to pre-crisis levels; and (3) The amount of crisis-resistance added since the crisis. That is, how the lessons learned have been incorporated into ongoing preparation and preparedness to avoid future problems.

The Tourism Bureau of Taiwan can also take this opportunity to use research effectively at this stage. Research can be conducted to survey potential tourists and travel partners in primary markets for readiness to travel and for information about their perception toward Taiwan. Retrieving information to place them back into promotion will allow the tailored marketing campaigns to correct damaged impressions.

The September 21 earthquake caused severe tangible and intangible damages. Using this integrated model, the flaws of the crisis management plan in Taiwan can be scrutinized by examining their proactive and reactive approaches. Most notable errors can be seen during the pre-event, prodromal, emergency, and intermediate phases associated with a proactive approach, as these phases were negligibly planned for. Virtually all of the activities carried out to assist with a crisis management plan in Taiwan were associated with parts of emergency relief, recovery and resolution (reactive approaches).

Many countries lack holistic reactive approaches for mitigating the stigmatization of tourism after the occurrence of disasters. The stigma-induced ripples and impact stroke the tourism industry the most as mass media extensively report the negative images of the affected areas. Proposing the integrated approach with a secondary impact which is mainly caused by mass media reports can contribute to a crisis management plan. In this model, we applied Ichinosawa's (2006) risk amplification and stigmatization model to the crisis management plan in Taiwan. In the first phase, source of stigma derived from the occurrence of risk for a place. The stigma formatted because of information flow, formation of public perception and marking on the place in the second phase. Then, stigma rippled and effected beyond the place itself, resulting impacts on other places, things and people, etc. In the fourth phase, stigma can be mitigated from this reactive approach via a comprehensive crisis management plan.

The governmental authority of Taiwan did take some actions to restore the tourism industry using reactive strategies, such as recast "the Big Taiwan Earthquake" to " the Chi Chi Earthquake" through foreign media in the early stigma ripples and effect stage. In addition, the message of "Taiwan thanks the world" was disseminated through international media right after the earthquake. In order to decrease negative media coverage, more than a thousand international media and tour wholesaler representatives were invited for familiarization tours to the areas affected by the earthquake during 1999-2000 (Tourism Bureau of Taiwan, 2000). "Tour Taiwan at ease" was the international marketing theme to lure foreign travelers to visit Taiwan, and other promotional activities, such as price deductions, new events, and destinations, were also carried out to stimulate the motivations to travel to Taiwan in the stigma mitigation stage, which led to significant revitalization of the tourism industry (Min, 2003). The Taiwanese government made efforts to offer loans to help earthquake impacted hotels, travel agencies and recreations to rebuild their facilities. The authority of Taiwan reacted to the disaster as best as they could to minimize the impact and maximize the revitalization.

Without a secondary impact approach in a crisis management plan, severe social impacts and economic devastation can occur. With the integrated approach, the physical and secondary impact can be controlled simultaneously. The integrated approach can have a positive effect on tourism recovery in the long-term.

CONCLUSION

The magnitude of the September 21 Earthquake was so serious that the routine operations of the tourism industry were not only disrupted, it also jeopardized the tourism industry. Disaster induced crisis is different from other crises because of quick-onset with no lead-time for deducing casualties. Thus, there is a need to tailor responses to individual crises rather than to try to plan for every individual situation. Heath (1998) stated that "no crisis has exactly the same form, the same time limitations, the same demand for resources . . . or the same temporal, social and economic threats." This indicates the difficulty in developing a general model to understand crisis management and how to prevent or limit the effects of crises. The characteristics of the disaster highlight the need for the development and ongoing review of destination crisis management plans to become a routine component of every tourism organization's agenda.

In the case of Taiwan the initial risk was of the earthquake itself and its immediate and grievous physical results, such as the health and injury of people, building infrastructure damage, and the destruction of nature. The next stage is the massive flow of information that immediately follows in the form of sensational news reports. The most powerful and influential channel of information flow during this time was television. In the case of the US, although TV news programs had barely begun to pick up the news from Taiwan, TV stations began to compete in obtaining and broadcasting sensational video footage which had been reported by residents. The news of the earthquake disaster then flowed into and through various communication channels, such as radio, newspaper and the Internet. Since Taiwan is a small island country located in Far East Asia and is a place both unfamiliar and distant to most international tourists, many people may have fostered unrealistic risk perceptions, which could have aroused negative reactions toward Taiwan as a tourism destination.

Strong risk-related concerns regarding a certain place usually put a "mark" on it, which can negatively alter its identity. To take Taiwan as the example, the US's TV stations extensively covered the damage in Taichung on a daily basis, frequently with shocking film. TV reporters dispatched to Central Taiwan often finished their reports by saying "This report is from Taiwan." It was partly true because the base facilities of the TV staff were indeed located in Taiwan, but the reporter was imprecise as many of the other cities in Taiwan suffered relatively minor damage (Taiwan He@dlines, 2000). The image of Taiwan changed from "Formosa" into an earthquake disaster zone, and consequently its market value as a tourist destination declined.

Therefore, in order to both help the local people of Taiwan in regaining their livelihoods and to assist with the recovery of international tourism, there is a need to more deeply understand the mechanisms and compound effects of the risk-induced stigmatization process and the vulnerabilities inherent in the local environment and situation. To recover the physical facilities of the disaster area promptly, more attention needs to be emphasized on media communications in order to control the secondary impact on destination image and reputation. After a thorough review of the literature, an integrated crisis management model has been chosen to accommodate the need for the September 21, 1999 earthquake and the emerging secondary impact on reputational disaster model to create an Innovative Integrated Crisis Management Model specifically for the tourism industries in Taiwan. Hopefully, Taiwan can have better proactive and reactive ability to handle the earthquake disaster by adopting this Innovative Integrated Crisis Management Model (Moe and Pathranarakul, 2006; Preble, 1993 & 1997; Faulkner, 2001; Wilks and Moore, 2005; Ichinosawa, 2006) in the future since there is a high probability of another earthquake.

There is a need to have a crisis management plan in place which establishes appropriate strategies and guidelines to prevent, prepare, and mitigate the damage caused by unexpected and non-routine events. Each crisis situation is unique, making it impossible to have a single formula, but having a blueprint can assist in saving time, energy and other resources for a tourist destination in crisis (Sonmez et al., 1999). To recap, the purpose of establishing a crisis management plan is to facilitate tourism recovery from negative occurrences via protecting and rebuilding a positive destination image, reassuring potential visitors of the safety of the area, and re-developing the functionality of the destination to help local travel and tourism industries recover their business. Crisis management is needed to retain the confidence of travelers and the tourism industry, and also to minimize the impact of a disaster on a destination. The case of Taiwan, hopefully, not only helps the tourism industry of Taiwan to deal with disasters more promptly, but also provides some guidelines to help the tourism industry in other countries to handle disasters.

REFERENCES

Baloglu, S. & McCleary, K.W. (1999). A Model of Destination Image Formation. *Annals of Tourism Research, 26(4)*, pp.868-897.

Burnett, J. J. (1998). A strategic approach to managing crisis. *Public Relations Review, 24*(4), 457-488.

Dimanche, F. & Lepetic, A. (1999). New Orleans tourism and crime: A case study. *Journal of Travel Research, 38(1)*, pp.19-23.

Directorate-General of Budget, Accounting and Statistics (DGBAS) (2000). *Quarterly national economic trends Taiwan area,* Republic of China: Executive Yuan.

Durocher, J. (1994). Recovery Marketing: What to Do after a natural Disaster. *Cornell Hotel and Restaurant Administration Quarterly, 35(2)*, pp.66-71.

Faulkner, B. (2001). Towards a framework for tourism disaster management. *Tourism Management, 22,* pp.135-147.

Fink, S. (1986). *Crisis Management: planning for the inevitable.* New York: American Management Association.

Fischhoff, B., Nightingdale, E. & Iannotta, J. (2001). *Adolescent Risk and Vulnerability: Concepts and Measurements.* Washington, DC: Institute of Medicines, National Research Council.

Gartner, W.C. & Shen, J. (1992). The impact of Tiananmen square on China's tourism image. *Journal of Travel Research, 30(4)*, pp. 47-52.

Gee, C. and Gain, C. (1986), Coping with crises. *Travel & Tourism Analyst,* June pp. 3-12.

Goltz, J.D. (1999). *The "921" Chi-Chi, Taiwan Earthquake of September 21, 1999: Societal Impacts and Emergency Response.* Retrieved December 13, 1999 from http://www.eeri.org/reconn/taiwang/taiwang.html

Huan, T.C., Beaman, J. & Shelby, L. (2004). No-escape natural disaster: mitigating impacts on tourism. *Annals of Tourism Research, 31(2)*, pp. 255-273.

Huang, J.H. & Min, J.C.H. (2002). Earthquake devastation and recovery in tourism: the Taiwan case. *Tourism Management, 23*, pp.145-154.

Huang, Y.C. & Ralston, L.S., (2001). "How a Crisis Marketing Plan can Help Taiwan Recover its Tourism Industry After the 1999 Earthquake," *the 32nd TTRA (Travel and Tourism Research Association) Annual Conference*, Fort Myers, Florida.

Ichinosawa, J. (2006). Reputational disaster in Phuket: the secondary impact of the tsunami on inbound tourism. *Disaster Prevention and Management, 15(1)*, pp.111-123.

Lee, Y. F. & Harrald, J. R. (1999). Critical issue for business area impact analysis in business crisis management: Analytical capability. *Disaster Prevention and Management, 8(3)*, pp.184-189.

Lepp, A. & Gibson, H. (2003). Tourist Roles, Perceived Risk and International Tourism. *Annals of Tourism Research, 30(3)*, pp.606-624.

Luhrman, D. (2005). *Crisis guidelines for the tourism industry*. Retrieved September 31, 2006, from the World Tourism Organization Web site: http://www.world-tourism.org/market_research/recovery/ Crisis and Disaster Management Guidelines.pdf

Mansfeld, Y. (1999). Cycles of war, terror, and peace: determinants and management of crisis and recovery of the Israeli tourism industry. *Journal of Travel Research, 38(1)*, pp. 30-36.

Milo, K. J., & Yoder, S. L. (1991). Recovery from natural disaster: Travel writers and tourist destinations. *Journal of Travel Research, 30(1)*, pp. 36-39.

Min, J.C.H. (2003). A study of post-disaster tourist behavior and effective marketing strategies: The case of September 21st earthquake. *Journal of Tourism Studies, 9(2)*, pp. 141-154.

Mitroff, I. I. (1988). Crisis management: Cutting through the confusion. *Sloan management Review, 29(2)*, pp.15-20.

Mitroff, I. I., & Pearson, C. M. (1993). From crisis prone to crisis prepared: A framework for crisis management. *Academy of Management Executive, 7(1)*, pp. 48-59.

Moe, T. L., & Pathranarakul, P. (2006). An integrated approach to natural disaster management: Public project management and its critical success factors. *Disaster Prevention and Management, 15(3)*, pp. 396-413.

Peters, M., & Pikkemaat, B. (2005). Crisis management in Alpine Winter Sports Resorts–The 1999 avalanche disaster in Tyrol, *Journal of Travel and Tourism Marketing, 19(2/3)*, pp. 9-20.

Preble, J. F. (1993). Crisis management of financial institutions. *American Business Review, 11(1)*, pp. 72-79.

Preble, J. F. (1997). Integrating the crisis management perspective into the strategic management process. *Journal of Management Studies, 34(5)*, pp. 769-791.

Reisinger, Y. & Mavondo, F. (2005). Travel Anxiety and Intentions to Travel Internationally: Implications of Travel Risk Perception. *Journal of Travel Research, 43*, pp.212-225.

Ritchie, B. W. (2004). Chaos, crisis and disaster: A strategic approach to crisis management in the tourism industry. *Tourism Management, 25*, pp.669-683.

Roberts, V. (1994). Flood Management: Bradford Paper. *Disaster Prevention and Management, 3(2)*, pp.44-60

Roehl, W.S. & Fesenmaier, D.R. (1992). Risk Perceptions and Pleasure Travel: An Exploratory Analysis. *Journal of Travel Research, 30(4)*, pp.17-26

Sonmez, S.F. & Backman, S.J. & Allen, L.R. (1994). *Managing Tourism Crises: A Guidebook. Clemson University*, Clemson, South Carolina. pp. 5.5 & 6.2 & 8.1 & 9.1& 10.1 &11.1 & 12.1 & 13.1 & 14.1 & 15.1 & 16.1

Sonmez, S.F. & Graefe, A.R. (1998). Influence of Terrorism Risk on Foreign Tourism Decisions. *Annals of Tourism Research, 25(1)*, pp. 112-144

Taiwan He@dlines (1/11/2000). *Liberty Times*. Retrieved January 11, 2000, from http://www.taiwanheadlines.gov.tw

Taiwan Is As Beautiful As Ever–A Government Statement. Taiwan He@dlines (11/17/1999). Liberty Times. Retrieved November 17, 1999, from http://www.taiwanheadlines.gov.tw/ad/unaffected.htm

Tourism Bureau of Taiwan (1999). *1998 annual report on tourism*. Taipei: Tourism Bureau.

Tourism Bureau of Taiwan (2000). *1999 Annual report on tourism*. Taipei: Tourism Bureau.

Tsaur, S.H., Tzeng, G.H. & Wang, K.C. (1997). Evaluating Tourist Risks from Fuzzy Perspectives. *Annals of Tourism Research, 24 (4)*, pp. 796-812.

Wilks, J., & Moore, S. (2005). *Tourism risk management for the Asia pacific region: An authoritative guide for managing crises and disasters*. Retrieved September 10, 2006, from the World Tourism Organization Web site: http://www.world-tourism.org/

Yavas, U. (1987). Foreign Travel Behavior in a Growing Vacation Market: Implications for Tourism Marketers. *European Journal of Marketing, 21 (5)*, pp.57-69.

Yu, L., Stafford, G., & Armoo, A. K. (2005). A study of crisis management strategies of hotel managers in the Washington, D.C. Metro Area. *Journal of Travel and Tourism Marketing, 19(2/3)*, pp. 91-105.

Repositioning a Tourism Destination:
The Case of New Orleans After Hurricane Katrina

Harsha E. Chacko

Marianne Hawkins Marcell

SUMMARY. This paper is a case study of the repositioning of New Orleans as a tourism destination after the devastating effects of Hurricane Katrina in August 2005. It examines the event from a post-disaster marketing viewpoint and first outlines the tourism industry in New Orleans before Hurricane Katrina, including visitor profile, destination image, and positioning statements. The article then recounts the effects of the hurricane on the tourism infrastructure. The effectiveness of recovery marketing strategies, including the repositioning strategies undertaken by the city's tourism marketing organizations, is examined. The disaster management frameworks as discussed in the literature are revisited and extended to include the lessons learned for post disaster market repositioning.

INTRODUCTION

August 29, 2005, the day that Hurricane Katrina made landfall, will go down in history as the worst natural disaster to befall the United States of America in recent memory. The subsequent storm surge overwhelmed coastal communities in the states of Louisiana and Mississippi, leaving behind death and destruction of a magnitude unimaginable in a modern economically advanced nation. The event was widely covered by today's round the clock television news media as flood waters inundated 80% of the city of New Orleans, which re-mained under water for several days. The images of the massive scale of the flooding were combined with those of human misery as thousands of New Orleanians, mostly poor and African American, were rescued from rooftops or seen huddled without food and water in two of the city's most famous landmarks, the Superdome and the Convention Center. The former, a prominent building on the skyline of New Orleans, was well known to many Americans as the host of ten Super Bowls (the final game of the American Football Championships) and the latter was one of the largest convention centers in the U.S., hosting hundreds of thousands of

Harsha E. Chacko (E-mail: hchacko@uno.edu) is Professor in the School of Hotel Restaurant & Tourism Administration of University of New Orleans, New Orleans, LA 70148 USA. Marianne Hawkins Marcell (E-mail: mhmarcel@uno.edu) is a Research Analyst in the School of Hotel Restaurant & Tourism Administration of University of New Orleans, New Orleans, LA 70148 USA.

conventioneers over its 20 year life span. In the days and months following Katrina, these images of desperation combined with those of lawlessness and looting in one of America's favorite destinations has brought a flourishing tourism industry to its knees. However, a less known fact is that, despite all this, the main tourism infrastructure of New Orleans remained intact with only minor damage. This presents an opportunity and a challenge for the city's tourism marketers who have to answer this critical question: How do you promote and attract tourists to a destination that has a relatively intact infrastructure but a completely devastated destination image?

PURPOSE

Although much has been written about the effects of a crisis on a variety of tourism destinations (see literature review) there has never been an event that mirrors the unique circumstances of Hurricane Katrina in the United States. The purpose of this paper is to describe the events of Hurricane Katrina and its effects on the city of New Orleans, specifically focusing on strategies developed by tourism marketers to reposition the city.

In addition to a review of the literature on the effects of crises and disasters on tourism destinations, this article will cover four major sections. The first section will be a narrative of vital tourism statistics for the city of New Orleans before the hurricane including a visitor profile, tourism demand generators, tourism related infrastructure, marketing strategies and advertising campaigns, and image and positioning statements. The second will be an account of the effects of the hurricane on the tourism infrastructure, and visitation. In addition, the intense, worldwide coverage of the event and the negative effects on the image of the city will be reported. The third phase will critically examine the effectiveness of recovery marketing strategies undertaken by the city's tourism marketing organizations. This section will focus on repositioning but will include discussions on product renewal, target marketing, advertising, and personal selling. The final section will revisit the disaster management frameworks as discussed in the literature and extend them to

include strategies for post disaster market repositioning.

NEW ORLEANS AS A TOURISM DESTINATION

With its rich cultural heritage, abundance of unique food and many opportunities to enjoy local art, music and festivals, New Orleans has long enjoyed the status of a world famous tourist destination. Often cited for its "European" charm and the unique French Quarter historic district, tourists have visited the city for years to partake of the distinct experience New Orleans has to offer as a vacation venue. In a perceptions study conducted by the University of New Orleans (UNO) Hospitality Research Center (2005a) in January 2005, just seven months before Hurricane Katrina, New Orleans ranked sixth among the top U.S. vacation destinations in a nationwide phone survey of U.S. residents. Respondents cited their most recalled images of New Orleans to be of Mardi Gras and food/restaurants. In 2004, tourism was one of the city's main economic engines and prior to Hurricane Katrina hospitality and leisure employment in New Orleans accounted for 80,827 jobs generating $30 million in state income taxes (UNO Hospitality Research Center, 2005b). The hospitality industry also produced $158.6 million in state tax revenue and even channeled $10 million a year to the New Orleans school system (New Orleans Metropolitan Convention and Visitor Bureau, 2005). Visitation to New Orleans peaked in 2004, when 10.1 million visitors came to the city, spending $4.9 billion (UNO Hospitality Research Center, 2005b). Hurricane Katrina interrupted data collection in 2005, and visitation was only measured from January 1 through August 26, 2005. At that point, New Orleans had seen 6.6 million visitors who spent $4.2 billion. Had Katrina not occurred, it is projected that visitation for 2005 would have been on par with 2004–somewhere within the statistical range of 10 million visitors, with much higher expenditures than in the previous year.

Just prior to Hurricane Katrina, the New Orleans metropolitan area had 265 operating hotels with an inventory of 38,645 rooms. Average annual occupancy in 2004 was 63.7% with an average daily rate of $111.19 (Louisiana Office of Tourism, 2006). Occupancy rates tended to rise in the spring and fall, which makes up New Orleans' peak convention season, and to decrease in the summer and winter months. The leisure market accounted for 75% of visitation while the remaining 25% was from the corporate and convention business markets (see Table 1 for a visitor profile).

Also, in 2004, the New Orleans Metropolitan Convention and Visitors Bureau booked approximately 950 meetings, accounting for approximately 1.5 million room nights (New Orleans Metropolitan Convention and Visitor Bureau, 2006). Ninety-three of these were major conventions or trade shows held at the Ernest N. Morial Convention Center, which boasted 1.1 million square feet of meeting space.

THE UNIQUE CIRCUMSTANCES OF HURRICANE KATRINA

Crises and disasters have affected numerous tourism destinations in the recent past. Natural phenomena such as the tsunami in Asia or earthquakes in Turkey and Iran or man made events such as September 11, 2001 and civil wars in Lebanon and Africa have had detrimental effects on tourism. Faulkner (2001) addressed the distinction between the definitions of a crisis versus that of a disaster. He developed a continuum with crises located at one end and disasters at the other end and posited that there could be much debate as to where specific catastrophic events would be located along the continuum. A crisis was broadly defined as "induced by the actions or inactions of the organization" (p.137) while a disaster was considered to be an "induced natural phenomena or external human action" (p.137). The Chernobyl nuclear accident and the Exxon Valdez oil spill would be classified as crises while the Kobe earthquake and the Lockerbie plane crash were disasters. The uniqueness of the events surrounding Hurricane Katrina in New Orleans arises from the fact that it could be placed at any point on the continuum, including at either end. It is well known, as recounted by thousands of New Orleanians who rode out the storm in their homes, that the city had weathered a night of gale force winds with relatively little damage or loss of life. Nevertheless, at that point, by Faulkner's definition it would have been classified as a disaster. However, it was not until the next morning, when the man made (poorly designed by the U.S. Corps of Engineers, a federal agency) concrete levee walls (dikes) that surround and protect the city breached, did the flood waters inundate 80% of New Orleans and create a crisis of gigantic proportions. In addition, there was a total failure in federal, state, and local government authorities to prepare for and react in a timely manner to the needs of the residents of this beleaguered city. Thus, Hurricane Katrina can be described as an induced natural phenomenon (a disaster) followed by the inactions of organizations (a crisis) and will only add to the debate on the differences between a crisis and a disaster and for the purposes of this article the terms will be used interchangeably.

LITERATURE REVIEW

There are two major aspects to the literature on the effects of disasters and crises on tourism. The first group includes mostly case studies of specific events and their effects on various tourism destinations while the second group offers a broader perspective, dealing primarily with policy development, planning, and crisis management modeling. Among the destination case studies a variety of crises and disasters were enu-

TABLE 1. New Orleans Visitor Profile–2004

Purpose of visit:	
Leisure	75.4%
Assoc/Convention/Trade Show	12.5%
Corporate meeting/Business	12.0%
Duration of stay:	
Daytrippers	14.0%
Overnight Visitors	86.0%
Mode of Transportation:	
Personal vehicle (Automobile)	59.8%
Airplane	38.1%
Other	2.1%
Visit frequency:	
First time visitor to New Orleans	34.5%
Repeat visitor	65.5%

Source: University of New Orleans Hospitality Research Center, 2005b. Used with permission.

merated. Bierman (2003) identified five types of events that could affect a tourism destination, including war and conflict, crime, terrorism, natural disasters, and health related crises. He provided examples of eleven specific case studies ranging from political conflict in Fiji to the 1999 earthquake in Turkey. Other case studies included the Indian Ocean tsunami of 2004 (Henderson, 2005); SARS (Henderson & Ng, 2004; Wen et al. 2005); Bali bombings in 2002 (Hitchcock & Putra, 2005); terrorists attacks on September 11, 2001 (Stafford et al. 2002); U.K. Foot and Mouth disease (Williams & Ferguson, 2005); Asian financial crisis (Henderson, 1999); political turmoil (Ioannides & Apostolopoulos, 1999; Richter, 1999); and floods (Faulkner & Vikulov, 2001). A common theme among these case studies was the enumeration of crisis management strategies used and the evaluation of the applicability of different crisis management models.

The second group of articles in the literature discussed broader aspects of crisis management. These included the definitions and typologies of crises and disasters; the stages in a crisis; and the suggested responses of organizations during a crisis (i.e., crisis management). Sausmarez (2004) discussed the challenges pertaining to the development of a broad crisis management policy for the tourism industry. Crises such as the Foot and Mouth disease in Britain and the Asian financial crisis in Malaysia forced their respective governments to recognize the contribution of tourism to their national economies thus providing incentives for the development of crisis management plans. Page, Yeoman, Munro, Connell and Walker (2006) detailed the use of scenario planning by Visit Scotland, the Scottish National Tourism Organization, to a potential avian flu pandemic and illustrated the complexity of information flow during a crisis in addition to evaluating the potential negative economic impact. Evans and Elphick (2005) reviewed the pros and cons of various crisis management typologies (Booth, 1993; Seymour & Moore, 2000) and models (Arnold, 1980; Booth, 1993; Clarke & Varma, 2004; among others) and discussed the impact of the 9/11 terrorist attacks on a tour operator in the United Kingdom.

Faulkner (2001) identified the phases or stages in a crisis. These were pre-event, prodromal (when a crisis is inevitable), emergency, intermediate recovery, long-term recovery, and resolution (when normalcy returns). He also developed a framework that included elements of disaster management responses and strategies. Young and Montgomery (1998) and Bierman (2003) focused on the communications and marketing aspects of crisis and discussed the important marketing messages that needed to be disbursed to stakeholders when a destination is in the recovery stage. While much of the literature on crisis management and tourism focus on disaster management strategies and overall community mass emergency plans, this case study will examine the event from a post disaster marketing viewpoint. After all, although the majority of New Orleans tourism infrastructure is largely intact, the mass media images of the distressed and unrepaired residential areas continue to dominate the news coverage even one year after the event and the destination image continues to be battered by the news media. For the visual media, the Hiroshima-like backdrop of the devastated Ninth Ward, an area that bore the brunt of the levee breach, can frame a story better than the almost normal hustle and bustle of the tourists on Magazine Street and in the French Quarter.

POSITIONING

Market positioning is a communications strategy and is defined as "the way a product is defined by consumers on important attributes—the place the product occupies in consumers' minds relative to competing products" (Kotler, Bowen, & Makens, (2005) p. 280). According to Pike and Ryan (2004, p. 334), "a major objective of any destination positioning strategy will be to reinforce positive images already held by the target audience, correct negative images, or create a new image." Thus, positioning is a communications strategy that is the natural follow-through of market segmentation and target marketing. Selection of a positioning strategy that creates a distinctive place in customers' minds is essential in preventing the following pitfalls (Lovelock, 1991):

1. The destination is forced into a position of competing directly with a stronger

competitor. For example, a destination that is further from the source of its visitors may be relegated to a secondary or tertiary level of competition with destinations that are closer to the market.

2. The destination's position is so unclear that its target market does not recognize the message that is being sent to them. This often happens when a destination tries to be all things to all people.

3. The destination has no identity or has a negative image in customers' minds and does not create customer demand.

With intense competition for the tourist dollar, most destination marketers are constantly developing and refining their market positioning strategies. Chacko (1997) discussed the application of six different positioning approaches to tourism destinations including, positioning by product attributes, price, competition, product class, user, and application. While positioning strategies may be carefully planned and orchestrated, the major problem during a catastrophic event is that the mass media coverage of the disaster has an overwhelming impact on a destination's market position. With the proliferation of international satellite, cable and Internet channels for news and vivid graphics, the negative publicity after a natural disaster is instantaneous and widespread. So it was when Hurricane Katrina arrived in New Orleans.

POSITIONING NEW ORLEANS PRE-KATRINA

There are two major organizations responsible for the overall marketing of the New Orleans tourism and hospitality industry. The first is the New Orleans Metropolitan Convention and Visitors Bureau (NOMCVB) whose primary mission is to bring in meetings, conventions, tradeshows and tour groups to the city and supply customers for the many hotels, restaurants, attractions and other providers of tourism goods and services. This is mainly accomplished by a group of 22 salespeople who solicit business from various tourism intermediaries such as meeting planners and tour operators.

While personal selling is the primary sales strategy used by the NOMCVB, the second organization, the New Orleans Tourism Marketing Corporation (NOTMC), which has a similar broad goal of spurring New Orleans visitation, uses most of its two million dollar budget for advertising and positioning the city to the leisure market. Since effective positioning must be based on a thorough knowledge of the needs, wants, and perceptions of the target market, along with the benefits offered by the destination, an importance performance analysis was conducted based on the data gathered from visitors to New Orleans. Visitors were asked to rate the importance of certain destination attributes when planning a trip and then were asked to rate the performance of New Orleans on those same attributes. The city performed extremely well on the attributes labeled Unique, Entertainment, Friendliness of people, Exciting, and Popular but did poorly on Safety, Cleanliness, and Affordability (UNO Hospitality Research Center, 2005b).

In order to capitalize on the strengths of New Orleans as an exciting and unique destination, intertwined with food and music, tourism marketers for the city created a new positioning statement, "happenin' every day" (Figure 1).

This is typical of positioning with respect to a product class (Chacko, 1997) where a destination is associated with experiences that are extraordinary and/or unique. In addition, as part of the 2005 summer campaign (just two months before Katrina) marketers produced a television commercial, featuring well-known and talented local musicians from New Orleans, titled "Do They Play Jazz in Heaven?" The appeal of the message was more emotional rather than rational (Kotler, Bowen, & Makens, 2005) and included the lines "do they play jazz in heaven, in New Orleans we know they do." These and other messages reinforced New Orleans' well-established position as an exciting and popular yet authentic destination with great food and music. However, there would have to be major shift in positioning strategy after the arrival of Katrina produced hundreds of hours of negative publicity in the mass media.

FIGURE 1. Sample of New Orleans Advertising Pre-Katrina

Source: New Orleans Tourism Marketing Corporation/Peter A. Mayer
Advertising, New Orleans (2006). Used with permission.

KATRINA AND ITS EFFECTS ON NEW ORLEANS TOURISM

On August 29, 2006, the storm New Orleans always feared, Hurricane Katrina, roared ashore as a category three (winds of 111-130 mph) hurricane. The storm's winds took out trees and power lines, and some rooftops, but the worst was yet to come. Within hours, the levees that protect the city from the waters that surround it began to give way, and the bowl-shaped city began filling up. The flooding continued for two days until the water level in the city and Lake Pontchartrain reached equilibrium.

Some areas were inundated with as much as 20 feet of water. Rescue workers scrambled frantically to evacuate stranded people from rooftops via boat or helicopter and delivered them to the Superdome and Convention Center. Food and water were in short supply and communication was non-existent. As panic and desperation began to overtake those who were stranded, chaos and lawlessness began to proliferate. The City of New Orleans was truly in a

state of disaster. To make matters worse for the tourism industry, the national and international media was airing every detail, repeatedly. Not only was the physical infrastructure of the city being washed away by the storm and subsequent flooding, but also the perception of the city as a viable tourism destination was being eroded every time the negative images were replayed.

After about a week, the flood waters were finally pumped out of the city. While residents of the outlying metropolitan area were able to return and begin rebuilding homes and businesses, New Orleans still had a long road to recovery ahead. This was potentially devastating to the tourism industry, as it was estimated that for every day there was no tourism in New Orleans, the city was losing $15.3 million (Northington, 2006). Not only was the loss due to the lack of tourism operations immense, but the City of New Orleans also faced the possible loss of the huge economic impact from the many festivals and events that it hosts. These events, such as Mardi Gras and Jazz Fest contribute to

New Orleans' cultural economy as well as enhance the image of New Orleans as a tourist destination. Whether New Orleans would be in shape to handle these events, after Katrina, was tenuous at best.

However, there was one beacon of hope for the tourism industry. The French Quarter, the oldest and best known area of the city, where over 58% of all tourists visited in 2004, was relatively unharmed. In addition, much of the city's hotel room inventory was located in the Central Business and Warehouse Districts that also saw minimal flooding. However, the tourism industry was far from secure.

Conventions that were scheduled for the imminent future began canceling. Not only had the Convention Center and Superdome endured tremendous wear and tear by the evacuees who had been temporarily housed in them, but meeting planners also lacked confidence that the city would be repaired in time to handle their meetings. Cancellations for the short term were understandable, but the magnitude of the crisis began to be realized when conventions set far off into the future began canceling. It was becoming clear that there was a perception that New Orleans was not capable of handling major conventions for some time into the foreseeable future. As it would turn out, New Orleans would not host another major convention until June 2006.

Meanwhile, the hotel industry was having difficulties of its own. Although many of the hotels in the French Quarter and Warehouse District remained unscathed, hotels throughout the city did suffer wind damage, thus severely limiting room inventories. The few rooms that were available began filling immediately with insurance adjustors, government workers and contractors. Many hotel rooms were also being occupied by hotel employees who had lost their own homes and by other displaced New Orleans residents subsidized by the Federal Emergency Management Agency. Room inventory in September 2005 was only 12,000 but slowly rose each month and by January 2006, room inventories had risen to 27,000, some 11,500 rooms short of pre-Katrina inventories (Louisiana Office of Tourism, 2006).

In addition to the problems of wind and water damage, some hotel operations had to remain limited because it was difficult to find employees. Many of the industry's frontline employees lived in areas of the city that were the hardest hit, and they could not return to New Orleans because they had no where to live. Those that did find housing found that their rents had increased dramatically as did their need for higher wages.

Restaurants were in a situation similar to that of hotels. Those that remained undamaged by the storm were able to reopen as soon as they passed inspection by the Board of Health. However, lack of employees and higher operating costs forced restaurants to operate at reduced hours with limited menus. As of July 2006, the Louisiana Restaurant Association reported 44% of metropolitan (including suburban) area restaurants had been recertified to open (but only 33% within the city boundaries). Staffing issues remain one of the industry's biggest challenges, and are fundamental to restoring the restaurant experience tourists have come to expect in New Orleans.

The biggest hurdle facing the New Orleans' tourism industry, however, is the perception that the city is somehow tarnished as a tourist destination. "By virtue of the power of the media and the tendency for negative images to linger, the recovery of destinations usually takes longer than the period required for the restoration of services to normalcy" (Faulkner, 2001, p. 142).

REPOSITIONING

An adage in the field of market positioning is that *perception is reality*. To a large extent it does not matter what is reality, people's perceptions are what is important to them. With so many prevailing negative perceptions of New Orleans the city's tourism marketers knew they had to develop a repositioning strategy. As stated by Ries and Trout (1993):

> The basic approach to positioning is not to create something new and different, but to manipulate what's already there in the mind, to retie the connections that already exist. (p. 5)

Lewis, Chambers, and Chacko (1995, p. 358) outlined the steps in the procedure for repositioning and have been adapted below:

1. Determine the present position
2. Determine what position you wish to occupy
3. Ensure the product is truly different from the former position
4. Undertake repositioning strategy
5. Continue to measure if there is a position change in the desired direction

THE PRESENT POSITION–PERCEPTION

Research and measurement of tourism in New Orleans after Hurricane Katrina has been challenging, yet interesting. Whereas the focus of research prior to Hurricane Katrina was on measuring the industry and profiling the visitors to New Orleans, in an attempt to prevent further loss to the industry, the focus has now sharply shifted to measuring potential visitors' perceptions of New Orleans.

In January 2006 (five months post-Katrina), the New Orleans Tourism Marketing Corporation conducted a perceptions study. In a nationwide telephone survey, 46.4% of respondents indicated they still believed some neighborhoods still had standing flood water from Hurricane Katrina in the streets, and 41.6% believed the water was not safe to drink. In spite of media coverage that the French Quarter remained intact after the storm, 47.6% of respondents indicated they believed the historic districts, such as the French Quarter, were severely damaged or destroyed by Hurricane Katrina. In addition, 45.6% of respondents believed that there was a lack of police presence in New Orleans due to layoffs related to Hurricane Katrina (Market Dynamics Research Group, Inc., 2006a). In March 2006 (seven months post-Katrina), a similar perceptions study of a panel of 5,000 online travelers, 22% indicated they believed that some neighborhoods of New Orleans still had standing flood water from Hurricane Katrina, 14% believed New Orleans is not safe to visit due to contaminated air or drinking water, and 12% indicated that the historic districts in New Orleans, such as the French Quarter, are still

destroyed or devastated (Market Dynamics Research Group, Inc., 2006b).

Better results were obtained when the perceptions of meeting planners were measured between October 2005 and January 2006. The results were positive, with over three-quarters (77%) of meeting planners indicating they were optimistic that New Orleans would recover sufficiently to regain its status as a major destination city (Travel Career Connexxions, 2006). Furthermore, the optimism seems to have increased over time. In interviews conducted during October 2005, only 17% stated that they were "very optimistic" about the city's recovery. Later interviews show this level of optimism increasing to the low 30% range where it remains. Although meeting planners fully expect a recovery, they believe it will be a slow process. One-third (33%) of planners expect a recovery within 1 to 2 years, while 61% believe the recovery process will extend beyond 2 years.

THE DESIRED POSITION–REALITY

Obviously, the reality on the ground in New Orleans is very different from the perception of potential leisure travelers. There is no standing water on the streets and the tap water in the city was declared safe to drink by city health officials as early as January 2006. Although the number of police officers declined from 1,680 to 1,469 (12.6%) the ratio of police officers to residents has now increased from 1:289 to 1:130 due to the smaller population in the city (New Orleans Metropolitan Convention and Visitor Bureau, 2006). Airline and ground transportation is more than adequate to handle travelers and the hotel room inventory has rebounded to around 80% of pre-Katrina levels. Most importantly, the main generators of tourism demand, such as the French Quarter and the Convention Center, are fully functional. However, recovery in many of the flooded neighborhoods is painfully slow and the media continues to frame their news coverage in these environments, continually undermining any positive messages about the city. Given this reality, the challenge was to find the appropriate marketing position for New Orleans.

REPOSITIONING NEW ORLEANS

It is of vital importance to the survival of the tourism industry in New Orleans to counteract the negative images that were continually played out in the national media in the days and months following hurricane Katrina as "tourism demand presents a higher elasticity index per level of perceived risk than any other industry because of the hedonistic . . . benefits customers ascribe to its products and services" (Gonzalez-Herrero & Pratt (1998, p. 86). Although there is a belief that it is best to let the public gradually forget about a crisis (based on the theory that "time will heal") this is not an effective strategy, nor is it a viable strategy given the continuing media attention focused on New Orleans. City tourism marketers realized that a proactive stance was necessary to rebut negative media and decided that there had to be a concerted effort to get media coverage that reflected the reality of the undamaged areas of the city. Various tourism industry stakeholders both private and public pooled their resources to open The New Orleans Media Center to put out messages that reinforced the fact that tourism infrastructure was still viable. This Center was located at a downtown hotel and to attract media correspondents it offered high-speed and wireless Internet service, cable news access, computer resources, and general office services. Members of the media could use this facility for broadcasts and news conferences and were also given daily updates of the progress of the recovery efforts in the city. A New Orleans flair was added by offering musical performances and food tastings.

For the advertising strategy, marketers identified the most promising initial target market to be those visitors who had previously visited New Orleans. After all, as Table 1 shows, 65.5% of visitors in 2004 were repeat visitors to the city and it would be easier to convince them to come back rather than go after first time visitors. This is similar to the proposition by Braun-LaTour, LaTour, and Loftus (2006) that "reminding consumers of their past connection with a brand may be a particularly effective way to repair the brand's image after a crisis situation" (p. 107). The repositioning campaign asked visitors to "Come fall in love with New Orleans all over again." This was common to both print and electronic media advertising which featured New Orleans' homegrown celebrities of national stature including actors, artists, chefs, and jazz musicians (see Figure 2 for one example).

According to Lewis, Chambers, and Chacko, (1995) the three basic rules of persuasion proposed centuries ago by Aristotle were *logos*–logic and reasoning; *pathos*–emotions; and *ethos*–source credibility. New Orleans marketers hoped this advertising message fulfilled the two latter rules with references to emotions (falling in love) emanating from credible messengers. The television version also featured a moral appeal (Kotler, Bowen, & Makens, 2005) with the celebrities thanking Americans for their charitable support and urging them to visit New Orleans to help the recovery process.

While advertising may be appropriate for the leisure market it is usually not as effective with tourism intermediaries such as convention and meeting planners, tour operators and travel agents. Two of the most important criteria by which these intermediaries are evaluated are the volume of attendance at an event, such as a convention or tradeshow, and also the smooth operation of the hundreds of details that go into the planning of such events. Therefore, negative publicity, especially about basic concerns such as the availability of potable water and personal safety, weigh heavily on the decision to select a destination in crisis recovery mode. Since the responsibility of dealing with these intermediaries fell within the purview of the NOMCVB, officials of the organization devised new personal selling and public relations strategies. A plan was put into place to re-establish contacts with all their clients, especially since 2.2 million hotel room nights of definite bookings were cancelled in the days following the storm (New Orleans Metropolitan Convention and Visitors Bureau, 2006). Clients were apprised of the progress of the recovery including the reopening of the various tourism industry entities and supporting businesses.

The public relations strategy included the production and distribution of a free DVD titled "Make Way for the Rebirth" providing visual evidence that the tourist areas, such as the French Quarter, were intact and that many businesses were open. In addition, live testimonials from corporate and convention meeting planners, of national repute, reporting their confidence in the city to host meetings were featured including one from the meeting planner who was going to bring a 16,000 person convention to New Orleans as early as June 2006. Unlike the pre-Katrina advertising strategy, the messages of this public relations piece were based on *logos*–logic and reasoning (showing that New Orleans would be able to host meetings and conventions) and *ethos*–source credibility (using nationally known meeting planners to spread the message).

An advertising campaign targeted to meeting planners, who had previously been to New Orleans, featured the byline "New Orleans, just as you remember it," and displayed photographic evidence of time stamped French Quarter scenes before and after the storm (with no discernable difference). In addition, a direct email campaign

was mounted, also to travel intermediaries, showing images of the undamaged areas of New Orleans (New Orleans Metropolitan Convention and Visitors Bureau, 2006).

The final piece of the repositioning effort was the use of the Internet websites of the New Orleans Metropolitan Convention and Visitors Bureau and the New Orleans Tourism Marketing Corporation. Both sites prominently featured links to sections of the website that provided frequent updates on the progress of the recovery in the tourism industry including the states of event facilities, airports, cruise lines, local transportation. In addition, important city statistics, the new Emergency Preparedness Plan, and the reconstruction of levees and flood protection were also highlighted. A map of New Orleans, reiterated the fact that the airport, French Quarter, and downtown hotels suffered

FIGURE 2. Sample of New Orleans Advertising Post-Katrina

Source: New Orleans Tourism Marketing Corporation/Peter A. Mayer Advertising, New Orleans (2006). Used with permission.

FIGURE 3. Map of New Orleans from the NOMCVB Website

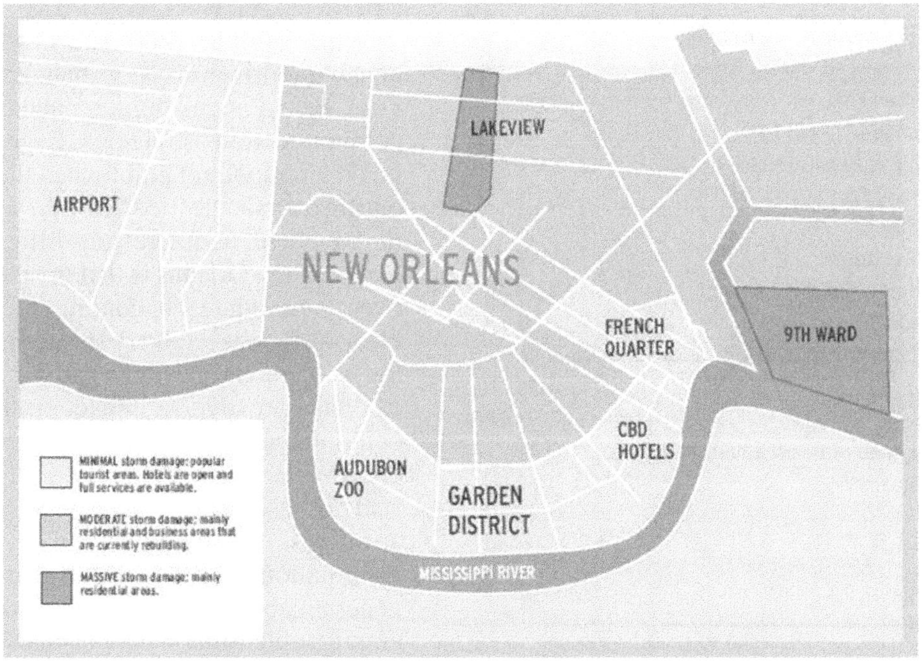

Source: http://www.neworleanscvb.com/docs/NeighborhoodMap.pdf. Used with permission.

minimal damage and were open for business but still showed the higher damage levels in the residential neighborhoods such as the Ninth Ward and Lakeview (Figure 3). These efforts also ensured that New Orleans would not indulge in any denial of the scope of the disaster as seen in other cases (Cammisa, 1993; Murphy & Bailey, 1989).

CONCLUSIONS

Three major lessons can be learned from the New Orleans post Katrina marketing experience. First, the creation of a location for members of the media to receive updates from local officials so that the perpetuation of disaster "myths" can be mitigated is of vital importance. The New Orleans Media Center provided an attractive place for media correspondents to congregate and to conduct their business. Second, identifying and using opinion leaders in the dissemination of positive elements of a destination in crisis recovery is vital to offset negative publicity from emanating from the mass media. The use of nationally reputed and respected meeting planners and other tourism intermediaries has helped to allay some of the fears of this important market segment. In fact, while New Orleans lost 70% of its business booked through travel intermediaries in 2006, it is expected to lose only 30% in 2007, and less that 5% in 2008 (New Orleans Metropolitan Convention and Visitors Bureau, 2006). Third, using affective advertising (Braun-LaTour et. al. 2006), by capitalizing on the emotions and connections with previous visitors to New Orleans seems to be an effective strategy. This was exemplified by the "Fall in love with New Orleans all over again" advertising campaign. However, there should not be an over reliance on this strategy unless it is clear that advertising is an effective communications vehicle. In the case of New Orleans, approximately 25% of visitors had seen or heard advertising prior to their trip (Table 2).

TABLE 2. 2004 New Orleans Visitor Sources of Information/Advertising

Primary Source of Information:	
Just knew about New Orleans	46.5%
Internet	27.7%
Friends	24.2%
Job/Business/Company	15.0%
Convention	8.4%
Family	4.2%
Travel Agent	4.2%
Advertisements	4.1%
Guide Shows	2.7%
Seen or heard advertising about New Orleans:	
Yes	25.3%
No	74.7%
Where seen or heard advertising:	
Magazine	50.2%
TV	47.1%
Internet	1.6%
Mail	0.8%

Source: University of New Orleans Hospitality Research Center, 2005b. Used with permission.

This case study contributes to the literature on the effects of crises and disasters by examining the marketing efforts of a destination during the recovery stage after tremendous and continuous negative publicity. Hurricane Katrina has turned out to be the most expensive natural disaster for the United States with damage and recovery estimates ranging from $100 billion to $200 billion over the long term. Almost a year later, it continues to be a news story in the U.S. media especially since the hurricane season is a predicted annual occurrence unlike other natural disasters such as tsunamis or earthquakes. Indeed, the intense negative media coverage in just the seven weeks following Hurricane Katrina was calculated to be equivalent to five years of pre-Katrina ad equivalency (New Orleans Metropolitan Convention and Visitor Bureau, 2006). Quarentelli (1984) discussed the role of media during disasters and noted that television, in particular, was prone to perpetuate disaster myths and research has borne that out in the case of New Orleans. It is difficult for tourism marketers to effectively compete with the mass media that has world wide, 24-hour

coverage but what can be done is to try and restore confidence by publicizing the positives and reporting the progress of the recovery (Bierman, 2003).

While Faulkner (2001) developed a comprehensive tourism disaster management framework he did not elaborate much on marketing communications strategies. Page et al (2006) made an important point when they noted that during a crisis the media would set the pace of the coverage. An interesting difference with regard to New Orleans is that the media, with its overwhelming reach, continues to set the pace even during the recovery stage. Since positioning is a mental concept, negative media "noise" can have an adverse impact on the deliberate communications strategies of tourism marketers. While the uniqueness of these circumstances in New Orleans provide the outline for an interesting case study, it is also contributes to a limitation of the method, namely reduced generalizability. Indeed, there was even debate among some Americans who questioned the efficacy of rebuilding a city that was below sea level and prone to disasters annually. Under these circumstances, New Orleans faces a long road to recovering its destination image. However, given its use of a repositioning strategy and the vanguard efforts of the city's tourism marketers, New Orleans has taken the first steps toward regaining its status as a preeminent tourism destination. Further research must be conducted to examine the recovery of this city especially in terms of the destination image from the perspectives of visitors, tourism intermediaries, and local residents.

REFERENCES

Arnold, W. (1980). *Crisis communication.* Dubuque, Iowa: Gorsuch Scarisbrook.

Bierman, D. (2003). *Restoring tourism destinations in crisis: A strategic marketing approach.* Oxford, U.K: CABI Publishing.

Braun-Latour, K. A., Latour, M. S., & Loftus, E. F. (2006). Is that a finger in my chili?: Using affective advertising for post crisis brand repair. *Cornell Hotel and Restaurant Administration Quarterly.* 47, 106-120.

Booth, S. (1993). *Crisis management strategy: Competition and change in modern enterprises.* New York, NY: Routledge.

Cammisa, J. V. (1993). The Miami experience: Natural and manmade disasters, 1992-93. In expanding responsibilities: A blueprint for the travel industry. *24th Annual Conference Proceedings of Travel and Tourism Research Association* (pp. 294-295). Whistler, BC.

Chacko, H. E. (1997). Positioning a tourism destination to gain a competitive edge. *Asia Pacific Journal of Tourism Research.* 1, 69-75.

Clarke, C. J., & Varma, S. (2004). Strategic risk management: the new competitive edge. *Long Range Planning.* 32, 414-424.

Evans, N., & Elphick, S. (2005). Models of crisis management: An evaluation of their value for strategic planning in the international travel industry. *International Journal of Tourism Research.* 7, 135-150.

Faulkner, B. (2001).Towards a framework for tourism disaster management. *Tourism Management.* 22, 135-147.

Faulkner, B., & Vikulov, S. (2001). Katherine, washed out one day, back on track the next: A post-mortem of a tourism disaster. *Tourism Management.* 22, 331-344.

Gonzalez-Herrero, A., & Pratt, C. B. (1998). Marketing crises in tourism: Communication strategies in the United States and Spain. *Public Relations Review.* 24, 83-97.

Henderson, J. C. (1999). Managing the Asian financial crisis: Tourist attractions in Singapore. *Journal of Travel Research.* 38, 177-181.

Henderson, J.C., & Ng, A. (2004). Responding to crisis: Severe Acute Respiratory Syndrome (SARS) and hotels in Singapore. *International Journal of Tourism Research.* 6, 411-419.

Henderson, J. C. (2005). Responding to natural disasters: Managing a hotel in the aftermath of the Indian Ocean tsunami. *Tourism and Hospitality Research.* 6, 89-96.

Hitchcock, M., & Putra, I. N. D. (2005). The Bali bombings: Tourism crisis management and conflict avoidance. *Current Issues in Tourism.* 8, 62-76.

Ioannides, D., & Apostolopoulos, Y. (1999). Political instability, war, and tourism in Cyprus: Effects, management, and prospects for recovery. *Journal of Travel Research.* 38, 51-56.

Kotler, P., Bowen, J. T., & Makens, J. C. (2005). *Marketing for hospitality and tourism.* Upper Saddle River, NJ: Pearson Education Inc.

Lewis, R. C., Chambers, R. E., & Chacko, H. E. (1995). *Marketing leadership in hospitality.* New York: Van Nostrand Reinhold.

Louisiana Office of Tourism (2006). Memorandum: Monthly Lodging Data by Smith Travel Research. July 5. Baton Rouge, LA: Author.

Lovelock, C. H. (1991). *Services marketing (2nd Ed.).* Englewood Cliffs, NJ: Prentice-Hall Inc.

Market Dynamics Research Group (2006a). Wave 1 Interim Report. New Orleans, LA: Author.

Market Dynamics Research Group (2006b). Wave 2 Interim Report. New Orleans, LA: Author.

Murphy, P.E. & Bailey, R. (1989). Tourism and disaster planning. *Geographical Review.* 79 (1), 36-46.

New Orleans Metropolitan Convention and Visitor Bureau (2005). *Tourism: The industry that drives Louisiana's economy.* New Orleans, LA: Author.

New Orleans Metropolitan Convention and Visitor Bureau (2006). *State of Tourism.* New Orleans, LA: Author.

Northington, M. (2006) Director of Research, Louisiana Office of Tourism, Personal Communication, January 15.

Page, S., Yeoman, I., Munro, C., Connell, J., & Walker, L. (2006). A case study of best practice: Visit Scotland's prepared response to an influenza pandemic. *Tourism Management.* 27, 361-393.

Pike, S., & Ryan, C. (2004). Destination positioning analysis through a comparison of cognitive, affective, and conative perceptions. *Journal of Travel Research.* 42, 333-342.

Quarantelli, E. L. (1984).Organisational behavior in disasters and implications for disaster planning. Monographs of the National Emergency Training Center. 1, 1-31.

Richter, L. K. (1999). After political turmoil: The lessons of rebuilding tourism in three Asian countries. *Journal of Travel Research.* 38, 41-45.

Ries, A., & Trout, J. (1993) *Positioning: The battle for your mind.* New York: Warner Books.

Sausmarez, N. (2004). Crisis management for the tourism sector: Preliminary considerations in policy development. *Tourism and Hospitality Planning and Development.* 1, 157-172.

Seymour, M., & Moore, S. (2000). *Effective crisis management: worldwide principles and practice.* London: Cassell.

Stafford, G., Yu, L., & Armoo, A. K. (2002). Crisis management and recovery: How Washington, D.C., hotels responded to terrorism. *Cornell Hotel and Restaurant Administration Quarterly.* October, 27-40.

Travel Career Connexxions (2006). Travel Career Connexxions Opportunities Newsletter. http://www.travelconnexxions.com/opportunities032106.html#1. Retrieved August 1, 2006.

University of New Orleans (2005a). New Orleans Perception Study. New Orleans, LA: Author.

University of New Orleans (2005b). 2004 New Orleans Visitor Profile. New Orleans, LA: Author.

Wen, Z., Huimin, G., & Kavanaugh, R. R. (2005). The impact of SARS on the consumer behavior of Chinese domestic tourists. *Current Issues in Tourism.* 8, 22-38.

Williams, C., & Ferguson, M. (2005). Biting the hand that feeds: The marginalisation of tourism and leisure industry providers in times of agricultural crisis. *Current Issues in Tourism.* 8, 155-164.

Young, W. B., & Montgomery, R. J. (1998). Crisis management and its impact on destination marketing: A guide to convention and visitors bureaus. *Journal of Convention and Exhibition Management.* 1, 3-18.

Backpacking Your Way into Crisis:
An Exploratory Study into Perceived Risk
and Tourist Behaviour Amongst Young People

Philippa Hunter-Jones

Alice Jeffs

Denis Smith

SUMMARY. Risk and tourism have become more closely interlinked in recent years. Recognising the complexity of tourist behaviour, research by Cohen (1972) classified tourists according to the degree of novelty or familiarity sought. Whilst the subject of extensive debate, many questions remain including to what extent perceived risk can be used as an indicator of tourist roles. Focusing upon the growing youth tourism market, backpackers in particular, travel patterns and attitudes towards risk were questioned and possible responses to a crisis differentiated through an exploratory qualitative study. The findings challenge both the resilience of the market alongside Cohen's (1972) typology suggesting backpackers exhibit different roles (drifter and explorer) dependent upon the risk in question. Given the exploratory nature of the work, the paper concludes calling for further targeted research.

INTRODUCTION

There are some tourist attractions that are so obviously based on 'risk' in its broadest sense. Anyone who has visited Las Vegas will be immediately aware that risk is a major pillar of the city's tourist 'appeal.' Similarly, there are a range of adventure holidays that have 'risk' at their core. However, not all tourists want to be exposed to risk and many want security and safety as core elements of their travel agenda. Indeed according to Richter and Waugh (1986) "political serenity, not scenic or cultural attractions, constitute the first and central requirement of tourism," (p. 231), a claim backed up by the later work of Pizam and Mansfeld (1996, p.1) who argue that: "the effects of wars, criminal activities, terrorist attacks and violent acts aimed specifically against tourists have been devastating to tourist destinations."

Philippa Hunter-Jones (E-mail: P.Hunter-Jones@liverpool.ac.uk) is Lecturer in the Marketing Division at University of Liverpool Management School, Chatham Street, Liverpool, L69 7ZH, UK. Alice Jeffs is a Yield Analyst working for MyTravel, 25 Argyll Street, Ashton-Under-Lyne, Lancashire, OL6 6RQ UK. Denis Smith (E-mail: denis.smith@lbss.gla.ac.uk), is Professor of Management in the Department of Business and Management at the University of Glasgow (Gilbert Scott Building, Glasgow, G12 8QQ UK).

Yet there is also a sense that some destinations have shown an ability to recover quickly. Indeed, some areas that have been exposed to a major crisis may also generate a market for a new type of tourist. In Nepal, the campaign by Maoist rebels to unseat the monarchy has resulted in a loss of over 8,000 lives since 1996. Even so, holiday agents believe that the chance of meeting rebels has led to a significant rise in the number of trekkers to the region (Khadka, 2004). This pattern is repeated in a more general context when reflecting upon the estimated 22% growth in UK outbound travel between 2000 and 2005 (Mintel, 2006), a period when the international tourism map has been particularly threatened. After the terrorist attacks of September 11th 2001, there was an influx of tourists to New York, many of whom wanted to pay their respects to the victims at the site of the World Trade Centre.

Clearly, trying to understand tourist behaviour and perceptions of risk is a complex process. Various authors have attempted this, with Mitchell and Greatorex (1993) reflecting upon the wider services environment, while Mitchell and Vassos (1997) focused more upon holiday purchases. Yet despite this, Mo, Howard and Havitz (1993), and more recently Lepp and Gibson (2003), continue to lament the paucity of academic research exploring the perceived risks associated with international tourism. Understanding how different market segments respond to a particular form of crisis may play a pivotal role in enabling destination marketers to redefine their consumer base at a critical time. Whilst a review of the full range of market segments is clearly beyond the scope of this paper, it is felt that some exploratory insights can be provided by investigating the perceptions held by one tourism segment, the youth tourism market. At the heart of this study is a questioning of the extent to which perceived risk can be used as an indicator of tourist roles.

'Pack All Your Troubles . . . .'– Youth Tourism and Risk Acceptance

Currently, the multi-million dollar youth tourism market is recognised as a major growth sector within international tourism (Cooper, Fletcher, Fyall, Gilbert & Wanhill, 2005) and an indictor of future travel trends (Hall, 2005).

It also represents a diverse segment and one that may take a number of different guises. In concert with the heterogeneous nature of tourism in general, various approaches to classifying the segment exits. The application of a tourism typology framework is a particularly useful tool as such is able to characterize differences among tourists across a range of factors, be it socio-demographic, activities, lifestyles and values for instance. Applied within many contexts, it is the work by Cohen (1972) which has proved the most useful when exploring the youth tourism market. The basic premise of this early work suggests the existence of four identifiable categories of tourist: the organized mass tourist; the individual mass tourist; the explorer; and the drifter, categorization determined by the degree tourists seek out novelty or familiarity in their travel experiences. Crudely put, the organized mass tourist seeks familiarity, whilst at the opposite end of the spectrum, the drifter is energised by novelty.

According to O'Reilly (2006, p. 1005) Cohen's drifter "has least contact with the tourism industry, has no fixed itinerary or timetable, travels on a more limited budget, and is more of a risk-taker." Backpackers, invariably referred to by the academic community as drifters, long-haul, long-term, independent travelers, budget travelers are often commonly associated with Cohen's drifter category (see for instance Mo, Howard & Havitz 1993; Lepp & Gibson, 2003; Loker-Murphy & Pearce, 1995; O'Reilly, 2006; Uriely, Yonay & Simchai, 2002). In terms of the contemporary backpacker, there are some general characteristics that can be applied. Most backpackers are students under 24 taking gap years or are young people on career breaks. The segment is also one that is economically important. The student travel market alone is estimated to account for 20% of all international travel (FIYTO, 2006). They tend to travel on limited budgets, operate independently of tour operators, have flexible itineraries and aim to travel to multiple destinations. Many fund their trip by working or volunteering during their travel. They also represent a high-risk group who are vulnerable due to their age, attitudes, naivety and generally low levels of experience as travelers. In recent years backpacking has grown in popularity, in fact according to Mintel (2003), between 1999 and 2007 a 12% increase in the growth of the 15-24 year olds backpacking market is estimated, facilitated in part by a growing infrastructure of low cost airlines, budget accommodation and the Internet.

Yet the increasing popularity of backpacking has led some authors, including notably Cohen (2004), to question whether the contemporary backpacker is comparable to the original drifter tourist type (Cohen, 1972) or instead exhibits characteristics more akin with mainstream tourism activity. One vehicle for testing this is to explore perceived risk as an indicator of tourist roles. Understanding the relationship between perceived risk and backpacking is complicated. As backpacking has increased in popularity so too has the negative media attention regarding the safety and security of this community. It is easy to assume that media coverage of these risks will influence tourist activity. The nature of this influence is less clear-cut for whilst many people may perceive backpacking to be dangerous, this perception of risk may not be sufficient to deter activity. Indeed Morgan and Dimmock (2006) argue that the presence of 'risks' may serve to fuel the desire to travel. Citing participation in outdoor adventure tourism activity, these authors argue that perceptions of risk are more likely to result in "feelings of excitement, arousal, challenge and fun" (Morgan & Dimmock, 2006, p. 175) and to encourage, rather than deter, engagement. Whether such findings are transferable to crisis situations is not obvious, and further work is needed in this area. In order to explore the relationship between tourism and the potential for adverse outcomes in travel, it is necessary to highlight some key areas of synergy between the two bodies of work.

Incubating the Potential for Harm– Coping Within New Environments

Despite having a long-term association, the study of tourism, risk and crisis management has only really become more formalized within relatively recent years. Much of the work has considered definitions and meanings associated with risk and crisis alongside providing case studies of an increasingly diverse range of examples. Rather than rehearse the debate here, we point the reader towards the work edited by

Laws and Prideaux (2005) and to their typology of crisis terms in particular (Laws & Prideaux, 2005a, p. 6) which provides the premise for our discussion.

Work within the literature on risk has long recognised that there are a number of processes that allow problems to be 'incubated' over time (see, for example, Turner, 1976; 1978; Reason, 1990; 1997). Decisions taken at discrete points in 'space' and 'time' can generate impacts that will emerge later. There is also recognition that adverse outcomes rarely, if ever, have a single root cause. There are several important elements that allow adverse outcomes to be incubated that have a relevance to our present discussion.

The first of these relates to the processes by which information is 'codified,' interpreted and communicated. A failure to recognise uncertainty in the environment can generate problems around decision making. Exposure to new environments presents travellers with a heightened vulnerability. Such environments invariably contain new cultural, psychological, physical, physiological, emotional, environmental and microbiological experiences which tourists adjust to with differing degrees of success (Wilks & Page, 2003). The manner in which this 'information' is codified and interpreted is an important element in generating risks for the tourist.

A second issue concerns the way in which organisations and individuals respond to warnings about hazards that are outside of their control and, in particular, how 'weak signals' (Turner, 1978) around risks are dealt with. Health and safety risks for example can have a serious impact upon tourist destinations arrivals. Many popular destinations for British backpackers carry health risks and result in visitors being advised to take precautions including malaria treatments, vaccinations, the use of mosquito nets and so on. Crime may also pose a threat to safety. These represent recognised everyday risks, reported in the travel media of guidebooks, travel programmes, Websites, etc. They can be anticipated and planned for accordingly.

Weak signals are also a major problem at the 'industry-level' and this adds to the difficulties around effective pre-planning. Perhaps the best examples of such major shocks come from geo-physical events which may happen without warning, even though they often occur within generally well-known hazard zones. The Indian Ocean tsunami of 2004 illustrates quite tragically the problems facing tourists who are caught up in a crisis situation. Terrorist attacks are also an example of this type of hazard. Both of these crisis examples invariably take the Industry off guard and often provoke a knee jerk reaction to the problem rather than being based upon a pre-conceived (and tested) contingency plan. Such volatility can be apparent even where tourists have not been directly targeted. Commenting upon the September 11th terrorist attacks Floyd, Gibson, Pennington-Gray and Thapa (2003, p. 20) note that "consumer confidence in the safety and security of travel decreased significantly," the 29% decline in international arrivals to the US adding an additional pressure to an already shaken economy.

Understanding tourist perceptions of natural disaster[1] is also complicated and the tourist reaction to these events is variable. Reporting on Hurricane Ivan, Buckley (2004) found that even though the hurricane affected many tourists (and locals) in the Caribbean, particularly in Jamaica and Grenada and destroyed up to ten metres of beach in some areas of Jamaica, it had not deterred tourists from visiting. In contrast, holiday cancellations related to the Severe Acquired Respiratory Syndrome (SARS) outbreak resulted in a 1.2% decline in international tourism arrivals in 2003, a 41% drop in East Asia alone in April 2003 (Wilder-Smith, 2006). That said, such a drop may be more of a reflection of the unprecedented World Health Organisation (WHO) advice against non-essential international travel than necessarily consumer response.

The third issue that is relevant to our discussion is the ill-structured nature of the problem that can face both the individual and organisations within the tourist industry. Both the examples of natural disaster and terrorist threat will be typified by contradictory information flows and these will require effective information processing and decision making capabilities. Given the uncertain nature of the problems facing tourists and their lack of local knowledge, then these limitations will exacerbate the problems around decision making. For many complicated issues, such as disease outbreaks, which have complex dynamic properties, effective decision making is made all the more difficult due to issues around knowledge, information flows, communication and interpretation. These factors can lead to, what Turner (1976, 1978) described as the 'minimisation of emergent danger.' At the level of the individual, this may manifest itself as a mindset that says 'it couldn't happen to me.' Organisations also appear to suffer from a similar problem (see Mitroff, Pauchant, Finney & Pearson, 1989; Pauchant & Mitroff, 1992) and one that results in a failure to recognise that they may be prone to crisis.

What the literature on adverse events suggests is that there are a range of factors that can generate conditions that will allow an adverse event to escalate into a 'crisis.' In some respects, individuals and organisations can become authors of their own misfortune as they fail to take account of their own role in generating those adverse conditions that may befall them. For tourism organisations to better anticipate the consequences of adverse conditions, understanding consumer perceptions of what constitutes travel risks may provide one route towards this.

Unpacking the Problem of Travel Related Risks–Research Methodology

An initial study was undertaken to explore the perceptions of risk in young tourists. The basic steps employed in developing the methodology were guided by the work of Uriely, Yonay and Simchai (2002) whose analysis of Israeli backpackers employed a qualitative methodology to distinguish between type and form-related attributes in an attempt to deconstruct the contemporary nature of the activity. For this study three research parameters were established. First the sample population was to consist of those aged 15-24, an age range representative of the main backpacking market (Mintel, 2003). Second, the travel was to be specifically leisure travel. Third, the window of reflection was to be the main holiday-taking activity undertaken within the two years prior to the interview. Quota sampling techniques were applied and 20 informants recruited, 10 with previous backpacking experience, 10 without from the city of Manchester,

UK, a city including a population in excess of 40,000 students, an age-range complimentary to that sought. Since the sample population comprised UK based students, the generalizability of the findings may well be limited to similar populations.

Face-to-face, semi-structured interviews were conducted over a twelve month period beginning in the spring of 2005. The interview schedule, developed taking account of the work by Floyd, Gibson, Pennington-Gray and Thapa (2003), included informant profiling by age, gender, travel propensity and patterns of holiday-taking including motivations, choice and inhibitors. The four research themes explored by Mo, Howard and Havitz (1993) and Lepp and Gibson (2003) war and political instability, health concerns, crime, and terrorism provided a framework for questioning supple- mented by one further category, natural disasters, explored through the work of Peters and Pikkemaat (2005). Once piloted and the question wording altered accordingly, the interviews were conducted in a location convenient to the informant (usually home), in most instances tape recorded (with permission) and analysed using template analysis (Saunders, Lewis & Thornhill, 2003).

RESULTS

Table 1 illustrates the profile of respondents noting an equal gender split and an age range of 19 to 24. All of the respondents were holiday-takers. Those without previous backpacking experience were united in their tendency to consume package holidays, their profiles reflective of Cohen's (1972) organized mass tourist. Those with experience of backpacking tended to exhibit very individual patterns of consumption, visiting a wide range of destinations for a varying period of time with a differing number of travel partners. The five literature based research themes were re-classified as four sources of hazard and are used as the basis for categorising the results: war and political instability; health; crime and terrorism; and natural disasters. During the interviews one additional factor arose out of the discussions, namely the

range of pre-travel influences. To provide a contextual setting for the results that follow, this issue is discussed first. As the sample included both backpackers and non-backpackers, the discussion explores both actual (the former group) and suggested (the latter group) risk avoidance strategies. Whilst such an approach was selected to widen the data capture net, future research may benefit from a more focused sampling strategy.

TABLE 1. Profile of Respondents

Name	Backpacking Career	Age
John	Yes–Australia for 2 months alone, Western Europe for 5 weeks with girlfriend.	23
David	Yes–Twice, inter-railing around Europe, once for 2 months with 2 friends, once for 6 weeks with 5 friends.	22
Matthew	Yes–6-8 week trips around Europe, climbing based.	23
Richard	Yes–inter-railing around Europe for 2 months with 2 male friends.	22
Paul	Yes–Europe for one month with 1 friend, Australia for 2 months alone.	21
Laura	Yes–5 months, Hong Kong, Singapore, Malaysia, Thailand, Australia, New Zealand, with 3 female friends.	19
Rebecca	Yes–1 month around Europe with 1 male and 1 female friend. 3 weeks Greek island hopping with 1 female friend.	22
Rachel	Yes–3 weeks, organised tour in group of 13, around USA.	22
Vicky	Yes–Australia for 2 months alone.	20
Debbie	Yes–Europe for 2 months with 2 friends, 1 male, 1 female.	23
Robert	No–package and independent holidays with friends and family from 2-8 weeks.	21
Ben	No–package holidays.	22
Michael	No–package holidays.	22
Oliver	No–package holidays.	20
George	No–package holidays.	21
Helen	No–package holidays.	21
Beth	No–package holidays.	20
Julia	No–package holidays and flight only.	22
Clare	No–package holidays.	21
Anna	No–package holidays.	19

Source: Primary data.

Pre-Travel Influences

Respondents who had no previous experience of backpacking were found to be less likely to take responsibility for their own safety–instead placing a greater emphasis upon the role of the travel intermediary. As Cavlek (2002 p. 494) notes "potential tourists view tour operators as strong signals of travel safety or risks." Non-backpackers Julia, Helen, Beth, Ben, Oliver and Clare, all argued that they would expect the travel agent to make them aware of any risks to their safety. Richard was the only backpacker to concur with this. This reliance on external expertise is an important issue as it assumes that the travel agents themselves have the knowledge and information needed to give such advice. Such assumptions are potentially powerful pre-cursors of crisis. Those with backpacking experience were more likely to undertake their own research into travel risks. Many of them would echo the reasons cited by a sceptical Robert (non-backpacker) who observed that:

> travel agents generally don't have a clue about destinations out of brochures. Unless you go to specialist agents you know like Trailfinders, you won't find anyone who really knows what off beat places are like.

This view is consistent with Mohsin and Ryan's (2003) claim that major sources of information for backpackers are word of mouth, the internet (especially significant here being the direct experiences of fellow travellers), and consulting travel guides, (the Rough Guide and Lonely Planet series mentioned most frequently). It also mirrors Cohen's (1972) drifter tourist role whereby institutional support is rejected in favour of individuality.

War and Political Instability

Without exception, war was cited as the most significant factor influencing destination choice. Contrary to the STA travel survey (Mintel, 2003), which claimed that crises such as SARS and the Iraqi war had no impact upon the travel aspirations of over two-thirds of student respondents, 90% of whom stated that they would not cancel their travel plans, no respondent in our sample said that they would visit a war zone or destination under imminent threat of war. Whilst all respondents felt that a trip to a potential conflict zone would place personal safety and security at too high a risk, two added an additional justification. The first comment was made by Paul who stated that: ". . . if you visit such a place it's like you are endorsing the conflict." Another comment was made by Anna who stated that:

> . . . these places have got enough problems feeding their own without tourists being there. Look at what happened after the tsunami–people trying to help just added more strain.

In the light of recent events, it is not surprising that every respondent made reference to Iraq, "crisis," "human tragedy," and "political crisis," terms frequently quoted in this context. Other destinations also seen to be subject to the potential for crisis included areas surrounding Iraq, Iran, and the Middle East in general. Responses were consistent in both groups, those respondents who had previous backpacking experience did not derive any additional comfort from that experience about the risks that they would face. Interestingly though, when approached from the perspective of the role of political stability in destination choice, a different pattern of responses emerged.

Consistent with the argument proposed by Hall and O'Sullivan (1996, p. 117) that, "perceptions of political stability and safety are a pre-requisite for tourist visitation," all respondents voiced their anxieties over visiting destinations perceived to be politically unstable. However, it was recognised by twelve respondents, drawn from both groups that as there are degrees of political stability, the extent of influence depends upon the perceived level of risk that they hold. Interestingly, respondents were more forgiving of instability in Eastern European destinations than further afield. For example, John commented that:

> political instability, I suppose there's degrees of that (. . .) maybe Eastern European countries, some of those could be

classed as politically unstable but I'd definitely visit those.

Vicky concurred with this view, stating that:

> I want my next trip to be around the former Soviet states. It seems really chaotic in places and I suppose that's part of the attraction really.

In contrast Zimbabwe (John, David, Ben and Michael), a regular source of discussion within the British media, the Sudan (John), Colombia (Michael) and Bolivia (Beth and Laura), were each cited as destinations in political crisis which offered little attraction to respondents.

Health

Health concerns also proved to be significant to the majority of respondents. All noted that developing countries offered a heightened health risk. Destinations that were associated with illness, disease and hygiene related hazards included: Africa (John, Rebecca, Rachel, Mathew, David, Julia, Beth, Helen, Clare, Anna and Michael), South America (Robert, Beth, Rachel and Rebecca, Oliver and George), India (Rebecca, David, Richard and Paul), Egypt (Rachel), Asia (David, John, and Rebecca) and Thailand (Beth and Robert, Debbie and Vicky). One respondent (Beth) identified Peru and Australia as high-risk destinations with regard to animal and insect bites, such as poisonous snakes and spiders. Such a comment illustrates well the complexity of health-related perceptions and diversity of situations categorised as such.

Interestingly, respondent responses can be categorised into two types broadly reflective of the earlier literature review: *everyday* types of hazard and *crisis* situations, that is, hazards that are widespread within a geographical area and unusual. In terms of *everyday* types of hazard, whilst the risk of contracting malaria featured highly within responses, in no instance was it sufficient to prevent respondents from visiting a destination: "malaria is just one of those things you hear about all the time. I know it's a big deal but it doesn't really have any influence on my choices" (Debbie). In terms of the *crisis* type of hazard, this, in contrast, evoked a con-

siderable amount of fear and uncertainty in travel decisions. Similar to the earlier work by Carter (1998), respondents were especially concerned about contracting infectious diseases linked with epidemics and natural disasters. A comment made by Rachel summarised much of the concern regarding epidemics "if there was an epidemic like SARS then obviously I wouldn't travel." Whilst Robert highlighted the perceived health consequences of natural disasters:

> there's no way I'd go to Thailand or Indonesia or anywhere that was affected by the tsunami (. . .) I'm frightened of the diseases that are there because of the tsunami (. . .) what I've read in papers and seen on the news scares me (. . .) diseases are rife there now.

The differentiation in severity between *everyday* and *crisis* situations was often performed in a sub-conscious manner. When explored further, the perceived management of these situations was found to play a central role in framing perceptions. The perceived management of malaria received a favourable response (Robert, Paul, Vicky, Debbie, Anna and Clare) whilst, in contrast, the perceived management of SARS, the UK based Foot and Mouth outbreak of 2001, and the disease spread following the tsunami and hurricanes all came in for strong criticism.

Crime and Terrorism

Given the high media profile crimes committed against British backpackers receive, it was anticipated that perceptions of crime would play a significant role in determining destination choice. However, the interview findings suggested otherwise. The belief that crime exists everywhere was commonly voiced:

> There's crime all over and tourists are targets, so it wouldn't stop me going anywhere, I'd just be more cautious in some places. (John)

> there's crime in every place, you can just as easily get your drink spiked somewhere like Newquay or even Manchester. (Rachael)

Everywhere has a certain amount of crime. (Julia)

Despite these comments, respondents did acknowledge the need to modify behaviour in order to reduce the risk. Safety precautions commonly noted included not walking alone at night, leaving valuables in safety deposit boxes and wearing money belts, although the extent to which respondents followed their own recommendations was questionable.

Comments captured within the crime theme shared a number of common characteristics. Crime was seldom associated with a broader crisis-type of context but was rather perceived as being reflective of wider societal norms. Respondents found it difficult to disentangle crime from terrorism, a problem Tarlow (2006) highlighted as common to research in this area. Developing countries, large cities and ports each received recognition as potential havens for possible crimes against individual travellers, whilst developed nations, such as the UK and North America, were perceived as being of high risk due to terrorism. The consequences of such perceptions are illustrated by contrasting the comments about South Africa with New York. All those who considered South Africa as risky in terms of crime, said they would visit but behave more cautiously:

> I've got friends and family that live in South Africa, there's a really big problem with crime there (. . .) it doesn't put me off going (. . .) I've been before, but I think about it and act differently when I'm there, like I won't go anywhere on my own or anything like that. (Robert)

In contrast Richard, Debbie and Oliver each voiced concern about future travel to New York for reasons expressed by Debbie:

> I love going to New York and I know it's full of crime but this terrorist situation has really put me off the place. Weird really, doesn't bother me being mugged or attacked but being part of a terrorist attack does.

Generally the role that terrorism plays in the travel decision making process was found to be similar for both data sets. Contrary to the observations by Sonmez and Graefe (1998) that the threat of terrorism often induces a desire to choose an alternative, safer, destination, two-thirds of respondents, drawn from both data sets, claimed that such a threat had little influence over their patterns of tourism consumption. The view expressed by David helped clarify thinking here "terrorism doesn't concern me, you can't do much about it can you?" John, Rebecca and Laura, who were all experienced travellers, shared the view that terrorism is largely unpredictable and consequently they were more ready to ignore the influence of such events on their travel decision making. Their ambivalence was explained by Laura: "I'm kind of more worried about terrorism in England or North America to be honest!" a comment that was made prior to the London attacks of 2005. It also has a resonance with the findings of Browne (2004) who, reporting a survey of Spanish tour operators, found that the Madrid bombings of 2003 had minimal effect on the tourism industry. Where concern was voiced, the September 11th attacks on New York and the Bali bombings provided the most common backdrop to such concern.

Influence of Natural Disasters

The majority of respondents claimed that the threat of natural disasters had little impact upon their travel decisions. Indeed responses suggested something of an ambivalence towards the potential consequences of these events. Most respondents agreed that "natural disasters are few and far between" (John) and are "out of our control, you don't know what might happen where" (Rebecca). Where concern was voiced, it was generally in relation to pressure from family members to avoid certain locations:

> we're going back to Thailand this summer and my mum really doesn't want me to go to that side of the Island but I would go back there (. . .) I'd just generally be aware of it. (Laura)

and was also linked to the consequences of any disaster:

it's not the disaster, like the tsunami, that worries me, it's more the after effects, like the diseases. (Robert)

How knowledgeable respondents were in this area is questionable, however. They utilised only a small range of disasters to exemplify their responses: the Asian Tsunami, SARS, Hurricanes Charley and Ivan.

CONCLUSIONS

Understanding the relationship between perceived risk and tourist behaviour is complicated. As the literature review demonstrated, there is evidence that whilst destinations blighted by conflict are less attractive to tourists, in some instances adverse events can also provide an attraction themselves, even becoming a reason for potential tourism activity. Determining how best to position destinations presents marketers with a greater challenge than ever before. This paper has reported on the preliminary exploration of this process by investigating the travel behaviour of young people. Drawing upon the seminal work of Cohen (1972), this paper has begun to explore the extent to which perceived risk can be used as an indicator of young people tourist roles.

An initial finding, linked to pre-travel influences, would seem to suggest that young people draw extensively on 'experience' and expertise in the decision making process. In this study, for those who have experience of backpacking, the experiential element is the most important and there is a suggestion that tour operators and travel agents do not have the additional expertise necessary to help them to make informed choices. The rejection of institutionalised support at the pre-travel phase might also be interpreted as an endorsement of Cohen's (1972) drifter category. This rejection of support alongside inexperienced backpacker reliance on the (perceived) 'expertise' of the agents may well have an important bearing on the potential for the incubation of an adverse event.

Another finding to emerge from this exploratory study is, perhaps not surprisingly, that war and political instability proved to be the most influential risks to pre-travel decisions. Regardless of travel history, no respondent

would visit a war zone or destination on the verge of war. What is significant though is the varying pattern of destinations mentioned. Iraq, Iran and the Middle East were all commonly associated with war, much to the exclusion of many other destinations. This pattern of responses endorses the earlier claim by Enders, Sandler and Parise (1992), reported also in Lepp and Gibson (2003), of the existence of a "generalization effect" whereby neighbouring destinations, subject to perceptions of heightened risk, albeit at a sub-conscious level, may suffer economic consequences of this perceived risk.

Respondents also spoke of the importance of varying degrees of political instability as a factor shaping travel behaviour. Endorsing the work of Carter (1998), Westernised and developed destinations such as Europe, Australia and New Zealand were seen to be politically stable environments to visit. Interestingly those respondents who acknowledged the political vulnerability of some central and eastern European destinations often saw this as a motive to visit. This pattern of responses sends out confusing signals as, contrary to our earlier observations, it suggests backpackers as more comfortable with familiarity than novelty, as explorers rather than drifters when perceptions of political risk are heightened.

Of the remaining hazard types, the relationship between terrorism and tourist roles provides possibly the most interesting finding. Overall terrorism was identified as the least significant risk influencing the decision making process, respondents conscious that threats exist at home not just abroad. These findings are particularly difficult to interpret. The widening net of criminal and terrorist activities appears to have prompted the emergence of a de-sensitised consumer who seeks novel experiences where novel is actually represented by the absence of terrorism. To explore the explorer/drifter role further, the reasoning behind this mindset requires further exploration. Questioning the sense of familiarity prompted as a consequence of the Global War on Terror might present one way forward.

Of the two remaining risk areas, respondents voiced most concern in relation to health matters, in particular the risk of disease as a significant factor influencing the decision-making process. Interestingly, established health risks, those *familiar* to the respondent presented less of a threat than ad hoc *novel* occurrences. This once again questions the backpacker resolve suggesting more of an explorer rather than drifter role in this context. In contrast, natural disasters were considered unpredictable, uncommon and not worth worrying about. It would be interesting to explore further whether respondent ambivalence is reflective of the intrinsic association of such crises as presenting remote or novel risks, risks commonly recognised as an integral part of drifter tourism.

Overall, what this research has indicated is that the perceptions of even one tourism segment may differ concerning the nature of the risks associated with travel destinations. As an exploratory study, this research raises more questions than it answers. What it does attempt to do is to contribute further to the debate regarding how youth travellers perceive, and are influenced by, risk when making travel decisions. It also attempts to add to the body of literature developing in the tourist roles arena, if only to once again qualify the complexity of conducting research in this area and the need for further targeted work.

NOTE

1. There has been considerable debate within the literature over the precise meaning of a 'disaster.' For the purposes of our present discussions, a disaster will be considered to have a geo-physical trigger (e.g., earthquakes, tsunami, disease outbreak, etc.), thus differentiating it from the wider concept of a crisis.

REFERENCES

Browne, D. (2004). *Spain bounces back from Madrid bombings* Retrieved April 12, 2004, from http://www.travelmole.com/news.

Buckley, G. (2004). *Holiday*. [Television]. London: BBC. [Shown 20/12/04 BBC 1].

Carter, S. (1998). Tourists' and travellers' social construction of Africa and Asia as risky locations. *Tourism Management*, 19, 349-358.

Cavlek, N. (2002). Tour Operators and Destination Safety. *Annals of Tourism Research*, 29(2), 478-296.

Cohen, E. (1972). Towards a Sociology of International Tourism. *Sociological Research*, 39, 164-182.

Cohen, E. (2004). Backpacking: Diversity and Change. In: G. Richards, & J. Wilson (Eds.), *The Global Nomad: Backpacker Travel in Theory and Practice* (pp. 43-59). Clevedon: Channel View.

Cooper, C., Fletcher, J., Fyall, A., Gilbert, D., & Wanhill, S. (2005). *Tourism. Principles and Practice* (3rd Edn). Harlow: Pearson Education Ltd.

Enders, W., Sandler, T., & Parise, G. (1992). An Econometric Analysis of the Impact of Terrorism on Tourism. *Kyklos*, 45, 531-554.

FIYTO (Federation of International Youth Travel Organisations) (2006). *Federation of International Youth Travel Organisations*. Retrieved May 10, 2005, from http://www.fiyto.org

Floyd, M. F., Gibson, H., Pennington-Gray, L., & Thapa, B. (2003). The Effect of Risk Perceptions on Intentions to Travel in the Aftermath of September 11, 2001. In: C.M. Hall, D.J. Timothy, & D.T. Duval (Eds.), *Safety and Security in Tourism: Relationships, Management and Marketing* (pp. 19-38). New York: The Haworth Hospitality Press.

Hall, C. M., & O'Sullivan, V. (1996). Tourism, political stability and violence. In: A. Pizam., & Y. Mansfeld (Eds.), *Tourism, Crime and International Security Issues* (pp. 105-121). Chichester: John Wiley and Sons.

Hall, C.M. (2005). *Tourism. Rethinking the Social Science of Mobility*. Harlow: Pearson Education Ltd.

Khadka, N. S. (2004). *Trekkers Drawn to Nepal Rebels*. Retrieved January 2, 2005, from BBC News website: http://news.bbc.co.uk/1/hi/world/south-asia/3375091.stm.

Laws, E. & Prideaux, B. (Eds.) (2005) *Tourism Crises. Management Responses and Theoretical Insight*. London: The Haworth Hospitality Press.

Laws, E. & Prideaux, B. (2005a). Crisis Management: A Suggested Typology. In E, Laws. & B, Prideaux (Eds.), *Tourism Crises. Management Responses and Theoretical Insight* (pp. 1-8). London: The Haworth Hospitality Press.

Lepp, A., & Gibson, H. (2003). Tourist roles, perceived risk and international tourism. *Annals of Tourism Research*, 19, 606-624.

Loker-Murphy, L., & Pearce, P.L. (1995). Young Budget Travelers: Backpackers in Australia. *Annals of Tourism Research*, 22(4), 819-843.

Mintel. (2003). *Youth Travel and Backpacking–International*. Retrieved September 20, 2004 from: http://reports.mintel.com.

Mintel. (2006). *Holidays–The Impact of Terrorism and Natural Disasters–UK*. Retrieved May 9, 2006 from: http://reports.mintel.com.

Mitchell, V. W., & Greatorex, M. (1993). Risk perception and reduction in the purchase of consumer services. *The Service Industries Journal*, 13(4), 179-200.

Mitchell, V. W., & Vassos, V. (1997). Perceived risk and risk reduction in holiday purchases: A cross-cultural and gender analysis. *Journal of Euro-Marketing*, 6(3), 47.

Mitroff, I. I., Pauchant, T. C., Finney, M., & Pearson, C. (1989). Do (some) organizations cause their own crises? Culture profiles of crisis prone versus crisis prepared organizations. *Industrial Crisis Quarterly*, 3, 269-283.

Mo, C.-m., Howard, D. R., & Havitz, M. E. (1993). Testing an international tourist role typology. *Annals of Tourism Research*, 20(2), 319-335.

Mohsin, A., & Ryan, C. (2003). Backpackers in the Northern Territory of Australia–Motives, Behaviours and Satisfactions. *International Journal of Tourism Research*, 5, 113-131.

Morgan, D., & Dimmock, K. (2006). Risk Management in Outdoor Adventure Tourism. In: J.Wilks., D. Pendergast, & P. Leggat (Eds.), *Tourism in Turbulent Times* (pp. 171-184). Oxford: Elsevier Science Ltd.

O'Reilly, C.C. (2006). From Drifters to Gap Year Tourist. Mainstreaming Backpacker Travel. *Annals of Tourism Research*, 33(4), 998-1017.

Pauchant, T. C., & Mitroff, I. I. (1992). *Transforming the crisis-prone organization. Preventing individual organizational and environmental tragedies*. San Fransisco: Jossey-Bass Publishers.

Peters, M. & Pikkemaat, B. (2005). Crisis Management in Alpine Winter Sports Resorts–The 1999 Avalanche Disaster in Tyrol. *Journal of Travel and Tourism Marketing*, 19(2/3), 9-20.

Pizam, A., & Mansfeld, Y. (Eds.) (1996). *Tourism, Crime and International Security Issues,* Chichester: John Wiley and Sons.

Reason, J. T. (1990). *Human error*. Oxford: Oxford University Press.

Reason, J. T. (1997). *Managing the risks of organizational accidents*. Aldershot: Ashgate.

Richter, L., & Waugh, L. (1986). Terrorism and Tourism as Logical Companions. *Tourism Management*, 7, 111-119.

Saunders, M., Lewis, P., & Thornhill, A. (2003). *Research Methods for Business Students*. Harlow: Pearson Education Ltd.

Sonmez, S., & Graefe, A. (1998). Influence of Terrorism Risk on Foreign Tourism Decisions. *Annals of Tourism Research*, 25(1), 112-144.

Tarlow, P.E. (2006). Terrorism and Tourism. In J.Wilks, D. Pendergast, & P. Leggat (Eds.), *Tourism in Turbulent Times* (pp. 79-92). Oxford: Elsevier Science Ltd.

Turner, B. A. (1976). The organizational and inter-organizational development of disasters. *Administrative Science Quarterly*, 21, 378-397.

Turner, B. A. (1978). *Man-made disasters*. London: Wykeham.

Uriely, N., Yonay, Y., & Simchai, D. (2002). Backpacking Experiences. A Type and Form Analysis. *Annals of Tourism Research*, 29(2), 520-538.

Wilder-Smith, A. (2006). Tourism and SARS. In: J.Wilks, D. Pendergast, & P. Leggat (Eds.), *Tourism in Turbulent Times* (pp. 53-61). Oxford: Elsevier Science Ltd.

Wilks, J., & Page, S. (Eds.) (2003). *Managing Tourist Health and Safety in the New Millennium*, Oxford: Elsevier Science Ltd.

Crisis Management in Tourism: Preparing for Recovery

Christof Pforr

Peter J Hosie

SUMMARY. Anticipating and preparing to deal with the threat of crises precipitated by disaster from natural and people-made catastrophes is an important challenge facing tourism. As an industry tourism is particularly susceptible to such negative events putting the sector under almost constant threat of a crisis. Before the catastrophes of 9/11 and the Asian Tsunami of 2004 crisis management in tourism was essentially a reactive response, as opposed to a state of proactive anticipation. A review of the emerging literature on crisis management in tourism is given to identify the foci of the current academic discourse. More systematic input by human resource management was identified as a way to assist tourism businesses in preparing for and dealing with crises. By discussing crisis management within a services management context, a contribution is made to the debate on the need for proactive crisis management within the tourism industry. A central plank to this position is that the preparation stage of crisis management in tourism is the actual beginning of any strategic response to recovery. Well conceived and executed human development is promoted as an initiative and key component of crisis preparation and management. Developing the potential of human capital at the industry and enterprise level to deal with crisis management is a way of reducing the vulnerability of tourism enterprises to crises. Measures are suggested that may be taken to prepare tourism businesses for crisis situations.

INTRODUCTION

The globalization of business and international communications has led to crises rapidly achieving considerable prominence. Tourism is an industry which is highly susceptible to negative events and, since there is always a crisis somewhere in the world, the sector appears to be under an almost permanent threat of yet another crisis looming. As McKercher and Hui (2004: 101) observed, crises are inevitable, "episodic events that disrupt the tourism and hospitality industry on a regular basis." Coles (2004: 178) added "when not in crisis, destina-

Christof Pforr (E-mail: Christof.Pforr@cbs.curtin.edu.au) is Research Director and Senior Lecturer, Tourism Management, in the School of Management at Curtin University of Technology, Perth, WA 6845 Australia. Peter J Hosie (E-mail: p.hosie@curtin.edu.au), is a Adjunct Senior Fellow in the School of Management at Curtin Business School at Curtin University of Technology, Perth, WA 6845 Australia.

tions are in an extended program of practically pre-event limbo, almost waiting for the important trigger event to take place."

As crises in tourism are not a new phenomenon, perhaps only our perception of such threats have changed. Maybe it just the recent frequency of these negative events, which has brought 'crisis' to the media headlines and also to the forefront of our consciousness. Possibly this is attributable to our sense of an increase in the frequency and intensity of crises, as it seems as though the half life between the occurrence of catastrophes is constantly shortening. Global mass communication's penchant for rapidly sensationalizing negative events might also contribute to why crises are embedded in our consciousness. Whatever the underlying reason for crises having so much prominence, this heightened sensitivity serves to engender fear in potential tourists by increasing perceptions of personal risk.

Tourism brings considerable commercial benefits to enterprises and also generates extensive economic activity. The enormous growth of international tourism in the past 50 years, partly as a consequence of technological advancements in transportation, has resulted in a much stronger interconnectedness and complexity within the tourism system. Hence, this has made the industry in many regions around the world an important factor in their socio-economic development. Tourism is now in the 'big business' league based on more than one billion international tourists (WTO, 2006).

According to the World Tourism Organization (2006), an estimated $US 682 billion was spent by tourists in 2005, up by $US 49 billion or 3.4% on the previous year. Global spending on tourism is estimated to average more than $US 2 billion a day, an increase of $US 49 billion on 2005. When the spending on foreign passenger transportation of $US 130 billion is added, the total expenditure generated by tourism is more than $US 800 billion which represents some 6% of global export of all goods and services (WTO, 2006). Consequently, crises are likely to have a much stronger negative impact compared to the past and will affect a much larger portion of the population. Considering the enormous economic value of tourism it is no surprise that a heightened sensitivity and

concern for crisis management in the sector has emerged.

Travel is a particularly volatile sector of the tourism business which is inherently susceptible to external shocks. Competently managed organizations should therefore prepare for potential risks to their establishments in particular and industry in general. Part of this preparation takes the form of developing well considered managerial responses beginning with formulation and execution of the strategic planning processes. A host of internal and external factors in the travel industry are capable of creating a crisis which can have unpredictable impacts on the demand for travel. As such, crises of many complexions are bound to occur in this industry. Gurtner (2005: 197) considered that "[g]iven the sensitivity of the tourism industry and its strong reliance on perceptions of safety, security and stability", the "prospective remuneration on effective crisis management has made it topical amongst relevant authorities and stakeholders." Thus, there is an obvious need and demand 'on the ground' for guidance and strategies how to deal with crises in the tourism industry.

Despite an increase in activity in the past years, there are, in comparison, still only a few publications on crisis management specifically in the field of tourism, which discuss the concept systematically and holistically (e.g., Beirman, 2003; Dreyer, Dreyer, & Obieglo, 2001; Faulkner, 2001; Glaesser, 2003, 2006; Henderson, 2004; Mansfeld & Pizam, 2006; Santana, 2004). Ritchie (2004: 680) noted that a "small but growing body of research on crisis and disaster management has been conducted in the tourism industry. This may be due, in part, to the chaotic and complex nature of these incidents and an inability by some managers and researchers to understand such phenomena." A more systematic and robust conceptual approach has long been overdue to questions such as how tourism businesses react to crisis, which measures are taken and what impact they have, how businesses can prepare for such situations, and which strategies can be employed to deal with and to overcome crises.

There are *four* distinct aspects to this paper. The *first* part reviews the literature on crisis management in tourism in order to identify the foci of the current academic discourse which is mainly informed by the management and marketing literature. In the *second* part a discussion is undertaken of the management literature on crisis management. An important aspect of this investigation is the identification of models of crisis management suitable for applying to tourism. A particular emphasis is given in the *third* part to human resource management (HRM) and the application of human resource development (HRD) as a service. The *fourth* part concerns the intersection of the pertinent issues from the crisis management literature in tourism with the emerging role of HRD in preparing for crisis management. A contribution is made to this field by locating the common elements between these disciplines and suggesting how these may be usefully integrated. A natural fit was evident between crisis management literature in tourism and the application of HRD to prepare for crisis management. The central argument made in this paper is that preparation for any potential crisis in tourism is a strategic key to recovery, where preparation is seen as an integral part of any crisis recovery phase.

Tourism is conceived of and referred to in this paper from a macro perspective, as an industry sector rather than an individual enterprise. International and national enterprises are more likely to have access to designated HRM expertise which will not be available to smaller scale operation. It is worth noting that many tourism enterprises do not necessarily have formerly designated HRM departments. Smaller scale operations would need to draw on the advice and expertise from government and industry bodies when initiating HRM planning to deal with crises.

AN OVERVIEW OF CRISIS MANAGEMENT IN TOURISM

A growing sensitivity and awareness towards crisis in the tourism industry is indicated by a sharp increase in the number of publications in the past five years dealing with crisis management in the field of tourism. In this context 'preparedness' and 'sensibilization' and the 'initial response' to crises are core themes where communication, information and confidence in the destination are vital to effectively

managing a crisis. In particular, industry associations and government authorities, for example the World Tourism Organization and the Pacific Asia Travel Association, have taken a leadership role, although these are more concerned with reactive crisis management, than with the development of specific response patterns, resulting in practical advice on how to respond to a crisis. Many South East Asian countries, for instance, have shown a preference for reactive crisis management as opposed to proactive planning (Chien & Law, 2003; De Sausmarez, 2004; Henderson, 1999a, 2003a, 2003b). This government driven approach is very context specific with its focus on a particular destination and an emphasis on information and communication management to foster effective coordination and collaboration amongst the relevant stakeholders.

For Cushnahan (2004) such a contextualization of crisis management is crucial as it highlights the importance of customizing crisis management approaches. Similarly, Ritchie, Dorell, Miller and Miller (2004: 202), in line with Coombs (1999), noticed that "all crises are different and crisis managers need to tailor responses to individual crisis, rather than try to plan for every individual situation." Thus, it becomes clear that crisis management strategies have to be positioned in the context of the respective environment of socio-cultural, economic, political, historic and physical characteristics. Common measures of reactive crisis management in the past have included government aid packages (e.g., for the accommodation and transport sectors), the promotion of domestic tourism and in particular the marketing of specific niche products as well as the development of new forms of tourism, such as sustainable tourism and ecotourism (Henderson, 2002a; 2003a). For example, a comparative case study between Thailand and Indonesia, revealed that crisis recovery can be enhanced by strong, good infrastructure and aggressive marketing (i.e., Thailand) while additional problems such as social and political instability (i.e., Indonesia) had the opposite effect (Henderson, 1999b).

Coordination and collaboration between key stakeholders also appear to be crucial for the effective management of a crisis situation (Henderson, 2003a; King, 2000; McKercher &

Chon, 2004). Santana (2004) emphasized the significant role played by the media in the associated information management and communication processes in the aftermath of a crisis. A positive relationship with the mass media is specifically regarded as critical in the recovery phase to maintain destination image. In this context Ritchie et al. (2004) considered that it is particularly important to manage communication and perceptions through a well considered crisis communication and marketing strategy. Part of such a strategic approach to communications involves the establishment of a common language to define and describe a crisis.

SEMANTICS OF DISASTER AND CRISIS

A clear, accessible and agreed upon definition of crises is lacking in the literature. Several authors have attempted to define a crisis and have come up with a variety of terms and concepts often used synonymously (e.g., Faulkner, 2001; Glaesser, 2003; Pender & Sharpley, 2004; Pizam, 1999; Prideaux, Laws & Faulkner, 2003). More prominent examples include disaster, negative event, catastrophe, problem or turning point, risk, chaos, vulnerability, safety and security. Considering this diversity it is therefore no surprise that a definitional approach to crisis appears to be a difficult undertaking. In an attempt to provide an insight in the complexity of the discourse Santana (2004: 307) concluded that "the literature provides no generally accepted definition of crisis and attempts to categorize types or forms of crises have been sparse." Some authors remain fairly vague and provide more generalized statements of the nature of crises. For example, Ritchie et al. (2004: 202) posited that "crises are indefinite, numerous, unexpected and unpredictable" and Prideaux (2004: 282) stated that "[h]istory tells us that disasters and crises are usually unforeseen, occur regularly, act as a shock on the tourism industry and are always poorly handled." Other commentators use more precise semantics. Of these, Faulkner (2001: 136) differentiated between the terms crisis and disaster and argued that a crisis describes a situation "where the root cause of an event is, to some extent, self inflicted through

such problems as inept management structures and practices or a failure to adapt to change," while a disaster can be defined as a situation "where an enterprise . . . is confronted with sudden unpredictable catastrophic changes over which it has little control." McKercher and Hui (2004) referred to disasters as either natural events such as floods, typhoons and earthquakes or as human induced events (war and terrorism). In the context of tourism Coles (2004, p. 175) added that these

> [e]vents unfold at a variety of spatial scales that impact on local tourism sectors and can cause temporal market disturbances of varying duration . . . Such events take a variety of forms from natural landscape disasters to episodes of famine, disease and pestilence to wars, terrorist atrocities and political instability.

Thus, crises arising either within (endogenous) or outside (exogenous) the tourism sector can have a significant impact on tourism often seemingly beyond the control of its managers and executives (Brookfield, 1999; Sonnenberg & Wöhler, 2004).

There is a need to establish common ground on the conceptualization and definition of disasters and the crises they precipitate. In general terms, disasters may be defined as "multi-level, complex and damaging systems related events that unfold over time and space, through an emergent complex interaction of elements, involving structures, connection and networks and which are shaped by ideological, economic and social factors to generate impacts on elements of society that change the performance of the 'normal' order of the societal setting" (Smith, 2003, p. 11). Such negative events can take many forms including accidental and deliberate causes, initiated from internally as well as externally to the tourism industry. Not only do deliberate acts have considerable impact on tourism, major economic events like the Asian economic crisis in 1997 can also have a profound negative effect. Such shocks, either natural, people-made or a hybrid of these, should be viewed as an important concern of vigilant managers in the tourism industry as they can rapidly lead to crisis if managers are not equipped or have the wherewithal to take timely and decisive action (Evans & Elphick, 2005).

Natural disasters come in many forms–storms, floods, tsunamis, fires, volcanic eruptions, avalanches, hurricanes, typhoons and epidemics. Crises precipitated by disasters, such as the Tsunami in 2004, which affected large parts of coastal South East Asia or the severe bush fires in Australia's capital Canberra (2002) and Cyclone Katrina in New Orleans (2005), often occur without warning, with effects that are severe and sometimes catastrophic on the government and business communities. Conversely, disasters attributable to people, can emanate from accidents and hostile acts, such as fires, arson, explosions, political upheaval, riots, insurgency, disease, crime, terrorism or war. Acts of terrorism, for instance, have had major effects on tourism destinations. Such acts may be defined as "a systematic and persistent strategy practiced by a state or political group against another state or group through a campaign of acts of violence . . . to achieve political, social or religious ends" (Pizam & Smith, 2000, p. 123). These 'shadowy, mobile, and unpredictable' forces have become an integral part of travel and tourism, particularly in an international context (Pizam & Smith, 2000). Over the past 20 years, terrorism and serious criminal activities have impacted heavily on the tourism industry in Paris (1986), Tel Aviv (1990), Kenya and Tanzania (1998), Kenya (2001), New York and Washington (2001), Bali (2002 and 2005), Madrid (2004), Jakarta (2003), Morocco, Saudi Arabia (2003/2004), London in 2005 and, most recently, in Egypt (2006) and Mumbai (2006). Evans and Elphick (2005) noted that during the Gulf War in 1991 the countries in the Middle East and the eastern Mediterranean suffered a severe decline in the number of tourist visits, a scenario repeated by the attacks in Dahab, Egypt in 2006.

In 2006, the perennial hot spots of conflict, Israel and Lebanon, are once again at war. The terrorist bombings in London in July 2005 during the European peak holiday season and again on Bali in October of the same year also had a devastating effect on tourism in these regions. A quantitative analysis of major international terrorism events during the period from 1985 to 1998 by Pizam and Smith (2000) documented the severity of damage, motive, effect on tour-

ism demand and length of this effect. Wider lessons for the travel industry were found by Pizam and Smith (2000, p. 135) to include the need to "integrate crisis management with strategic planning processes, prepare detailed contingency plans, define decisional roles and responsibilities, and to retain a degree of flexibility." A similar review for the period 1998 to 2006 would probably reveal a dramatic increase in the incidence of international terrorism events.

Moreover, health related threats, such as the Severe Acute Respiratory Syndrome (SARS) and Avarian (bird) flu epidemics in South East Asia (in 2003 / 2004), as well as the foot and mouth outbreak in Britain in 2001 (Coles, 2004; Frisby, 2002), have severely impacted on tourist mobility. The negative consequences of crises for the tourism industry are often felt in destinations far away from where they have taken place. In the context of SARS, for instance, Hall, Timothy and Duval (2004, p. 2) argued that it "was not only spread internationally through modern aviation services but also resulted in a number of countries issuing travel warnings regarding travel to some destinations in East Asia and health security measures at their own borders."

From these negative events a pattern of tourist behavior has emerged suggesting that an increase in perceived risk associated with a destination is reciprocal to its demand (Floyed, Gibson, Pennington-Gray & Thapa, 2004). However, McKercher and Hui (2004, p. 102) have emphasized that "[f]ortunately, most tourists have relatively short memories and will resume travelling when they feel the immediate threat has passed. As a result, history suggests that disasters tend to have no lasting impact on tourist flows." While the tumultuous past years confirm that disruptions definitely have affected travel destinations in the short term, this has not altered global or regional traffic flows, which indicate that tourism consumer confidence remains high (WTO, 2006). This continuing demand may be explained by a displacement effect. Tourists may be well be choosing safer destinations and avoiding areas of perceived danger. Despite the resilience of tourists to negative events there is still probably a threshold limit to the amount of risk that can be absorbed before travel will be adversely affected. These events are by their nature unpredictable in relation to their geographical location, timing and scale and hence provide unforeseen problems for tourism industry managers.

CRISIS MANAGEMENT AND RESPONSE IN TOURISM

Santana (2004, p. 318) has argued that a "crisis is not an event. It is a process that develops in its own logic." Some authors position these negative events at the centre of crisis management.

A clear, concise and accepted definition of crisis management in the literature is yet to emerge. Glaesser (2003, 2005) argued that the common ground established so far is, at best, an agreement on the underlying processes. These are usually subdivided in two or three stages, either crisis prevention and crises coping or crisis precaution, crisis avoidance and crisis coping. For Peters and Pikkemaat (2006, p. 10) "[c]risis management in tourism deals with the recognition of crisis within the destination and the recovery and rebuilding after crisis." This classification represents a broadly based interpretation of what constitutes a crisis. Santana (2004, p. 308), however, has suggested a more encompassing interpretation of the concept:

> Crisis management can be defined as an ongoing integrated and comprehensive effort that organizations effectively put into place in an attempt to first and foremost understand and prevent crisis, and to effectively manage those that occur, taking into account in each and every step of their planning and training activities, the interest of their stakeholders.

A crisis presents a risk to an establishment, putting the assets of people, information, and property of an organization under threat (Caudron, 2002). Assets invariably have local, national and international significance and accordingly are an important consideration for the protection of the tourism system. Crises in tourism are by their nature very complex and not well understood as tourism is susceptible to host of internal and external dynamics (Henderson,

2006). While the importance of crisis management in tourism is self evident, nonetheless questions remain about what constitutes a crisis in the first place and if there is consensus in the debate of how to manage a crisis.

In the context of this debate, crisis management has emerged as an integral part of contemporary tourism business (e.g., Goodrich, 2002; Henderson, 2002a; Tate, 2002). The majority of accounts dealing with the phenomenon focuses on particular events or issues, such as the impact of negative events on specific sectors within the tourism and hospitality industry, for instance hotels (Chien & Law, 2003; Henderson, 2003a; Henderson & Ng, 2004; Israeli & Reichal, 2003), restaurants (Green, Bartholomew & Murman, 2004) and travel agents (Lovelock, 2004), but most frequently the airline industry (Aderighi & Cento, 2004; Henderson, 2003b; Ray, 1999; Gillen & Wall, 2003). Another theme evident in the literature concentrates on communication, information management and the powerful role of mass media in crisis in the aftermath of a major negative event (Glaeßer, 2005; Santana, 2004; Hall, 2002; Mason, Grabowski & Du, 2005). The reporting of risk factors pertinent to tourism, such as war and political instability, health concerns, crime, terrorism and natural disasters appear to be particularly powerful in influencing tourist destination choices (Floyed et al., 2004). As McKercher and Hui (2004, p. 102) stated, "[o]f course, media coverage influences psychological proximity." Hall et al. (2004, p. 2) argued in this context that "[t]ourist behaviour and, consequently, destinations, are deeply affected by perceptions of security and the management of safety, security and risk."

Furthermore, crisis management is also discussed within a specific geographic context. South East Asia appears to be taking centre stage with a focus on the financial crisis in South East Asia (Henderson, 1999a; 1999b; King, 2000) and health related threats such as SARS (Chien & Law, 2003; Henderson, 2003a; Henderson & Ng, 2004; Mason et al., 2005; McKercher & Hui, 2004). Hong Kong, Singapore and Malaysia have emerged as the main regions being studied. In an Australian context, particular natural disasters such as the Katherine floods (Faulkner & Vikulov, 2001) or the Canberra bush fires (Armstrong & Ritchie,

2005) have dominated the recent debate in the literature on crisis management. However, terrorism and political instability also appear to be an issue of concern with Bali (Henderson, 2002b; Hitchcock, 2001) but also more traditional political hot spots such as Egypt (Aziz, 1995) and Israel (Israeli & Reichal, 2003; Mansfield, 1999) having received particular attention. Following 'September 11' as a key crisis, the United States is frequently used as a prompt for discussing crisis management in tourism (Blake & Sinclair, 2003; Stafford, Yu, & Armoo, 2002; Fall, 2004; Taylor & Enz, 2002). Aktas and Gunlu (2005, p. 445) took a different approach, classifying some of the above events as politically motivated threats, economic, socio-cultural, environmental or technological crises with varying degrees of impact, scope and duration. Whatever the cause, these events have had a sudden and unanticipated effect of tourism destinations.

Crises emanating from unexpected events require specific arrangements or specific actions by organizations. As a result, "effective crisis management requires organizational responses which are outside a firm's ordinary repertoire of management activities" (Reilly 1993, p. 45). Rises in the incidence of global terrorism and major criminal activities, when combined with the omnipresent threat of natural catastrophes, are driving the need for high quality preparation to manage crises. Terrorist threats and natural catastrophes are high on the agenda for these never before experienced events, and consequently, the application of a well considered response strategy is a vital component of crisis management planning. The ability to successfully deal with a disaster is an important management competency which determines the capacity to avoid or reduce the consequences of the impact of the ensuing crisis.

Essentially, crisis management planning in tourism is about preparing for events that the organization has normally not previously experienced. Two approaches to crisis management have been identified by Pauchant and Mitroff (1992). First is the *proactive* stage which takes place before a crisis when, as a result of careful monitoring, a potential crisis is recognized and attempts are made to avoid the problem altogether or at least to minimize the consequences.

Second, the *reactive* approach is about crisis management after the actual crisis has occurred. Containing any damage is the priority to ensure the organization returns to stasis, a state of stability, in which all forces are equal and opposing and will therefore neutralize each other. A proactive approach to preparing for and managing crises is arguably more effective than the passive approach often evident in tourism business. Such a position is informed by different crisis management models.

CRISIS MANAGEMENT MODELS

There are several crisis management models identified in the literature, such as by Evans and Elphick (2005), Caplan (1970), Arnold (1980), Slatter (1984), Smith (1990) and Booth (1993). Seymour and Moore (2000), and Clarke and Varma (2004) have distinguished two crisis typologies, the 'Cobra' and 'Python' descriptors. A Cobra crisis is typified by a sudden disaster, such as 9/11, and a Python crisis gradually creeps up on an organization, such as poor quality or high costs. A Cobra crisis essentially leads to a defensive response which relies on a known and trusted approach, whereas a Python crisis triggers a bureaucratic approach, where a crisis is not identified, but is negotiated when recognized. Lessons to be learned from previous crises experience using these typologies include, according to Evans and Elphick (2005, p. 148), the preparation of detailed contingency plans, the definition of decisional and informational roles and responsibilities and the retaining of a degree of flexibility in order to react swiftly and decisively at an operational level without being tempted to rush into more strategic level decision-making. According to Heath (1998), crisis management should broadly aim to plan and provide for possible crisis events which may occur (the pre-crisis stage), to reduce or mitigate the impacts of a crisis by improving the response management (the crisis stage) and to swiftly and effectively determine the damage caused by a crisis (the post-crisis stage).

Of the crisis management models discussed in the literature, Faulkner's (2001, p. 44) Tourism Disaster Management Framework can be regarded as one of the most appropriate for systematically analyzing crisis management processes in tourism. Crisis management is segregated by Faulkner into a *pre-event phase*, when disaster contingency plans are developed and scenarios and probability assessment studies are undertaken. During this phase it may still be possible to avert or minimise a disaster before reaching the so-called *prodromal phase*, where avoidance is no longer possible and the previously developed contingency plans need to be activated. During the *emergency phase* the disaster's effects precipitate actions to protect people and property in the tourism destination. Short-term and immediate needs of people have to be addressed by emergency and rescue teams in the *intermediate phase*, during which a clear media communication strategy is also crucial. In the *recovery phase* a more long-term perspective is taken where affected areas and damaged infrastructure will need to be rebuilt. Finally, during the *resolution phase*, the crisis management process is evaluated and improved if necessary. This connects resolution and review to an ongoing strategy of risk assessment and includes contingency planning as a basis for managing future crises. Unfortunately, events do not always unfold in such a logical sequence and this leads to inadequate time to prepare for avoiding crisis and a neglect of contingency planning. Overall Faulkner's (2001) framework is an appropriate schema for analyzing complex crisis management steps in natural and people-made disasters in tourism. Nevertheless, the unanticipated crises can and do occur and those involved are often forced to confront the situations without the help of any formal guidelines or prior experience or preparation.

Henderson (2006) has applied Faulkner's model to the terrorist attack on Bali in 2002. The crisis was found to have commenced at the emergency phase and progressed quickly to the intermediate phase. A turning point was found to be reached when international daily arrivals stabilized and exceeded departures which signaled the beginning of the long-term (recovery) phase. However, the resolution of the crisis still remained a distant reality. Predictably, the initial response to the crisis was action followed by the pursuit of recovery. Imperatives which followed included the rebuilding of the physical environment and destination image, which were accompanied by a re-evaluation of target markets, which is still in progress. No evidence was detected by Henderson of any formal attempts to identify threats or devise plans preceding the attacks. Also, the Bali bombings do not seem to have increased awareness of the need to prepare for future attacks although, as Henderson highlighted, advance planning is critical for dealing with terrorist attacks due to the limited duration of the *prodromal phase* when terrorists have struck.

Another model of crisis management developed by Smith (1990) has been further extended by Smith and Sipika (1993). There are three distinct aspects to their crisis management process, *crisis of management*, *operational crisis* and *crisis of legitimation*. It enables the stages of crises to be tracked and adds to Faulkner's model by including the critical role of learning in crisis management. A feedback loop represents the resolution of the crisis and allows for lessons to be learned (double loop learning) before organizations are able to return to the pre-crisis stage. The first *pre-crisis period* (equivalent to Faulkners' *pre-event phase*) of Evans and Elphic's model (2006) concentrated on raising the awareness of employees and management of the potential scenarios that may occur. An application of this model of crisis management to a UK tour operator provided a good illustration of its potential utility (Evans & Elphick, 2005).

Western organizations concerned with crisis management have consistently adopted a four-stage model, such as the MPRR (mitigation, preparation, response, recovery), or the PPRR (prevention, preparation, response, recovery) as shown in Figure 1 (Heath, 1993). Both the MPRR and PPRR are iterative models and intended to provide ongoing opportunities for learning. HRD focusing on crisis management relates closely to the 'preparation' aspect of both the MPRR and the PPRR models. The prevention, preparation, response and recovery aspects of the latter depict a flow of events, which can be applied to many tourism-relevant areas, such as organizations and infrastructure. The sequence logically begins with the 'preparation' phase, equivalent to Faulkner's (2001) pre-event phase, which is emphasized as the component of management that can actively be promoted in organizations through HRD. Pre-

FIGURE 1. The PPRR Crisis Management Model (Hosie & Smith, 2004)

Hosie, P. and Smith, C. (2004). Preparing for crisis: Online security management education. Research and Practice in Human Resource Management, 12(2): 90-127. Used with permission.

paredness is integral to crisis management as it forms the foundation upon which recovery of the operation can occur. However, as stochastic events like 9/11 have shown crisis management may actually begin with a 'response,' when the 'preparation phase' is inadequate. As such, the preparation, response and recovery elements of this crisis management model are interrelated and, therefore, have a crucial relationship to the 'learning' purpose. Learning is therefore an axiomatic and critical recurrent feature of this model.

Some years back, Meyers and Holusha (1986, p. 22) suggested that the "essential point of crisis management is to break the sequence of the unmanaged crisis and to redirect events. Proper preparation can prevent some crises and minimize the impact of those which cannot be avoided." Regrettably, 18 years later De Sausmarez (2004, p. 158) observed that "few countries appear to make any advance preparations or provision for their tourism sectors in anticipation of a crisis. Instead, they tend to wait until after the event before starting to consider what action to take." One exception is Nankervis' (2000) integrated framework for the assessment of tourism vulnerability to a possible crisis at sectoral, organizational and

individual levels and the extent and duration of such impacts. This model includes threats and opportunities to tourism in the political, economic, social, physical and commercial arena. Nankervis' model goes some way towards systematically capturing and interpreting the macro and micro complexity of crisis situations in tourism. One way of reducing the vulnerability is to recognize the capacity to build human resource capital to deal with crisis management.

CRISIS MANAGEMENT AND HRD

Contemporary conceptualizations of crisis management need to be able to deal with broader issues of prevention and mitigation, as well as with issues related to response and recovery (Heck 1991; Rosental & Pijnenberg, 1991). Terrorist acts during the early years of the 21st century, for instance, have focused the attention of organizations on how to manage crises. Corporate initiatives to learn from these events have stemmed from the realization that senior management needs to be better prepared for such acts. Effective managerial response to crises in organizations is crucial for effective institutional functioning as disruptions to the operation of employees and establishments can dramatically impinge on corporate productivity. Corporations and governments have a moral and legal responsibility to ensure that their employees have been provided with appropriate HRD to undertake their work safely, to avoid compensation and risk liabilities (Hosie, 1993, 1994). Attacks on the people, information, and property of organizations can be prevented or their impact can be minimized through a well conceived and systematically tested crisis management plan. This approach serves to lay the foundation for conceiving crisis management as a service industry to protect people and organizations.

Implicit in preparing for extraordinary events is the realization that organizations need to be prepared for crises that may be anticipated but also those that are yet to be experienced. HRM professionals also have a critical role to play in assessing the corporate culture, and in particular how much denial there is about the need for crisis management HRD at all levels of an organization. An important part of these systems and activities involves initiating targeted HRD of key personnel. Crisis leadership principles should be promoted by HRM professionals as a key aspect of crisis management (Mitroff, 2004). Such planning should involve quality HRD initiatives to maximize the power of human capital available to organizations, conceived of within a services management framework. At the industry level this may take the form of developing policies and guidelines for distribution to a wider spectrum of smaller tourist enterprises. Specifically trained HRD specialists may also be funded and deployed by national tourism agencies. Attention has been focused on the necessity for the professional HRD of personnel in security technology, security management, and security risk for government, private organizations, and community services (Caudron, 2002; Smith, 2001; Smith, 2002a). Consequently, organizations now require high quality security and risk HRD programs in order to exercise crisis management strategies. In Mitroff's view there is potential for HRM professionals to take a more active role in crisis management, provided that they understand the phenomena and are motivated to take on this role. To become proactive in crisis management it is necessary to change an organization's corporate culture (Mitroff, 2004). Proactive companies, it is argued, have a tendency to follow the principle of not harming any individual to guide their conduct. In contrast, reactive corporations, do what is right, but only if it is cost effective. Ironically, Mitroff (2004) has argued that reactive companies, whose foremost concern is making money– without regard for employee and client wellbeing– invariably end up being less profitable. Thus, resources invested in HRD initiatives to change corporate culture related to crisis management ultimately pay off from both an ethical and business perspective.

It is argued here that HRD is an important aspect of any well conceived and executed preparation for crisis management. HRD refers to "the integrated use of training and development, organization development, and career development to improve individual, group and organizational effectiveness" (McLagan, 1989, p. 3). These activities and processes are intended to have impact on organizational and individual learning (Steward & McGoldrick, 1996, p. 1). An important aspect of HRD is therefore training, which is a "planned process focused on changing knowledge, skills or attitudes to achieve identified and measurable outcomes" (Tovey & Lawlor, 2004, p. 25). Such preparation in the form of deep and double loop learning has become increasingly important to industry and governments of all persuasions. Deep learning experiences are achieved by integrating crisis management concepts and practices to support the crisis management model adopted. Such learning is logically situated within the context of the crisis management literature.

The role of iterative and deep learning is crucial to crisis management as it provides the means through which organizational processes and outcomes can be achieved (Smith, 2001). Richardson (1994) distinguishes between single and double loop learning taking into consideration learning approaches in relation to crisis management. Single loop learning refers to learning from the managerial responses themselves in line with the accepted framework of an organization's objectives and roles. In contrast, double loop learning actually questions the implicit systems, roles and objectives within an organization in relation to response to the crisis to envisage new scenarios. Double loop learning provides a more rigorous and wide ranging basis for future strategic changes that may sometimes be contrary to an organization's cultural norms. Double loop learning needs to be embedded into every cycle of an organization's crisis management process to ensure that deep learning and subsequent change occur in management policies and practices. Organizational learning resulting from double loop learning is therefore a complex undertaking which takes time and commitment by all concerned to be achieved. Deep organizational learning is more likely to result when there is constant iterative design of learning opportunities about crisis management. Creating and maintaining a suitable organizational configuration will assist to embed the necessary culture into an organization's repartee. As such, crisis management needs to be treated as part of businesses' mainstream functions not as an ancillary activity. Part of this process is the infusion of learning about how to respond to and manage crises into the business culture. A suitable reward and incentives scheme needs to be embedded into the HRM practices to change and reinforce desirable behaviors.

In this context, successful planning involves preparing to mobilize the collective efforts of a large number of staff to react to a crisis (Harrison, 2000). Successful planning needs to fully engage the hearts and minds of as many staff as possible in preparing how to react to an actual crisis. In the pre-crisis period, organizations need to envision the potential scenarios that may occur. Although crises are likely to be unexpected it is still possible to prepare for such events by developing a well conceived crisis management contingency plan. In particular, executives and managers must drive policy development and subsequently regularly review the veracity of such plans. Preparedness for crises must become an integral part of the strategic consciousness of organizations in tourism. However, many enterprises are ill prepared for such events. Perhaps the reason organizations do not plan for crises may be attributable to the myths about planning. On the other hand, a general complacency can arise about the crisis management policies organizations employ since such plans may provide a level of comfort when the reality is that employees do not fully understand how to implement them (Bland, 1998). A state of active anticipation needs to be experienced from the shop floor to the top floor. Consequently, executives and line managers must formally allocate crisis management functions which have to be appropriately recognized and rewarded. HRM departments have hereby a critical role to play as organizations now require high quality security and risk HRD programs in order to exercise crisis management strategies as a service function for the effective management of crises.

One powerful way of testing the *pre-event* or *pre-crisis period* readiness of businesses is through simulation scenario learning. *Pre-event* disaster contingency plans can be tested by proposing a realistic risk scenario and challenging staff to implement the response phase before returning to the pre-crisis stage (*pre-event phase*). Real time scenario simulations permit staff to test the authenticity of contingency plans against key performance indicators. A capacity to manage a crisis scenario simulation may be evaluated by general performance indicators devised from the extant literature (Table 1).

One critical indicator of the preparedness of an organization for crisis is the quality and responsiveness of internal and external communications. Another broader indicator is the capacity of a corporate culture to accept feedback to ensure double loop learning occurs to adapt to future challenges. An important but vital aspect of simulation learning is the debriefing phase. Reactive and passive responses need to be excised from any responses and replaced by proactive approaches.

Developing the capacity of human capital goes beyond the provision of reactive and periodic training experiences to the necessity of keeping key personnel constantly learning. Responses to threats must be rapid, effective and well informed to avoid tragedy (Caudron, 2002). Priorities for meeting crisis change by the minute, rather than by the day, so institutions that are more efficient users of technology are likely to become 'learning organisations' (Senge 1990, Price 2001) with greater potential to survive and thrive. Effective preparation to monitor, manage and respond to crises can be orchestrated by the emerging trend to utilize appropriate learning technology. As Caudron (2002: 30) accurately observed: "technology in all its various forms has taken up a permanent and vastly more influential residence within the training function." A trend to utilize learning technologies includes videoconferencing, web conferencing, learning content management systems and the use of digital storage technologies (e.g., CD-ROMs, DVDs). Many tourism organisations are geographically disbursed making the delivery of learning using technology an efficacious way to reach employees distributed across the world. There is likely to be an increasingly rapid uptake of the use of online learning for organisations preparing for crisis management as distributed online technologies are appropriate for delivering learning in large and small enterprises. This would permit a range of tourism businesses to have ready access to critical information to avert crises in the form of consistent, high quality training on crisis management.

CONCLUSION

Tourism is very vulnerable to an enormous number of potential crises emanating from a variety of scenarios. These external shocks which

TABLE 1. Crisis Response and Management Indicators of Preparedness

Crisis management plan
° Was a detailed and realistic contingency plan available to deal with crises?
° Was the macro and micro complexity of the crisis situation systematically captured and interpreted in the political, economic, social, physical and commercial arena?
° Were decisional roles defined and responsibilities clearly described?
° Was the crisis management with the businesses integrated with the strategic planning processes?
° Was each and every step of the planning and training in the interest of the stakeholders?
° Was there an ongoing integrated and comprehensive effort to effectively understand the crisis and manage what occurs?
° Was a degree of flexibility retained to react swiftly and decisively at an operational level but not hurried for strategic level decision making?
Information and communication management
° Were communication and perceptions managed through a crisis communication and marketing strategy?
° Was information and communication management used to foster effective coordination and collaboration amongst the relevant stakeholders?
° Was any rebuilding of the physical environment and destination image accompanied by a re-evaluation of target markets?
° Was a positive relationship established and / or maintained with the mass media throughout the recovery phase?
Preparation–HRD
° Was a capacity to build human resources capital to meet crises evident?
° Was training and development used to improve individual, group and organizational effectiveness?
° Did these activities and processes have the intended impact on organizational and individual learning?
° Were crisis leadership principles developed?
Effectiveness and organizational culture
° How effective was the capacity to avoid or reduce the consequences of the impact of the ensuing crisis?
° Was a state of active anticipation experienced by all levels of staff?
° Was it possible to reduce or mitigate the impacts of the crisis (the pre-crisis stage), by improving the response management (the crisis stage) and to swiftly and effectively determine the damage to the business caused by the crisis (the post-crisis stage)?
° Did the debriefing session question the implicit systems, roles and objectives within an organization in relation to response to the crisis to envisage new scenarios?
° Was it possible to challenge organization's cultural norms?
° Is double loop learning embedded into every cycle of the crisis management process to ensure that deep learning and subsequent changes in management policies and practices occurs?

are inherently unpredictable, make the preparation to meet crises an integral part of the industry's operations. This paper began with a review of literature on crisis management in tourism which was intended to identify foci of the current academic discourse. The literature into crises management in tourism appears rather *ad hoc* and fragmented by presenting various issues in different contexts. Despite an increase in research activity driven by the frequency of negative events impacting on the tourism industry there is, however, still a considerable lack in clarity on the impact of crises on the sector (Prideaux et al., 2003). There is

also only limited scholarly activity and documentation on the development of models and frameworks of crisis management to prepare stakeholders for negative events but also guide their response when a crisis situation arises. Prideaux et al. (2003) and Faulkner (2001, p. 146) emphasize the need for more information and the necessity for a conceptual framework "to structure the cumulative development of knowledge about the impacts of, and effective responses to, tourism disasters."

As traditional indicators provide inadequate time to take remedial action, it is unrealistic to rely on identifying how to best deal with crisis by simply monitoring them *post hoc* (De Sausmarez, 2004). One key argument in this paper was therefore that proactive crisis management should form an integral part of contemporary tourism business by making a case for using preparation for any potential crisis in tourism as a strategic key to recovery. Ritchie (2004) argued along the same lines demanding proactive planning, effective implementation of strategies as well as the monitoring and evaluation of outcomes. In this context, Faulkner (2001) offered one of only few proactive and strategic crisis management approaches, the Tourism Disaster Management Framework. Other crisis management models also show promise, such as those by Nankervis (2000), Smith (1990), Smith and Sipika (1993) as well as Hosie and Smith (2004) which need to be verified or refuted with practice and hard data.

Drawing on the above it was argued here that HRD is an important aspect of any well conceived and executed preparation for crisis management. Common ground was identified in the literatures on tourism crisis management with the emerging role of HRD in preparing for crises. Particular emphasis was therefore given to the application of HRD through the HRM service function in suggesting how it may usefully be integrated to benefit tourist enterprises. An organization's capacity to respond to a crisis can have a significant impact on its short and long term survival. Developing the capacity of human capital to respond to and manage crises has become a major risk mitigation issue for organizations and nation states. Thus, resources invested in HRM initiatives to change corporate culture to deal effectively with crisis situations benefit organizations in both ethical and business perspectives (Mitroff, 2004). One way of reducing the vulnerability of tourism businesses is therefore to recognize the capacity of human capital built through HRD to deal with crises. Quality HRD initiatives should thus be a vital aspect of any crisis management strategy (Ang & Hosie, 2006).

In the future it will be of particular importance to emphasize proactive HRM strategies and subsequent application of HRD as tourism in 'post crisis' is by the nature of the industry seemingly perpetual tourism in 'pre crisis.'

REFERENCES

Aderighi, M. & Cento, A. (2004). European airlines conduct after September 11, Journal of Air Transport Management, 10: 97-107.

Aktas, G. & Gunlu, E. A. (2005). Crisis management in tourist destinations, in: W. F. Theobald (Ed.) Global Tourism (3rd ed.) (pp. 440-457). Amsterdam: Elsevier.

Armstrong, E. A. & Ritchie, B. (2005). Destination burning: Strategies for tourism industry recovery immediately after a major bushfire event. In P. Tremblay & A. Boyle (Eds.) Sharing Tourism Knowledge (pp. 12-14). Proceedings of the 2005 CAUTHE Conference, Darwin: Charles Darwin University.

Arnold, W. (1980). Crisis Communication. Gorsuch Scarisbrook: Dubuque, Iowa.

Aziz, H. (1995). Understanding attacks on tourists in Egypt, Tourism Management, 16(2): 91-95.

Beirman, D. (2003). Restoring Tourism Destinations in Crisis: A Strategic Marketing Approach (Wallingford: CABI).

Bennett, S. & Reilly, P. (1993). Using interactive multimedia to improve operator training at Queensland Alumina Limited. Australian Journal of Educational Technology, 14(2): 75-87.

Blake, A. & Sinclair, M. T. (2003). Tourism crisis management: US response to September 11, Annals of Tourism Research, 30(4): 813-832.

Bland, M. (1998). Communicating Out of a Crisis. Macmillan Business: London.

Booth, S. (1993). Crisis Management Strategy, Competition and Changes in Modern Enterprises. Routledge: London.

Brookfield, H. (1999). Environmental damage: Distinguishing human from geographical causes. Environmental Health, 1(2): 3-11.

Caplan, G. (1970). The Theory and Practice of Mental Health Consultation New York: Basic Books Inc.

Caudron, S. (2002). Training in a post-terrorist era, Training and Development, American Society or Training and Development (ASTD). Feb: 25-30.

Chien, G. C. L. & Law, R. (2003). The impact of the Severe Acute Respiratory Syndrome on hotels: A case study of Hong Kong, International Journal of Hospitality Management, 22: 327-332.

Clarke. C. J. & Varma, S. (2004). Strategic risk management: The new competitive edge. Long Range Planning, 32(4): 414-424.

Coles, T. (2004). A local reading of a global disaster. Some lessons on tourism management from an annus horribilis in South West England. In C. M. Hall, D. J. Timothy & D. T. Duval (Eds.). Safety and Security in Tourism. Relationships, Management and Marketing (pp. 173-198), New York: Haworth Press.

Coombs, T. (1999). Ongoing Crisis Communication. Planning, Managing and Responding. Thousand Oaks: Sage.

Cushnahan, G. (2004). Crisis management in small-scale tourism, Journal of Travel and Tourism Marketing, 15(4): 323-338.

De Sausmarez, N. (2004). Crisis management for the tourism sector: Preliminary considerations in policy development, Tourism and Hospitality Planning and Development, 1(2): 157-172.

Dreyer, A., Dreyer, D., & Obieglo, D. (2001). Krisenmanagement im Tourismus, München: Oldenbourg-Verlag.

Evans, S. & Elphick, S. (2005). Models of crisis management: An evaluation of their value for strategic planning in the international travel industry. International Journal of Tourism Management Research, 7(3): 135-150.

Fall, L. (2004). The increasing role of public relations as a crisis management function: An empirical examination of communication restrategising efforts among destination organisation managers in the wake of 11th September, 2001, Journal of Vacation Marketing, 10(3): 238-252.

Faulkner, B. & Vikulov, S. (2001). Katherine, washed out one day, back on track the next: A post-mortem of a tourism disaster, Tourism Management, 22: 331-344.

Faulkner, B. (2001). Towards a framework for tourism disaster management, Tourism Management, 22: 135-147.

Floyed, M. F., Gibson, H., Pennington-Gray, L., & Thapa, B. (2004). The effect of risk perceptions on intentions to travel in the aftermath of September 11, 2001, Journal of Travel and Tourism Marketing, 15(2/3): 19-38.

Frisby, E. (2002). Communicating in a crisis: The British Tourist Authority's response to the foot-and-mouth outbreak and the 11th September, 2001, Journal of Vacation Marketing, 9(1): 89-100.

Gillen, D. & Lall, A. (2003). International transmission of shocks in the airline industry, Journal of Air Transport Management, 9(1): 37-49.

Glaesser, D. (2003). Crisis Management in the Tourism Industry, Amsterdam, Butterworth-Heinemann.

Glaesser, D. (2004). Crisis Management in the Tourism Industry, Butterworth-Heinemann: Oxford.

Glaeßer, D. (2005). Krise oder Strukturbruch? In H. Pechlaner & D. Glaeßer (Eds.) Risiko und Gefahr im Tourismus (pp.13-28). Berlin: Erich Schmidt Verlag.

Glaesser, D. (2006). Crisis Management in the Tourism Industry (2nd Ed.). Oxford: Butterworth Heinemann.

Goodrich, J. N. (2002). September 11, 2001 Attack on America. A record of the immediate impacts and reactions in the USA travel and tourism industry, Tourism Management, 23(6): 573-580.

Green, C. G., Bartholomew, P. & Murman, S. (2004). New York Restaurant industry: Strategic responses to September 11, 2001, Journal of Travel and Tourism Marketing, 15(2/3): 63-80.

Gurtner, Y. K. (2005). Adversity and resilience: A case study of crisis management in a tourist-reliant desti-

nation. In P. Tremblay & A. Boyle (Eds.) Sharing Tourism Knowledge (pp. 196-198). Proceedings of the 2005 CAUTHE Conference, Darwin: Charles Darwin University.

Hall, C. M. (2002). Travel safety, terrorism and the media. The significance of the issue-attention cycle, Current Issues in Tourism, 5(5): 458-466.

Hall, C. M., Timothy, D. J. & Duval, D. T. (Eds.) (2004). Safety and Security in Tourism. Relationships, Management and Marketing. New York: Haworth Press.

Harrison, S. (2000). Public Relations: An Introduction (2nd ed.). Business Press: London.

Heath, R. (1993). Dealing with complete crisis-the crisis management shell structure. Safety Science, 30: 139-150.

Heath, R. (1998). Crisis management for managers and executives. Financial Times Publishing: London.

Heck, J. P. (1991). Comments on "The Zeebrugge ferry disaster." In U. Rosenthal & B. Pijnenberg (Eds.), Crisis Management and Decision Making. Kluwer, Dordrecht.

Henderson, J. C. (1999a). Tourism management and the Southeast Asian economic and environmental crisis: A Singapore perspective, Managing Leisure, 4: 107-120.

Henderson, J. C. (1999b). Southeast Asian tourism and the financial crisis: Indonesia and Thailand compared, Current Issues in Tourism, 2(4): 294-303.

Henderson, J. C. (2002a). Managing a tourism crisis in South East Asia: The role of national tourism organizations, International Journal of Tourism Research, 3(1): 85-105.

Henderson, J. C. (2002b). Terrorism and tourism: Managing the consequences of the Bali bombings, Journal of Travel & Tourism Marketing, 15(1): 41-58.

Henderson, J. C. (2003a). Case study: Managing a health-related crisis: SARS in Singapore, Journal of Vacation Marketing, 10(1): 67.

Henderson, J. C. (2003b). Communicating in a crisis: Flight SQ 006, Tourism Management, 24(3): 279-287.

Henderson, J. C. (2004). Tourism and Crisis, London: Thompson Learning.

Henderson, J. C. & Ng, A. (2004). Responding to crisis: Severe Acute Respiratory Syndrome (SARS) and hotels in Singapore, International Journal of Tourism Research, 6: 411-419.

Hitchcock, M. (2001). Tourism and Total Crisis in Indonesia: The Case of Bali, Asia Pacific Business Review, 8(2): 101-120.

Hosie, P. & Smith, C. (2004). Preparing for crisis: Online security management education, Research and Practice in Human Resource Management, 12(2): 90-127.

Hosie, P. (1993). Technologically Mediated Learning: The future of training in Australia. Australian Journal of Educational Technology, 9(1): 69-86.

Hosie, P. (1994). Human resource managers and training–A peek into the future. In Nankervis, A. & Compton, R.

(Eds.) Readings in Strategic Human Resource Management (pp. 259-277), Thomas Nelson, Australia.

Israeli, A. & Reichal, A. (2003). Hospitality crisis management practices: The Israeli case, International Journal of Hospitality Management, 22(4): 353-372.

King, B. (2000). Institutions, research and development: Tourism and the Asian financial crisis, International Journal of Tourism Research, 2(2): 133-136.

Lovelock, B. (2004). New Zealand Travel agent practice in the provision of advice for travel to risky destinations, Journal of Travel and Tourism Marketing, 15(4): 259-280.

Mansfeld, Y. & Pizam, A. (Eds.) (2006). Tourism, Security and Safety. Oxford: Butterworth Heineman.

Mansfield, Y. (1999). Cycles of war, terror and peace: determinants and management of crisis and recovery of the Israeli tourism industry, Journal of Travel Research, 38(1): 30-36.

Mason, P., Grabowski, P. & Du, W. (2005). Severe Acute Respiratory Syndrome, tourism and the media, International Journal of Tourism Research, 7: 11-21.

Mazzarol, T. & Hosie, P. (1997). Long distance teaching: The impact of offshore programs and information technology on academic work. Australian Universities Review, 40(1): 20-24.

McKercher, B. & Chon, K. (2004). The over-reaction to SARS and the collapse of Asian tourism, Annals of Tourism Research, 31(3): 716-719.

McKercher, B. & Hui, E. L. L. (2004). Terrorism, economic uncertainty and outbound travel from Hong Kong. In C. M. Hall, D. J. Timothy & D. T. Duval (Eds.) Safety and Security in Tourism. Relationships, Management and Marketing (pp. 99-116), New York: Haworth Press.

McLagan, P. (1996). Great ideas revisited: Creating the future of HRD. Training and Development, 50(1): 60-65.

Meyers, G. & Holusha, J. (1986). When it Hits The Fan: Managing the Nine Crises of Business. Boston: Houghton Mifflin.

Mitroff, I. I. (2004). Crisis Leadership: Planning for the Unthinkable, University of Southern California.

Nankervis, A. (2000). Dreams and realities: Vulnerability and the tourism industry in Southeast Asia: a framework for analysing and adapting tourism management toward 2000. In K. S. Chon (Ed.) Tourism in Southeast Asia: A New Direction (pp. 49-63). New York: The Haworth Hospitality Press.

Pauchant, T. & Mitroff, I. I. (1992) The Crisis-prone Organisation. San Francisco, CA: Jossey-Bass Publishers.

Pender, L. & Sharpley, R. (2004). International tourism. The management of crisis. In L. Pender & R. Sharpley (Eds.) The Management of Tourism (pp. 275-287), London: Sage.

Peters. M. & Pikkemaat, B. (2005). Crisis management in alpine winter sports resorts–The 1999 avalanche disaster in Tyrol, Journal of Travel and Tourism Marketing, 19(2/3): 9-20.

Pizam, A. (1999). A comprehensive approach to classifying acts of crime and violence at tourism destinations, Journal of Travel Research, 38(1): 5-12.

Pizam, A. & Smith, G. (2000). Tourism and terrorism: A quantitative analysis of major terrorist acts and their impact on tourism destinations. Tourism Economics, 62: 123-138

Price, A. (2001). The principles of human resource management. Oxford: Blackwell Publishing.

Prideaux, B. (2004). The need to use disaster planning frameworks to respond to major tourism disasters: Analysis of Australia's response to tourism disasters in 2001, Journal of Travel and Tourism Marketing, 15(4): pp. 281-298.

Prideaux, B., Laws, E. & Faulkner, B. (2003). Events in Indonesia: Exploring the limits to formal tourism trends forecasting methods in complex crisis situations, Tourism Management, 24: 475-487.

Ray, S. J. (1999). Strategic Communication in Crisis Management. Lessons from the Airline Industry. Westport CT: Quorum Books.

Reigeluth, C. M. (1999). What is instructional-design theory, and how is it changing? In C. M. Reigeluth (Ed.) Instructional-design theories and models: A new paradigm of instructional theory (pp. 425-459). Hillsdale, NJ: Lawrence Erlbaum Associates.

Reilly, A. H. (1993). The technology of effective crisis management: More than the daily routine, The Journal of Technology, Management Research, 4(1): 45.

Richardson, B. (1994). Crisis management and the management strategy: Time to 'loop the loop.' Disaster Prevention and Management, 33: 59-80.

Ritchie, B. W. (2004). Chaos, crises and disasters: A strategic approach to crisis management in the tourism industry, Tourism Management, 25: 669-683.

Ritchie, B. W., Dorell, H., Miller, D. & Miller, G. A. (2004). Crisis communication and the recovery for the tourism industry: Lessons from the 2001 foot and mouth disease outbreak in the United Kingdom, Journal of Travel and Tourism Marketing, 15(4): 199-216.

Rosental, U. & Pijnenberg, B. (1991). Crisis Management and Decision Making. Kluwer: Dordrecht.

Santana, G. (2004). Crisis management and tourism. Beyond the rhetoric. In C. M. Hall, D. J. Timothy & D. T. Duval (Eds.) Safety and Security in Tourism. Relationships, Management and Marketing (pp. 299-322). New York: Haworth Press.

Sausmarez, N. D. (2004). Malaysia's response to the Asian financial crisis: Implications for tourism and sectoral crisis management, Journal of Travel and Tourism Marketing, 15(4): 217-231.

Senge, P. M. (1990). The fifth discipline: The art and practice of the learning organization. New York: Doubleday.

Seymour, M. & Moore S. (2000). Effective Crisis Management: Worldwide Principles and Practice. Cassell: London.

Slatter, S. (1984). Corporate Recovery. Penguin: Harmondsworth.

Smith, C. L. (2002a). Security Science–An emerging applied science. SCIOS, 37(2), 8-10.

Smith, C. L. (2002b). A method for understanding students' perceptions of concepts in the defence in depth strategy (pp. 19-27). Proceedings of 3rd Australian Information Warfare and Security Conference.

Smith, C. L. (2001). Security Science as an applied science? Australian Science Teachers Journal, 47(2): 32-36.

Smith, D. (1990). Beyond contingency planning: towards a model of crisis management, Industrial Crisis Quarterly 4: 263-275.

Smith, D. & Sipika, C. (1993). Back from the brink–Post crisis management. Long Range Planning, 261: 28-38.

Smith, P. L. & Ragan, T. (1999). *Instructional design.* New York: John Wiley & Sons.

Price, A. (2001). *The principles of human resource management.* Oxford: Blackwell Publishing.

Sonnenberg, C. & Wöhler, K. (2004). Was bewirkt Sicherheit bzw. Unsicherheit? Prädiktoren der Reisesicherheit. In W. Freyer & S. CroB (Eds.), Sicherheit in Tourismus: Schutz vor Risiken und Gefahren. Dresden: FIT-Verlag.

Stafford, G., Yu, L. & Armoo, A. K. (2002). Crisis management and recovery. How Washington, D.C. Hotels responded to terrorism, The Cornell Hotel and Restaurant Administration Quarterly, 43(5): 27-40.

Stewart, J. & McGoldrick, J (Eds.) (1996). Human Resource Development: Perspectives, Strategies and Practice London: Pitman.

Tate, P. (2002). The Impact of 9/11: Caribbean, London and NYC case studies, Travel and Tourism Analysis, 5: 1-25.

Taylor, M. S. & Enz, C. A. (2002). GMs' Responses to the Events of September 11, 2001, Cornell Hotel and Restaurant Administration Quarterly, February: 7-20.

Tovey, M. D. & Lawlor, D. R. (2004). Training in Australia: Design, delivery, evaluation, management (2nd Ed.), Prentice-Hall, Sydney.

World Tourism Organisation (WTO). United Nations. Retrieved on 14/7/2006 from: http://www.world-tourism.org/newsroom/Releases/2006/july/twobillion.html

Developing a Research Agenda for Tourism Crisis Management, Market Recovery and Communications

Jack C Carlsen

Janne J Liburd

SUMMARY. This article focuses on the need to develop a comprehensive research agenda for crisis management and market recovery in tourism. A review of the literature on research into risk, crisis and disaster management indicates that research has emerged on an ad hoc basis. Analysis of a database of over 2400 relevant references supports the need for a research agenda that will focus on crisis management and market recovery and communications, rather than prevention. The BEST Education Network research agenda on risk and crisis management for sustainable tourism is then presented as a basis for further development of a crisis management and market recovery research agenda. In particular, it elaborates on research issues related to the communication during tourism crises, assessing strategies for market recovery and understanding these issues from the DMO's perspective.

INTRODUCTION

As risk and crises in tourism are escalating in the last decade, so too has the need to understand all aspects of their effects and the responses of all tourism stakeholders, especially Destination Management Organisations (DMOs). Whilst effects of risks, crises disasters have received increasing attention in the tourism literature, response and recovery strategies; their effectiveness is less well understood. Furthermore, there is much confusion in the tourism lexicon of tourism risk, crisis and disasters and a lack of clear conceptual and theoretical framework for researching this topic. This article reviews the research efforts to date and develops a research

Jack C Carlsen (E-mail: jack.carlsen@cbs.curtin.edu.au) is Professor at Curtin University, P.O. Box U1987, Perth, Western Australia, 6845. Janne J Liburd (E-mail: liburd@sitkom.sdu.dk) is affliated with the University of Southern Denmark, Niels Bohrsvej 9, Denmark, DK 6700.

The authors wish to thank Mr René Baretje and Dr Michael Hughes for the CIRET data provided for this article. The authors also acknowledge the contribution of the academics and professionals to the tourism risk and crisis research agenda during the Business Enterprises for Sustainable Tourism [BEST EN] Think Tank V in Jamaica, 2005.

agenda, with emphasis on questions related to crisis management, market recovery and communication as well as understanding the role of DMOs in managing the process.

Tourism is often the first sector to be impacted by disasters and crises and the first sector that community leaders look towards in the recovery phase. This makes it vital to understand the recovery process from a range of perspectives, including the role of broadcasting, marketing and communications. According to the United Nations World Tourism Organisation [UNWTO] (2005) "There is limited understanding of the importance of the tourism sector in supporting the general recovery from disaster" (p v.). This understanding must extend to the importance of human resources, the dual role of broadcasters (both as portals for mis-information and recovery communications) and also to the linkages between DMOs, tourism sector stakeholders, government and the media. The UNWTO highlighted the need for leadership in disaster response and recovery, especially in view of that fact that many destinations (especially DMOs in Lesser Developed Countries) lack the financial and technological resources for recovery marketing strategies and are located on the 'wrong side' of the global communications divide i.e. without access to many forms of modern communication.

The article draws upon extant literature, secondary data as well as findings from a focus group to develop a research agenda for crisis management, market recovery and communication. The limited literature on the topic and the paucity of research into the effectiveness of crisis management and market recovery strategies is reviewed in the next section. The method for firstly analysing the focus of extant literature on the topic and gaining agreement through a focus group on the key questions that should underpin the research agenda on this topic is then described. Finally, the research agenda for crisis management, market recovery and communication is discussed. The article demonstrates that there is consensus in the literature, analysis and focus groups as to the critical need for research in this increasingly important area of tourism management, especially for analysing and understanding the role of DMOs in crisis management.

LITERATURE REVIEW

Prior to 2000, there were only a few books and journal articles addressing the topic of crisis management. Security incidents in the Middle East and other destinations triggered academic interest in the 1990s followed by the first edited book on the topic titled Tourism, Crime and International Security Issues (Pizam and Mansfield 1996), as well as a more recent contribution by the same authors (Mansfield and Pizam 2006). Continuing disasters and crises around the time of the new millennium have given rise to a growing body of literature on this topic. It is apparent that prevention and management of risk and crises pervade the literature, whereas impacts and recovery have received much less attention. Most of the literature is prescriptive in nature, describing strategies and techniques for assessing and managing risk and preventing crises, or descriptive in terms of the immediate, short-term effects on tourism destinations.

Authors such a Ketelhohn (1989), Murphy and Bayley (1989), Cohn (2001), Glaesser (2003), Beirman (2003) and Lynch (2004) have produced guidelines, case studies and strategies for tourism crisis management and market recovery. Faulkner and Russell (2000) have distinguished between crises and disasters based on whether the cause is due to some internal organizational failure to act (a crisis) or an external event over which the organisation has no control (a disaster).

However, there has been virtually no research as to the effectiveness of these prescriptive strategies, nor have there been any real attempts to understand the scope of crisis management for the purposes of research. It is timely, therefore, to review not only what has been done to date in this topic area, but also to develop a clear and concise research agenda for crisis management for the long term development of knowledge in this area. Gartner (2005:17) has stated that "we know very little about the long-term effects" when referring to the exogenous forces that impact on tourism. Likewise, Cohen (2005: 81-114) finds that although terrorism and other security incidents have been investigated by academics, natural disasters "... have been given little attention by tourism researchers" and calls for a bridge to span the gap between tourism and disaster research, beginning with conceptualisation and location within the prevalent theoretical approaches to disaster studies. Cohen's work on the Tsunami disaster in Thailand provides a useful insight into the true nature of disasters and the impacts they can have not only on tourists, but also the host population. The interface between tourism and disasters, especially natural disasters lacks theoretical parameters, inhibiting our ability to analyse and compare the impacts on tourism destinations and response by tourism authorities.

Steene (1999) found when suggesting a research program for risk management within tourism and travel that "very little has been done when it comes to concrete research and publications concerning risks within the service sector in general and tourism and travel in particular (p.15). Until the 21st century, a significant professional focus on risk and crisis management was primarily confined to the airline industry, travel insurers, a small coterie of specialist management consultants and very few tourism academics. Santana (2003: 304) finds that

> *Research on crisis management has been largely overlooked in comparison to other issues that promote "success." The net result of such emphasis is that managers are not prepared technically, psychologically, and emotionally to deal with a common feature of business operations and management today: crisis.*

Ritchie (2004:680) also finds that "a small but growing body of research on crisis and disaster management has been conducted in the tourism industry" and suggests this is "due, in part, to the chaotic and complex nature of these incidents and an inability by some managers and researchers to understand such phenomena." Whether this research gap is due to the focus on other aspects of tourism management or the inability of tourism organisations to participate in such research, it is evident that a crisis management research agenda is needed.

It must be noted that these disasters and crises and their subsequent impacts can be studied from a range of business, humanities and environmental perspectives. Tourism research is as much a socio-cultural phenomena as it is an economic one, and takes place within finite environmental boundaries. It is necessary therefore when putting together a research agenda on this topic to identify the range of discipline areas and existing theoretical frameworks that are relevant. Relevant business disciplines include economics, management, marketing, finance, law, accounting, planning, politics and information technology. Relevant humanities disciplines include geography, history, anthropology, sociology, archeology and philosophy. The 'hard' sciences involving study of the physical environment require input from engineers, geologists, hydrologists, seismologists, biologists, ecologists and other natural and environmental scientists. Thus the assessment, management and monitoring of risk and crises as it applies to tourism requires a multidisciplinary team if it is to be inclusive of all relevant actors and forces. It also requires an understanding of the systemic and dynamic nature of global tourism risks and the ability of people to respond when risks are realized in tourism destinations.

Perhaps to accommodate this need for a holistic approach to tourism research, Faulkner and Russell (2000) recommend a systems approach to understanding the topic, and have applied chaos theory to the study of disasters. They argue that traditional Newtonian, positivist approaches to tourism research are appropriate for relatively stable systems, but expose gaps in the understanding of turbulence in tourism development and the dynamics of change. Tourism risks, disasters and crises create turbulent operating environments for tourism operators and DMOs; hence, a more complex and comprehensive research paradigm is required to understand their immediate as well as flow-on effects.

The UNWTO in collaboration with the World Economic Forum in Davos in January 2005 completed a study of global tourism and disaster response and the feasibility of establishing a disaster response network (World Economic Forum 2006a). In two comprehensive volumes, global risks to tourism are mapped and disaster response networks are identified. Importantly, the UNWTO recognizes the need to understand the 'ripple effects' of disasters, those unforeseen outcomes that lead to 'risk conflation' of amplification of the initial societal, geopolitical or environmental impacts. Examples include the escalation in oil prices following Hurricane Katrina, or the outbreak of Avian Influenza in one location disrupting travel to multiple destinations in Asia and North America. Thus there is a need to study three key elements of risk as they apply to tourism: causality, connectivity and complexity (World Economic Forum 2006b). For some disasters, risk conflation effects are known and can be accounted for in business planning and insurance assessment, e.g., cyclones or flooding. However some other risk conflation effects are largely unknown, e.g., terrorist attacks, so any risk management exercise is mainly speculative. The scale of risk is also broad and can range from large scale loss of population and decline of a destination to short-term loss of revenue for small businesses and temporary decline in real estate values.

To date, the business perspective and the management discipline pervade the literature, yet there is no theoretical framework for the study of this topic area. Pizam and Mansfield (2006) have moved toward a theory of tourism security over the last decade by developing a typology, concepts, propositions and empirical generalizations that apply to security incidents such as wars, terrorism, crime and civil unrest. Their extensive list of research questions provides the variables, metrics and building blocks for a positivist approach to developing a theoretical framework for researching tourism security. Whilst this initiative should be welcomed and adopted by those that take a positivist, deductive approach to research, it could be argued that a universal set of theories on this topic will be difficult to identify. This is because crises by their nature are geographically, demographically and temporally discrete, so that the boundaries of study are not fixed but vary dramatically. For example, there is no doubt the September 11, 2001 terrorist incident was a global crisis, with ramifications (or risk conflation) for all sectors of business and society, including tourism. The range of research tools and approaches for understanding the effects of this event would be vastly different to those needed to research the effects of civil unrest on tourism in, for instance, Fiji. There would always be some need to change the

boundaries of the study to suit the event being researched, thereby limiting extrapolation of any research findings and replication of research in 'similar' settings. Indeed, whereas some immediate effects could be identified and studied, risk conflation effects would certainly vary for discrete locations, types and magnitudes of disasters and crises.

Tarlow (2006) and Cunliffe (2006) argue that these risks and security are essentially social constructs, so that a social theory for study of this topic is required. The overarching issue is to what extent risks and security are social constructs, enmeshed within philosophical and cultural belief systems and set in modernist, materialistic contexts. Cunliffe (2006) and to some extent Tarlow (2006) and Cohen (2005) all argue that human actions (or inaction) can precipitate and perpetuate risk and security incidents by increasing exposure and vulnerability and impeding response and recovery strategies. Thus, the human dimension should not be overlooked when researching the causes and effects of crises and disasters.

Moreover, Cunliffe (2006) provides a framework for understanding the risk environment, in a circumstantial as well as a physical sense. Three aspects of the risk environment are identified: socio-physical environment, planning environment and economic environment. The interaction of hazard, exposure and vulnerability within the risk environment provides the framework for researching and managing risk and crises. Santana (2003) provides an anatomical analysis of a tourism destination that developed rapidly, causing many environmental problems and precipitating extensive beach pollution from untreated sewage. Consequently, a series of beach-related diseases were contracted by tourists that were extensively reported in the media causing a subsequent fall in tourist arrivals of 40 percent. This is a classic case of a known hazard that was not adequately addressed, exposing tourists in the destination to increased health risk and the destination vulnerable to a crisis in tourism. Failure of legal, social, planning and economic controls resulted in exacerbation of a problem and a period of crisis.

Some authors (Faulkner 2001, Santana 2003, Ritchie 2004, Evans and Elphick 2005) use strategic planning for crisis and disaster management taking a staged, iterative approach to understand and respond in a structured and ordered way. Mistilis and Sheldon (2006) take this approach one step further by developing a knowledge framework and examine how different forms of knowledge and information can be used to deal with tourism risk, crisis and disaster. Recognizing that strategic planning is a means to an end, not an end in itself, the continuous capture, processing and dissemination of tacit and explicit knowledge by stakeholders in tourism destinations is important Similarly Pforr (2005) supports a proactive, strategic approach to crisis management in tourism organizations to prevent a situation where "tourism in post-crisis is always tourism in pre-crisis" (2005:9).

This review indicates that literature has developed on an ad hoc basis, in response to the risks, disasters and crises as they have occurred. This has produced a disparate body of knowledge which is largely descriptive in nature, and limited in terms of the implications for other destinations. The problem with this approach is that every destination is different in terms of its level of preparedness, risk recognition and ability to respond, so the highly contextualised knowledge has limited utility for DMOs. Most importantly, research findings need to be related to the needs of DMOs in terms of lessons learned, management and resource implications to underpin sustainable tourism development.

It is also apparent that the terms risk, crisis and disaster have been used interchangeably, or have been used as a suffix for the generic disciplinary category, management. There is an immediate need for compartmentalising the research to clarify the definitions, concepts and typologies associated with the topic area. This will also help to dispel misunderstandings and confusion. For example, it is not appropriate to use the term 'disaster management' because, as Faulkner and Russell (2000) explain, disasters are external and unpredictable events, so the notion that DMOs can somehow 'manage' disasters is an anathema. Crises emerge from a lack of preparedness for a disaster and the inability of DMOs to respond in a co-ordinated and strategic way. The lower the level of DMO risk and crisis awareness and preparedness, the longer the crisis will persist, causing unneces-sarily prolonged damage to the viability and sustainability of the destination.

METHOD

Two approaches were used to develop the research agenda. Firstly, analysis of the Centre International de Recherches et d'Etudes Touristiques [CIRET] database was conducted. The database contains an annotated bibliography and key theme analysis of over 60,000 references on tourism studies. CIRET is a not-for-profit organization that actively gathers and catalogues tourism related academic publications. CIRET analyses and categorizes publications using a standardized process based on a thesaurus of 1300 theme words. An annotated reference is created for each publication including a list of one or more theme words associated with its content. The aim is to provide researchers with access to a comprehensive database of tourism publications (Baretje, 2004). An electronic database of over 2400 disaster and crisis management references categorized by theme words was analyzed.

The NUD*ist software package (using INVIVO coding processes) was used to analyze the reference list. NUD*ist enables text searches of imported plain text documents. Text searches can be used to return results indicating the number of 'text units' containing the search term. A text unit is defined by the user and may be a whole document, a paragraph or a single line of text within a document. Each text unit containing the desired words is 'coded' against the search term and a 'node' is generated. Text units may be associated with more than one 'node.' A 'node tree' may then be constructed within NUD*ist where 'nodes' are grouped according to how they relate (e.g., as categories and subcategories). The software also enables analysis of how respective 'text units' are related in terms of the nodes and categories of nodes they are associated with.

The database files were formatted and converted to plain text and imported into NUD*ist. Individual references with associated theme words were defined as 'text units.' Consequently, all searches returning the number of 'text units' containing search terms equated with the number of referenced articles with the given terms. The CIRET thesaurus (available online), used to originally categorize the references, was used as the source for search terms to ensure consistency with the original categorization process. The theme words allocated to each reference by CIRET were capitalized while the remaining reference details were in lower case. This allowed text searches within NUD*ist to specifically target the theme words based on capitalization, ensuring search results did not include references with search terms occurring outside the theme word categories. Where a text search resulted in matching references, a node was created using the search term as the label. Each node was linked to all articles categorized by the given theme word used as a search term. The list of references for any given node may be accessed and read. This enabled search results to be manually checked for consistency by ensuring references linked to particular nodes containing the desired theme word. The theme word analysis is presented in the findings section below.

The second approach was based on the use of the nominal group technique (NGT) at the Business Enterprises for Sustainable Travel Education Network (BEST EN) Think Tank V in June 2005 (see also Tourism Review International Volume 10, Issue 1-2). BEST EN is an international consortium of tourism educators and researchers committed to furthering knowledge on the principles and practice of sustainable tourism (see http://www.besteducationnetwork.org). BEST EN accomplishes this through annual Think Tanks where educational materials and research agendas on topical issues related to sustainable tourism are developed. Approximately 45 academics and tourism professionals met over several days in June 2005 to identify the major issues to be included in such an agenda on risk and crisis management for sustainable tourism. The applied group discussion methodology deserves further attention due to its usefulness in idea generation, identification of key objectives and democratic decision making (Jurowski and Liburd 2002). In brief, the nominal group technique (NGT) encourages the development of individual views that are debated and given consideration by the group (Chapple and Murphy 1996). It was developed by Delbecq and van de Ven in 1968 who synthesized studies related to social

psychology, management science, and social work (Ho, Lai, and Chang 1999). Within the highly structured technique are elements of brainstorming and brainwriting, as well as voting techniques that balance participation among group members. The nominal group technique begins with the articulation of the problem or question by a facilitator. Here, participants were asked: What are the key research themes and subject matter of relevance to tourism risk and crisis management? It is important that the problem be a distinct task that gives the participants a specific question to which they can respond (Roth et al. 1995). Once all group members clearly understand the question the process proceeds through five distinct steps:

1. Silent generation of ideas
2. Reporting of generated ideas
3. Clarification of ideas
4. Ranking of ideas
5. Presentation and discussion of the results of the voting process

Hence a combination of primary and secondary sources was used to identify key themes, find where research is needed and then develop research questions. Analysis of themes and expert opinion enabled prioritization of research areas, with two of the six categories of research identified by BEST EN presented below being directly relevant to the topic of this volume. The CIRET database analysis also verifies the views expressed in the literature concerning the need for more research into tourism crisis management.

FINDINGS

CIRET Database Analysis

Based on analysis of over 2400 references in the CIRET database, it is evident that the majority of publications are in the 'management' and 'disaster' themes (Table 1). Some 59 percent of the publications are on the theme of disasters and tourism, followed by management and tourism (53 percent) and prevention (47 percent). Interestingly, 'impacts' are less well studied (24 percent), as are 'crises' (17 percent) whilst 'research' almost fails to even register in the thematic analysis. Whereas there may be some definitional confusion in the analysis of this literature (especially confusion between disasters and crises), it nonetheless indicates that crisis management and market recovery research has largely been overlooked in the literature, so a clear and focussed research agenda is a timely contribution to the field.

Further analysis of the CIRET database also supports the need for crisis management and market recovery research, as it is lacking in comparison with 'prevention' literature, which dominates (Table 2). 'Risk management' is well studied within a management theme (66 percent) but 'crisis' (30 percent) and 'recovery' (27 percent) are less well documented.

The same is true of research in these themes (Table 3), where the limited literature on research indicates that 'management' (73 percent), 'disaster' (60 percent) and 'prevention' (53 percent) are well researched, but 'impacts' (17 percent), 'recovery' (13 percent) and 'crisis' (10 percent) are under-researched.

TABLE 1. Key Themes in the Literature

Key Theme	F	% of TOTAL
Management	1265	52.7%
Disaster	1408	58.6%
Prevention	1124	46.8%
Research	30	1.2%
Impacts	575	23.9%
Crisis	415	17.3%
TOTAL Pubs	2401	

Note: literature contains multiple themes, so percentages sum to more than 100
F = frequency

TABLE 2. Management Themes in the Literature

Theme	F	Management theme %
Risk Management	830	65.6%
Prevention	1124	88.9%
Recovery	340	26.9%
Crisis Management	380	30.0%
TOTAL management	1265	

Note: literature contains multiple themes, so percentages sum to more than 100
F = frequency

TABLE 3. Research Themes in the Literature

Theme	F	Research theme %
Management	22	73.3%
Disaster	18	60.0%
Prevention	16	53.3%
Impacts	5	16.7%
Crisis	3	10.0%
Recovery	4	13.3%
TOTAL research	30	

Note: literature contains multiple themes, so percentages sum to more than 100
F = frequency

NGT FINDINGS

Six categories of research emerged from the NGT, two of which posit a number of research questions to inform the crisis management and market recovery research agenda (Dwyer and Sheldon 2006). These six research categories are described below and consist of:

1. Clarification of definitions, concepts and typologies.
2. Risk identification and assessment.
3. Managing recovery and restoration.
4. Marketing and promotion during and after the crisis.
5. Rebuilding the destination.
6. Sustainable tourism development from a risk management perspective.

Clarification of Definitions, Concepts and Typologies

A need for clearer definitions of the terms of crisis and disaster was identified. For research to develop in this field, a commonality of terms and concepts is needed.

- Definitions of terms such as: risk, hazard, crisis, disaster, etc., are needed.
- Tourism destinations face various typologies of crisis. Examples are: severity of impact, geographic spread of impact, type of impact, source of impact, etc. Secondary research to identify and classify a compre-

hensive list of typologies would allow the field to move forward more easily.

Risk Identification and Assessment

Very little is known about the nature of tourism crises. Faulkner (2001) has classified crises into pre-event, prodromal, emergency, intermediate, long term and resolution. However, there are more dimensions that can clarify and provide deeper understanding of the nature of risk and crisis for a destination. The BEST EN Think Tank suggested that more work is needed on:

- How risks affecting tourism are identified, assessed, reduced, avoided or transferred.
- How risks are forecast.
- Who identifies and assesses these risks.
- How these risks are communicated to tourism stakeholders (government, industry, destination managers, community, tourists).
- The distinction between real and perceived risks for different stakeholders.
- How important is safety in tourists' choice of destination or activity.

Managing Recovery and Restoration

There is growing pressure for governments to assist tourist victims of crises quickly, demanding solidarity, flexibility and expertise. For example, the UNWTO has a Crisis Action Team made up of the world's top experts in the areas of communications, marketing, promotion, safety and security.

The research issues pertinent to this topic are:

- Analysis of roles and responsibilities in the recovery process, especially the role of the DMO.
- Exploration of ways to restore confidence in the destination; what are the roles of tourism stakeholders?
- What role does perception play in the recovery cycle?
- What are the forces that shape perception in a tourism crisis?
- What is the role of travel advisories, and what is their real impact on travel behaviour?

Marketing and Promotion During and After the Crisis

After the crisis is over, and sometimes during the crisis, decisions must be made regarding if, and how to market and promote the destination. Specific research issues are:

- Exploration of the ethical responsibilities in marketing and promotion activity during crises, including corporate responsibility.
- Should destinations be marketed during a crisis?
- How does this marketing and promotion differ compared to 'normal' times?
- Is there a role for de-marketing?
- Exploration of the media's role in restoring confidence in the destination.
- Understanding the impact of crisis on destination reputation and image.
- Exploration of strategic marketing approaches to destination crisis and management.

Rebuilding the Destination

The infrastructures and superstructures of destinations are often in ruin after a crisis–particularly after a natural disaster. Research needed to assist in rebuilding the destination includes:

- Tools to assess tourism's role in the future socio-economic development of the region–should the tourism industry be re-built to same scale and type?
- Assessment of different scenarios for tourism product and market development and the necessary planning processes.
- Analysis of sources of financing, humanitarian aid and investment for re-building.
- Understanding the role of communication methods and technologies in rebuilding the destination.
- Identifying the roles of different tourism stakeholders in the recovery process–including the community.
- Investigating how the tourist industry can engage with other industries in the recovery process.

Sustainable Tourism Development from a Risk Management Perspective

The BEST EN Think Tank participants felt there was a need for a meta-analytical approach to risk management for tourism. This has its own research implications and the following were identified as topics for research:

- Integration of systems approach into research on crisis management.
- Consideration of sectoral balance–both within the economy and within the industry.
- Integration of life cycle concepts and temporal dimensions? into research.
- Exploration of the importance of tourism recovery to community quality of life.
- The need to develop integrative case studies to share success stories and failures, and to identify lessons for destination stakeholders.

DISCUSSION

Based on the literature analysis and focus group findings the emergent research agenda should focus on crisis management and market recovery rather than prevention, which has already been well documented. As the type and frequency of disasters that are visited on tourism destinations continue to expand, the pursuit of a risk and prevention research agenda threatens to become a nebulous process, crossing many disciplines in the health, technology, biology and social sciences as well as the business research domains. In contrast, crisis management and market recovery research findings can be internalised by any DMO or tourism operator. Hence, the boundaries and scope of the research agenda are clearly defined, at least in conceptual and demographic terms, and confined in disciplinary terms to the management sciences.

For the purposes of this article and this volume, we will further discuss the research agenda as it relates to two topics relevant to the theme of this collection, that of (i) managing recovery and restoration and (ii) promotion and marketing during and after a crisis. Specific key research questions will be posed to further develop the research agenda. In addition, one research question from the Risk Identification and Assessment category of the BEST EN research agenda on how these risks (and indeed disasters and crises) are communicated to tourism stakeholders will be discussed as it relates closely to crisis management and market recovery.

There is evidence that in at least one recent disaster, the 2004 Indian Ocean tsunami in Southern Thailand, that the risk was not communicated at the insistence of those in the tourism industry, even though it was identified many years before the disaster (Cohen 2005). The response and recovery and many destinations impacted by the 2004 Indian Ocean tsunami have not been well-documented or analysed, apart from descriptive case studies and indications of recovery in Thailand (de Sausmarez 2005, Gurtner 2006) and the Maldives (Carlsen 2005, 2006). There is also an increasing awareness of the importance of the natural environment in providing protection from the destructive forces associated with such disasters (Cohen 2005, Handley 2005).

It is also apparent that marketing strategies and their effectiveness are also in need of deeper investigation. For example, Beirman (2003) has addressed the vexing question of marketing during a crisis, and whether DMOs should continue marketing efforts as before, change the message or be suspended altogether while victims can be cared for and infrastructure repaired. His recommendation, based on several case studies of terrorist attacks and natural disasters was that it depends on whether the crisis is ongoing (such as war or insurgency) or the result of a one-off disaster (such as a tsunami). Hence marketing of destinations during and after a crisis will benefit from definitional and conceptual clarification of risk, disasters and crises as well as learning the lessons of research from other destinations (Beirman 2003, Carlsen 2006).

Consequently, the key question in the context of crisis communication research is: how are all of the elements of tourism risk, disaster and crises (vulnerability, impacts, response, duration and consequences) communicated to tourism stakeholders (government, industry, destination managers, community and tourists)? A subsequent question is: what is the morality of not communicating these risks? Research to date indicates that although there appears to be some effective crisis communication strategies (see for example Beirman 2003, PATA n.d., PATA 2003, Carlsen 2005, 2006), mis-communication and non-communication are also characteristics of tourism risk, disaster and crisis (see for example Cohen 2005, Santana 2003). This problem is exacerbated when the true extent of the stakeholders is realised and political and social forces come into play to impede or prevent effective communication.

Focusing on recovery management and communication, the following key questions evolve: can strategic communication be adopted as a method that proficiently maps perceptions and influence networks, formulates shared objectives and strategies, develops themes and messages, and focuses on "doable tasks" for DMOs? Secondly, what are the relevant channels for internal and external communication, and how can successful and effective communication be monitored? Strategic communication builds on in-depth knowledge of other cultures and factors that motivate human behavior and shape perceptions. Rather than considering what perceptions are and establishing an a priori meaning or essence to them, the objective is to investigate what they do and how they work between people as instruments in creating, transforming and communicating meaning during and after a tourism crisis.

A final key question related to the issue of marketing research is: do new collaborative marketing structures between relevant stakeholders hold promises for recovery and restoration processes? Finding new ways to harness strategic marketing and communication and the flexibility and creative imagination of relevant tourism stakeholders, media and governments could help underpin the long-term sustainability of a destination. Any new collaborative marketing and promotional programs will require new methods and metrics for monitoring their success, beyond the traditional indicators of tourist arrivals and occupancy rates. If new higher yield markets are targeted, then more reliable indicators of yield such as length of stay and average expenditure should be employed.

Socially desirable outcomes including the introduction of more ethical marketing practices and increased corporate social responsibility may emerge from a tourism crisis. Governments, DMOs and tourism stakeholders may demonstrate increased concern for the welfare and security of visitors and all those involved in tourism after a crisis. They may also demonstrate greater awareness of the environment in the wake of natural disasters, and undertake demarketing of certain areas to facilitate environmental rehabilitation.

CONCLUSION

Despite increasingly frequent crises since 2001 and increasing academic and professional work on the topic, the authors have identified a need for a more comprehensive research agenda on crisis management, market recovery and communications for destination management organisations. It is evident that a range of disciplinary perspectives, ad-hoc approaches and descriptive methods characterise the emergent literature on crisis management and market recovery and that a clear research framework is lacking. The main emphasis in the literature has been on management of risk and crisis in the pre-event, prodromal and emergency phases (Faulkner 2001), with many descriptive and prescriptive publications on how to prepare a response to tourism risk or crisis. Many of these include marketing and communication strategies which may have been effective in particular settings, and as such may provide guidelines for destinations managing recovery and restoration.

However, there has been virtually no rigorous, co-ordinated research effort into understanding the effectiveness of crisis management and market recovery strategies and the role and importance of communication in the recovery process. This is not due to any lack of research subjects, as many disasters and crises have been investigated over the last decade that includes descriptions of the impacts and recovery strategies. There is therefore an opportunity to re-visit these case studies from a research perspective to gain better insights into the outcomes of specific tourism crisis management and market recovery strategies. It may then be possible to relate the opportunities and outcomes that can be pursued, particularly by DMOs, in the post-crisis marketing environment. Some of these outcomes may indeed be serendipitous as crises by their nature are geographically, demographically and temporally discrete, so that the boundaries of study vary dramatically due to the contextualised nature of crisis. Nonetheless, they are important to broader social, economic and environmental outlook for destinations, and indeed their long-term sustainability. Marketing and communication assume primacy in the crisis situation, so it is essential that the strategies, creativity and opportunities that inevitably emerge in these situations are well researched and recorded. The research agenda of the BEST Education Network should foster collaborative research on these critical issues, and represent a starting point for future research.

REFERENCES

Baretje, R. (2004, 13/8/2004) *Centre International de Recherches et d'Etudes Touristiques (CIRET) [http://www.ciret-tourism.com/.* accessed 20/11/2006].

Beirman, D (2003) *Restoring Tourism Destinations* in Crisis. Cambridge: CABI Publishing.

Carlsen, J (2005) 'Crisis Communication and Tourism Recovery Strategies for the Maldives.' BEST Education Network Think Tank V, University of West Indies, Jamaica, June 16-19. University of Western Sydney: Sydney. ISBN 1741080843.

Carlsen, J (2006) Post-Tsunami Tourism Strategies for the Maldives. *Tourism Review International.* Vol. 10, Nos. 1/2, pp 69-80.

Chapple, M. and R. Murphy. (1996) The Nominal Group Technique: Extending the Evaluation of Student's' Teaching and Learning Experiences. *Assessment & Evaluation in Higher Education*, 21(2): 147-160.

Cohen, E. (2005) 'Tourism and Disaster: the tsunami waves in Southern Thailand.' In W. Alejziak and R. Winiarski (Eds.) *Tourism in Scientific Research.* Academy of Physical Education in Krakow: Poland, pp 81-114.

Cohn, R (2001) 'The PR Crisis Bible.' Cited in Brent Ritchie J. R and G. Crouch (2003) The Competitive Destination: A sustainable tourism perspective. UK: CABI, p. 230.

Cunliffe, S. K (2006) Risk management for tourism: Origins and Needs. *Tourism Review International.* Vol. 10, Nos. 1/2 pp. 27-38

de Sausmarez, N. (2005) 'The Indian Ocean Tsunami.' *Tourism and Hospitality Planning and Development*, 2 (1) pp 55-59.

Dwyer, L and P. Sheldon (2006) Introduction: Managing Risk and Crisis for Sustainable Tourism. *Tourism Review International.* Vol. 10, Nos. 1/2, pp 1-6.

Evans, N. and Elphick, S (2005) 'Models of Crisis Management: an Evaluation of their Value for Strategic Planning in the International Travel Industry.' International Journal of Tourism Research, 7, pp 135-150.

Faulkner, B. (2001) 'Towards a framework for tourism disaster management.' *Tourism Management*, 22 (2), pp. 135-147.

Faulkner, B and R. Russell (2000) 'Turbulence, Chaos and Complexity in Tourism Systems: A Research Direction for the New Millennium' in B. Faulkner. G. Moscardo and E. Laws (eds.) *Tourism in the 21st Century.* London: Continuum.

Gartner, W. (2005) 'A Synthesis of Tourism Trends.' In J. Aramberri and R. Butler (Eds) *Tourism Development: Issues for a Vulnerable Industry.* Clevedon: Channel View Publications, pp 3-22.

Glaesser, D. (2003) *Crisis Management in the Tourism Industry.* Oxford: Butterworth Heinemann.

Gurtner, Y (2006) 'Understanding Tourism Crisis: Case studies of Bali and Phuket.' *Tourism Review International*, Vol. 10 Nos.1-2, pp 57-68.

Handley, S (2005) 'Vanishing Point.' *CNN Traveller*, July-August 2005, pp 64-68.

Ho, E.S.S.A., Y. Lai and S.I. Chang. (1999) An integrated group decision-making approach to quality function deployment. *IIE Transactions*, 31: 553-567.

Jurowski, C. and Liburd, J.J. (2002) A multi-cultural and multi-disciplinary approach to integrating the principles of sustainable development into human resource management curriculums in Hospitality and tourism. *Hospitality and Tourism Educator*, 13(5): 36-50.

Ketelhohn, W (1989) 'Doing Business in Turbulent Environments,' cited in Brent Ritchie J. R and G. Crouch (2003) *The Competitive Destination: A sustainable tourism perspective.* CABI: UK p 231.

Lynch, M. (2004) *Weathering the Storm. A Crisis Management Guide for Tourism Businesses.* Leicester: Matador.

Mansfield, Y and Pizam, A. (2006) *Tourism, Security and Safety from Theory to Practice.* Oxford: Elsevier Butterworth-Heinemann.

IMistilis, N. and Sheldon, P (2006) Knowledge Management for *Tourism Crisis and Disasters. Tourism Review International.* Vol. 10, Nos. 1/2 pp. 39-46.

Murphy, P. and R. Bayley (1989) 'Tourism and Disaster Planning' *Geographical Review*, Vol. 79, No. 1 pp 36-46.

PATA (n.d.) The Project Phoenix Story, CD-ROM, Bangkok: PATA.

PATA (2003) *Crisis It Won't Happen to Us*! Bangkok: PATA.

Pforr, C. (2006) Tourism in Post-Crisis is Tourism in Pre-Crisis: A Review of the Literature on Crisis Management in Tourism. School of Management

Working Paper Series (01/2006). Perth: Curtin University.

Pizam, A and Mansfield, Y. (1996) *Tourism, Crime and International Security Issues*. New York: John Wiley & Sons.

Ritchie, B. W. (2004) Chaos, crises and disasters: a strategic approach to crisis management in the tourism industry, *Tourism Management*, 25, pp 669-683.

Roth, P. L., L.L.F. Schleifer, & F.S. Switzer (1995). Nominal Group Technique–an aid in implementing TQM. *The CPA Journal*, 65(5): 68-69.

Santana, G. (2003) 'Crisis Management and Tourism: Beyond the Rhetoric.' *Journal of Travel & Tourism Marketing*. Vol. 15, No. 4, pp 299-321.

Steene, A. (1999) Risk Management within Tourism and Travel–Suggestions for Research Programs. *Turizam*, Vol. 47 No. 1, pp 13-18.

Tarlow, P. (2006) Disaster Management: Exploring ways to Mitigate Disasters before they Occur. *Tourism Review International*. Vol. 10, Nos. 1/2 pp 17-26.

United Nations World Tourism Organization [UNWTO] (2005) 'Evolution of tourism in the tsunami-affected destinations' TF2/MKT Report: Madrid.

World Economic Forum (2006a) *Disaster and Response: The Tourism Dimension*. Available online at http://www.world-tourism.org/risk/index.htm accessed 9/8/2006.

World Economic Forum (2006b) *Global Risks 2006*. Available at http://www.fd.nl/GetBlob.asp?DirectID =Globalrisks&MimeType=accessed 9/8/2006

INDEX

Avian flu 87
    investigators assessment
        of likelihood 91
    related content on websites 91
    statistics 2003-2006 90
Backpackers *see* Youth tourism
Bali bombings 2002
    market recovery following 140-141
Brand
    meaning 129-130
Canada 113-126
    destination choice 114-115
    image 115-116
    image and decision making 123
    legislative change, and 124
    marketing competiveness 123-124
    proposed stratification of focus
        groups 116-118
    recruiting script and screener 126
    research methodology 116-118
    research results 118-123
    stratification of focus groups 119
    weekend travel destination, as 113-126
        statistics 114
    WHTI passport requirements 113-126
Canberra 175-189
    ACT tourism industry 177
    bushfire 178
        impacts on tourism industry
            178-179
    campaign messages developed
        in response to possible
        misconceptions 186
    consistency of messages within
        marketing campaign 184-185
    consultation with stakeholders 184
    destination recovery after major
        bushfire 175-189

heart recovery marketing campaign
    175-189, 179-181
        messages from broadcast
            campaign 182
        messages in print
            campaign 181
        messages received in Sydney
            market 183
        stakeholder consultation 186
    honesty and openness 185-186
    marketing campaign, access to
        funding 183-184
    marketing campaign, rapidity
        of development and
        implementation 182-183
    monthly door count data 2002-2005 179
    negative perceptions 177
    use of messages to correct destination
        image perception 185
Communications
    research agenda 265-282
Complexity or chaos theory
    tourism crises, and 4
Crisis
    meaning 96, 205
Crisis communications plan 176, 181-182
Crisis communication training
    tourism organisations, for 187
Crisis management 194-198, 249-264
    changed trading environment 197
    CIRET database analysis 270-271
    concepts, clarification of 271-272
    crises, effect 195
    crisis recovery 198
    crisis, semantics of 252-254
    deeper investigation, need for 273
    definitions, clarification of 271-272
    disaster, semantics of 252-254

enhanced tourism disaster
    management framework 197
general theories 194
growth in tourism, and 250
human resource development
    250, 257-259
human resource management 250
indicators of preparedness 260
literature review 266-269
marketing during and after crisis 272
models 254-257
new collaborative marketing
    structures 274
NGT findings 271-273
overview 251-252
phases of 7
post-crisis 195
PPRR model 256
preparing for recovery 249-264
pro-active practice 201
promotion during and after crisis 272
rebuilding destination 272
recovery 272
research agenda 265-282
        key themes in literature 271
        method 268-270
        themes in literature 271
research findings 270-271
response, and 253-254
restoration 272
"ripple effect" 196
risk assessment 272
risk identification 271
Taiwan *see* Taiwan
typologies, clarification of 271-272
Crisis recovery strategies
    risk perception, and 15-27
Cyclone Larry 163-168
    counter disaster plan 165
    immediate impacts 164-165
    North Queensland, and 163-174
    perceptions of tourists, and 167
    post crisis recovery 163-168
    research methodology 167-168
    sustainable tourism development from
        risk management perspective 272
    tourism in North Queensland,
        and 166-167

Destination choice 114-115
    image, and 115-116
Destination disaster management 74
Destination image
    natural disasters, and 31-32
Destination marketing organization
    (DMO) 45-57
    action planning and implementation 55
    crisis organizational learning for 52-55
    crisis strategies 45-57
    importance of 55-56
    primary role 73
    reflection, and 45-57
    research methodology 88-90
Destination recovery 175-189
    Canberra 175-189
    research design 176-177
Destination websites 83-93
    avian flu related content 91
    avian flu statistics 2003-2006 90
    communicating tourism crises
        through 83-93
    conceptual framework 87-88
    evaluations 90-91
    inadequacy of 92
    investigators assessment of likelihood
        of avian flu 91
    research findings 90-91
    tourist arrivals 90
    WTO status 90
Disaster
    definition 205
Disaster management framework 7-10
Disaster risk management
    literature on 85-87
Emergency
    meaning 96
Greek passenger ship industry 191-202
    background 192-194
    cabotage date brought forward 200
    categorization of potential issues and
        crisis 199
    crisis management 191-202
    crisis management teams, types 200
    indices 192-194
    key companies 193
    liberalization of ferry route
        licensing 200

new rules for crews 201
research findings 199
research method 198-199
research sample 198-199
"ripple effect" 200-201
statistics 192
Human resource development
crisis management, and 250, 257-259
Hurricane Katrina 223-235 *see also* New
Orleans
advertising after 232
desired position-reality 230
effect on New Orleans
tourism 228-229
literature review 225-226
New Orleans advertising before 228
positioning 226-228
present position-perception 230
repositioning 229-230
repositioning tourism
destination 223-235
unique circumstances 225
Image 115-116
affective 116
cognitive 116
destination choice, and 115-116
government policy effects on 115
Indian Ocean tsunami 2004
speed of recovery 142
Issues management 194-198
London 95-111
Action Plan 99
ATOC Campaign 101-102
Christmas 106
crises, effect on 96
devolution, and 98
events campaign 105-108
GILT 102-104
iconic destination, as 109
large-scale investment in 108
lessons learned 108-110
LTAG 100
LTRG 99-100
New Year 106
organisation of tourism 98-99
plan for future action 108-110
Plan for Tourism 107
post-crisis marketing plan 99-108

post-disaster marketing
response 95-111
proposals for future development 109
research methods 99
short-haul campaign 104-105
target markets 105
terrorism 21 July 2005 110
TIRP 100
totally London month 102-104
tourism 95-111, 97-99
tourism statistics 98
Maldives 139-149
analysis of visitor arrivals 146
arrivals trends for top four emerging
markets 2001-2005 146
arrivals trends for six major markets
2001 to 2005 146
communications strategy 143
guest testimonial from Universal
Resort 145
Indian Ocean tsunami 2004 139-149
impact of 143
limitations 146-147
market recovery strategies 143-144
market segmentation 153-154
marketing actions and outcomes 144
MTPB 140
new markets 148
percentage changes in top ten arrivals
2004/2005 147
research methods 142
Thailand 151-161
tourism 142-143
tourism market recovery 139-149
Market recovery
research agenda 265-282
research method 268-270
Market segmentation
crisis management 154
incentives 153
literature review 152-154
long haul markets 156
long-term strategy 157
recommendations for future study 159
regional market 157
sensitivity to crises 159
terminology 152
trip descriptions 158

understanding 153-154
Marketing orientation 59-71
    airline sector 60
    barriers in airline sector 69
    centralization 63-64
    definition 61
    factors driving 68
    future research 68
    integrative model statistics 67
    Kohli and Jaworski on 62-63, 66, 68
    leadership 62-63
    limitations of research findings 69
    literature review 61-64
    managing crises during post-crisis
        phase 59-71
    MARKOR scale 64
    nature of 64
    path diagram of integrative model
        results 67
    potential advantages of crises 60
    research method 64-65
    research premises 61-62
    research results 65-66
    research sample 64-65
    role of 59-71
    structural equation analysis 66
    unidimensionality 65
Marketing recovery strategies 1-13
    tourism crises, and 1-13
MICE sector 151-161
Montenegro 127-137
    Balkans, and 129
    branding post-conflict
        destinations 127-137
    civil war and Yugoslavia
        tourism 1990-1991 131
    creation of national icon 130
    Crna Gora 131-133
    destination branding 127-137
    disintegration of Yugoslavia,
        and 127-137
    eco-destination, as 135
    primary attractions for European
        visitors 134
    public-private sector processes and
        partnerships 134
    recreating 127-137
    Serbia, and 132
    SWOT analysis 133
    Tourism Master Plan 133
    tourist destination, as 127-137
    "wild beauty" 131-133
Natural disasters 29-43
    CFA model 37
    destination image 31-32
    dominance dimension 39
    emotional reaction, impact of 33-34
    future research 41
    limitations of research 41
    maximum likelihood estimates 38
    meaning 30
    model measurement 35-36
    over-arousal 40
    over-stimulation 40
    paired-samples t-test 35,36
    perceived risk 33
    proposed study model 34-35
    ripple effects 31
    risk on travel intention 32-33
    sampling 34-35
    statistical analysis 35
    structural equation model of PAD on
        intention 38
    structural model specification 36-37
    survey development 34-35
    tourism, in 30-31
    travel intention, and 29-43
    vulnerability of tourism 39
New Orleans 223-235 *see also*
    Hurricane Katrina
    advertising post-Katrina 232
    desired position-reality 230
    effect of Hurricane Katrina on tourism
        228-229
    map from NOMCVB website 233
    Media Center 233
    positioning 226-228
    present position-perception 230
    repositioning 230-232, 229-230
    repositioning tourism
        destination 223-235
    sample of advertising pre-Katrina 228
    tourism destination, as 224-225
    visitor sources of information/
        advertising 233
    visitor profile 2004 225

North Queensland
    Cyclone Larry *see* Cyclone Larry
Organizational learning 45-57
    analyzing data 55
    asking questions 52-53
    challenging values, beliefs and
        assumptions 53
    collecting data 55
    definition 47-49
    dialogue 54
    DMOs, for 52-55
    double loop 49-50
    Faulkner and Vikulov on 47
    four forms of knowledge 52
    Henderson on 47
    identifying values, beliefs and
        assumptions 53
    interpreting data 55
    reflection 54
    reflection as part of process 50-52
    role of 47-50
    single loop 49-50
    tourism crisis management, and 45-57
Recovery marketing plan 181-182
Recovery marketing strategies 141
Risk 15-27
    catastrophic 15-27
    crisis recovery strategies, and 15-27
    importance of 25
    meaning 15-16
    natural disasters, and *see* Natural
        disasters
    probability and impact timeline 21
    real 17-21
    stealth 15-27
    vulnerability, concept of 20
Risk perception 15-27
    airline safety 18
    crisis recovery strategies, and 15-27
    dimension of consequences 17
    importance of 25
    inconsistent trends 20
    interviews for data collection 21-22
    means: catastrophic risks vs. stealth
        risks 23
    means: tourists vs residents 22-23
    natural disasters and *see* Natural
        disasters

    nuclear power 17
    personal invulnerability, sense of 17
    results of research 22-24
    risk characteristics influencing 17
    risk vulnerability, perception of 24-25
    scenarios after crisis or disaster
        recovery 19-20
    top ten risk ranking 24
    trends after crisis or disaster 18-19
    X-rays 17
Rotorua 73-82
    analysis of local tourism industry 79
    colonisation of New Zealand, and 75
    conceptual framework 80
    crisis acknowledgement 77
    evolution as tourism destination 80
    government resources, reliance
        on 75-77
    image problems 76-77
    independence from central
        government 76
    infrastructure investments 78-79
    initiatives for recovery 78
    legislative history 75-76
    marketing as tourism destination 79
    "marketing dependence" 80
    New Zealand tourism industry, and 76
    recovery efforts 77-80
    reflections on negative tourism
        images 79
    sanatorium of the earth 74-75
    self-inflicted crisis 73-82
    situation analysis 1987 76
    turnaround in destination
        competiveness 81
Serbia
    Montenegro, and 132
Social networks
    tourism crises, and 4-7
Taiwan 203-221
    crisis management planning to restore
        tourism after disasters 203-221
    earthquake 1999 203-221
        definition of crisis and
            disaster 205
        destination image 206-207
        emergency phase 215-216
        epicentre 205

impacts on tourism 204-205
initial risk 219
Innovative Integrated Crisis
    Management Model 220
integrated crisis management
    framework 216
intermediate phase 216
literature review 205-216
long-term (recovery)
    phase 216
model development 215-219
perceived risk 206-207
pre-event phase 215
prodromal phase 215
reactive strategies 219
resolution phase 216
sequence of events 204
summary of crisis management
    framework 208-214
summarization of crisis
    management plans 207
Thailand 151-161
    data analysis 155-158
    data collection 154-155
    external crises, and 152
    market segmentation in time of crisis
        151-161
    MICE sector 151-161
    research findings 155-158
    research methodology 154-155
    tourist descriptors 155-158
Tourism
    demand 83-84
    statistics 83
Tourism crises 1-13
    avoidance factors 10
    boundaries, role of 3-4
    Chinese word for crisis 3
    complexity or chaos theory 4
    conceptualization of effect on
        destination system 6
    destination websites, and 83-93
    disaster management framework 7-10
    effect on intentions to travel 10
    Faulkner's tourism disaster
        management framework 9
    marketing recovery strategies,
        and 1-13

natural disasters 1-2
phase model 8
phases of crisis management 7
range of recovery challenges 8-9
recovery 1-13
social networks 4-7
systems perspective 3-4
terrorism 2
tourist system as network of
    organisation 6
wider systems perspective 11
Tourism crisis management 45-57 *see also*
    Crisis management
        crises evaluation processes 51
        dialogue 54
        holistic framework 48
        organizational learning, and 45-57
        reflection 54
        reflection as part of process 50-52
        strategic framework 48
Tourism disaster framework 96-97
Tourist descriptors 155-158
Travel intention
    natural disasters, and 29-43
Trip descriptors 158
Youth tourism 237-247
    coping within new
        environments 239-240
    crime, and 243-244
    "experience" 245
    health 242
    incubating potential for harm 239-240
    natural disasters, influence of 244-245
    perceived risk 237-247
    political instability, and 242-243
    pre-travel influences 242
    profile of respondents 241
    research methodology 240-241
    research results 241-245
    risk assessment, and 238-239
    terrorism, and 243-244
    tourist behaviour 237-247
    unpacking problem of travel related
        risks 240-241
    war, and 242-243
Yugoslavia
    disintegration, Montenegro,
        and 127-137

#0202 - 030817 - C0 - 297/210/16 - PB - 9780415850469